A MEDITERRANEAN VALLEY

Frontispiece. The 'Other Italy': a woman working her fields in the upper Biferno valley in 1953. (Photograph: Frank Monaco)

A MEDITERRANEAN VALLEY

LANDSCAPE ARCHAEOLOGY AND *ANNALES* HISTORY IN THE BIFERNO VALLEY

GRAEME BARKER

WITH MAJOR CONTRIBUTIONS BY
RICHARD HODGES
CHRIS HUNT
JOHN LLOYD
MARLENE SUANO
PETER TAYLOR
CHRIS WICKHAM

&

SPECIALIST CONTRIBUTIONS BY
GILL CLARK
JOHN GIORGI
SUSAN LUKESH
CAROLINE MALONE
TIM REYNOLDS
DERRICK WEBLEY

LEICESTER UNIVERSITY PRESS
LONDON AND NEW YORK

LEICESTER UNIVERSITY PRESS
A Cassell imprint
Wellington House, 125 Strand, London WC2R 0BB, England
215 Park Avenue South, New York, NY 10003, USA

First published in 1995

British Library Cataloguing in Publication Data
A CIP catalogue record for this book is available from the British Library

ISBN 0 7185 1906 X

Library of Congress Cataloging-in-Publication Data

Barker, Graeme.
  A Mediterranean Valley : Landscape Archaeology and *Annales* History
in the Biferno Valley / Graeme Barker ; with contributions by Richard Hodges
  . . . [et al.] ; and specialist contributions from Gill Clark . . . [et al.].
    p.   cm.
  Includes bibliographical references and index.
  ISBN 0–7185–1906–X
  1. Biferno River Valley (Italy) – Antiquities. 2. Land settlement – Italy –
Biferno River Valley – History. 3. Landscape archaeology – Italy – Biferno
River Valley. 4. Excavations (Archaeology) – Italy – Biferno River Valley.
5. Biferno River Valley (Italy) – History.
I. Hodges, Richard. II. Clark, Gillian. III. Title.
DG975.B542B37   1995
937'.7–dc20   94–32222
                                                                CIP

Typeset by Mayhew Typesetting, Rhayader, Powys
Printed and bound in Great Britain by Redwood Books, Trowbridge, Wiltshire

In memoriam

Derrick Webley (1922–1994)

CONTENTS

NOTE ON COMPANION VOLUME
THE BIFERNO VALLEY SURVEY: THE ARCHAEOLOGICAL AND GEOMORPHOLOGICAL RECORD

Please note that this volume is accompanied by a companion volume containing the specialist supporting data collected by the archaeological project, entitled *The Biferno Valley Survey: The Archaeological and Geomorphological Record*. This volume, edited by G. Barker, is also published by Leicester University Press, ISBN 0 7185 2375 X. The contents of this volume are as follows:

1. The survey gazetteer
2. The geomorphological fieldwork: the sediment descriptions
3. Test excavations and geophysical survey at Samnite and Roman sites
4. Catalogue of Samnite and Roman finds
5. The slags
6. The quernstone remains
7. The faunal data

References in *A Mediterranean Valley* to specialist data in the companion volume are given within parentheses as **II** followed by the relevant chapter, figure or table number.

LIST OF CONTRIBUTORS

Chapter One	Graeme Barker
Chapter Two	Graeme Barker
Chapter Three	Graeme Barker
Chapter Four	Chris Hunt
Chapter Five	Graeme Barker, with a contribution by Tim Reynolds
Chapter Six	Graeme Barker, with contributions by Gill Clark, Chris Hunt, Caroline Malone, Tim Reynolds and Derrick Webley
Chapter Seven	Graeme Barker, with contributions by Gill Clark, Chris Hunt, Susan Lukesh and Derrick Webley
Chapter Eight	Graeme Barker and Marlene Suano, with contributions by Gill Clark, John Giorgi and Derrick Webley
Chapter Nine	John Lloyd, with contributions by Graeme Barker, Gill Clark and Derrick Webley
Chapter Ten	John Lloyd, with contributions by Graeme Barker, Gill Clark and Derrick Webley
Chapter Eleven	Richard Hodges and Chris Wickham, with a contribution by Graeme Barker
Chapter Twelve	Graeme Barker with Peter Taylor
Chapter Thirteen	Graeme Barker

Institutional Affiliations of Contributors

G. Barker   School of Archaeological Studies, University of
                   Leicester
G. Clark   British School at Rome
C. Hunt   Department of Geographical Studies, University of
                   Huddersfield
R. Hodges   British School at Rome/Department of Archaeology
                   and Prehistory, University of Sheffield
J. Giorgi   Environmental Section, Museum of London
J. Lloyd   Institute of Archaeology and Wolfson College,
                   University of Oxford
S. Lukesh   Center for Old World Archaeology and Art, Brown
                   University
C. Malone   Department of Classics and Archaeology, University
                   of Bristol
T. Reynolds   Department of Archaeology, University of Cambridge
M. Suano   Faculty of Philosophy, Letters and Human Sciences,
                   Sao Paulo University
P. Taylor   Independent solicitor, Manchester
D. Webley (dec.)   Formerly of the Agricultural Development and
                   Advisory Service, Ministry of Agriculture and
                   Fisheries, Bangor
C. Wickham   School of History, University of Birmingham

Companion volume: *The Biferno Valley Survey:
the Archaeological and Geomorphological Record*

LIST OF ILLUSTRATIONS

Frontispiece: the 'Other Italy': a woman working her fields in the upper Biferno valley in 1953.

LIST OF TABLES

PREFACE AND ACKNOWLEDGEMENTS

The project described in this book set out to document the long-term settlement history of a typical Mediterranean landscape, to try to understand how and why it developed in the way it did. The fieldwork and subsequent analysis drew together a group of scholars from a variety of disciplines in the humanities and sciences, particularly archaeology and cognate disciplines, who applied their specialisms within an integrated methodology. The landscape selected was the Biferno valley in the modern political region of Molise, a particularly beautiful though little-known part of central-southern Italy (Figs. 1, 4). The cornerstone of the project was an archaeological field survey or field-walking programme to map the archaeological evidence for changing settlement patterns from prehistoric to recent times. The archaeological survey was integrated with geophysical analyses and excavations of prehistoric, classical and medieval settlements discovered during the programme, scientific investigations of environmental history, and documentary studies. The principal fieldwork was undertaken during the 1970s, though aspects of the investigation continued throughout the 1980s, and the book also integrates our findings with other archaeological work undertaken in the valley in the 1980s and 1990s.

Scholars have discussed aspects of the development of human settlement in the Mediterranean region ever since classical times. However, as described in Chapter One, the project drew its particular inspiration from three seminal studies of different aspects of Mediterranean landscape history, one by an historian, one by an archaeologist and one by a geographer: Fernand Braudel's *La Méditerranée et le Monde Méditerranéen à l'Époque de Philippe II* (Braudel, 1949), John Ward-Perkins' landscape archaeology and field survey of South Etruria (Potter, 1979), and Claudio Vita-Finzi's *Mediterranean Valleys: Geological Changes in Historical Times* (Vita-Finzi, 1969). To them must be added, for the particular regional context of central and southern Italy (the 'Mezzogiorno') , Carlo Levi's *Christ Stopped at Eboli* (1947). Levi's story of peasant life in the Mezzogiorno before the last war provided a particularly poignant starting-point for our study of the history of the Italian *contadino* or peasant farmer, whom he described as 'cut off from History and the State', with a history 'so old that no one knows whence it came and it may have been forever' (Levi, 1947: 2). Was such a perspective true? The frontispiece of the book illustrates a woman working her fields in the upper Biferno valley in the 1950s. In this project we hoped to write her history and prehistory.

The landscape history described in this book in fact begins with a lakeside encampment of palaeolithic scavengers three-quarters of a million years ago, and ends with the problems facing modern farmers over how best to protect their livelihoods whilst husbanding the landscape for their successors. Although – as Chapter Three describes – the methodologies of the project would certainly be improved if the fieldwork were to be undertaken again, the scale of the geographical unit and the length of the timescale studied by the project make it unique in Mediterranean landscape studies.

It is my great pleasure to acknowledge here the support of the many funding institutions which provided research grants for the fieldwork and specialist analyses, without whose continued commitment the project could not have been undertaken. The principal grants for the fieldwork were from the following organizations: the American Philosophical Society, the British Academy, the British School at Rome, the Leverhulme Research Fund, the National Geographic Society, the National Museum of Brazil, the Regione Molise (the Regional Government of Molise), the Social Science Research Council, the Superintendency of Antiquities for Molise, the University of Cambridge (Crowther-Benyon Fund), the University of Oxford (Craven Committee) and the University of Sheffield (Research Fund). The principal grants for the subsequent analyses of the material were from the British Academy, the British School at Rome, the University of Oxford (for John Lloyd, from the Craven Committee, the Institute of Archaeology and Wolfson College), and the University of Sheffield (Research Fund).

During the fieldwork, we received enormous hospitality and kindness from the farmers and shepherds whose land the teams searched for potsherds, and the administrative councils of the *comuni* of Boiano, Campomarino, Casacalenda, Guglionesi, Larino, Petrella and Termoli also provided invaluable support for the team in terms of the free accommodation they supplied for us (which included several schools, an empty bank, a medieval tower, and an ex-prison). The Archaeological Superintendency for Molise provided storage facilities for the project's finds in their stores in the Roman theatre at Saepinum, and invaluable liaison with the police and civic authorities within whose territory we were working.

An archaeology-driven project such as this depends on teamwork from start to finish, and it is a great pleasure to thank the many staff and students who worked in the Biferno valley team. Those who were involved in the principal fieldwork are listed below. It is very pleasing to see how many of those who worked as undergraduates or postgraduates in the team have gone on to successful careers in professional archaeology.

Gino Andreoli, Howard Bailey, Giles Barker, Ian Bethune, Angela Brady, Simon Browning, Anna Buchanan, Miranda Buchanan, Corinne Campion, Pamela Campion, Sarah Carlisle, Judith Cartledge, John Cherry, Ann Chippindale, Chris Chippindale, Gill Clark, Catherine Dagg, Ken Dash, Christine Davies, Margaret Deith, Anna Doberski, Ann Dolan, Mandy Dunn, Janet Gabriels, Chris Gosden, Colin Green, Francis Green, Richard Grove, Peter Hayes, Mary Haynes, Agnes Hetherington, Ann Hill, Pat Hinchcliffe, Debbie Hodges, Richard Hodges, Philip Howard, Paul Huston, Helen Jackson, Bridget Jenkinson, Rogan Jenkinson, Christopher Jones, Tim Lawson, Lesley Levine, Richard Linington, John Lloyd, Vicki Lloyd, Carl McChesney, Rod McCullagh, Lucy McGarrell, Alan McPherron, Ailsa Mainman, John Macnish, Michael Mannix, Vicki Mattocks, Stefan Milik, Nigel Mills, Margaret Morris, Graeham Mounteney, Fiona Mountford, Charles Mundy, Sally Nash, Janet Newton, Ann Nolan, Ian Page, David Parsons, Alison Pitt, Julia Randall, Howard Reeves, Elisabetta Rossi, John Russell, Cliff Samson, Kevin Shaw, Jane Shiren, Poppy Singer, Andrew Slade, Peter Smith, Marlene Suano, Roger Suddaby, Sheila Sutherland, Peter Taylor, Robin Torrence, Alan Turner, Phil Turner, Keith Wade, Hafed el Walda, Bruce Watson, Derrick Webley, Joan Webley, Robert Whieldon, Chris Wickham, Don Williamson, Duncan Wilson, Stephen Wilson, Jane Zott

In the analysis of the data, the project also drew on the expertise of a wide range of specialists. In addition to those listed on the title page of this book, I would particularly like to thank here those whose findings are fully presented in the companion volume, *The Biferno Valley Survey: The Archaeological and Geomorphological Record*, whose work underpins much of the story described in this volume: Claudia Agrippa, Paul Arthur, Donald Bailey, Enrica Boldrini, Amanda Claridge, Gianfranco De Benedittis, John Drinkwater, Richard Linington, David Peacock, Jenny Price, Paul Roberts, Chris Salter, Alwyne Wheeler, and Olwen Williams-Thorpe. John Lloyd would also like to acknowledge the assistance of Paul Roberts, Alison MacDonald and Vicki Lloyd in the preparation of Chapters Nine and Ten in this volume and Chapter Four of the companion volume, of John Hayes and Philip Kenrick in the preparation of Chapter Four of the companion volume and of Sally di Cicco, Jill Hale, Lyn Selwood and Alison Wilkins in preparing the illustrations accompanying his text. We are also grateful to the many colleagues who commented on drafts, especially Tim Potter for his detailed comments on the book as a whole, but also Neil Christie, Caroline Malone, David Mattingly, Simon Stoddart, and (on Chapters Nine and Ten specifically) Ed Bispham, John Patterson, and Dominic Rathbone.

In bringing the project to its final publication, I would particularly like to acknowledge the commitment and talent of Deborah Miles, who has prepared all of the illustrations in this volume except those accompanying Chapters Nine and Ten; the permission of Frank Monaco to reproduce some of the beautiful photographs he took of women working around Cantalupo Mandela in the upper Biferno valley in the early 1950s (frontispiece, and Figs. 14, 15); the help of Valerie Scott, librarian of The British School at Rome, and of her assistants, in the final compilation of the bibliography; and the encouragement and support of Vanessa Harwood and Frances Pinter of Leicester University Press in seeing the book through the press.

The Biferno valley project began twenty years ago, and I am very conscious that this book and its companion volume have been a long time coming. In the survey we stumbled upon an extraordinary wealth of settlement archaeology in a region that had never been systematically explored hitherto, and we were also given a remarkable *carte blanche* by the Italian authorities to carry out excavations on sites of different periods that we had found, in a way which would be very unlikely to happen today. Several of the staff members of the project learned the hard lesson that beginning a new field project (in my case, the UNESCO Libyan Valleys Survey) immediately after completing the fieldwork of another one, before the latter's analysis is well advanced, results in a whole flock of pigeons coming home to roost at the same time! In the protracted process of preparing the Biferno valley study for publication, I would like to thank the many scholars in Britain, Italy and elsewhere who collaborated in the project for their forbearance. Above all I would like to thank the three Archaeological Superintendents of Molise who oversaw the project – Adriano La Regina, Bruno d'Agostino and Gabriella d'Henry – for their continued patience and goodwill. Their kindness and friendship over the past twenty years have been a constant support.

Graeme Barker
Leicester, May 1995

CHAPTER 1

APPROACHES TO MEDITERRANEAN LANDSCAPE HISTORY

Graeme Barker

ARCHAEOLOGY AND *ANNALES* HISTORY

In 1949 the French historian Fernand Braudel published an extraordinary survey of 16th-century life across the Mediterranean basin, *La Méditerranée et le Monde Méditerranéen à l'Epoque de Philippe II*. The majestic sweep of its narrative embodied 'total history' of a kind rarely if ever attempted before, going completely against the grain of the narrative political history that had been the norm in France hitherto, and it became a cornerstone of the French movement of *Annales* history that had begun with the writings of his mentors Lucien Febvre and Marc Bloch on French agrarian history.

The story that unfolded consisted of the interplay between different kinds of histories operating at different timescales. At one end of the scale were *événements*, the short-term occurrences of political and military history characterized by Braudel as 'surface disturbances, crests of foam that the tides of history carry on their strong backs' (1972: 21). In the middle were what he termed *conjonctures*: 'there can be distinguished another history, this time with slow but perceptible rhythms . . . the history of groups and groupings' – social and economic changes developing over a generation or so, within the lifetime of the actors. At the other end of the scale were long-term processes, the *longue durée*, factors such as the role of climate, seasonality, and topography on farming and communications, for example, and the effects of technology on production systems – 'a history whose passage is almost imperceptible, that of man in his relationship to the environment . . . those underlying currents, often noiseless, whose direction can only be observed by watching them over long periods of time' (1972: 20). As influential on long-term historical process were people's thought processes, *mentalités* – the religious, ideological and behavioural systems that bound societies together in particular ways. History amounted to the interweaving of these different rhythms of time.

As several archaeologists have argued in recent years, the goals of archaeology are in many respects parallel to the goals of Annaliste history, and archaeological data are well suited to this kind of holistic analysis (Bintliff, 1991; Hodges, 1986; Knapp, 1992). Proponents of 'Annaliste archaeology' have generally pointed to its potential for investigating long- and medium-term processes of change. Certainly archaeology has command of immense time sequences, and the methodologies of environmental archaeology and landscape analysis in particular are ideally suited to the investigation of the *longue durée*. Long-lived ritual and ideological systems, *mentalités*, also can frequently be studied very effectively using archaeological data. Despite the many problems to be resolved concerning the identification of 'groups and groupings' using material culture, archaeologists are generally well placed to investigate Braudel's *conjonctures*, social and economic trends amongst the societies they study, though the timescales of these processes may vary from a generation to a century to a millennium or more depending on the period of antiquity and the chronological framework in which it is studied.

Événements are generally more difficult. Precise correlations between an historical event and archaeological data, as in the case of Pompeii's destruction by Vesuvius, are absolutely rare. The identification of historical events such as military actions in archaeological data is generally more difficult than was previously thought, when by circular reasoning destruction layers actually dated very loosely by pottery to several centuries could be confidently assigned to an historical event somewhere within those centuries, providing convincing archaeological proof for it in the process! However, whilst Binford (1986) has argued that we should distinguish between 'archaeological time' (long-term) and 'ethnographic time' (short-term) in recognition of this difficulty, single-episode events can sometimes be convincingly recognized with care, and developments in chronological techniques such as dendrochronology are increasingly allowing prehistoric as well as historic archaeologists to assign specific natural events and individual (if often impersonal) human actions to narrow time frames.

Archaeologists frequently comment that one of the attractions of their data is that all societies, and all segments of society, create archaeology by their actions, whereas much historical source material was written by the literate minority, frequently with a bias towards their own concerns. In many ways the dichotomy between historical and archaeological data is unreal: documents, no less than potsherds, are material culture, and historians and archaeologists probably need to concentrate more on developing a unified theory of material culture for the study of the past than arguing over differences in their data. It remains true, however, that the links between human behaviour and the archaeological data created by it are frequently ambiguous to say the least, and this is compounded by the fact that the data as recovered by excavation or survey are the outcome of a complicated set of natural and cultural processes of discard, burial, attrition and survival that are also poorly understood. Nevertheless, the strengths of archaeological data – the timescale they represent and the range of social actions from which they derive – suit them ideally to Braudel's model of history (and for archaeologists, prehistory as well as history), as the complex interplay between different forces operating at different timescales in particular landscapes.

A major criticism of Braudel has been that, for all his discussion of the interweaving of different temporal rhythms, he was unwilling to explore explicitly the possible relationships between them in explanations of change. In reality, particularly in *La Méditerranée*, he placed most emphasis on the *longue durée*, a 'structure' of history which for many historians has seemed simply environmental determinism by another name. However, the same criticism cannot be levelled at his students such as Georges Duby, Jacques Le Goff, and Emmanuel Le Roy Ladurie, even though they are deliberately (and unashamedly) inconsistent in their use of Braudel's concepts of time – Braudel's *conjoncture* is Le Roy Ladurie's *longue durée*. Moreover, as the case studies in Knapp's *Archaeology, Annales and Ethnohistory* (1992) demonstrate, archaeologists can profitably attempt not only to characterize their data in terms of different kinds of historical process operating at different timescales, but also to measure their respective roles in maintaining stability or instigating change. As John Moreland (1992: 125) argues in his study of the emergence of medieval villages in central Italy, 'although people worked within and through structures, they were not structure-bound. They could and did take action, and even used facilities . . . that constituted elements of structure to further their own ends'. As his own and the other case studies in Knapp (1992) and Bintliff (1991) confirm, to investigate the long-term relationship between structure and agency, the most appropriate scale of archaeological analysis is generally at the level of the *region* rather than the single *site*. To conduct regional landscape analysis effectively, archaeologists need to apply the interdisciplinary methodologies of 'landscape archaeology', the study of ancient settlement patterns and of the relationship between settlement and landscape in antiquity.

UPLANDS AND LOWLANDS: THE 'SLOW-FURLING WAVES' OF MEDITERRANEAN HISTORY

Part One of *La Méditerranée* described the components of the Mediterranean landscape: the mountains, plateaux and plains; the seas and coasts; the neighbouring regions of the 'greater Mediterranean'; the nature of the

Mediterranean climatic regime; the evidence for climatic change. In Part Two Braudel addressed a series of major social and economic themes and their interplay with this landscape – farming, mining, transport, trade. Perhaps the most important theme of all, he wrote, was the changing relationship between the lowlands and uplands.

In his opening chapter on the role of the Mediterranean landscape in shaping past human settlement, Braudel lamented how the lowlands had tended to dominate most previous analyses of Mediterranean history: 'the historian is not unlike the traveller. He tends to linger over the plain, which is the setting for the leading actors of the day, and does not seem eager to approach the high mountains nearby. More than one historian who has never left the towns and their archives would be surprised to discover their existence' (Braudel, 1972: 29). Instead, he went on to argue that the mountains, plateaux and plains of the Mediterranean landscape have always been inextricably related in the history of human settlement.

The most obvious example of linkage, he wrote, had been in the practice of transhumant pastoralism, the movement of herders and their stock from winter grazing on the lowlands to summer grazing in the uplands (the herders' settlements being based at either end of the system). In the period of his survey this form of pastoralism was practised on a huge scale in many Mediterranean countries, amply documented in the archives because the herds and flocks were big business, the property of the State, the Church, or leading families. Alongside such long-distance transhumance, however, he pointed to the likelihood of smaller-scale movements of stock between lowlands and uplands carried out by families or groups of families at a subsistence level rather than for market production. In the dramatic topography of the Mediterranean, such movements need involve only a few hours' or a day's walk. He described the changing relationship between lowlands and uplands, farmers and shepherds, as the ebb and flow of perhaps the most important 'slow-furling wave' (1972: 88) in the *longue durée* of Mediterranean history. The investigation of this relationship is a central theme running through the present study.

Braudel's thesis for the 16th-century, of a complex and oscillating interplay between environment, land use and society, provides an ideal model to test for the earlier periods of Mediterranean history using regional archaeological landscape analysis. It provided the stimulus for the ensuing study of one particular Mediterranean valley, the Biferno valley in the modern political region or *regione*, of Molise in southern Italy (Figs. 1, 4). Chronologically, the project follows Braudel's dictum that the relationship between people and landscape needs to be studied over the longest timespan possible – in the case of the Biferno valley, some three-quarters of

Fig. 1 The regions of peninsular Italy.

a million years. Inevitably, therefore, its methodology depends most on landscape archaeology and its related disciplines rather than documentary research.

LANDSCAPE ARCHAEOLOGY AND FIELD SURVEY IN ITALY

Classical archaeology in Italy has always been dominated by the 'Great Tradition' of classical art and architecture. Even today a university course on 'ancient topography' in an Italian department of archaeology will usually deal predominantly with the layout of the major imperial cities and the details of their monumental architecture. The strength of the tradition is not surprising in the face of the overwhelming wealth of standing monuments of the Roman period surviving throughout Italy, quite apart from in the ancient urban centres such as Rome, Ostia, Pompeii and Herculaneum. The predominant focus for the archaeological investigation of the ancient world has inevitably been urban. In Britain, by contrast, the longevity and strength of our own tradition of fieldwork in landscape archaeology are explicable given the wealth of our visible archaeological data – settlements, tombs, field systems and so on – in the countryside, that first drew the attention of antiquaries such as Aubrey and Stukeley and which were incorporated into Ordnance Survey mapping from an early stage in its history.

It is no accident, therefore, that from an early period British archaeologists working in Italy have tended to focus as much on the countryside as on the city. Pioneering fieldwork on the major cities and cemeteries of the Etruscan civilization was published by George Dennis in 1848. In 1901 Thomas Ashby took up a scholarship at the newly founded British School at Rome and in 1906 became Director, remaining in post until 1925. During this time he carried out intensive fieldwork on the lowlands immediately surrounding Rome, the 'Roman Campagna', publishing a series of major articles on the Roman roads and the archaeological monuments along their routes. His studies culminated in his classic synthesis *The Roman Campagna in Classical Times*, published in 1927.

John Ward-Perkins was Director of the British School from 1946 to 1974. Though principally a Roman archaeologist, he had extraordinarily wide research horizons: his career embraced fieldwork in Britain and Libya as well as Italy, he conducted excavations of prehistoric, Roman and medieval sites, and within classical archaeology his research contributed to a very wide range of social and economic issues including art and architecture, technology and trade, religious systems, urban and rural settlement forms, and more besides. The South Etruria Survey which he directed was an important role model for the Biferno Valley Survey.

When Ward-Perkins became Director after the last war, he was struck by the amount of damage to the archaeological landscape of south Etruria (the part of the Roman Campagna immediately north of Rome) by the suburban expansion of the post-war boom and, above all, by the steady replacement of traditional ploughing technologies by mechanized deep ploughing. Traditional ploughs pulled by oxen, horses and donkeys tend to scratch the surface down to about 20 centimetres' depth (Fig. 19), whereas the massive ploughs in use throughout Italy today pulled by caterpillar tractors commonly go down to almost a metre (Fig. 20). The destruction of the archaeological record of south Etruria as farmers switched from the old technology to the new in the 1950s was fearful, as we were to find in the Biferno valley in the 1970s (Fig. 23).

Ward-Perkins initiated a series of projects involving field-walking. His enormous personal contribution apart, he also encouraged others (especially PhD students) to survey an area by walking over the newly ploughed fields, picking up archaeological artefacts on the surface. Other residents and staff at the British School at Rome, together with friends, often helped. Ancient sites being destroyed by deep ploughing were represented on the surface by concentrations of artefacts, particularly fragments of pottery. By making systematic collections of these materials, and mapping their location carefully, his project was able to build up maps of settlement at different times in the past. The system worked particularly well for the Roman period (Fig. 2), when many people lived in the countryside, on farms made of the kind of robust materials that have survived as fragments in the ploughsoil through millennia – tile roofs, brick and stone walls, plaster floors and so on. They also used pottery that was well made and durable, and manufactured in relatively large quantities, and which is also very distinctive, so very visible to the archaeological teams walking the fields.

The field-walking also recorded prehistoric, Etruscan and medieval settlements, and Ward-Perkins and his collaborators carried out a series of excavations of settlements of different periods – a bronze age encampment, an iron age village and cemetery, a Roman farm, an early medieval estate centre, and medieval churches. He encouraged palynologists and geomor-phologists to research the history of forest cover and river sedimentary history, research which cast light not simply on the changing climate and environment but also on the changing pattern of human impact on the landscape in terms of forest clearance and agricultural practices. The field survey was published in a series of papers (e.g. Duncan, 1958; Jones, 1962, 1963; Ward-Perkins, 1962, 1964, Ward-Perkins et al., 1968), and the excavations and environmental studies were generally published as separate monographs or papers (e.g. Christie, 1991; Judson, 1963; Potter, 1972, 1976), but the best overview of the project was provided by Tim Potter in his 1979 synthesis The Changing Landscape of South Etruria. The book is a landmark in the development of European landscape archae-ology, and eloquent testimony to the power of this kind of archaeology to write Braudelian history.

The principal fieldwork for the South Etruria Survey was conducted in the 1950s and 1960s, though the British School has maintained an active programme of archaeological fieldwork in the area ever since. In the

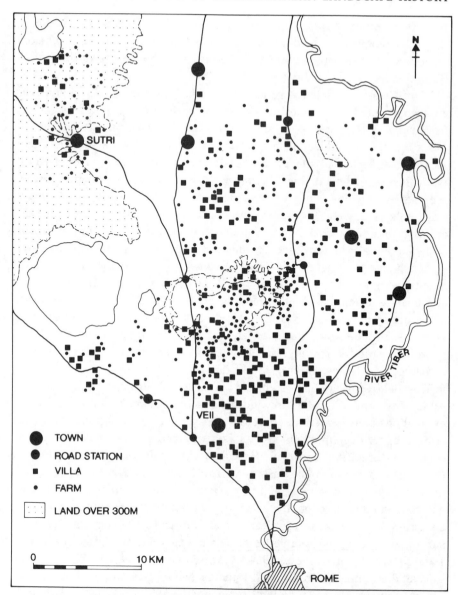

Fig. 2 The South Etruria Survey: the Roman landscape *c.*100 AD.
(Adapted from Potter, 1979: fig. 35)

following decades a number of regional survey projects was developed
elsewhere in Italy using field-walking methodologies developed from the
kind employed by Ward-Perkins in south Etruria. Reports on many of
those conducted in the 1970s are included in Barker and Hodges (1981),
and on those of the 1980s in Barker and Lloyd (1991). The Biferno Valley

Survey has been the largest of these, and closest to the South Etruria model in its integration of an extensive programme of excavation and palaeo-environmental research with the field-walking to provide a regional landscape archaeology.

THE FORMATION OF THE MEDITERRANEAN LANDSCAPE: CLIMATE OR PEOPLE?

The third major study that provided the context for the Biferno valley project was the model for Mediterranean alluviation (the deposition of river sediments) published by Claudio Vita-Finzi in 1969, *The Mediterranean Valleys: Geological Changes in Historical Times*.

For centuries, Mediterranean geographers and historians have pointed to the evidence for significant landscape change in the past. Areas whose prosperity in classical times was proverbial were now decayed. The ruins of once great cities stood in the midst of impoverished countryside. Rivers known to have been navigable in classical or medieval times were now silted up. The present delta of the River Tiber now lies a couple of kilometres beyond Rome's great port of Ostia, once built at its mouth. What had caused such changes? Once modern geological reasoning replaced biblical notions of great floods and deluges in the last century, speculation centred on the rival strengths of two possible factors that might have affected stream flows: climatic change or human actions (deforesting the landscape for agriculture and timber, allowing animals like sheep and goats to denude vegetation, and so on). Vita-Finzi provided the first scientific investigation of the scale and nature of Mediterranean landscape change, with a clearly argued model of causation.

For his doctoral thesis at Cambridge, Vita-Finzi travelled round the Mediterranean basin, mapping geomorphological exposures with evidence for valley alluviation and collecting archaeological artefacts and charcoal samples from the exposures to enable him to date them. He concluded that there had been two major phases of sedimentation, which he termed the Older and Younger Fills (Fig. 3). The first he dated by the presence of flint and chert tools of middle palaeolithic form to the last glaciation, to about 50,000 years ago, the second from its relationship to buried archaeological features (such as Roman water-control dams near Lepcis Magna in Tripolitania) and inclusion of Roman and medieval potsherds to historical times. He concluded that, at some stage in the historical period, many streams which had hitherto been engaged primarily in downcutting began to build up their beds, steepening and smoothing out their longitudinal profiles. The aggradation did not produce a single continuous alluvial

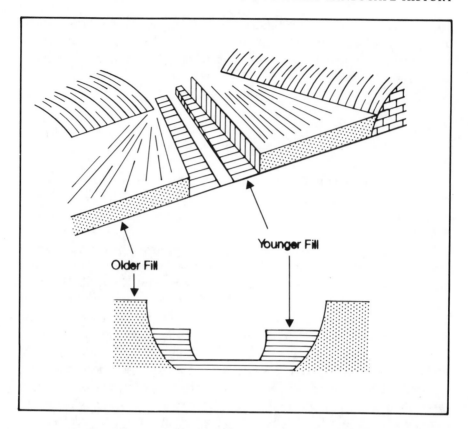

Fig. 3 Vita-Finzi's model of Younger Fill alluviation. (Adapted from Vita-Finzi, 1969: fig. 37)

surface, but rather a stairway of surfaces separated by breaks of slope where the ground was steep. At some stage after the formation of these sediments, downcutting took place (which he noted in places was still in operation today), incising stream channels into the alluvial fill, flattening the longitudinal profiles of the valleys and restoring their stepped character. 'It is this sequence of events – valley filling followed by down-cutting – which has given the Mediterranean valleys their characteristic form: a well-defined channel cut into a broad, smooth valley floor' (Vita-Finzi, 1969: 91).

The nature, chronology and reasons for the formation of the Younger Fill are critical issues in any study of Mediterranean landscape change. Although he recognized that the Older and Younger Fills differed in texture, degree of stratification, and colour, Vita-Finzi concluded that climatic change rather than human agency was a more convincing explanation for both phases of alluviation given the ubiquity and broad contemporaneity of the two sets of phenomena he had observed around the Mediterranean. He ascribed the Older Fill to glacial conditions, and the Younger Fill to a more recent time of cold, wet weather, the 'Little Ice Age'. Since then, a variety of earlier and later episodes of alluviation during the last 10,000 years has been identified by geomorphologists in various parts of the Mediterranean basin, as well as many examples of the 'classic' Younger Fill (which has been dated increasingly to classical rather than medieval times), and generally ascribed to human impact on the environment rather than climatic change (e.g. Davidson, 1980; Gilbertson et al., 1983, 1992; Pope and Van Andel, 1984; Van Andel et al., 1985; Wagstaff, 1981). Proponents of the original thesis, however, point out that the classic Younger Fill sediments are significantly different in their scale and characteristics from earlier and later aggradations, suggesting that, whilst land-use systems may well have been a critical factor in their genesis, climatic change may still have been a stimulus.

In order to evaluate the respective roles of climate and people in shaping the Mediterranean landscape, we need to investigate Mediterranean valleys with integrated methodologies linking geomorphology, archaeology and history, so that we can compare like with like: reliable evidence for environmental change with reliable evidence for settlement process. The need for this kind of study to advance the debate stimulated by Vita-Finzi's pioneering study provided a further critical context for the Biferno Valley Survey.

SELECTING THE STUDY REGION

After graduating in archaeology, I undertook a PhD on the prehistory of central Italy, based at the British School at Rome. The thesis concentrated on the transition from hunting to farming, as a contribution to the British Academy's Major Research Project on the Early History of Agriculture directed by Eric Higgs at Cambridge, who was my supervisor, although whilst in Rome my fieldwork was overseen by John Ward-Perkins. The study area was defined as the five main regions of central Italy: Toscana (Tuscany) and Lazio (Latium) on the western or Tyrrhenian side of the peninsula, Marche and Abruzzo on the eastern or Adriatic side, and Umbria in the centre (Fig. 1).

I had selected the area because it hadn't been worked on recently by a British student, for whom regional syntheses of Italy's prehistory have a remarkably long pedigree (Barfield, 1971; Barker, 1981; Peet, 1909; Stevenson, 1947; Trump, 1965; Whitehouse, 1992). The most recent thesis had been written by Ruth Whitehouse in the late 1960s, and was published as a series of important papers putting forward new chronologies and ideas about the beginnings of farming in southern Italy (Whitehouse, 1968a, 1968b, 1969, 1971). A striking feature of the Whitehouse and Barker PhDs was that the boundaries of southern Italy and central Italy drawn by the two theses met on the western side of Italy somewhere on the borders of Campania and Basilicata (subconsciously around Eboli, the town 'beyond which Christ stopped' in Carlo Levi's famous study of the Italian south, or Mezzogiorno), but not on the eastern side (Fig. 4). On this side, the region of Molise was no-man's-land, a blank area on both sets of thesis maps of prehistoric settlement. It was noticeable also in Radmilli's 1962 *Piccola Guida della Preistoria Italiana*, an atlas of known prehistoric sites, that Molise was a complete blank.

The heritage in Italy – archaeological, artistic, archival – is controlled and protected by a system of *soprintendenze*, or superintendencies. Each region has its Archaeological Superintendency, which undertakes appropriate conservation works to the monuments in its care, monitors planning applications for their effect on archaeological sites, conducts archaeological research (especially rescue work), and oversees fieldwork and museum studies in its territory by other archaeologists from Italian and foreign universities and museums and the foreign schools in Rome. (With few exceptions such as the Gruppo Archeologico Romano, amateur archaeologists are rarely permitted by the state to undertake fieldwork, especially excavation.) Molise is the youngest of the Italian regions. Until the 1960s it was administered with the neighbouring region to the north, Abruzzo, the entire region being known collectively as the Abruzzi. The case for it to be an autonomous region was formally recognized in 1966, but its first elected administrative council only took office in 1970. Until its own Archaeological Superintendency was established in that year in the capital town of the newly autonomous region of Campobasso, the archaeology of Molise was administered at a distance by the single Superintendency for Abruzzo and Molise in Abruzzo's capital town, Chieti. With no Superintendency of its own, and no university, it was perhaps inevitable that, until the establishment of the autonomous region, far less archaeological research had been carried out in Molise than anywhere else in Italy.

Given the wealth of material known to the north and south, it seemed to me highly likely that the almost total absence of published evidence for prehistoric finds in Molise reflected absence of fieldwork rather than absence of settlement. Certainly the area was known to have been occupied in classical times. Molise, at least the inland mountainous part of it, was known to have been the heartland of Samnium, the homeland of the Samnite tribes that the ancient historians describe as the most deadly

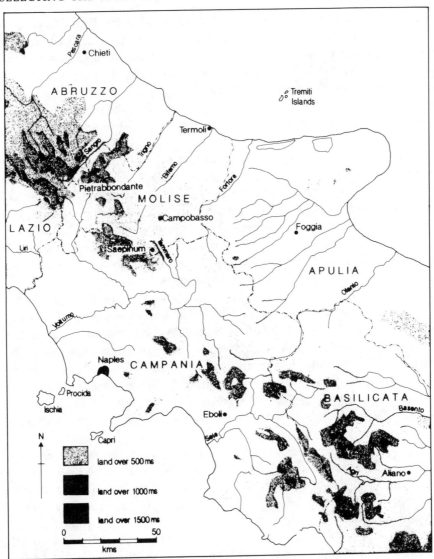

Fig. 4 Central-southern Italy: the natural landscape, the modern political regions, and places mentioned in Chapter One.

and unforgiving enemies of the Romans in their attempt to establish hegemony over the peninsula during the first three centuries BC. In 1967 E. T. Salmon had published a masterly synthesis of Samnite history and culture. Whilst depending for the most part on the ancient sources and epigraphic material, he also introduced into his narrative such archaeological research as had taken place to date on the best known

Samnite and Roman monuments of Molise, notably the Pietrabbondante sanctuary in the northern mountains and the Roman town of Saepinum in the inland basin of the upper Tammaro river. Most of this research had been undertaken in the 1960s by a young Italian archaeologist, Adriano La Regina, working from the Chieti Superintendency, who in 1970 was appointed the first Archaeological Superintendent for the new autonomous region. In 1974 he invited me to develop an archaeological survey in Molise.

The Biferno river is the principal river system of Molise: to the north, the Trigno forms the boundary with Abruzzo, and to the south, the Fortore forms the boundary with Apulia (Fig. 4). The headwaters of the river rise in an intermontane basin on the northern side of the Matese mountains, the part of the Apennine chain in this region of the peninsula, which rise to almost 2000 metres, and reach the sea near the port of Termoli some 75 kilometres away. With a total catchment measuring some 100 kilometres in length by 30 kilometres in width, a topography rising from sea level to almost 2000 metres, and a geological structure that is typical of the eastern side of the Italian peninsula, the valley seemed an ideal study area for the regional analysis planned. In addition, a major construction programme was near completion in the early 1970s of a new road down the valley, the Bifernina, dramatically improving access. The Biferno valley therefore offered a coherent and accessible sample of Mediterranean upland and lowland landscapes, ideally suited for an investigation of the ebbs and flows in settlement relationships between the two, and the impact of these on the natural environment.

The field survey and excavation programme began in September 1974, and the principal fieldwork continued every summer until 1978, though material studies and other fieldwork (geomorphological especially) continued throughout the 1980s. Colleagues from Sheffield who joined the Biferno survey also continued working in Molise afterwards. John Lloyd, the project's Roman specialist (now at the University of Oxford), excavated the Samnite and Roman villa of Matrice during the first half of the 1980s, and Richard Hodges, the medieval specialist for the project and latterly Director of the British School at Rome, has been excavating at the medieval monastery of San Vincenzo al Volturno in the northern mountains of Molise ever since the completion of the Biferno Valley Survey (Hodges, 1993). Italian colleagues have been extremely active in Molise through the same period, especially in the Biferno valley. As the following chapters integrating all these investigations describe, from being a blank area on the archaeological map of Italy thirty years ago the Biferno valley has become one of the most intensively investigated landscapes in Italy.

MOLISE AND THE MEZZOGIORNO

Southern Italy – the Mezzogiorno – has long been a byword in Europe for economic stagnation and social deprivation, the Achilles heel of the Italian post-war economic miracle. The European Union's 'index of well-being' for the region is a third the European average. Since 1950 land reform, the investments of the Cassa per il Mezzogiorno or 'Fund for the South' and other policies of industrial incentives have attempted to transform and modernise the Mezzogiorno. The visible results are new industrial complexes by the major cities, sprawling new coastal resorts of tourist hotels, new roads and motorways, and irrigation schemes to provide water for industry, agriculture, and population centres. Few of these projects, however, have created long-term employment, and the underlying social and economic fabric of the Mezzogiorno remains little changed. 'It represents the stunted noonday of Italy at its most tragic: scarred by erosion and earth tremors, tormented by drought, silenced by fascism, weakened by emigration . . . the developmental problems of these gaunt hills . . . are to do not only with topographic and climatic obstacles but also with centuries of feudal history, which have bred among the people a resigned, fatalistic mentality' (King, 1990: 41).

Though on its northern fringe, Molise is as firmly in the Mezzogiorno's grip as more notorious problem regions such as Calabria or Basilicata. Molise is spectacularly beautiful, though hardly visited by tourists (both foreign and Italian) apart from the beach resorts, and sophisticated Italians tend to caricature Molise as a cultural backwater. La Molisana, the main spaghetti manufacturer of the region, ran a national poster campaign a few years ago with the catchwords 'What? Decent pasta? From Molise?!!' Population densities are amongst the lowest in Italy: in 1978 there were some 320,000 inhabitants, with an average density of about seventy people per square kilometre. The Church and the Christian Democratic Party have been all-powerful influences on the fabric of ordinary life. The recent history of Molise has been characterized by some of the highest unemployment rates, the most extreme disparities between rich and poor, and the most intense rates of emigration of any in the Mezzogiorno – many Molisani have more family in Buffalo or Bedford than at home.

In 1935 the painter, writer and doctor Carlo Levi was punished by Mussolini for his anti-fascist writings by banishment from Rome to the remote village of Aliano in Basilicata in the heart of the Mezzogiorno (Fig. 4). The book he wrote about his experiences, *Christ Stopped at Eboli*, is by far the most eloquent account of the terrible conditions of poverty, deprivation and exploitation of the southern Italian *contadino*, the peasant or subsistence farmer, towards the middle of the 20th century. He looked back to:

> that other world, hedged in by custom and sorrow, cut off from History and the State, eternally patient, to that land without comfort or solace, where the peasant lives out his motionless civilisation on barren ground in remote poverty, and in the presence of death ... No one has come to this land except as an enemy, a conqueror, or a visitor devoid of understanding. The seasons pass today over the toil of the peasants, just as they did three thousand years before Christ; no message, human or divine, has reached this stubborn poverty ... Of the two Italys that share the land between them, the peasant Italy is by far the older; so old that no one knows whence it came, and it may have been here forever ... There should be a history of this Italy, a history outside the framework of time, confining itself to that which is changeless and eternal, in other words, a mythology. This Italy has gone its way in darkness and silence, like the earth, in a series of recurrent seasons and recurrent misadventures. Every outside influence has broken over it like a wave, without leaving a trace. (Levi, 1947: 12–13)

Watching the *contadini* at work in their fields, Levi felt he saw in their faces both the tragedy and the nobility of the resilience of this Other Italy in its ability to withstand the forces of history. 'I was struck by the peasants' build: they are short and swarthy with round heads, large eyes, and thin lips; their archaic faces do not stem from the Romans, Greeks, Etruscans, Normans, or any of the other invaders who have passed through their land, but recall the most ancient Italic types ... History has swept over them without effect' (1947: 137).

Christ Stopped at Eboli is an eloquent and moving account of the plight of the southern Italian *contadino* before the last war. It was extremely influential in shaping public opinion in Italy, leading to the foundation of the Cassa per il Mezzogiorno to facilitate state investment in the Mezzogiorno. To the dry academic, of course, its story of a peasant Italy motionless in remote poverty, of five thousand years of changeless toil 'cut off from History and the State', reads as poetic licence. Braudel's concept of Mediterranean landscape history as a complex and oscillating interplay between environment, land use and society, ebbs and flows that 'govern the life of man, which is never simple' (1972: 88), provides an inherently more plausible model for us to test in the earlier periods of Mediterranean settlement. Yet the frontispiece of this book, a photograph by Frank Monaco of a woman working in her fields in the upper Biferno valley in the early 1950s, is resonant of Levi's reflections on the antiquity of peasant life in the Mezzogiorno 'so old that no one knows whence it came, and it may have been here forever'. The project described in the following chapters set out to tell her story.

CHAPTER 2

THE BIFERNO VALLEY: THE MODERN LANDSCAPE

Graeme Barker

THE MODERN LANDSCAPE: TOPOGRAPHY AND GEOLOGY

The Biferno river has a measured length of 83.5 kilometres and a catchment of 1311 square kilometres (Lalli, 1978: 36). The study area for the archaeological survey was principally defined by the watershed of the Biferno river and its main tributary stream, the Cigno, but in the lower valley we also included the catchment area of the small stream north of the Biferno, the Sinarca, and limited survey took place on the floors of the high basins of the Matese mountains (Fig. 5). The area of study forms an approximate rectangle lying at an angle of 45 degrees some 75 kilometres long by 30 kilometres wide. It encompasses a range of topography and geology that is typical of the eastern side of the Italian peninsula. The topography rises from sea level to the high Apennines, 2000 metres above sea level. The geology (Fig. 29) includes the three principal components of the Adriatic side of the peninsula – Pliocene marine sands in the lowlands, a mixture of conglomerates, sandstones and clays in the middle valley, and limestone in the mountains – together with alluvial soils in the river valley and in a major intermontane basin at the head of the valley that is also typical of Apennine topography.

The Apennine chain that forms the backbone of the Italian peninsula is at its narrowest at the Matese – some 20 kilometres wide. The Hon. Keppel Craven, one of the very few English gentlemen whose Grand Tour in the early 19th century included Molise, ascended the Matese and described how 'the view from its summit, when favoured by a clear atmosphere and serene weather (circumstances of rare occurrence), is extremely extensive; embracing both seas, and, it is said, occasionally the coast of Dalmatia beyond the Adriatic' (Craven, 1838: 130). The structure of the Matese is typical of the limestone Apennines: steep ridges rising to some 2000 metres above sea level enclose a series of karstic basins (*altipiani*), the floors of most of which are at about 1000 metres above sea level. Formed by limestone solution, they have flat floors which are a

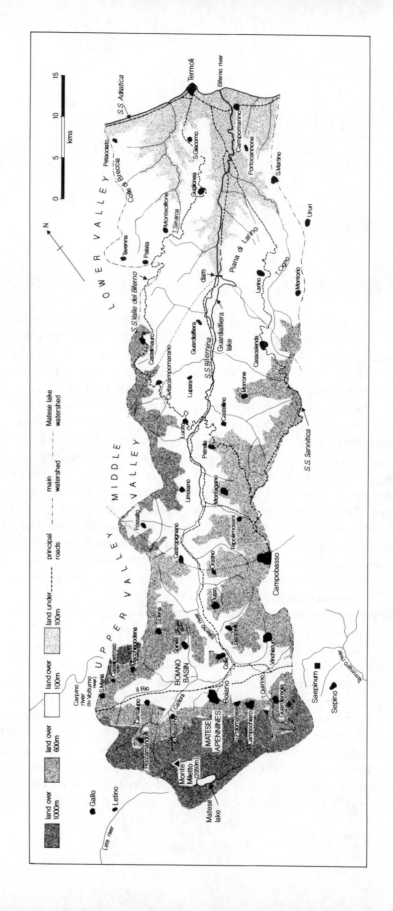

Fig. 6 The Matese mountains: the Lago del Matese *altopiano*, summer grazing for transhumant flocks. (Photograph: Graeme Barker)

combination of sediment accumulation and lateral solution by flood-waters (Fig. 6). The Matese has five principal basins, the largest of which has an enclosed catchment which feeds the only permanent lake, named after the mountain. Three others lie to its west, and provide the head-waters of the Lete river, which flows westwards out of the Matese into the Volturno. The ridge on the northern side of all four basins rises to the summit of the Matese, Monte Miletto (2050 metres above sea level), which forms the watershed between the Adriatic (Biferno) and Tyrrhenian (Volturno) river systems (Fig. 4). The fifth basin lies at 1400 metres above sea level on the northern flank of Monte Miletto and has been developed into the ski resort of Campitello.

The tributary streams of the Biferno river gather in a large intermontane basin north of the Matese named after its principal settlement, Boiano (Roman Bovianum). The floor of the basin, at about 500 metres above sea level, is covered by fine alluvial sediments, intermixed with colluvial sediments at the margins where erosion has brought down sediment from the basin sides; the most notable example of this phenomenon is the spectacular fan of sediment almost covering the eastern end of the basin (Fig. 29). As his carriage came down into the basin from Campobasso, Craven was moved by the magnificent vista before him (Fig. 7): 'the serrated peaks of the towering Matese, the magnificent forests that stretch

Fig. 5 The Biferno valley: topography and modern settlement.

Fig. 7 The Boiano basin, looking south from Colle Sparanise across the basin to the Matese mountains. Colle Sparanise was the site of a small rural sanctuary of the pre-Roman Samnite period, and there was a major Samnite sanctuary on the opposite side of the basin at the foot of the wooded slopes of the Matese (see Chapter Nine). (Photograph: Graeme Barker)

along its indented and precipitous flanks, and the transparent rills that issue from its roots and meander over a surface of verdure such as is never seen in the summer of the South' (Craven, 1838: 165). The principal stream of the Biferno, il Rio, meanders south-eastwards across the centre of the basin for some 15 kilometres, joined by the Torrente Callora near Boiano. The other main stream is the Torrente Quirino, the waters of which gather in the heights of the Matese and flow through a spectacular gorge at their foot before egressing onto the basin floor to join the Rio/Callora system, making the Biferno river proper on the northern edge of the Boiano basin. East of the Callora a low watershed separates the Boiano basin from the adjacent intermontane basin called the Piano di Sepino, named after the Roman town of Saepinum on its southern edge. The headwaters of the Tammaro river rise in this basin and flow southwards round the Matese into the Calore and thence the Volturno rivers (Figs. 4, 5).

On the southern side of the Boiano basin there is a band of gravels and conglomerates, with discontinuous patches of sands interspersed with limestone outcrops, forming a steep, rugged and broken terrain. 'Its aspect, on this side, is as impressive as gloomy: dark and yawning recesses, extending apparently into the bowels of the mountain, protrude huge

Fig. 8 The middle valley: outcrops of limestone amidst an unstable landscape of sands and clays. Looking northeast from near the southern watershed, towards Petrella Tifernina and across to the northern watershed on the other side of the 'Biferno gorge'. The Bronze Age settlement of Fonte Maggio (G1) is at the foot of the forested hill to the left of Petrella. (Photograph: Graeme Barker)

buttresses of naked rock into the flat; while these narrow glens are thickly clothed with impenetrable thickets, which appear to climb up the higher fissures as far as the most elevated point, Monte Miletto' (Craven, 1838: 159). The limestone hills and associated gravels extend northwards round the western end of the Boiano basin. Across the rest of the northern side of the basin, however, the topography changes markedly to gentle rolling hills rising to some 600–700 metres above sea level, as the underlying geology changes to sands.

From its point of egress from the Boiano basin, the Biferno river winds north-eastwards for some 75 kilometres to the sea. For the first two-thirds of this length, to the site of a former bridge called the Ponte del Liscione, it flows through a landscape made of soft sands and clays, interspersed with outcrops of limestone (Fig. 8). In this part of the valley the river flows down a narrow channel of alluvium about 100 metres wide, descending from 450 metres above sea level as it leaves the basin to about 90 metres above sea level at the Ponte del Liscione. The topography on either side is steep, the

Fig. 9 The lower valley: looking southeast across the Biferno floodplain below the Ponte del Liscione dam, with the dissected plateau of the Piana di Larino beyond and the hills around Larino in the distance. (Photograph: Graeme Barker)

watershed being 200–300 metres higher than the river in the upper section, rising to 500 metres or more downstream, though in general the rate of climb is sharper on the northern than on the southern side of the valley. The steepness of the topography and the soft and unstable nature of the geology combine to make this part of the Biferno landscape very liable to *frane*, or landslips (Figs. 111 and 112). 'The main track winds for some miles through a series of hills so barren and repulsive to the eye, that I could fancy myself among the clay mountains of Basilicata' (Craven, 1838: 139).

Some 20 kilometres from the sea, the Biferno river passes though a narrow gap in the hills at the site of the Ponte del Liscione. In the late 1960s and early 1970s the bridge was replaced by a dam almost 500 metres wide by 60 metres high, one of the largest in Europe, upstream of which there is now a lake, the Guardialfiera lake, some 8 kilometres in length. The modern Bifernina crosses the lake and dam in spectacular fashion on raised piles (Figs. 10, 110).

Below the dam the river meanders across a wide flood plain, reaching the sea near Termoli (Fig. 9). The topography on either side is generally much gentler and more rolling than upriver. North of the river, the land rises to a ridge 300–400 metres above sea level, crowned by the two major villages of Montecilfone (405 metres) and Guglionesi (369 metres). Between Guglionesi and the sea, the landscape consists of an extensive rolling plateau generally at about 100–150 metres above sea level, dissected by the tributaries of the Sinarca stream; the same landscape extends westwards from the Sinarca to the Colle Serramano/Colle di Breccia ridge, the limit of the survey area. On the southern side of the lower Biferno, the dominant topographical feature is another dissected plateau at the junction between the Biferno and the Cigno, its major tributary, the Piana di Larino (Larino plain), named after the principal town of this part of the valley. The plateau rises gently from about 30 to 200 metres above sea level, with the topography then changing to steeply rolling hills around Larino (341 metres), the northern end of the ridge of hills from Campobasso which form the southern watershed of the Biferno system. East of the Cigno, the topography of the lower valley is also characterized by rolling plateau lands. The geology of the lower valley is dominated by alluvial sediments, which form not only the floodplain of the Biferno but also the dissected plateau (Fig. 29). The Guglionesi and Sinarca plateaux are composed of a variety of gravels, sands, and clays, generally of Pliocene age. The plateau lands east of the Cigno are of similar composition and origin.

The boundary between the lower valley and the rest of the valley is commonly defined by the Ponte del Liscione dam, built at the natural topographical and geological division between the steeply sided, V-shaped valley upstream and the wide, flat-bottomed floodplain downstream. In his study of the economic geography of the modern settlement systems of the upper and middle valley, Ranieri (1956) drew the boundary with the lower valley at the Ponte del Liscione gap, extending it to the watershed westwards to Civita Campomarino and southwards to Casacalenda. The boundary also correlates broadly with the significant rainfall boundaries, the lower valley having less annual rainfall and markedly drier summers than the rest of the valley (see below). The same definition of the lower valley has been used in this study.

The boundary between the upper and middle valley is less easy to define, because the geology from the Boiano basin to the dam is basically the same. One important division generally used in Mediterranean environments is the limit of olive cultivation; in the case of the Biferno valley, olives are grown inland as far as Petrella and Lucito. However, the 800-millimetre rainfall isohyet is probably a more useful boundary between the intermediate environment of the middle valley and the significantly wetter, colder and more mountainous interior. This boundary runs westwards from the capital town of Campobasso past the villages of Oratino and Castropignano on either side of the valley, and then curves northwards approximately along the 600-metre contour (Fig. 5). In this study, therefore, the upper valley is defined broadly as the area of the Boiano basin and the upper stretches of the Biferno as far as this line, and the middle valley as the remaining section to the Ponte del Liscione dam. However, the upper/middle division has to be seen as rather arbitrary, the division between the lower valley and the remainder being clearer and, as we shall see, generally more significant in the valley's history.

SETTLEMENT AND COMMUNICATIONS

As discussed in the following section, the dominant form of settlement in the Matese mountains traditionally has been of a seasonal character, but two of the upland basins on the southern side support villages: Letino (1046 metres) and Gallo (877 metres) (Fig. 5). In the Boiano basin, the main town is unusual in its location at the edge of the alluvial sediments – most of the villages are further upslope, often situated on isolated limestone outcrops. There are very similar settlements on the northern side of the basin where the geology is similar. The villages on the sandy soils either side of the Biferno's egress route from the basin are generally more extensive settlements than the limestone hilltop villages. All these villages, like most of those further down the valley, are medieval foundations, the result of the shift common throughout Italy from dispersed Roman settlement on the plains to nucleated hilltop villages, the process of *incastellamento* that forms a critical part of our settlement analysis (Chapter Eleven).

Although the Boiano basin can seem isolated, cut off from the outside world by the Matese on the one side and the unstable landscape of the upper Biferno on the other, in fact communications to the western side of the peninsula are relatively easy. Before modern times it was relatively simple in most weathers for travellers to bypass the Matese by crossing the low watersheds separating the Biferno from the Volturno and Tammaro rivers. From spring to autumn it was also possible to cross the Matese from one *altopiano* to another, following the shepherd tracks that linked the mountains with the communities either side. 'Rugged and impracticable as the passage over the highest extremities of the Matese may seem, it is in use at almost every season of the year by the natives of the south and northern sides of the mountains, who drive their beasts of burden, laden with various articles of commerce or produce, close to the most elevated of its pinnacles. The ascent [from the south] does not employ more than five hours; and much less is required to descend into the valley of Boiano' (Craven, 1838: 166).

The villages of the middle stretches of the valley, where the geology is dominated by laminated sands and clays, are almost invariably situated on limestone outcrops overlooking the valley, often at the ends of spurs projecting from the watershed ridge (Fig. 8). Until the construction of the

Bifernina along the valley bottom, communications in this part of the valley were generally extremely difficult. 'Except the high road to Naples, [Campobasso] is provided with no direct or efficient means of communication with the rest of the kingdom, and the coast of the Adriatic. A road originally intended to secure this last advantage, by communicating with the little sea port of Termoli on that sea, has hitherto been carried no farther than fourteen miles beyond Campobasso, in the direction of Larino' (Craven, 1838: 141). The road to which Craven refers, now called the Sannitica, was completed in the following decades as the principal route of the Biferno valley, winding along the main southern watershed ridge from Campobasso towards Termoli, crossing the Biferno about six kilometres from the sea (Fig. 5).

The villages on the right-hand side of the valley were connected to the Sannitica by roads along the spurs on which they are located; tracks led down from them to the river, but crossings were few. In medieval times there were isolated bridges such as the Ponte San Antuono (Fig. 10), now submerged in the Guardialfiera lake, but few lasted long before the pressure of the torrential waters of the winter and spring floods. Between 1845 and 1881 no bridge existed across the Biferno upstream of Porto-cannone. The river could be forded, with some difficulty, in summer. In winter, villages only a few kilometres apart were isolated from each other, the settlements on the left side of the river in particular being more or less totally cut off from news of the outside world (Perrazzelli, 1976: 77–78).

Towards the end of the 19th century a second major route was constructed, now the SS Valle del Biferno, branching off the Sannitica a few kilometres north of Campobasso, crossing the Biferno between Petrella and Lucito, and then following the northern watershed of the valley down to Termoli (Fig. 5). Apart from this route over the river, for much of this century there have been only two other significant river crossings between the Boiano basin and the Ponte del Liscione, the first being the road from Campobasso via Oratino and Castropignano to the Trigno valley, the second linking Casacalenda with Guardialfiera. The dramatic improvement in communications brought about by the construction of the modern valley road is demonstrated partly by the varying distances of the Sannitica, Valle del Biferno and Bifernina from Campobasso to Termoli (80, 100 and 65 kilometres respectively), but more particularly by travel times: by car, the journey from Campobasso to Termoli now takes some three-quarters of an hour using the Bifernina, but two or three hours along the tortuous curves of the other two roads. As our project discovered, the difficulties of communication between the middle valley and the upper and lower zones were as significant in antiquity.

The settlement system of the lower valley consists of the main

Fig. 10 The Ponte San Antuono medieval bridge, one of the main crossings of the Biferno river – now submerged under the Guardialfiera lake, with the modern Bifernina and one of its link roads in the distance. (Photograph: Graeme Barker)

population centre Termoli, with a few villages that all tend to be rather substantial settlements with populations of some several thousand people. This compares with the inland part of the valley, where there are the two major towns of Campobasso, the regional capital, and Boiano, together with large numbers of hill villages with populations of one or two thousands or even a few hundreds (Table 1). Communications in the lower part of the valley have generally been easier than upriver given the gentleness of the topography and the adjacency of the Adriatic. The natural movement of communications is inevitably along the line of the coast,

Table 1 1978 population figures for the Biferno valley *comuni*.
(Source: Lalli, 1978: 195–8)

Upper valley		Middle valley		Lower valley	
Baranello	3064	Casacalenda	3425	Campomarino	3972
Boiano	6928	Castelmauro	3188	Guglionesi	5821
Busso	1484	Castellina	1063	Montecilfone	2396
Campobasso	41782	Guardialfiera	330	Montenero	2757
Campochiaro	754	Limosano	1337	Petacciato	2845
Cantalupo	1050	Lucito	1391	Portocannone	2423
Casalciprano	831	Lupara	1082	S. Giacomo	866
Castelpetroso	1944	Montorio	932	S. Martino	4433
Castropignano	1533	Morrone	1432	Termoli	15659
Colle d'Anchise	1061	Petrella	1620	Ururi	3495
Guardiaregia	1052	Providdenti	234	Macchiagódena	2425
Macchiagódena	2425				
Montagano	513				
Oratino	1193				
Ripolimosano	1935				
Roccamandolfi	1409				
S. Angelo	877				
S. Polo Matese	426				
Spinete	1666				
Vinchiaturo	2539				

whether by sea or along the littoral itself. Today the principal road and rail routes of the eastern side of the peninsula pass through Molise along the coast, along the line of a principal road of Roman times. A reflection of the openness of this part of the Biferno to the Adriatic sphere was the settlement here of Albanian refugees from the Turks in the 15th and 16th centuries. Their major settlements in the valley were Montecilfone and Petacciato on the western side of the valley and Campomarino, Porto-cannone, and Ururi on the eastern side.

Like the rest of the Mezzogiorno, very large areas of Molise were marshy and poorly drained when proper records began to be made in the early 19th century (Del Re, 1836), and much of the population was affected by malaria. Torelli's map of the distribution of malaria in Italy (1882) shows most of the Biferno valley as affected, the area around Larino being the worst. A detailed study of the problem in Molise concluded that virtually everybody living in the vicinity of the river from Boiano to Termoli had malaria (Pietravalle, 1890). The number of deaths from malaria in Molise at that time was amongst the worst anywhere in Mezzogiorno. It was recognized that the construction of the railway in the mid-19th century had generally exacerbated conditions by impeding natural drainage in the lower valley in particular. Large-scale drainage works (*bonifica*) were undertaken here in the late 19th century, though still only a small fraction of the land identified as marshy by Del Re was improved. Malaria was only eradicated from the valley at the end of the last war.

ENVIRONMENT AND LAND USE

The dramatic topographical differences between the upper and lower valley are inevitably reflected in climate, environment and land use. Winter temperatures today average 3 degrees centigrade at Campobasso compared with 7 degrees at Termoli, and the respective summer temperatures are 22 degrees and 25 degrees (Simoncelli, 1972: 34). Spring temperatures on the coastal lowlands are comparable with those inland three months later. The rainfall regime is typical of the Mezzogiorno, in that most of it falls in autumn and winter, but the amount of rainfall varies considerably depending on altitude and exposure (Fig. 11). Records earlier this century for mean annual rainfall included a minimum of 644 millimetres on the coastal lowlands and a high of 1870 millimetres at Roccamandolfi in the upper valley (Simoncelli, 1972: 39).

The distribution of rainfall varies likewise from less than seventy days a year on the lowlands to over one hundred days at Boiano. Most of it falls in the autumn and winter, the period when landslips are common in the claylands. The summer is not as arid as elsewhere in the Mezzogiorno, but although nowhere in Molise receives more than 200 millimetres of rain through the summer, summer rainfall on the lowlands is frequently below 50 millimetres and in particularly bad summers the lowlands can be entirely rainless. In the uplands, much of the precipitation falls as snow. The recent records for Molise indicate averages of fifteen to thirty days of snowfall each year above 1000 metres' altitude, with the high mountains such as the Matese snow-covered in the winter from one to three months. Many of the interior villages are cut off for several days each year after heavy snowfalls, particularly if high winds cause drifting.

Patterns of land use have been changing significantly in the post-war period, but a useful guide to the major divisions in land use is the *Carta della Utilizzazione del Suolo* published in 1959 (Fig. 12). These maps were produced from air photographs (including those of the wartime air forces) at a scale of 1:200,000 for the whole of Italy in the 1950s. The lower valley has the classic radial pattern of land use around Mediterranean lowland villages, in which there is a gradation outwards from the settlement from intensive to extensive in terms of time and labour requirements (Chisholm, 1968). Thus olive and vine cultivation is dominant around the major settlements (together with garden plots not shown on the map); the intervening areas are given over almost exclusively to dry farming, in places interspersed with tree crops; and pasture and woodland lie beyond

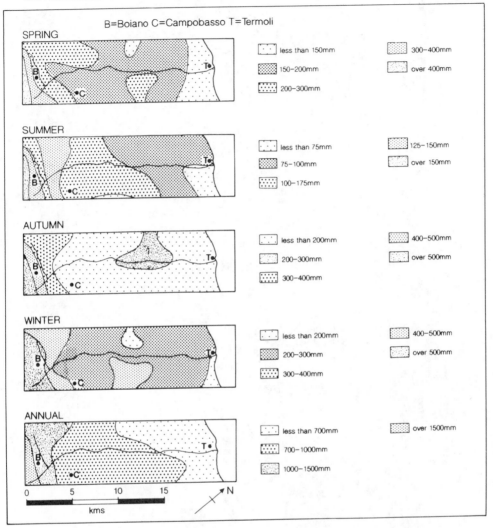

Fig. 11 Seasonal and annual patterns of rainfall in the Biferno valley.
(After Simoncelli, 1972: figs 26, 28, 31)

the arable land, mainly along the floor of the Biferno valley. Traditionally
olives and vines were grown in systems of polyculture or *coltura promiscua*
– that is, mixed together in rows with the intervening spaces used for
cereals and other crops (Fig. 13). The system was admirably suited to cope
with summer aridity – the roots of the vines, olive trees and annual crops
occupied different soil levels and so did not compete with each other for
water, and the trees also provided shade – and in winter it raised the
ground temperature by several degrees, making for a longer growing
season.

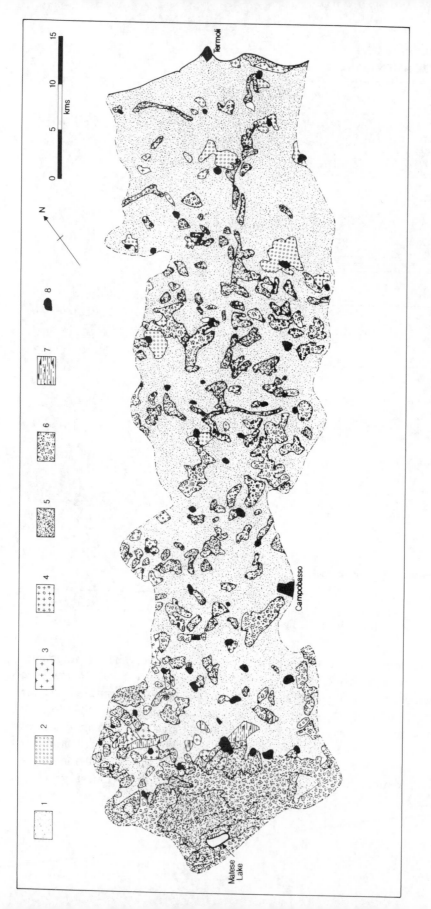

Termoli

Campobasso

Matese
Lake

N

0 5 10 15

kms

1 2 3 4 5 6 7 8

Fig. 13 Classic Mediterranean polyculture in the Biferno valley: olive trees with vines between, a fig tree in the background, and cereal cultivation on the intervening ground. (Photograph: Graeme Barker)

In the middle and upper valley, there is a somewhat similar pattern of intensive-to-extensive land use around the villages, but the principal difference is that olive cultivation diminishes rapidly inland from the dam, dying out beyond Lucito. The clay 'badlands' are frequently forested, and large areas of the valley floor are given over to tangled undergrowth and rough grazing, recorded as 'pasture/uncultivated land' on the 1959 map. In the upper valley the hill villages on the edge of the Boiano basin are surrounded by gardens, orchards and vineyards. The floor of the basin is for the most part given over to cereals and legumes, but the wettest areas of the alluvium are used for rice cultivation. The flanks of the Matese overlooking the basin are heavily forested, though there are also extensive areas of grazing at the margins between the forest and the cultivated zone.

Fig. 12 Simplified land use in the Biferno valley: 1. arable; 2. olives; 3. vines; 4. mixed olives and vines; 5. pasture and rough grazing; 6. woodland; 7. irrigated land; 8. settlements (identified in Figure 5). (Adapted from the *Carta della Utilizzazione del Suolo d'Italia*, 1959, foglio 15)

Fig. 14 Women harvesting in the upper Biferno valley in 1953. (Photograph: Frank Monaco)

In the Matese mountain, the floors of the major basins are shown as given over partly to crops and partly to pasture, the latter extending up the sides of the basin and over the crests above the tree line.

Not shown in the land-use map are the nature and scale of cultivation, and how it changes from the lowlands to the uplands. The settlement pattern of the lower valley includes large farms dotted across the landscape as well as the major settlements, whereas in the rest of the valley, and particularly around the Boiano basin, most farmers live in villages and travel out each day to cultivate their fields or tend their stock. As a rule, field sizes decrease steadily as the topography steepens and gets more broken, as do the size of landholdings, and the scale and efficiency of technology. Yields fall accordingly, and farming is increasingly at a subsistence level moving up the valley into higher altitudes, steeper topography and lower temperatures. The photographs taken by Frank

Fig. 15 A young shepherdess with her flock in the upper Biferno valley
in 1953. (Photograph: Frank Monaco)

Monaco near Cantalupo in the 1950s of women harvesting by sickle and of
a shepherd girl guarding the family flock, like the frontispiece photograph,
are eloquent witnesses to the harshness of peasant life in the upper valley
in the early post-war period (Figs. 14, 15). Inevitably, this area has suffered
most from the flight from the land, and most of the pasture/rough grazing
shown on the land-use map along the northern slopes of the Matese
consists of cultivation terraces abandoned during the course of this century
(Fig. 109). There are increasing areas of cultivable land abandoned to rough
grazing throughout the upper valley. Most marginal of all is the cultivation
of the Matese basin floors: the climate precludes the cultivation of the olive,
vine, and fig, soils are extremely stony, winters exceptionally harsh and
frosts late, and the few main crops consist of hardy cereals, potatoes and so
on.

Arable farming is combined with stock-keeping to varying degrees in the
valley. Apart from poultry and rabbits (the latter traditionally an important

source of meat for the Mezzogiorno *contadino*), most farms have a couple of pigs and sometimes a few cattle. Before mechanization, oxen, horses or donkeys were needed for working the fields: horses were commonly used in the lower valley for pulling carts, and donkeys as pack animals inland. The most numerous stock, however, were sheep and goats, which are far better adapted to the Mediterranean climate and vegetation than cattle.

Sheep and goat pastoralism in the Apennines divides into two major forms, *stanziale* (stalled) and *transumanti* (transhumant) (Barker and Grant, 1991). The commonest form in the valley is relatively small-scale *stanziale* husbandry, within a mixed farming system. The family has a small flock, from a score or so to a hundred animals, less commonly a few hundred animals. During the night they are kept on the farm or in the village, in a pen or (especially in winter) in a stall. By day they are taken away from the settlement by a shepherd to graze on vegetation within a couple of kilometres' radius – wasteland, roadside grass, fallow land, stubble fields after harvest, the rough grazing along the river floor. In the lower and middle valley in particular this kind of pastoralism is especially important for fertilising the arable land. In the upper valley, pastoralism is increasingly important as crop farming is more marginal. The villages of the Boiano basin in particular tend to have bigger flocks, because there is such extensive grazing on the abandoned terraces and, more particularly, in the Matese mountains. Much of the shepherding from these villages involves daily journeys into the Matese. Many of the shepherds, however, take their animals up to the Matese *altopiani* for the summer months, living in stone huts and overnighting their flocks in enclosures attached to them.

The Matese *altopiani*, and the higher pastures up to 2000 metres, are also used by transhumant shepherds (Fig. 6), who winter their flocks on the Tavoliere plain around Foggia in Apulia some 80–100 kilometres away (Sprengel, 1975: 283). The Matese is the smallest and southernmost of the Apennine summer pasturing area used by the Tavoliere flocks (Fig. 16). The other main direction of transhumance is from the Apennines to the Maremma coastal regions along the western littoral of central Italy. Today the flocks are transported between the winter and summer pastures by truck. Earlier this century and at the end of the last century many were taken by train to railheads and walked to the pastures from there. The traditional method, however, was to walk the flocks on foot, using droveroads or *tratturi*. During this century six major droveroads from the Tavoliere plain crossed the Biferno valley, cutting across the grain of the topography running more or less parallel to the coast before swinging inland to the Abruzzo mountains further up the peninsula. These wide swaths of grass were public land, protected from cultivation by the State. With the demise of transhumance on the hoof, the droveroads are

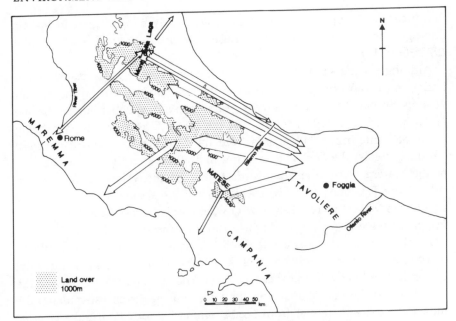

Fig. 16 Pre-war transhumance routes in peninsular Italy. (After Sprengel, 1975: 283)

Fig. 17 A droveroad (*tratturo*) crossing the Biferno valley. (Photograph: Graeme Barker)

disappearing, though traces of them could clearly be discerned in the air photographs used for the 1959 land-use map and were still visible in the 1970s (Fig. 17).

Although some landowners on the lowlands have large transhumant flocks, most transhumant shepherds in the Apennines are from the upland villages. Sprengel's excellent survey of transhumant shepherding in the late 1960s, published in 1975, found that the lower Biferno valley was being used for wintering by shepherds from the Monti della Laga of northern Abruzzo, whilst the flocks belonging to the villages on the northern flanks of the Matese were taken eastwards to the Ofanto valley on the eastern side of the Tavoliere plain, whereas those of the settlements on the other side of the Matese were taken down to Campania. Flocks from landowners in Apulia were also being brought up to the Matese.

As elsewhere in the peninsula, both the stalled and transhumant flocks of Molise are kept mainly for their meat and milk – the price for wool currently barely covers the shearing costs. The most visible activity of the shepherds in the mountains or in the lower villages is cheese-making: the milk is boiled and rennet from lambs' stomachs added to make *pecorino* cheese, which is mild when eaten fresh or very sharp when cured. The whey makes *ricotta*, a kind of cream cheese. However, the main profit in shepherding today is in the production of meat from very young (30–40-day-old) milk lambs, *abbacchio*, which is highly prized in Italy, fetching more than twice the price per kilo of mutton. The fourth product of sheep, their manure, is also valuable, the rents for grazing land taking this into account. The value of *abbacchio* is a principal factor preserving transhumant shepherding at a time when social factors mitigate strongly against it. Traditionally, the young men from the community took the sheep into the high pastures above the *altopiani* for the summer months, penning their flocks at night in rope enclosures and themselves sleeping in rough stone and turf shelters. Today the transhumant shepherds tend to use pre-fabricated metal huts as their living and working quarters, camping on the *altopiani* where they can be reached on a daily basis from their villages by truck. Wives occasionally now take part in what was almost invariably an exclusively male domain.

The antiquity of long-distance transhumance in the Apennines, as elsewhere in the Mediterranean, is the subject of much debate (Barker, 1989a). Large-scale transhumance clearly has to operate within a political context capable of protecting extensive areas of grazing and the droveroads connecting them, and has generally been a capitalist enterprise, whether State or private. The documentary evidence indicates that it goes back to the Roman period. In the last century Craven, travelling in the summer in the mountains north of Molise, reported seeing vast flocks 'plodding across the valleys of Abruzzo as far as the eye can reach', and along the access route the flocks 'slowly passed by the carriage for a mile or more' (Craven, 1838: 259). The zenith of the system was probably when Abruzzo and Molise were within the Kingdom of the Two Sicilies, when millions of animals walked the droveroads each year and the system was promoted by the government taxation office, the Dogana delle Pecore (Braudel, 1972: 85–9; Di Cicio, 1966), which controlled the gathering of the flocks at the ends of the droveroads and their distribution to the Tavoliere farms or to the high pastures. References to long-distance Apennine transhumance are common throughout the medieval period, the flocks being owned variously by the State, the Church, or noble families (Clementi, 1984; Sprengel, 1975). Some of the earliest medieval references, from the 8th century, are from the archive of Farfa abbey in the Sabine hills near Rome (Leggio, 1991). References are also common in the Roman period, from the late Republic through the empire (Gabba, 1985, 1988; Pasquinucci, 1979).

One of the most famous pieces of evidence for long-distance trans-humance in Roman Italy in fact comes from Saepinum, the Roman town immediately east of the Boiano basin. An inscription on the western gate (CIL.IX.2438), dated to the reign of Marcus Aurelius, registers a dispute between the town officials and the shepherds over tolls (Fig. 82). It records that similar notices recording the shepherds' rights were being set up along the droveroad, including at Bovianum. The modern droveroad also passes through Saepinum (Fig. 83) to Boiano, but it is impossible to say whether or not the other five droveroads now crossing the Biferno valley have their origins in Roman times. It seems unlikely there could be a one-to-one correlation, though it is interesting that the *pro Cluentio* speech by the orator Cicero mentions what seem to be transhumant shepherds below the town of Larinum (Larino), where one of the modern *tratturi* crosses (Barker *et al.*, 1978). The important point is the clear evidence for long-distance transhumance and the *tratturo* system in the Biferno valley in Roman times. The evidence for the development of pastoralism in general, and for transhumance, earlier than the Roman period is discussed in the ensuing chapters.

In the 1970s it was still common to see hand-cultivation in the upper valley (Fig. 18), and cultivation with a light plough drawn by a donkey, horse, or pair of oxen in the upper and middle valley (Fig. 19). In the lower valley, however, the 1960s and 1970s witnessed the change to mechaniz-ation that began elsewhere in Italy in the pre-war years, that has fundamentally changed the landscape (and has since extended to much of the middle valley). Animal traction gave way to heavy tractors with caterpillar tracks capable of not bogging down on heavy soils. The ploughs they pulled changed from light wooden ploughs with metal shares, or all-

Fig. 18 Hand cultivation in the upper Biferno valley in the 1970s.
(Photograph: Graeme Barker)

Fig. 19 Traditional ploughing technology in the middle Biferno valley in
the 1970s. (Photograph: Graeme Barker)

Fig. 20 Modern ploughing technology in the lower Biferno valley in the 1980s. (Photograph: Graeme Barker)

metal ploughs, capable of cultivating down to 15–20 centimetres, to single- or multi-shared steel ploughs which commonly reach down to 75–80 centimetres (Fig. 20).

The change has been accompanied by a dramatic extension of the cultivated zone, because the new technology has enabled farmers to plough slopes that formerly could only be cultivated by hand. In the lower valley, moreover, the heavy alluvium of the floodplain of the Biferno below the dam formerly given over to scrub and rough grazing has been drained and also taken into cultivation. Field boundaries have been bulldozed to make for larger and more efficient ploughing units. Polyculture has increasingly given way to monoculture, with separate vineyards, olive groves, and cereal fields. The trend has been in response to both the new technologies and their efficiency demands, and market forces in the form of subsidies from the Italian State and the EU. The development of vineyards has been particularly dramatic: to prepare the ground for the new roots it is ploughed down to over a metre's depth with a colossal share, and a lattice of concrete posts then established to support the vine rows, set at an appropriate distance to allow for mechanized cultivation in between. Apart from the dramatic increase in erosion rates caused by the new technologies (Chapters Four and Thirteen), the changing nature of land use in the valley during the 1970s had a major influence on the development of the archaeological survey.

CHAPTER 3

THE BIFERNO VALLEY SURVEY: METHODOLOGIES

Graeme Barker

In terms of landscape archaeology in general and field survey in particular, the Mediterranean region is typical of most parts of the world in that there is a large and growing literature on aspects of survey methodology and a number of publications presenting survey results (e.g. Barker and Hodges, 1981; Barker and Lloyd, 1991; Keller and Rupp, 1983), but the number of publications of regional studies in which the methodologies and data as well as the interpretations have been explicitly described are very few indeed. Yet, as Cherry *et al.* (1992) describe in their excellent account of the Keos Survey in Greece, full publication is essential because 'how decisions affecting a survey's eventual form are actually made is not widely agreed upon, nor are they often set out in detail in the final report; yet, they materially affect the character of the data acquired by the survey and, still more important, the types of archaeological problems they can be used to tackle' (1992: 13).

It is a commonplace that in any archaeological field project, the methodologies selected form the vital link between the general research aims and the nature of the data required to tackle them. As described in Chapter One, the Biferno Valley Survey took the British School's South Etruria Survey as its general role model in setting out to apply a group of archaeological methodologies in landscape analysis to a selected study area, to try to reconstruct and understand its settlement history. On the other hand, like most archaeological projects of this kind, the Biferno Valley Survey grew organically and altered focus within the overall research design as particular contributors joined the team, new and unexpected sets of data emerged, specific research problems came to the fore, and local circumstances changed – for example, new accommodation offered, the weather making ploughing unexpectedly late, or a request from the Superintendency to assist with a particular project in progress.

DEFINING THE SURVEY AREA

The rationale for the selection of the study area has already been described in Chapter One. Given that it had to be large enough to encompass a typical range of Mediterranean topography from coast to mountain, the catchment area of a medium-sized river seemed entirely appropriate. The Biferno was the only such river lying entirely within the boundaries of Molise and so was the obvious choice. The area selected for the survey consisted largely of the main catchment, but we did not take the watershed as an immovable boundary. Inland, I decided to extend the area of interest into the *altopiani* within the Matese mountain (Fig. 5) rather than stop at the Biferno's watershed on the first ridge: as the floors of the upland basins have been the only focus for substantial occupation in recent times (because they contain the principal cultivable soils and pastures in the mountains), it seemed very likely that we would need information about mountain settlement in antiquity from the same zones as well as from within the Biferno's watershed on the Matese. On the lowlands, the main catchment narrows substantially near the sea, so to obtain a more representative sample of lowland settlement data the study area was extended north to include the adjacent catchment of the Sinarca stream – on the dissected plateau near Termoli the watershed between the lower Biferno and Sinarca in any case is frequently imperceptible – and survey was also conducted outside the formal boundary to the south. The area of study thus defined measured some 75×30 kilometres, or 2250 square kilometres.

Regional archaeological surveys in the Mediterranean have differed enormously in scale, but the most impressive results in terms of settlement analysis have invariably been obtained from projects that were systematically intensive in the method of field-walking, developing the techniques pioneered in south Etruria (Cherry, 1983). Such methods are necessary to collect representative samples of the surface archaeology: for the Roman period, for example, this typically consists not only of the surface remains of large sites such as estate villas but also those of small sites such as cottages and huts. For many periods of antiquity, particularly in prehistory, the settlement remains left on the surface today are even more ephemeral. Clearly we needed to apply systematic and intensive methods of field-walking to get reliable data sets, but equally clearly it was unrealistic to attempt to cover the whole 2250 square kilometres.

Like almost all modern survey projects, therefore, we had to select a sample of the study area for analysis (Cherry, 1983; Mueller, 1975; Schiffer *et al.*, 1978). The main programme of field-walking was carried out between 1974 and 1978, for a total of fourteen weeks, normally employing a dozen students each day, making a total of just over 750 person-days. The archaeological survey covered just over 400 square kilometres, or 18 per cent of the total catchment of the study area, making this project one of the largest archaeological surveys in the Mediterranean (Fig. 21). In the first year, as a pilot exercise, three blocks of terrain were selected, in the upper, middle and lower valley respectively. In the middle years of the survey, work concentrated in the lower valley, where large continuous blocks of ploughed land across the low ridges and dissected plateaux were accessible to the survey teams. In the final season, work concentrated on the 'badlands' of the middle valley, which were investigated by a team led by John Cherry using a series of transects across them. We also returned to the upper valley in that year to investigate settlement at the western end of the Boiano basin using a limited set of transects.

The completed sample thus consists of a set of quite extensive blocks of terrain across the lower valley, and composites of blocks and transects in the middle and upper valley. Although it would have been better to have designed a single sampling strategy at the beginning of the project, we do at least have a relatively large sample of what is in any case a very large study area compared with most archaeological surveys, and one which spans the entire topography from the Apennines to the sea. On the other hand, the data base is undoubtedly biased towards the lower valley: the units investigated in the upper, middle, and lower zones consist of, respectively, 30 per cent, 25 per cent and 45 per cent of the total sample investigated. Moreover, the bias towards the lower valley may be further exaggerated by the 'filtering' effect of land use and topography further inland: as described in Chapter Two, field sizes are generally much smaller here than in the lower valley, and in parts of the upper valley the amount of uncultivated or abandoned land was visibly increasing through the lifetime of the project. Field-walking in parts of the middle valley was particularly difficult because of the steepness of the terrain.

FIELD-WALKING TECHNIQUES

Not all the 400 square kilometres were walked in the same way. In the most intensive system, used after the first two years, teams of students endeavoured to cover all accessible land in the unit to which they had been assigned. In the earlier years of the survey, particularly in the first year which was devoted almost entirely to field-walking (the second season was

Fig. 21 The archaeological survey: the IGM (Istituto Geografico Militare) map grid showing the twenty-three map units in which survey took place and the sampling strategy (for explanation, see text discussion): 1. intensive-level survey; 2. intermediate-level survey; 3. reconnaissance survey.

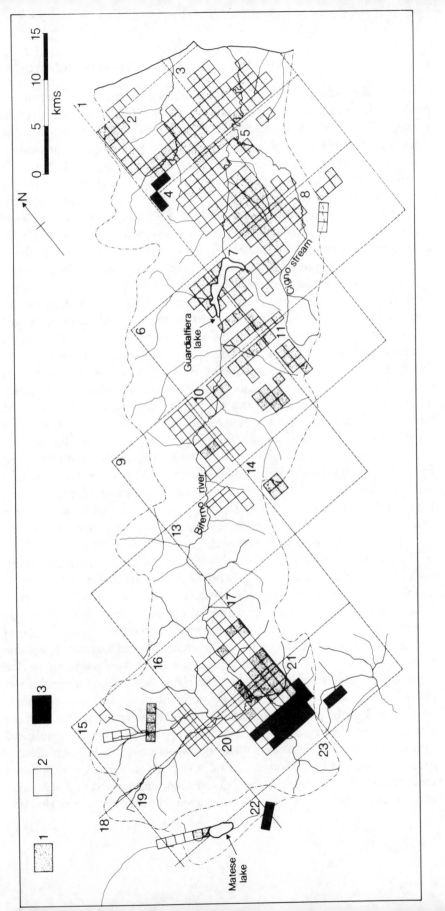

N

1 2 3

0 5 10 15
kms

Guardialfiera
lake

Biferno river

Cigno stream

Matese
lake

dominated by excavation), I was anxious to get preliminary results from all parts of the valley, and the coverage was generally less intensive: on average 50–75 per cent of the terrain of each unit was searched. In a few areas we also carried out what can be classified simply as reconnaissance work, for example in parts of the Matese mountain bordering with Campania. About 40 per cent of the study sample was walked with the first method, 50 per cent with the second, and 10 per cent with the third.

For the area in which they were working, each team had photocopies of the relevant part of the IGM (Istituto Geografico Militare) 1:25,000 topographical map. Field-walking was conducted in twenty-three of these, each of which measures about 90 square kilometres (Fig. 21). They marked the units they had searched on the photocopy (so the units not searched were also clearly demarcated) and all units with finds were assigned an individual number. One problem we encountered was that many of the last series of IGM maps published in the 1950s were not subdivided with a kilometre grid. As the four teams headed out of Boiano on the first day of the first season, I had assigned each team a letter (A–D), and each numbered its units sequentially, beginning A1, B1, C1, D1. Later on when all four teams were in the field and specialists were working elsewhere, the latter were assigned different sequences (E and G). With retrospect it would have been much simpler for the analysis of the results to have imposed a square kilometre grid on the entire map cover for the valley at the outset, assigned each square kilometre an individual number, and then had each finds unit numbered from one onwards within it, the system I have used in later surveys at Montarrenti (Barker et al., 1986) and Tuscania (Barker et al., 1993), instead of having sites with consecutive numbers in different parts of the survey area.

The recording system, like much else in the survey's methodology, underwent change during the fieldwork. At the beginning of the survey, a simple record sheet was used, half A4-sized, with seven small boxes (area/season; date; finder's initials; grid reference; feature type; finder's feature number; period) and two main spaces for text, one on the location/natural features of the unit and the other on the archaeological features. It became clear that much more consistency and precision were required in the information supplied under the last two headings – good team leaders provided excellent record sheets, but from other teams the descriptions became noticeably more laconic as the day got hotter (or wetter in some cases). The original record sheet was therefore replaced in the fourth and fifth seasons by a double-sided A4 record sheet designed by John Cherry, requiring much more information. The first page was divided as follows: unit number; date; initials of team leader; map number and grid reference; chronological periods tentatively recognized; description of the situation

Fig. 22 Field-walking in the Biferno valley: the members of the team are walking parallel to each other 15 metres apart, towards a typical concentration of surface archaeological material. (Photograph: Graeme Barker)

(topography, natural vegetation, local land use); general description of the unit, with sketch; extent of unit; features noted/nature of scatter/extent and nature of structures, ground plan etc. The reverse side had spaces for further details of the finds and the photographic record, and a checklist to note the presence and relative abundance of the archaeological materials observed (brick, tile, cut blocks, rubble, concrete, marble, mosaic, non-local stone, plaster, daub, pottery, pottery wasters, chipped stone, glass, metal, coin, mortar, industrial waste, human bone etc).

Each team selected a unit to be walked, normally a ploughed field or, in the huge ploughed areas of parts of the lower valley, a segment of a ploughed field demarcated by buildings, tracks, drainage ditches etc. They then traversed the unit in parallel lines walking fifteen paces apart, picking up all the archaeological artefacts (mainly potsherds, pieces of brick or tile, and chipped stone or flint) visible in a metre-wide strip (Fig. 22). All units with archaeological materials were numbered and assigned a record sheet, so some of these were distinct concentrations of artefacts ('sites'), others were fields with low densities of sporadic or 'off-site' material. If a field contained sites within it, these would be assigned separate numbers from those given to the sporadic material in the rest of the field.

In recent years off-site material has been recognized as a critical feature of the archaeological landscape. Ethnoarchaeological studies show that much of the behaviour of modern hunting-gathering and pastoral peoples creates discontinuous spreads of surface material over many hundreds of metres rather than discrete artefact clusters, and the same seems likely of much prehistoric behaviour in the past (Binford, 1978a, 1978b; Foley, 1981a, 1981b). The off-site surface material round classical and medieval sites is conventionally interpreted as evidence of manuring, as household rubbish (broken pots included) was dumped on the manure heap and incorporated into the straw and dung that was spread on the arable fields (Bintliff and Snodgrass, 1988). Undoubtedly this activity alone cannot be the only explanation of off-site material, which could presumably have been generated by a range of activities including cultivation practices, herding, hunting and gathering, and industrial activities such as charcoal-burning and lime-burning. However, the important point is that the intensity and extent of off-site material are likely to mirror in some way the intensity and extent of the land-use practices that created it. The Biferno Valley Survey took place before the importance of off-site archaeology had been widely discussed, and more recent Mediterranean surveys have adopted much more sensitive systems of recording it (Barker et al., 1993; Bintliff, 1992; Bintliff and Snodgrass, 1985; Cherry et al., 1992). However, the recording and mapping systems we used were sufficient to provide useful information on the general differences between site and off-site distributions across the landscape.

COLLECTION TECHNIQUES

When a distinct artefact concentration was found, the team defined its limits, and then collected the artefacts within them. For the majority of such sites, they attempted to collect all the materials visible on the surface. The very large/very dense classical sites presented a different problem: the site shown as Figure 23 is exceptional, showing the enormous sea of archaeological material marking the site of a substantial Roman farmstead or villa which was found by a survey team a few days after the farmer had practised deep ploughing on the field the first time, but many classical sites had abundant materials stretching over 100×100 metres or more. In this case, the teams were instructed to collect as much as possible of the fine wares, a large representative sample of the coarse wares, and a small representative sample of the tile and brick. More systematic sampling techniques at such sites, of the kind we have since employed at Montarrenti and Tuscania using grids and transects, would probably have

Fig. 23 The surface remains of a Roman villa in the first year of deep ploughing at site A249 in the lower Biferno valley; the figures are carrying out a geophysical survey.

produced more reliably representative samples than by leaving matters to a team's judgement. One important result of working in so large a survey area, and combining survey work with excavation, was that many survey teams were left in the field all day, rather than working with a vehicle nearby or being picked up at midday, so willingness to carry increasing weights of material all day was undoubtedly a factor, and I have no doubt that the total samples dutifully reported from some sites were not quite as total as they were meant to be!

The teams searched ploughsoil, fields with crops where they could see at least 50 per cent of the ploughsoil and where they would not be damaging the crop (such as vineyards, olive groves, and fields with rows of vegetables), and fields with thin pasture or fallow with soil visible between the clumps of vegetation. We also mixed the teams according to general experience (many students worked on the project for several seasons) and expertise (particular team members were good at spotting flint, others pottery, as other survey teams have found [Hodder and Malone, 1984]).

RELIABILITY OF THE SURVEY DATA

Field-walking at face value seems an extraordinarily simple technique, but the principal lesson we have learnt over the past two decades is that 'survey archaeology' is just as complicated as 'excavation archaeology' (Barker, 1991). The extent to which surface archaeological materials are found by survey teams depends on a complex range of factors. Large-scale geomorphological changes of the kind discussed in Chapter Four can mantle ancient sites under metres of sediment, or carry their materials hundreds of metres downhill. Systematic walking cannot be carried out in thick woodland, and is unlikely to be effective in growing crops (quite apart from the damage it will do). What a survey team can see on the surface of a ploughed field will also be affected by the condition of the soil – whether it is freshly ploughed or weathered (dry and dusty, or sticky after rain), by the harshness of the light and depth of shadows, the position of the sun, and by individual skill, experience, and commitment. There is still little quantitative data on the precise effects of particular biases (Ammerman, 1985a; Hodder and Malone, 1984).

Another major factor is the differential 'archaeological visibility' of particular groups of material: 'field survey cannot collect the settlement data of different periods in an unbiased way like some kind of enormous vacuum cleaner' (Barker, 1991: 2). The contrast between the success of field survey in Italy in documenting the classical landscape (Barker and Lloyd, 1991) and its comparative failure regarding early medieval settlement – and the Biferno Valley Survey is typical in this respect – is an obvious example of this, the predictable outcome of the positive and negative features of their respective data sets. In classical times, an abundant rural population lived in dispersed settlements, many built of durable materials such as brick and tile, and used pottery which was mass-produced, of high quality, and (the fine wares at least) capable of quite precise dating. In the early medieval period, a far smaller rural population lived mainly in nucleated settlements, particularly in hilltop locations which are frequently forested today and where excavations have shown that many of their habitations were of wood, and much of their pottery was poorly made and is difficult to date. The principal way early medieval settlements have been investigated successfully by recent landscape surveys has been by first pinpointing locations – usually densely forested hills – on the basis of documentary evidence and then excavating a series of test pits in the search for habitation evidence (Barker *et al.*, 1988; Hodges, 1982a; Moreland, 1986, 1987). Regional studies investigating prehistoric settlement have also had to define particular 'geomorphological windows' within the landscape offering the best potential for exposing occupation debris of the period or periods of interest in recognition of the likelihood that most of this archaeology has been deeply buried by alluviation or carried away by erosion (Ammerman, 1985b).

Survey archaeologists frequently cite the repeatability of survey as a major advantage of this approach compared with excavation, yet there are very few examples of survey archaeologists actually repeating survey to test the validity of their data. One salutary example from the Biferno valley was the site shown in Figure 23: a new team was sent back to the same general area the following year as an experiment, and the sea of potsherds and building rubble recorded in the ploughed field the previous year became a miserable collection of finds ('sporadic tiles, probably classical') in the same field, no longer deep ploughed and now under a tomato crop. A small classical site found as a dense concentration of large lumps of tile and pottery recently pulled up by deep ploughing in 1974 had become a large diffuse scatter of abraded material by 1978. These and other examples led me to comment once that in archaeological survey the surface sites 'can come on and off like traffic lights' (Lloyd and Barker, 1981: 291) in different soil, vegetation and survey conditions.

Various archaeologists have conducted experiments to see how artefacts move in ploughsoil from year to year in a single field as a result of ploughing, but there are very few examples of how reliable the data are at the regional scale, which is much more our concern. In order to gauge the scale of the problem in the Biferno valley, in the final days of the fieldwork in 1978 we re-surveyed 4 square kilometres in the upper valley which we had surveyed in the first year around the Samnite sanctuary of Colle Sparanise (recorded then as site C36). The results for the Samnite and Roman periods – excluding the off-site data – are shown in Figure 24. Although there are many discrepancies between the two sets of data, both incorporate the same principal feature of dense settlement in the immediate vicinity of the sanctuary and one or two small settlements per square kilometre around it, even though in 1978 we interpreted the central zone as evidence for a single substantial village rather than as a cluster of individual farmsteads. At Montarrenti in central Tuscany, systematic survey repeated over a larger area every year for five years produced similar results: whilst individual sites came and went, the settlement models that could be reconstructed from each year's survey data for the prehistoric, protohistoric, Roman and medieval periods stayed essentially the same (Barker *et al.*, 1986). These were both small experiments, and need

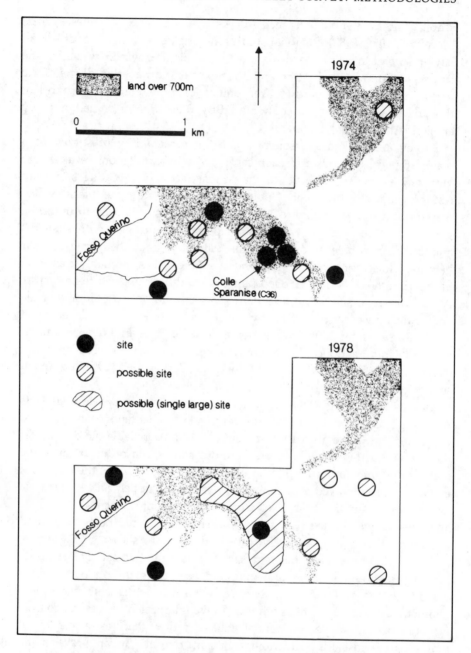

Fig. 24 Comparison of results from repeating survey in part of the
upper Biferno valley.

to be repeated, but they provide reasonable grounds for optimism concerning the reliability of survey data. Systematic archaeological survey cannot make 'real maps' of the ancient world, but it can provide reasonably reliable models of settlement forms, densities and patterns that are the critical data we need to understand the long-term settlement history of a region.

In total, the Biferno Valley Survey recorded almost 1200 units in the 400 square kilometres, roughly 3 per square kilometre. The experience of most systematic surveys tends to be 'the more you look, the more you find', particularly in the case of the very small sites measuring only a few metres across (Cherry *et al.*, 1992). In the site gazetteer of the Biferno Valley Survey (II: Chapter One), we have simplified the site measurements into three crude size categories: large (over roughly 100×100 metres); small (under about 50×50 metres); and medium (between the two). The overwhelming dominance of the second and third categories suggests that, whilst surface coverage could certainly have been more intensive, recovery procedures were effective and that we are likely to have a reasonably representative sample of the different kinds of surface archaeology of the different periods. Any survey methodology must be a compromise between scale and intensity, and I believe that the methodology we adopted achieved an acceptable degree of accuracy, intensity and coverage given our resources, with a geographical and chronological span of settlement data appropriate for our research objectives.

AUGERING AND GEOPHYSICAL SURVEY

Augering and geophysical survey were applied at a selection of sites located by the field-walking for two purposes: to investigate the possibility of intact archaeological deposits below the ploughsoil in order to identify representative sites for excavation, and to attempt to map outlying archaeological features around sites where we were excavating. The augering (Fig. 25) was with a simple screw auger 1.5 metres in length. It proved particularly effective at some sites with favourable conditions of soil composition, moisture and colour (e.g. Figs. 57, 61; II: Chapter Three). Pulling up compact samples of the subsoil lying below the loose ploughsoil enabled us to map the extent of dark charcoal-rich occupation deposits invisible from the surface – and in so doing allowed us to compare the distribution of this material with the distribution of surface artefacts as mentioned above.

In 1977 and 1978 geophysical survey was conducted at about a dozen sites discovered by the field-walking, mostly by staff from the Lerici

Fig. 25 Using a hand auger to investigate the nature and extent of archaeological deposits below the level destroyed by ploughing. (Photograph: Graeme Barker)

Foundation in Rome – in particular the then Director, the late Richard Linington, and his assistant Franco Brancaleone, aided by students from the Sheffield team. In 1978 sites were also investigated using a fluxgate gradiometer by Cliff Samson, then a technician on the staff at Sheffield. Although both magnetic and electrical resistivity surveying can be of value on a wide range of sites, and the two methods are often complementary in revealing different kinds of buried features, the Lerici team opted to use magnetic survey because the dryness of the soil in high summer, together with the fact that at most sites studied the soil had been recently ploughed, mitigated against electrical resistivity.

In favourable conditions the soil deposits within an archaeological site can exhibit sufficiently high susceptibility contrasts that the wide range of features cause observable variations in the local magnetic field strength: typical cases will be pits and ditches cut into rock or subsoil, and stone walls buried in sediment. In peninsular Italy, most topsoils overlying limestones, marls, marly limestones, sandstones, clays and most alluvial deposits tend to have fairly low susceptibilities. Most of these soils have a high iron mineral content, and on archaeological sites changes can occur in these minerals, resulting in considerable increases in susceptibility: soil from within the Roman town of Saepinum gave values four times higher than similar soils outside (Tite and Linington, 1986). In the development of such strong contrasts, the duration and intensity of past occupation are clearly important. Thus whilst for Roman sites the situation is normally favourable, for many prehistoric sites it is much less good. Thermo-remanent magnetism, by contrast, is important where intense heating has occurred, as with kilns and some hearths; the resultant magnetic variations can be very large. Strong changes can also occur with structures of brick and tile. As a rough guide, therefore, the strongest variations can be expected on long-occupied sites with massive constructions, whereas earth-filled pits and ditches can give weaker variations.

In 1977 the Lerici team used an absolute proton magnetometer, with a measurement height of 85 centimetres (Figs. 23, 26). In 1978 this was replaced by a differential proton magnetometer, with a measurement height of 50 centimetres. Each site was surveyed using squares measuring 20×20 metres, with measurements taken at metre intervals. Comparisons between the proton magnetometer and the Sheffield fluxgate gradiometer indicated that, whilst the latter was quick to use and adequate for sites with large shallow features, the former, though more laborious, was more sensitive for more complicated sites with weaker variations. The results of the geophysical investigations are described where appropriate in the ensuing chapters. In general, the combination of the lack of substantial buried features and low magnetic susceptibility on the neolithic sites examined was such as to make the proton magnetometer surveys ineffective, whereas useful results were obtained by this method on later prehistoric and more particularly classical sites (II: Chapter Three). The fluxgate gradiometer produced very helpful results from the major Roman settlement of San Giacomo and from the early medieval site excavated by

Fig. 26 Geophysical survey before excavation at the neolithic settlement of Monte Maulo. (Photograph: Graeme Barker)

the project, Santa Maria in Civita, where its lack of sensitivity to background noise such as changes in soil depth proved a positive advantage.

EXCAVATION

To complement the survey record of site distributions and densities, sites of each major period of settlement discovered during the survey were selected for excavation, in order to answer specific questions about settlement and land use. In part the excavations were to seek stratified artefact sequences, so that we could build up control typologies as yardsticks against which to classify the surface data. The second priority was to recover samples of animal bones and plant remains to inform on subsistence, particularly agricultural practices. All excavated sediments below ploughsoil were therefore screened through 1 centimetre and 2 millimetre meshes, to avoid the biases in archaeozoological material that can occur by hand collection on its own (Payne, 1972a). Substantial deposits were also washed in a froth flotation machine designed along the principles described by Jarman *et al.* (1972) for the recovery of carbonized plant remains (Fig. 27).

Fig. 27 Using a froth flotation machine to collect carbonized plant remains: the petrol-driven pump on the left produces a stream of bubbles through the tank, washing organic material out of the soil and into the sieves suspended from the tank rim. (Photograph: Graeme Barker)

The programme of excavation concentrated on sites discovered by the field-walking which were being destroyed by deep ploughing. The main excavations were on two neolithic settlements (Monte Maulo – B198; Ponte Regio – C63), two bronze age settlements (Fonte Maggio – G1; Masseria Mammarella – A113), an iron age settlement (Santa Margherita – A90), the Samnite/Roman rural sanctuary of Colle Sparanise (C36) and the medieval village of Santa Maria in Civita (D85). Test pits were also cut at a number of other sites (II: Chapter Three). In addition, during the survey the team was also invited by the Superintendency of Antiquities to sample midden deposits in three other classical sites for biological data: the main Samnite sanctuary in the upper valley at Campochiaro, the Roman town of Saepinum (being excavated by a team from the University of Perugia), and the principal Samnite sanctuary for the region, Pietrabbondante in upper Molise.

Although none of the main excavations was large-scale, the sample as a whole proved extremely productive in its information on settlement structure, particularly in combination with artefact gridding, augering and geophysical survey, and it also provided invaluable stratified samples of cultural material and biological data. Following the conclusion of the survey, further major excavations were conducted in the valley, particularly by Archaeological Superintendency staff at a series of iron age cemeteries and a major settlement of the same period in the lower valley, and by John Lloyd at the Samnite/Roman villa of Matrice in the upper valley. Since the early 1970s, too, Gianfranco De Benedettis has been excavating at the major Samnite settlement of Monte Vairano in the upper valley, and since our survey other members of the Superintendency have conducted further excavations on classical sites in the lower valley. In short, to flesh out the survey record for the Biferno valley, we now have excavated data from a reasonably coherent sequence of neolithic, bronze age, iron age, Samnite, Roman and medieval sites.

MATERIAL CULTURE STUDIES

All the artefacts collected by the survey and excavation teams were washed and marked in the following days by a finds team. They were then classified in a preliminary catalogue by myself and assistants from the finds team. During each season a full visual record was made of a substantial part of this material: most worked flints and most feature sherds were drawn, and the major groups of these were photographed in colour and black-and-white separately and with groups of associated body sherds if appropriate. The final catalogue of the finds is described in the companion volume (**II**: Chapters One, Four, Five and Six). The material is within the care of the Superintendency, stored at Saepinum, and the archive is in the care of the University of Leicester (School of Archaeological Studies).

Some of the specialist analyses took place during the fieldwork, some of them afterwards, either at Saepinum or in the British School at Rome where material was taken for temporary study. Material assigned to different periods was separated into different bags, but every care was taken to resist the temptation to store the material by period groups even though this can seem more convenient for the specialist. It proved particularly important to be able to consider all the material from a survey unit together as the specialist analyses progressed, and as more detailed knowledge of pottery fabrics and typologies was established. A great deal of surface survey material is difficult or impossible to classify to one period or another with absolute accuracy – some Roman and medieval coarse ware are very similar, small collections of featureless handmade prehistoric sherds can be difficult to assign to periods within prehistory, and some prehistoric and early medieval fabrics are almost identical. Inevitably, much of such material can only be classified very loosely by comparison and association with better dated assemblages (especially stratified assemblages from excavations). It was extremely important that the specialists working on material from adjacent periods were able to go back to such material together and come to an agreed conclusion about its status.

As with all Mediterranean multi-period surveys, the commonest finds from the surface sites were, from the prehistoric periods, chipped flint and chert and/or potsherds, and from the classical and later periods, potsherds and fragments of tile and brick. Rarer finds could include items such as worked stone, pieces of animal and/or human bone, fragments of building material, architectural fragments and coins. A variety of information was provided by this material. The most critical was the primary evidence for the likely period or periods of occupation of the survey unit from which they had been collected by the survey teams. Second was information about the possible function of the site – domestic, funerary, industrial and so on, and if possible its status within any hierarchy of settlement and social type we had established for the period. Third was information on systems of production and exchange operating within the valley and outside it: fragments of grinders from sources of stone outside the valley, for example (**II**: Chapter Six), pieces of obsidian from identifiable sources beyond mainland Italy (Chapter Six), or potsherds shown by visual or microscopic examination to be made from local or exotic clays and fillers.

The artefact collections from the surface and excavated sites also provided evidence for extractive technologies which contributed to our models of land use at different periods of antiquity. For the prehistoric periods some information can be extrapolated from the flint and chert chipped tools and from polished stone tools, and for these and later periods from grinding equipment. Other indirect agricultural evidence we searched for included fragments of pressing equipment for the production of olive oil and wine of the kind well documented for the classical period throughout the Mediterranean. However, the most important evidence for reconstructing systems of land use consisted of the collections of animal bones (II: Chapter Seven) and carbonized plant remains collected from the excavated sites. The specific techniques of analysis applied to this material are described where appropriate as the results are presented in the ensuing chapters.

PALAEOENVIRONMENTAL INVESTIGATIONS

Reconstructing how the physical environment has changed is of critical significance for a regional archaeological survey, for two reasons: to understand the modern distributions of the surface archaeological materials and sites, and to understand the settlement patterns of antiquity. Under the first heading, geomorphological investigation is essential if we are to understand whether blank areas of the archaeological map of a particular period are blank because the people of the time chose not to put their settlements there, or because those settlements, though once there, cannot now be found as surface traces because of sedimentation processes. Have processes such as erosion, colluviation or alluviation mantled these areas with sediments, covering the archaeological sites so deeply that ploughing cannot reach them and fetch their artefacts up to the modern surface? Or have these areas been stripped of ancient sites by erosion, which has carried away the surface sediments and the archaeological artefacts within them?

As well as allowing us to understand the integrity or otherwise of the various settlement systems of the past indicated by the surface survey data, palaeoenvironmental studies were also intended to provide the vital record of the nature of past environments and the impact of land-use systems on them, to address the critical issue of 'climate or people?' discussed in Chapter One. Valley sediment stratigraphies are especially useful in documenting how a river may have alternated its regime in the past. Further information on such changes can be gleaned from animal and plant remains trapped within the sediments. Preliminary geomorphological studies were carried out during the archaeological survey by Derrick Webley, and his initial findings then formed the basis of a more detailed investigation in the mid-1980s by Chris Hunt (Fig. 28), who also extracted a sediment core from the basin floor by the Matese lake for pollen analysis.

Fig. 28 Geomorphological fieldwork: (left) Derrick Webley at Geo 2 and (right) Chris Hunt at Geo 12. (Photographs: Graeme Barker)

We attempted to extract pollen from the settlement excavations, but it was insufficiently preserved to provide meaningful information. On the other hand, mollusc remains were preserved in small numbers at some of the prehistoric sites, and Chris Hunt has been able to provide comments on their implications for local environments. Samples of the sediments from these sites were also taken back to Sheffield for analysis in terms of particle size. The methodologies used in the geomorphological study, and the main results, are detailed in the following chapter and in **II: Chapter Two**, though specific information concerning particular settlements or periods of the past is presented elsewhere as appropriate.

DOCUMENTARY RESEARCHES

Although the focus of our study of settlement history in the Biferno valley was primarily archaeological, we attempted as far as possible to integrate the data we collected with the documentary record. References by the classical authors to the general region of Samnium are numerous and well studied (Salmon, 1967), and John Lloyd makes full use of this material as well as inscriptions from the valley in his account of Samnite settlement in Chapter Nine and Roman settlement in Chapter Ten. The medieval record for the region is much patchier, particularly for the early medieval period, as Chris Wickham describes in Chapter Eleven. Settlement patterns in the valley in the modern period were studied for the project by Peter Taylor using the resources of the libraries and state archives in Campobasso, and his findings are discussed in Chapter Twelve.

CONCLUSION

As I have described in this chapter, archaeological survey techniques have advanced considerably since we undertook the primary fieldwork in the Biferno valley, and there were undoubted weaknesses in the methods we used. On the other hand, the project collected a very large quantity of data from an entire transect of Mediterranean topography from the mountains to the sea, a scale of settlement information unrivalled throughout the Mediterranean basin. We collected it from an area which, when we started, was virtually a blank area on the archaeological map. We collected surface data from all major periods of the past, from early prehistory to the modern period. We were – again, uniquely, I think, for any Mediterranean regional study – allowed to conduct excavations on selected neolithic, bronze age, iron age, classical and medieval sites we had found, so that we have been able to integrate surface and excavated data for much of the valley's history. Integrating the archaeological survey, the excavations, the palaeoenvironmental data and the documentary studies has allowed us to assemble perhaps the most detailed long-term landscape history of any region in the Mediterranean. We have to be aware of the weaknesses of the data, but I believe that should not deter us from recognizing that as a result of this project and the excavations that have succeeded it in the valley, we are in a unique position now to reconstruct the evolution of a typical Mediterranean landscape, and attempt to understand its history.

CHAPTER 4

THE NATURAL LANDSCAPE AND ITS EVOLUTION

Chris Hunt

INTRODUCTION

The landscape of southern Italy in general and of the Biferno valley in particular has been in a state of flux throughout its history. Since earliest times, tectonics and climate change have led to the constant remodelling of the landscape, and since the end of the last glacial period especially, human activity superimposed on and influencing these natural processes has led to further substantial modification. While the landscape offers opportunities and constraints to human activity, this activity may in turn have a significant impact on the landscape. Human impact may include modification of vegetation and animal populations, soil profile modification, soil erosion and modification of river morphology and behaviour (Butzer, 1982). Some of these impacts leave easily preservable traces in the landscape which provide a record of human activity independent of (and thus a test for) normal archaeological techniques.

In southern Europe, landscape processes are often extremely active. Processes such as landsliding, colluviation and alluviation can have a significant effect on the preservation and visibility of archaeological sites. In any archaeological field survey, therefore, it is vital to be able to distinguish 'black holes' in the survey record caused by geomorphological processes from those determined by cultural and social factors. Likewise, areas of geomorphologically recycled artefacts must be distinguished from *in situ* archaeological remains. In the Biferno Valley Survey, therefore, environmental reconstructions were pursued in order to help understand the taphonomy of the archaeological record, to provide an environmental context for sites and the activities deduced to have occurred on them, and to provide an indication of changing patterns of human activity in terms of their impact on the landscape.

GEOLOGICAL BACKGROUND

In what is now peninsular Italy, the shallow waters of the Tethys Ocean persisted from its creation in the early Mesozoic some 250 million years ago until the Palaeocene, about 70 million years ago. During this time, an immense thickness of limestone was laid down. These limestones underlie the Biferno valley at depth and are overlaid by silty flysch (Ippolito, 1970). The Matese mountain, a great slab of Mesozoic limestone, is being thrust over the flysch deposits in a north-easterly direction (Ietto, 1971). Pressure from the south-west is forcing the flysch deposits to be folded and faulted, and to rise, thus forming the hills between the Boiano basin and the Adriatic Sea. These ongoing earth movements have caused the earthquakes which are known to have repeatedly struck the upper valley in the historical period.

The simplified geology of the Biferno valley is shown in Figure 29 (see also Lanzafame and Tortorici, 1976). Immediately to the north-east of the Matese lies the Boiano basin, a rapidly subsiding area which receives alluvial fan and lacustrine deposits from, and will eventually be overridden by, the Matese. The rest of the Biferno valley is incised into rocks of Tertiary and early Quaternary age. The generally unconsolidated Tertiary rocks, rapidly uplifted and deeply incised by the Biferno and its tributaries, are subject to extensive landsliding. There are numerous, well-developed examples of both deep-seated and superficial landslides, mudflows and rotational failures (Frazzetta and Lanzafame, 1977). The Pliocene and early Quaternary deposits, marine silts and sands formed just below or at sea level, are now strongly uplifted. Later Pleistocene (post-Tyrrhenian) deposits were laid down in a river valley with a geography approximately similar to that of the modern Biferno valley. These deposits are predominantly river-gravels, though lacustrine silts are known from the Boiano basin. Earth movements continued to affect deposition throughout the Pleistocene, uplift giving rise to a sequence of river terraces in the lower part of the valley, while folding has affected deposits of probable Pliocene and early Quaternary age in the Boiano basin.

BIOGEOGRAPHICAL BACKGROUND

Over recent years, great advances have occurred in our understanding of the evolution of the current distribution of the Italian fauna and flora. The Late Pliocene and Lower Pleistocene flora and fauna of Italy are well known from the work of a distinguished set of palynologists (Bertolani Marchetti et al., 1979; Follieri and Castelletti, 1988 and references therein;

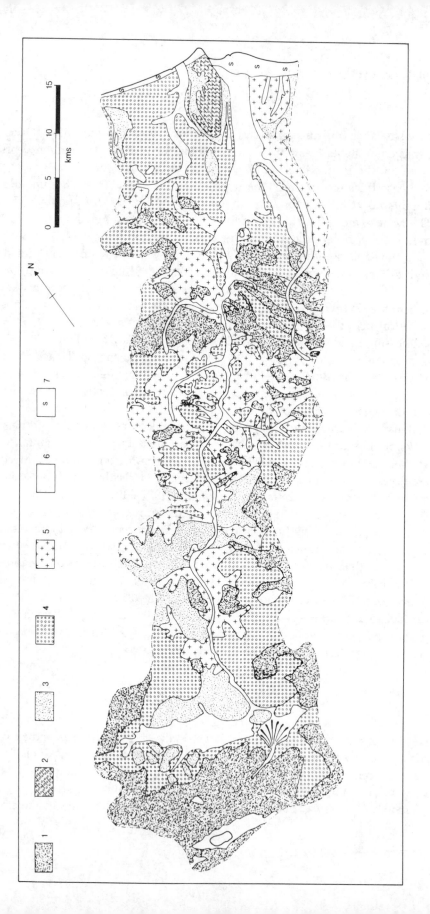

Lona and Bertoldi, 1972), malacologists (Esu, 1988 and references therein; Esu and Girotti, 1974) and mammal palaeontologists (De Giuli and Sala, 1988 and references therein). Two and a half million years ago, during the Late Pliocene, the climate was cool temperate and often wet, with cold winters. Much, possibly all, of the proto-Italian landmass was forested, with conifers such as pine, *Sciadopitys*, spruce, *Sequoia* and cedar dominant but also a great diversity of broad-leafed and other trees, many now extinct in Europe (Bertolani Marchetti *et al.*, 1979). The coastal forests were dominated by swamp cypress.

The Pleistocene period was marked by complex cycles of glacials and interglacials, with the major cycles around 100,000 years long. These cycles were already apparent in the Late Pliocene, but became increasingly marked as the Lower Pleistocene progressed. In general terms, the climate became drier and, at times during the Early Pleistocene, warmer. As a result of rising temperatures and aridity *Sciadopitys* became extinct in Italy (Bertolani Marchetti *et al.*, 1979). During the warm phases, coniferous species were still important, but the trees characteristic of mixed oak forest (especially oak, hornbeam, beech, fir, hazel, yew, ash, lime and elm) became more important. Exotics such as palms, hemlock, the tulip tree and wingnut were still present. A flora and mollusc fauna of this age were found during the Biferno valley project, in the Boiano basin. During cold phases the climate was cool, and forests were heavily dominated by conifers. The coastal areas remained covered with swamp cypress throughout this period (Bertolani Marchetti *et al.*, 1979).

Our knowledge of the later Lower Pleistocene and most of the Middle Pleistocene in Italy is still comparatively incomplete. Some time after one million years ago, during the later Lower Pleistocene, the climate changed considerably and the cold phases became more marked and increasingly cold and arid. Many of the temperate phases were also arid. These changes were probably brought about by changes in atmospheric circulation influenced, amongst other factors, by the continued rise of the circum-Mediterranean mountain belts, including the Apennines. The temperate phases were marked by diverse mixed oak forest and the cold phases by arid steppe vegetation with grasses, *Artemisia*, chenopods and crack pine (Follieri, 1958–61).

There have recently been substantial advances in our knowledge of the flora of the later Middle Pleistocene and the Upper Pleistocene, largely as the result of work of Follieri and her associates but also by a number of

Fig. 29 The Biferno valley: simplified geology. 1. limestone; 2. gravels and conglomerates; 3. sands; 4. sands/marls/clays/diluvial soils; 5. clays; 6. recent and Pleistocene alluvium; 7. coastal sands.

northern European palynologists (for instance, Alessio *et al.*, 1986; Bonatti, 1966, 1970; Follieri, 1958–61, 1979; Follieri *et al.*, 1988; Frank, 1969; Grüger, 1977; Kelly and Huntley, 1991; Napoleone and Follieri, 1967; Watts 1985). During temperate phases, mixed oak forest covered the lowlands, with beech and fir dominant at high altitudes and during cooler phases. The cold phases are marked by *Artemisia* and grass steppe at low altitude, with glaciation on the highest mountains (Orombelli, 1988), loess deposition, and periglacial activity to low altitude (Dramis, 1988). The last glacial maximum, around 18,000 years ago, conforms to this pattern. Subsequently, 14,000 or 15,000 years ago, temperature rise but continuing aridity led to the increase of grasses, juniper and broad-leafed trees and the decline of *Artemisia* (Alessio *et al.*, 1986; Harding, 1992) and the evolution of a 'parkland' landscape at low altitude, with grassy interfluves and trees along watercourses and in sheltered locations. At high altitudes in the Apennines, rainfall was sufficient to enable mixed oak forest to dominate the landscape (Watts, 1985).

Around 11,000 years ago, *Artemisia* steppe again became dominant during the Late Glacial stadial, a complex climatic phase characterized by low temperatures and variable humidity (Kelly and Huntley, 1991). About 10,000 years ago, the climatic amelioration of the early Holocene occurred. Temperatures rose, but rainfall at low altitude remained low until perhaps 8,000 or 7,500 years ago (Alessio *et al.*, 1986; Hunt and Eisner, 1991; Kelly and Huntley, 1991). Mixed oak forest became important, but well-drained areas retained a vegetation of grasses and herbs. At high altitude rainfall was sufficient for closed woodland (Watts, 1985). Rainfall increased and the forests at low altitude had become closed by 7,500 years ago, shortly before the transition to farming in central Italy (Kelly and Huntley, 1991; Harding, 1992).

Serious inroads into the forests were not made in many areas until the 3rd and 2nd millennia bc, the Copper and Bronze Ages respectively. From that time onwards, the pattern of vegetational change recorded in the pollen diagrams became localized to a considerable extent, though in many areas the maximum extent of clearance occurred in classical times, in the late medieval to early post-medieval periods, and from the late 19th century onwards (Bottema, 1974; Follieri and Castelletti, 1988; Harding, 1992; Hunt *et al.*, 1992).

The modern flora in the Biferno valley, as elsewhere in Italy, is the product of millions of years of natural processes, substantially modified by several millennia of human activity. If human disturbance had not occurred, one might expect that nearly all of the Biferno valley would be forested. The coastal belt, especially the dune belt, would be dominated by stone, maritime and umbrella pines, with species such as juniper, broom, rosemary, lentisk, *Phillyrea* and cistus as an understorey. At low altitudes away from the coast, there would have been evergreen oak forest with tall shrubs like juniper, olive, *Phillyrea*, manna ash and lentisk. At altitudes above 200–300 metres, there would have been deciduous forest dominated by oak, with sweet chestnut, hornbeam and hop-hornbeam especially prominent towards the base of the zone and accessory beech important towards the top. Other trees in this zone would have been poplar, ash, elm, lime and sycamore, with willows and alders beside the rivers. High altitudes, above about 1000 metres, would probably have had beech forest with some ash, elm, sycamore, box and yew where rainfall was low and silver fir and pine forests where it was wetter. High mountain tops, such as the Matese, might have supported a montane dwarf juniper and herb-rich grassland community if the soils were too thin or the situation too exposed for forests to survive.

Of course the actual flora of the valley today bears very little resemblance to this idealized model of climax vegetation. Virtually all of the valley has been farmed at one time or another and much of it is still under the plough or grazed (Fig. 12). Soils have been eroded and exhausted by millennia of farming. The coastal zone is still characterized by its pinetum, but the lowland evergreen oak forests have long gone. Most of the lowland is cultivated or used for winter grazing, but where land is abandoned or disused, for instance in places along the valley floor, a scrubby macchia of rosemary, cistus, broom, lentisk, juniper, evergreen oak, *Phillyrea*, acacia and tree heather has grown up and if left ungrazed and undisturbed would regenerate to evergreen oak forest. In what would have been the deciduous forest zone, very steep slopes such as where the river has cut a gorge through the middle section of the valley, as well as some marshy ground on the gorge floor and in the Boiano basin, are covered with young deciduous oak woods with some acacia, ash, sycamore and hazel. These woods have mostly been allowed to grow up since the last war and some appear to be managed for firewood extraction. Most of the land is, however, farmed. On the steep limestone slopes above the Boiano basin are dense oak-beech woods. The high land of the Matese is largely subalpine grassland with occasional junipers, the summer pastures of transhumant flocks; there are, however, occasional dense stands of beech-oak woodland on very steep ground and in places near the Matese lake.

THE PLEISTOCENE SUCCESSION

The Pleistocene and Holocene succession described below has been established on the basis of the investigation of some forty exposures in

Table 2 Sedimentary facies distinguished in the Biferno valley; terminology after Miall (1977) and Rust and Koster (1984)

Abbreviation	Description
Dm	Diamicton – an unsorted deposit with clasts of all sizes 'floating' in a muddy matrix
Gm	Clast-supported, commonly imbricated gravel with subhorizontal bedding
Gms	Muddy matrix-supported gravel without imbrication or internal stratification
Gt	Trough cross-bedded clast-supported gravel
Gp	Planar cross-bedded clast-supported or matrix-supported gravel
Ge	Epsilon cross-bedded, imbricated sheet
GFp	Planar gravel and sand/mud sheet
Sh	Horizontally stratified sand
Sm	Massive sand
St	Trough cross-stratified sand
Sp	Planar cross-bedded sand
Fm	Massive mud or fine sandy mud
Fl	Laminated silt or mud
P	Pedogenic concretionary carbonate
C	Cryoturbation and other frost disturbance

Pleistocene and Holocene sediments throughout the Biferno valley (Fig. 30), combined with geomorphological mapping. The exposures were selected to be representative of the succession, but it is acknowledged that given the relatively short period of time in the field and the chance nature of exposures in a largely vegetated landscape, the selection may be incomplete or subject to some form of sampling bias. The exposures are described in detail in the companion volume (**II**: Chapter Two).

A number of sediment facies can be distinguished in the deposits examined in the Biferno valley. These are briefly described and explained in Table 2. The Quaternary stratigraphy proposed for the Biferno valley on the basis of these facies is summarized in Table 3.

In the landforms and Pleistocene and Holocene deposits of the Biferno valley lies evidence of the palaeoenvironments and processes which shaped the landscape we see today. The broad form of the modern landscape, with the Matese mountains overlooking the Boiano basin and with hilly upland between the Boiano basin and the coast, was established by the end of the Pliocene, though relief was probably less pronounced than today and the coastal lowlands were under the sea at that time.

Figure 30 shows the Quaternary geology of the valley, and Figure 31 the altitude and locations of the Quaternary aggradations identified. The oldest terrestrial Pleistocene deposits in the Biferno valley are the Quirino gravels and De Francesco beds of the Boiano basin, the Gentile gravels of the

Table 3 Quaternary succession in the Biferno valley

LOWER BIFERNO	MIDDLE BIFERNO	BOIANO BASIN
Late Pliocene Marine deposition		Termine silts (Fm)
Early Pleistocene Marine deposition Guglionesi beds (GdP,FmP)	Gentile gravels (Gp,Ge,Fm) De Francesco beds (Gp,Ge,Fm)	Quirino gravels (Gp,Fm)
Marine/dune deposition major uplift/incision Santa Columba gravels (GeP,FmP,GdP)		Campochiaro gravel (Gm,Gp,Ge,Fm)
major uplift/incision		
?Middle Pleistocene Ripetello gravels, Castello gravels (GpC GeC Ge GFp) uplift/incision Paledri gravels (GpC) uplift/incision valley floor 10 (GtCP)	incision Moline gravels (GdP Gt)	
Last interglacial valley floor 9 (F1P)	Moline gravels (FmP)	
Interstadial during last glacial period valley floor 8 (GtP)		
?Glacial maximum valley floor 7 (FmC)		
Neolithic/Bronze Age? valley floor 6, 5 (Ge,Fm)	valley floor 5 (Ge,Fm)	valley floor 8,7 (GFp,Gp)
Late Samnite/Roman valley floor 4 (Gp,Ge,GFp)	valley floor 4 (Ge,Sh,Fm) Tre Archi beds (GFp)	valley floor 6(Gp,Ge,GFp)
Medieval valley floor 3 (Ge,Fm)	valley floor 3 (Ge)	valley floor 5 (soil)
Early post-medieval		valley floor 4 (Ge)
Late 19th century		valley floor 3(Gp,GFp,Fm)
1930–1950	valley floor 2 (Ge,Sp,Fl)	
1960–1975 valley floor 2 (Gp,Fm)		valley floor 2 (Gp,GFp)
modern valley floor 1 (Gp,Gt,Fm)	valley floor 1 (Gp,Fm,Fl)	valley floor 1(Gp,Gt,Fm)

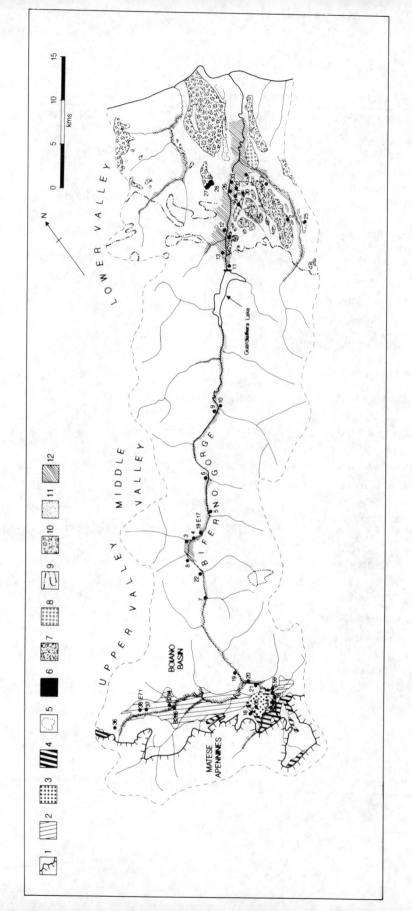

Biferno gorge and the Guglionesi beds of the lower valley. It is impossible to correlate these deposits accurately, but they reflect alluvial fan and lacustrine sedimentation in the Boiano basin, the presence of the Biferno gorge and a short-lived phase of marine regression and river-gravel deposits in what is now the lower valley. Deposition probably took place over a considerable period of time, and the climate varied from temperate to cold-arid.

After a substantial phase of earth movements and erosion, the sea retreated finally from the lower valley, and alluvial fan gravels – the Santa Columba gravels – were laid down. The Matese was also substantially raised by these earth movements and a great volume of alluvial fan gravels – the Campochiaro gravels – were laid down. The Campochiaro gravels contain pollen of extinct Fagaceae (*Tricolpopollenites liblarensis fallax*), Aquifoliaceae (*Tricolporopollenites margaritatus*), and exotic taxa such as *Sciadopitys*, *Rhus*, *Cedrus*, *Liquidambar*, *Juglans* and *Pterocarya*, as well as extinct terrestrial molluscs, and are thus of Lower Pleistocene age. They were laid down during a temperate forested phase and then a phase of subarctic climate, and are overlain by two substantial fossil soils.

During the Middle Pleistocene, at least three further phases of uplift occurred, and each time the Biferno incised its bed. Further terrace gravels – the Ripetello, Castello and Paledri gravels – were laid down in the lower valley and the Cigno valley, and coarse gravels – part of the Moline gravels – in the Biferno gorge. Most are coarse planar and trough cross-bedded gravels (that is, gravels with small scour features formed by the water flows moving dunes or bars downstream) with occasional *Pupilla muscorum*, probably laid down in cold-arid climates; some of the terraces have a cover of loess-like silts which are also likely to be the product of cold-stage conditions. However, the Castello gravels include a warm stage unit laid down by a meandering channel and with a temperate scrubby woodland and marsh mollusc assemblage including *Pomatias* spp, Clausiliidae, *Rumina decollata*, *Trichia striolata*, and *Helicella itala*.

The Biferno had incised almost to its current altitude in the lower valley by the cold stage preceding the last interglacial, but further earth movements occurred upstream, probably around the top of the Biferno gorge. Gravels and channel fills of this age are widespread in the gorge (part of

Fig. 30 The Quaternary geology of the Biferno valley. 1. front of Matese limestone massif; 2. ancient basin fill – Quirino and De Francesco beds; 3. Campochiaro gravels; 4. talus, scree; 5. Campobasso lake deposits; 6. Guglionesi beds; 7. Santa Columba gravels; 8. Ripetello gravels; 9. Paledri gravels; 10. Lower Pleistocene marine beds; 11. Castello gravels; 12. valley floor deposits. The numbered points refer to the location of the sediments described in the companion volume (II: Chapter Two).

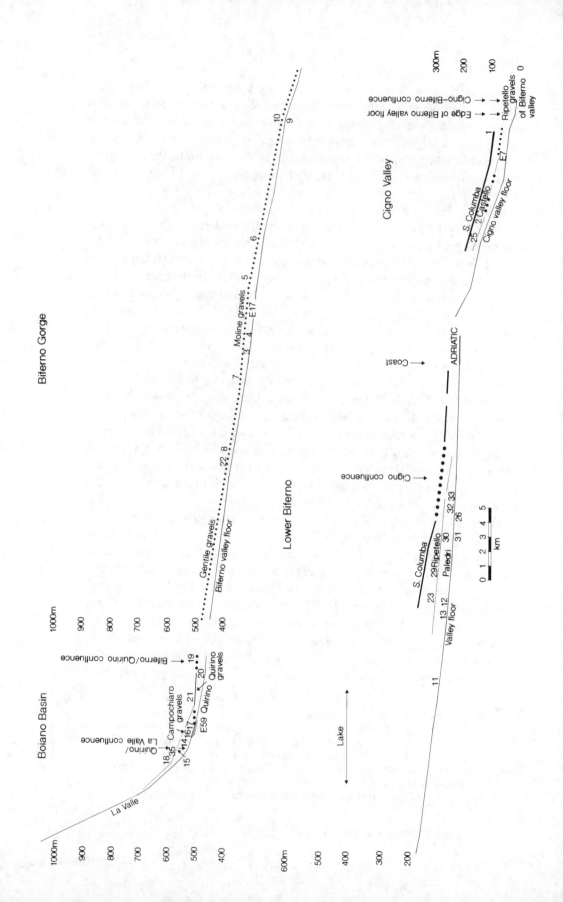

the Moline gravels) and are also found in the lower valley (valley floor 10), but although chert artefacts of middle palaeolithic type were found, the deposits are otherwise without fossils. However, the sedimentary style – epsilon cross-bedded fine gravels (that is, elongated S-shaped beds of gravel formed by large meandering river channels) and silty palaeochannel fills – is consistent with fully temperate conditions and a well-vegetated landscape during the last interglacial. Following the deposition of the fluvial sediments, pedogenic carbonates indicate a period of warm-arid climate.

The last glacial period is represented only in the lower valley (valley floor 8) by gravels with an interstadial pollen flora of grasses, sedges, herbs, birch and buckthorn, and trough cross-bedded, cryoturbated gravels of the ?glacial maximum (valley floor 7).

THE HOLOCENE SUCCESSION

The complexity and the poor dating control of the Holocene sediments, relying largely on derived artefacts, limit the interpretation of the valley floor deposits. Nevertheless, at least seven sedimentary units can be recognized, with the following chronology: 1, (broadly) neolithic/bronze age; 2, classical; 3, medieval; 4, early post-medieval; 5, 19th century; 6, early 20th century; and 7, late 20th century. These are distinguished firstly on stratigraphical grounds, since units overlie or lie adjacent to one another, and secondly by the artefact assemblages found within them.

The fluvial units are characterized by two main facies-groups. The first of these is in-channel gravels, characterized by a variety of bedding styles. Epsilon cross-bedding is common. This most probably relates to a meandering single-channel stream. Also common is plane bedding, probably associated with deposition in a low-sinuosity single channel or multi-channel river with large tabular lateral or medial bars. In a few places trough cross-bedding, sometimes with colluvial lenses, is present. This lithofacies is characteristically laid down in multi-channel rivers (Rust and Koster, 1984). The colluvial lenses result from mass-flows. The second main facies-group consists of usually plane-bedded sheets of silts, sands and gravels, laid down in an overbank or back-basin location by flood-waters. The aggradation of significant epsilon cross-bedded gravels is a slightly unusual feature of the sedimentation pattern of Holocene rivers in

Fig. 31 The altitudes of the Quaternary aggradations identified in the Biferno valley. The numbered points refer to the location of the sediments described in the companion volume (II: Chapter Two).

Italy. Experience suggests that aggradation is typically associated with low sinuosity single thread or multi-channel streams (Hunt *et al.*, 1992). It is suggested that the Biferno aggraded from a single meandering channel most probably as the result of high sediment input but cohesive (most likely well-vegetated) riverbanks.

MID-HOLOCENE DEPOSITS

The 'neolithic/bronze age?' fluvial sediments identified in the valley (Table 3) are only correlated very loosely by pollen in one case and by rather undiagnostic lithic artefacts and potsherds, though the latter can be assigned to the Bronze Age with a reasonable degree of confidence. In addition, soil development suggests that several centuries at least separate these sediments from those of the Samnite/Roman phase, the beginning of which can probably be dated to the last two or three centuries BC. The likelihood is, therefore, that the late prehistoric sediments date variously to the Neolithic (*c.* 4500–3000 bc), Copper Age (*c.* 3000–2000 BC) and/or Bronze Age (*c.* 2000–1000 bc), rather than to the Iron Age (the period *c.* 1000–500 bc). The pollen and molluscan evidence suggests small openings in a predominantly closed environment.

In the lower valley, about 2 metres of silts, clays and soil profiles (valley floor 5) rest upon epsilon cross-bedded gravels (valley floor 6) which contain epipalaeolithic/mesolithic artefacts. Pollen analysis of the silts gave spectra dominated by oak pollen with a variety of other trees including hornbeam, fir, yew, elm, hazel, pine, pistachio, buckthorn, hawthorn, sycamore, lime and ash. Herbaceous taxa are also present, including grasses, sedges, black bindweed, dandelion group, daisy group, wormwood, plantain, and others. These assemblages reflect species-rich mixed oak woodland and are comparable with mid-Holocene spectra from elsewhere in Italy (Alessio *et al.*, 1986; Hunt and Eisner, 1991). Mollusc assemblages contain woodland taxa such as *Pomatias elegans*, *Oxychilus cellarius*, and Clausiliidae, together with the open ground species *Helicella itala* and *Vallonia excentrica*. The plant macrofossil assemblages contain charcoal, leaves of trees and seeds of 'weeds' such as Polygonaceae and Chenopodiaceae. The presence of significant numbers of 'weed' pollen and plant fossils and open ground molluscs may reflect areas of naturally open ground such as gravel bars in river courses, landslide scars, and tree-fall scars, but it is tempting to equate them with clearances resulting from early agriculture, particularly given the presence of charcoal.

In the gorge, about a metre of river gravels and slackwater deposits, undated but most probably of middle Holocene age, is known from two sites (valley floor 5). An extremely small pollen assemblage, containing a

mixture of trees and open ground species, is possible evidence for contemporaneity with an early clearance. In the Boiano basin, coarse river
gravels containing bronze age potsherds and overbank alluvium of
probably mid-Holocene age are known from two sites (valley floor 7, 8).

SAMNITE/ROMAN DEPOSITS

The classical-period aggradation is by far the largest in the sequence prior
to those of this century. These sediments, identified in all three sections of
the valley, are dated by the occurrence of black glazed and Italian sigillata
pottery; the absence of later imperial wares of the 3rd to 5th centuries AD is
striking. Given the preservation of fine pottery in the sediments, and the
frequency of later imperial wares on the settlement sites discovered by the
survey, the absence of later imperial wares from the alluvial deposits seems
likely to be significant, rather than a function of survival and recovery,
suggesting that the classical aggradation can be broadly dated to the
Samnite and early Roman periods of occupation in the valley. These
sediments are much coarser than those of the preceding and ensuing
episodes of aggradation (Fig. 32).

In the lower valley, plane-bedded and epsilon cross-bedded gravels and
significant overbank deposits (sometimes over 3 metres thick) containing
classical-age potsherds are very widespread (valley floor 4). A major
aggradation of 3 metres of mostly epsilon cross-bedded gravels, containing
potsherds, brick and tile of classical age, is also known from the gorge
(valley floor 4). A small mollusc assemblage from the gravels contained
only open-ground taxa. Colluvial sequences up to 3 metres thick are also
known from the gorge. Tree-stump casts are common in the colluvial
deposits and the mollusc faunas are a mixture of sheltered habitat taxa
such as Clausiliidae, *Pomatias elegans*, *Oxychilus* spp and open ground
species such as *Helicella itala*. The associated potsherds range up to the 1st
century AD. In the Boiano basin, gravels and overbank alluvium containing
classical artefacts are widespread and up to 2 metres thick (valley floor 6).
At high altitude, trough cross-bedded gravels with colluvial lenses are the
dominant lithofacies. Lower in the basin, plane-bedded gravels and
overbank silt and gravel sheets are common, and by the entrance to the
gorge are epsilon cross-bedded gravels.

MEDIEVAL TO 19TH-CENTURY DEPOSITS

We found one example of Holocene alluviation which may correlate with
Vita-Finzi's model of a Younger Fill dating to the latter part of the 1st

Fig. 32 Valley floor sediments (Geo 12): (above) Derrick Webley is pointing to silts containing middle palaeolithic artefacts, which are overlain by coarse gravels of classical age; (below) sandy silts and sands of 19th/early 20th-century age overlie a series of coarse cobbly gravels formed in classical times. (Photographs: Graeme Barker)

Fig. 33 The San Martino beds in the Cigno valley. The figure with the ranging pole is pointing to the interface between the lower gravels and upper silts; charcoal from the base of the silts yielded a radiocarbon date of *c.* AD 700. (Photograph: Graeme Barker)

millennium AD. Construction work in 1977 for protective walling along the Cigno river to protect a road bridge at San Martino had cut back the river sediments, revealing a 7 metre high section with coarse gravels in the lower half and fine silts in the upper half (Fig. 33). Charcoal taken from the base of the silts yielded a radiocarbon date (HAR-2557) of 1230 ± 80 bp, or AD 720, indicating an early medieval date for its formation.

In the lower valley, over 2 metres of epsilon cross-bedded gravels and significant overbank sands and silts postdate alluvium with classical ceramics and predate sediments with late 20th-century artefacts, but contain no distinctive artefacts at the sites visited (valley floor 3). At one site in the gorge, sherds of the 13th century and a little later were recovered from around 2 metres of epsilon cross-bedded gravels (valley floor 3). In the Boiano basin, soils containing medieval potsherds (valley floor 5) overlay gravels containing Roman artefacts and at another site (valley floor 4) epsilon cross-bedded gravels contained sherds of early post-medieval age. Also in the Boiano basin planar gravels and overbank alluvium contained sherds of 19th-century age.

EARLY 20TH CENTURY DEPOSITS

In the gorge, over 4 metres of lacustrine sandy silts and epsilon cross-bedded gravels (valley floor 2) relate to the construction of an industrial weir at Santa Elena and the rapid infilling of the lake behind it with sediment. The weir is most probably of inter-war date: a piece of rubber tyre was preserved in the gravels below it and the construction style is typical of the earlier part of the 20th century. Robust tin cans of typical inter-war type were found in fluvial gravels upstream from the lacustrine deposits. The deposits that accumulated behind the dam are richly fossiliferous, containing a variety of woodland molluscs (*Oxychilus, Nesovitrea, Pomatias*), open ground species (*Hellicella, Truncatellina*), marsh taxa from the edge of the lake (*Vertigo, Cochlicopa*) and aquatic species (*Valvata, Acroloxus, Lymnaea*). Plant macrofossils reflect a similar range of habitat, with trees represented by oak and other charcoal and a poplar seed, weeds such as *Chenopodium* and marsh and aquatic plants like *Schoenoplectus*, Cyperaceae, *Najas*, and *Ranunculus*.

LATER 20TH CENTURY DEPOSITS

In the lower valley, up to 5 metres of mostly plane-bedded gravels and overbank alluvium (valley floor 2) are widespread. The deposits contain abundant artefacts from the 1960s and 1970s: polythene bags, tin cans, bottles and so on. Gabions and other flood-control structures were buried by this aggradation at two sites, at one by over 3 metres of gravels and overbank sediments. Similarly in the Boiano basin, gravels with planar and trough cross-bedding, and significant overbank alluvium, have overwhelmed flood-control structures to a depth of over a metre (valley floor 2). The deposits again contain artefacts typical of the period since 1960.

SEDIMENTS OF THE ACTIVE FLOODPLAIN

In most places in the Biferno valley, the river is a low-sinuousity single channel flanked by large tabular lateral bars, but on the higher slopes of some alluvial fans and occasional reaches downstream it is a multi-channel river with tabular medial bars. The modern floodplain (valley floor 1) contains much late 20th-century rubbish clearly accumulated over approximately the last 10–20 years. The Biferno has recently incised into its bed, but the causes and chronology of this appear complex. The river has incised 2–5 metres in the lower valley since the construction of the Guardialfiera dam in 1975. By the mid 1980s, aggradation was beginning to extend upstream from the lake that has formed behind the dam. In the

Biferno gorge, about 4 metres of incision has occurred after the breaching of the industrial weir at Santa Elena. The abandoned in-channel sediments appear to have stopped accumulating some time around the middle of the 20th century, because no modern plastic or other artefacts were found over several hundred metres of exposure. In the Boiano basin, 2–4 metres of incision have occurred and in-channel sediments that contain artefacts dating to the 1960s and 1970s have been abandoned.

PROCESSES OF LANDSCAPE CHANGE

The Quaternary deposits of the Biferno valley preserve fossil and sedimentary evidence of past processes and environments. In the environmental record described in the previous section can be seen the influence of tectonics, climate, sea-level change and human activity.

TECTONICS

Tectonics control large-scale sedimentation and erosion. Uplift leads to steepening of gradients, which may encourage landsliding and, more importantly, increases the erosive force of flowing water. Downwarping may lead to the formation of lakes or to marine incursions, each with their characteristic style of sedimentation.

Tectonics have affected the different parts of the Biferno catchment in different ways. Overthrusting by the Matese has led to the downwarping of the Boiano basin and the deposition of lacustrine sediments within this structural depression. Thrusting appears to have steepened the front of the Matese, which has led to several episodes of alluvial fan sedimentation in the southern part of the Boiano basin (Fig. 29). In the middle Biferno, thrusting and general upwarp of the Tertiary sediments have been offset by downcutting by the river, giving rise to the Biferno gorge. Lateral migration by the incising river has occasionally led to the preservation of fluvial sediments as terrace deposits. The complex structure of this area has led to rather uneven uplift of the various minor tectonic units, creating a number of independent minor basins of fluvial sedimentation separated by steep gorges lacking a sedimentary record. Correlation of the essentially unfossiliferous deposits of this region is thus fraught with difficulty.

In the lower Biferno, the last major episode of faulting and folding was of Mio-Pliocene age. A relatively planar unconformity was cut across the folded earlier Tertiary deposits; upon which a series of marine incursions laid down shallow marine silts and near-marine sands of Plio-Pleistocene (Calabrian-Tyrrhenian) age. The sea levels then fell and the early Biferno flowed across the sea bed for a short while, then sea levels rose once more and shallow marine sands were deposited before a number of phases of uplift raised the deposits as much as 350 metres above sea level. The Biferno incised into the sedimentary pile, and during phases of stillstand laid down enormous spreads of fluvial gravel. These gravel spreads are today represented by a series of huge terraces in the lower Biferno and Cigno valleys. The period of intense uplift was a time of rapid downcutting, today marked by steep bluffs.

CLIMATE

Upon this large-scale picture have been superimposed the effects of climate. Climatic changes govern the style and rate of erosion and sedimentation to a considerable degree, through a number of direct and indirect mechanisms. Changes in temperature and precipitation govern the nature and density of vegetation; which in turn influence such variables as soil stability and the degree and rapidity of run-off. These, together with factors directly controlled by climate – such as the timing and quantity of precipitation and the magnitude of frost disturbance of soils – control terrestrial erosion and sedimentation and thus water and sediment input to, and movement within, the fluvial system. The quantity and timing of water and sediment entering a river govern channel geometry and the pattern, type and rate of sedimentation or erosion. These factors in turn decide whether a river aggrades, maintains a steady rate, or incises.

In the Biferno valley, as elsewhere in Italy (Frank, 1969; Grüger, 1977; Watts, 1985), past climates have ranged between humid and semi-arid, and between warm-temperate and sub-arctic. There is ample sedimentological and biological evidence that climatic change has influenced sedimentation and erosion in the Biferno valley. Much fluvial sedimentation took place during times of soil instability caused by low temperatures and/or aridity. Phases of incision probably correlate, to a considerable extent, with phases of warm-temperate, humid climate, when stable soils and a dense vegetation cover led to run-off entering the rivers slowly, over an extended period. Under such conditions terrestrial erosion is slight, and with little sediment entering the river there is energy within the system to entrain material from the channel floor and incision occurs as a result.

SEA-LEVEL CHANGES

Sea-level changes may be the result of shifts in the earth's gravity field (the geoid), tectonic movements, or global (eustatic) processes such as those that were in response to glacial/interglacial cycles (glaciation causing a fall in sea level as seawater was taken up into the ice-caps).

The effects of geodetic sea-level change in the Mediterranean are unknown, although some authorities suggest that they may be of considerable significance worldwide. Certainly sea-level changes caused by tectonic movement are of great importance in this region, which was a zone of general uplift throughout the Pleistocene and the Biferno valley is no exception, as can be seen from the flight of tectonic terraces in the lower part of the valley. The effects of eustatic sea-level change can be seen in the lower part of the Biferno valley, where they are reflected by episodes of incision and aggradation, giving rise to some of the complexity of the lowest terraces and floodplain. Incision following eustatic sea-level fall is the most probable cause for the deep, gravel-filled trough which lies below the floodplain of the lower valley and which is still 15 metres deep as far upstream as the Ponte del Liscione dam (Manfredini, 1964).

HUMAN ACTIVITY

The activities of humans may have direct or indirect effects upon the fluvial system. Direct action includes the straightening of reaches, the building of water-control structures (dams, levees, canals) and the abstraction of water for drinking and irrigation. The indirect effects of human activities are more widespread: clearance of the landscape, either directly for agriculture and settlement, or inadvertently by forest fire or the effects of overgrazing, has effects similar to deforestation caused by climatic deterioration (Starkel, 1991). Forest clearance and agriculture may lead to the enhancement of soil-erosion rates and storm run-off and the reduction of base flow. Forest vegetation acts like a sponge, holding water and releasing it slowly to rivers. With the removal of forests, rivers typically become 'flashy', with major floods rapidly following rainfall and episodes where flow dries up or diminishes considerably during dry spells. Such rivers are inefficient transporters of a sediment load enhanced by soil erosion: this therefore accumulates in the watercourse, causing the river to build up its bed (aggrade). Similarly, colluvium may build at the foot of steep eroding hillslopes. Agricultural episodes thus leave widespread and easily preserved evidence in the landscape, such as spreads of colluvium and river terraces (Bell, 1982; Butzer, 1974).

The results of direct action can be seen in the Biferno valley in the form of dam construction, in the early part of the twentieth century at Santa Elena as well as, so spectacularly, within the last ten years at Ponte del Liscione. This has led to the rapid accumulation of lacustrine silts and sands upstream from the dams. Downstream from the dams, regulation of the river tends to cause incision, as can be seen already below the Ponte del Liscione dam. Breaching of the dams, a potentially catastrophic event (made more likely by the complete infill of the lake, which makes it less able to accommodate flood waves), would be followed by rapid incision through the lacustrine sediments.

There also seems to be convincing evidence for the repeated effects of clearance on landscape formation in the Biferno valley. Whilst the character and apparent age of the San Martino sediments in Figure 33 conform closely with Vita-Finzi's model of the Younger Fill, it is difficult to see climatic change as the prime mover behind the formation of the complex sequence of prehistoric, classical, medieval and post-medieval/modern sediments identified in the Biferno valley. In fact, they contain pollen, plant macrofossils and molluscs which generally show evidence of agriculture on the upper slopes of the valley and dense woodland beside the river contemporary with their formation. (The general exception to this pattern appears to be the Boiano basin, where the fluvial style suggests that most of the landscape was cleared.) The evidence of Holocene colluviation and aggradation in the Biferno valley seems above all a record of clearance episodes from later prehistoric times to today.

The near-absence of pre-classical aggradations in the valley argues either for extremely limited pre-classical clearance in the valley, or for earlier aggradations being comprehensively reworked and overwhelmed by the classical-period aggradation. Thick colluvial deposits in the Biferno gorge of classical age contain tree-stump casts and molluscan fauna of woodland species, indicating the presence of woodland beside the river, but far more numerous in these beds are the indicators of the open country beyond.

CONCLUSION

The Biferno valley owes much of its character to the very active geological processes which have taken place there during the last few million years. These processes, particularly upwarping in the Biferno gorge and lower Biferno, and downwarping in the Boiano basin, have made possible the preservation of the incomplete, but extensive, Pleistocene record discussed above.

The Pleistocene and Holocene sequence in the Biferno valley preserves a long, if discontinuous, history of environmental change. The early part of the sequence is dominated by tectonics, but in the Middle and Upper Pleistocene deposits, the effects of varying climatic conditions on sedimentation may be seen, and there may be evidence for Holocene climatic change along the lines of Vita-Finzi's 1969 model of 'Younger Fill' alluviation in the post-Roman period. People do not seem to have had a major influence on the environment until late pre-Roman (Samnite) and early Roman times, when intense agricultural activity caused widespread valley alluviation. The effects of these clearances were not subsequently exceeded until the late 20th century, which has witnessed the culmination of the second great agricultural expansion in the valley described at the end of Chapter Two (Fig. 20).

The natural landscape offers to human populations both opportunities (resources of food, water, space, raw materials and so forth) and constraints (natural hazards, difficult terrain, biological limiting factors). Although social, cultural, political and economic considerations are in most circumstances the major conditioners of human behaviour patterns, nevertheless environmental opportunities and constraints undoubtedly had (and still have) some level of impact upon the behaviour of most human groups. An important focus of interest in the following chapters is the extent to which at different times in the past, from early prehistory to recent times, the patterns of settlement and land use as indicated by the project can be seen to have been shaped by, or to have shaped, the sequence of environmental change described in this chapter.

CHAPTER 5

EARLY PREHISTORIC SETTLEMENT

Graeme Barker, with a contribution by Tim Reynolds

THE FIRST INHABITANTS

Molise is particularly fortunate in having the oldest (or at least, currently the most securely dated) evidence for human settlement in the European continent. In a locality called La Pineta, construction work in 1977–78 for a new bypass around the town of Isernia in the upper Volturno valley some 8 kilometres north-west of the watershed with the Biferno valley (Fig. 34) cut through a series of volcanic, fluvial and lacustrine deposits containing faunal remains and stone artefacts dated to some three-quarters of a million years ago (Coltorti *et al.*, 1982a, 1982b; Peretto *et al.*, 1983). The archaeological material was found on the upper surface of a long sequence of lake silts which had been covered rapidly by volcanic activity. Pumice from this phase was dated by K-Ar (potassium-argon) to 730,000 ± 40,000 bp (before the present). Palaeomagnetic dating confirmed the antiquity of the deposit: the earth's magnetic field changed from reversed to normal polarity 730,000 years ago (known as the Brunhes-Matuyama boundary), and the Isernia sediments containing the human artefacts were on the older side of the boundary. The bones and stone tools probably cannot be treated as an *in situ* butchering assemblage, but the physical condition of the volcanic materials in the archaeological layers suggests that the deposit has not been affected severely by the kind of fluvial activity that has so dramatically altered the clustering of materials at many comparable locations, creating palaeolithic 'living sites' where in reality none existed (Gamble, 1986).

The stone tools found at Isernia la Pineta were in many thousands, and divide into three typological groups: unmodified flint flakes, flint flakes fashioned into denticulated or notched tools, and choppers formed from limestone river cobbles. Microwear studies of similar (though much more recent) material from Britain suggest that there was probably little relationship between shape and function in such assemblages (Keeley, 1980): the same tool might be used for working wood, hide and meat, and both unmodified 'waste' or 'debitage' flakes and more elaborate tools were used in such activities with little apparent discrimination. Bone tools,

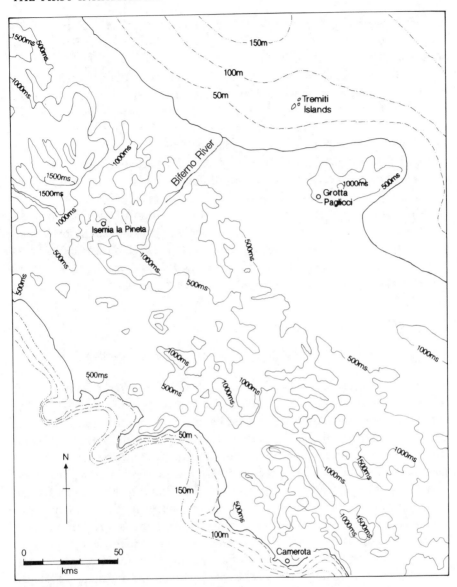

Fig. 34 Central-southern Italy, showing the location of the palaeolithic sites mentioned in Chapter Five, and the major environmental features of the cold stages of the Upper Pleistocene: winter snow-lines were at *c.* 500 metres above present sea level, summer snow-lines above *c.* 1000 metres, whilst sea levels were lowered by at least 100 metres compared with their present levels.

though less frequently preserved, seem to have consisted of unmodified and modified flakes and choppers, and were probably used much as stone tools (Biddittu and Segre, 1982).

The large number of bones at Isernia la Pineta was derived from a small number of species, in particular bison, rhinoceros, elephant, and bear, as well as hippopotamus, pig, goat, and a single specimen of a deer. As Gamble (1986: 156) points out, the Isernia la Pineta fauna is a 'classic lakeside death assemblage' and accords well with his subsistence model for the first palaeolithic groups in Europe of winter scavenging of big-game carcasses at riverside and lakeside locations, probably in conjunction with ambushes and stampedes (Fig. 35). Flake and core-tool assemblages of Middle Pleistocene date are known from a number of locations in peninsular Italy, including sites immediately north and south of Molise (Palma di Cesnola, 1982; Piperno and Segre, 1982; Radmilli, 1964, 1982; Segre et al., 1982), again especially from lakeside situations, and the faunas represented suggest similar systems of foraging, scavenging and ambush hunting (Piperno, 1992).

LOWER/MIDDLE PALAEOLITHIC SETTLEMENT

The lithic material collected by the survey teams amounted to almost three thousand pieces from 475 locations. As with most lithics collected by surface survey, it is impossible to date most of the material with any precision. Many of the individual findspots or field collections are very small – mostly under twenty pieces and often under ten. The raw materials used in every period were predominantly cherts varying in colour from grey to brown and a finer honey-coloured flint. From their appearance they were probably obtained locally, within the valley, in the form of river cobbles. Occupation over so many millennia has invariably left at most locations a palimpsest of surface materials which typologically are likely to be of different ages. Another real difficulty is that unmodified flakes were probably the dominant kind of lithic pieces discarded by most people in the valley from the earlier Palaeolithic to the end of the Bronze Age (the effective end of the systematic use of lithic tools). Unmodified flakes are very common in excavated upper palaeolithic assemblages in peninsular Italy, and are very common at the neolithic and bronze age sites we excavated in the valley.

In common with other surveys, too, we found that patination and weathering or abrasion could only be taken as a very general guide to age. Almost all the obviously palaeolithic forms of lithic artefact are both patinated and abraded, but a few localities yielded similarly classic types

Fig. 35 A reconstruction of the environment of the Isernia la Pineta camp *c.* 750,000 years ago. (Redrawn from a reconstruction by L. Scarpante published in Peretto *et al.*, 1983: 31)

which were neither patinated nor abraded, where deep ploughing in recent years has cut into Pleistocene terraces and brought previously buried material to the surface. On the other hand, none of the classic neolithic bladelets or pressure-flaked arrowheads was heavily patinated or abraded apart from a few water-rolled pieces from recent alluvial deposits in the valley bottom. It therefore seems reasonable to regard the majority of the abraded and patinated material as palaeolithic in origin (excluding doubtful finds from recent alluvial contexts), as well as the fresh material of similar forms from contexts such as terrace edges where the geomorphological evidence for similar antiquity is convincing.

The application of modern radiometric systems of dating to the European Palaeolithic over the past two decades has given little support to the traditional clear division between lower and middle palaeolithic industries. As a result, Gamble (1986) prefers to lump both as the Earlier Palaeolithic, in which two technologies can be recognized: one with simple reduction strategies for making cores, flakes and chopping tools, the other with more complex techniques of flaking and retouch. Both of these long-lived industries contrast dramatically with the revolutionary technological advances of the Upper Palaeolithic founded on the systematic use of blade cores from about 35,000 years ago. The lithic material likely to be of palaeolithic age found by the Biferno Valley Survey is mapped in Figure

36, divided where possible into the two general categories of Earlier and Upper Palaeolithic.

The most striking feature of the distribution is the predominance of palaeolithic finds in the lower valley – over 200 findspots, compared with about 40 in the middle valley and less than 20 in the upper valley. In part the predominance is a reflection of the biases in field-walking discussed in Chapter Three. On the other hand, whilst field-walking conditions were somewhat similar in the middle and upper valleys, the palaeolithic findspots differed markedly. Not only was the number of locations in the middle valley double that of the upper valley, but also their characteristics were very different: the individual collections in the upper valley were invariably very small, whereas several of the middle-valley collections were large assemblages with scores or hundreds of struck flakes and blades. It does therefore seem likely that the marked abundance and widespread distribution of findspots in the lower valley, together with the occurrence of fewer but larger sites in the middle valley, reflect a genuine preference in palaeolithic settlement, as well as biases in survival and recovery.

The richest 'earlier palaeolithic' collection (Fig. 37) is that from C292 in the middle valley. A total of 340 pieces was recovered here within an area of some 4000 square metres. The material, most commonly a brown chert, is worn and patinated to the extent that 33 pieces could not be attributed with confidence to human agency, whilst showing indications of manufacture. Among the remaining pieces, a total of 195 consisted of flakes, mainly with plain platforms, 5 were blade fragments and 6 were irregular cores, the latter for the production of flakes. The retouched tools included 38 flake side scrapers (single, double, and transverse forms, two with demi-Quina retouch), denticulates, a *limace*, burin, and end scraper, as well as irregularly retouched flakes. Much of the retouching was abrupt and steep-angled. The assemblage is broadly middle palaeolithic in character, and classically Mousterian in the absence of a Levallois element and of bifaces. There is no evidence for *in situ* knapping by the people who made the palaeolithic material, though there are signs of re-working at a much later date, probably in neolithic/bronze age times.

A further large collection of middle palaeolithic material was made at B289 in the middle valley, in the same locality as an assemblage of bronze age pottery and lithics on a terrace immediately overlooking the Biferno river. There were some 200 pieces likely to be palaeolithic in date, almost

Fig. 36 The distribution of palaeolithic artefacts found by the archaeological survey of the Biferno valley, together with the principal sites mentioned in the text.

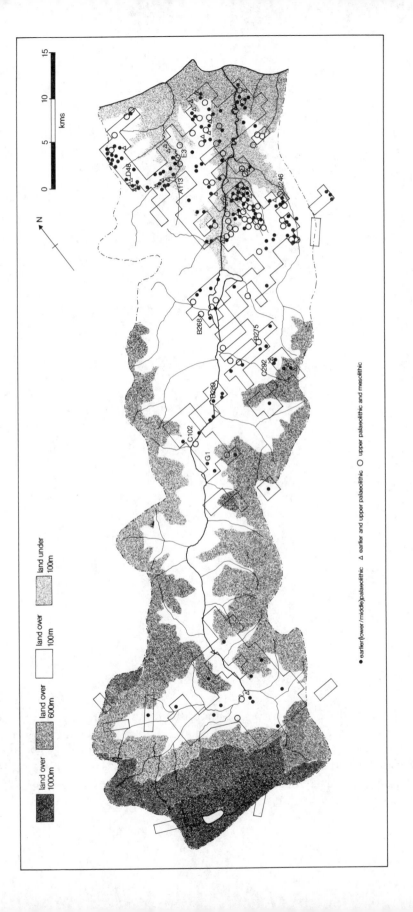

land over 1000m

land over 600m

land over 100m

land under 100m

N

0   5   10   15
kms

● earlier (lower/middle) palaeolithic   △ earlier and upper palaeolithic   ○ upper palaeolithic and mesolithic

D48

AT13

E3

D246

B268

B275

C292

B289

C102

G1

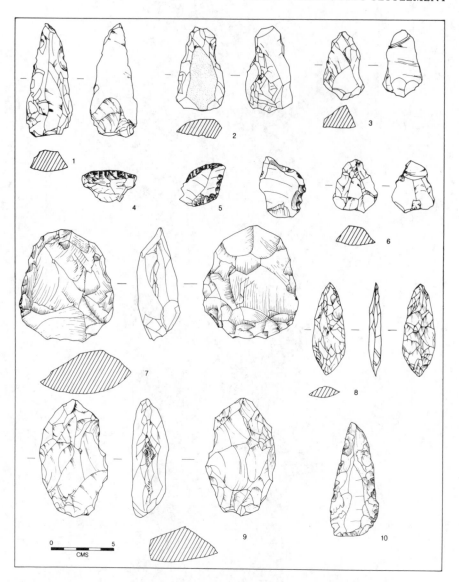

Fig. 37 Examples of earlier palaeolithic artefacts found by the survey.
[C292 (1–6), D48 (7), A278 (8), A275 (9) and C192 (10)]

all flakes, with 15 flake cores, mostly of the same brown chert as at C292.
Retouched pieces included side scrapers (2 with plano-convex retouch), a
burin, a backed knife, and three flake end scrapers. The Levallois technique
was present in this material. Again, there was no evidence for *in situ*
knapping in palaeolithic times, though material was re-worked at a later
date.

In contrast with these relatively large collections, most of the individual field collections made by the survey teams are small. However, their adjacent locations in many areas indicate preferred zones of settlement, the clusters of individual finds together making up 'off-site' or 'non-site' scatters of material of the kind discussed by Foley (1981a, 1981b) as typical traces left by mobile hunter-gatherers. One such zone is the high ground west of the Sinarca valley: the Colle di Breccia and Colle Serramano hills, the interlinking ridge, and the low spurs running down to the Sinarca (Fig. 36). There were also sporadic finds on the terraces of the Sinarca, and on the edge of the dissected plateaux of the lower valley below Guglionesi on the left side and below Larino on the right side of the river, between about 300 and 100 metres above sea level. Another preferred zone seems to have been the west-facing slopes of the high spurs and ridges of the middle valley, between about 500 and 750 metres above sea level.

In addition to the flake assemblages, the survey also found 3 hand-axes of lower/middle palaeolithic age (Fig. 37): at D48 on the edge of Colle Serramano we found a cordiform axe; there was a rolled and irregular ovate biface at A275 on the Larino plateau; and a triangular flake biface was found at G1 in the middle valley. The fact that the bifaces tend to occur in isolation might suggest that these pieces were portable multi-purpose tools that were taken off site to be used elsewhere, whilst the flake tool element was restricted for use at fixed locations.

Most lithic assemblages from middle palaeolithic sites in peninsular Italy consist of unworked flakes, different kinds of scrapers, notched and denticulated pieces. The percentages of tool types are very variable, and probably largely reflect the unspecialized nature of subsistence. The evidence of these assemblages, together with the locations of the sites and the nature of the faunal refuse found in them, suggest that people at this time exploited a wide variety of game in an unspecialized way, probably employing a mixture of ambush hunting and scavenging (Barker, 1981; Gamble, 1986). The faunal list from middle palaeolithic sites includes cattle, fallow deer, horses, ibex, pigs, red deer, and roe deer, together with occasional big game such as elephants and rhinoceros; there is no evidence for significant specialization on any one species or groups of species. There is also no definite evidence for plant gathering, although it is assumed to have been important.

As far as the Biferno valley is concerned, the lithic material suggests a pattern of consistent utilization of the lower elevations and a variety of subsistence tasks being practised there, with forays into the middle valley creating more task-specific 'sites' rather than the extensive 'off-site' spreads across the lower valley. It is impossible to translate the differences in the survey material into different kinds of subsistence activities, but it is interesting that their principal characteristics – the large flake assemblages in the middle valley, compared with numerous smaller collections in the lower valley, and the isolated bifaces – are somewhat reminiscent of the differences noted by Turq (1978) in earlier palaeolithic material between the Lot and Garonne rivers in France: chopping tools and debitage clustered on the river terraces, but flake tool assemblages more common on the intervening plateaux.

LATER PALAEOLITHIC HUNTER-GATHERERS

The Upper Palaeolithic in peninsular Italy is conventionally divided into two phases, the Earlier Upper Palaeolithic between c. 35,000 and 19,000 bp, and the Later Upper Palaeolithic between c. 19,000 and 9000 bp (Gamble, 1986). The best data on assemblage development and chronology have been collected from excavations of coastal caves in southern Italy, particularly from the Camerota caves (Fig. 34) in southern Campania and those of the Salento peninsula, the heel of the peninsula, in Apulia (Guerreschi, 1992). Probably the most important site, however, is the Grotta Paglicci (Fig. 34), a deep stratified cave on the edge of the Gargano peninsula overlooking the Tavoliere plain of northern Apulia some 60 kilometres south-east of the Biferno valley (Mezzena and Palma di Cesnola, 1972; Palma di Cesnola, 1975, 1984).

The earliest upper palaeolithic industries are termed Uluzzian, and like contemporary Chatelperronian/Lower Perigordian industries in France are characterized by numerous side scrapers and denticulated pieces fashioned with a predominantly middle palaeolithic technique of flint-working using flakes and the Levallois technique. Typical Aurignacian industries with nosed and carinate end scrapers and large blades have been found at several caves and have been dated from about 30,000 bp. The most widespread and long-lived lithic tradition of the Earlier Upper Palaeolithic is the Gravettian, in which the most distinctive characteristic is the frequency of backed blades and points and truncated tools. There was a general trend over time towards smaller backed blades, and this, together with changing types of end scraper and burin, has enabled archaeologists to sub-divide the Gravettian into different phases (Guerreschi, 1992; Palma di Cesnola, 1984). The industries of the Later Upper Palaeolithic are generally classified as Epigravettian, a term used because of their major similarity with the Gravettian assemblages in the frequency of backed tools. They have been divided into three chronological groups spanning the period 19,000 to 9000 bp on the basis of changing typologies, changes which for the most part are probably related to an increasing economy in the use of raw materials (Milliken, 1991): the early Epigravettian (19,000–16,000 bp), with many burins, relatively few short end scrapers, few denticulated tools and few geometric pieces; the middle or evolved Epigravettian (16,000–14,000 bp), with more burins, more short end scrapers, few denticulated and geometric tools; and the late or final Epigravettian (16,000–9000 bp), with many small backed and truncated tools, short end scrapers, denticulated and geometric tools.

The survey material cannot be assigned to these phases within the Upper Palaeolithic and Epipalaeolithic because the individual collections are small, and admixtures of earlier and later date are possible and frequently likely. Thus surface material in the vicinity of the late bronze age settlement at A113 in the Sinarca valley included a prismatic core of classic upper palaeolithic type, but no blades of the kind that must have been struck from it (were they taken away for use elsewhere?), together with another core of Levallois type, presumably middle palaeolithic. Only about twenty collections, all in the lower valley, have material that can be securely identified as upper palaeolithic, though abraded blades that may be of this period were found at over one hundred locations. A small selection of material of possible upper palaeolithic and epipalaeolithic age is shown in Figure 38. The principal feature is the lack of backed tools, the most characteristic elements of the cave assemblages. The age range of the material is indicated by the carinated scraper and blade core from B275 probably at one end of the chronological spectrum, the bladelet cores from B286 and C246 in the middle, and the geometric microlith (E3) and retouched bladelet (C102) at the other end.

If this material is correctly assigned, it suggests that upper palaeolithic settlement concentrated like that of the Middle Palaeolithic in the lower valley, but that forays now were also made not only to the middle but also to the upper valley. In the lower valley, the distribution of findspots extends from the higher ground west of the Sinarca valley across the Sinarca to the hills overlooking the Biferno, but clusters particularly on the Larino plateau on the eastern side of the river. In the middle valley there are findspots across the full range of the topography from terraces and isolated outcrops near the river at 200 metres above sea level to near the watershed ridge south of Casacalenda at about 650 metres. In the upper valley material was recovered on terraces overlooking the Biferno/Quirino confluence in the centre of the Boiano basin and on the fringes of the basin.

Pollen analysis indicates a predominantly open landscape in peninsular Italy during the period of upper palaeolithic settlement, dominated by *Artemisia* steppe in the cold and arid conditions, with pine forests in the major valleys and inland basins (Chapter Four). In maximum glacial conditions, permanent snowlines are presumed to have been about 1700

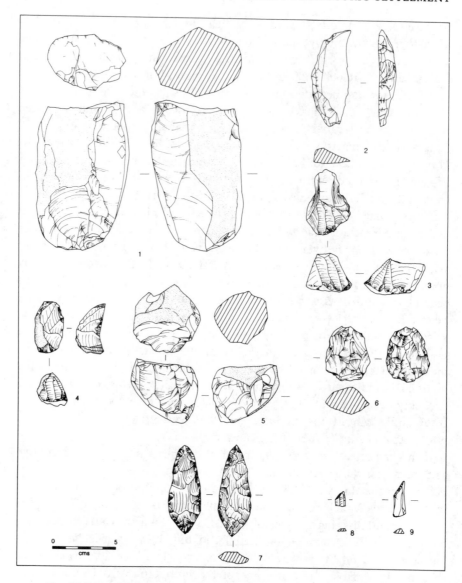

Fig. 38 Examples of upper palaeolithic/epipalaeolithic artefacts found by the survey. [B275 (1), B279 (2), B286 (3), C246 (4), A268 (5, 6), A278 (7), E3 (8), C102 (9)]

metres above present sea level, and winter snow-lines at about 500 metres above present sea levels (Malatesta, 1985). The enlargement of the world's ice-caps caused a fall in sea level, estimated at 120 metres below present levels at 17,000 bp (Shackleton *et al.*, 1984), creating substantial coastal plains beyond the present coast-line of the Italian peninsula (Fig. 34).

Annual mean temperatures are estimated as some six degrees centigrade below present levels (Peterson *et al.*, 1979).

In 1981 one of us (GB) put forward a model of upper palaeolithic subsistence in central Italy, arguing that it was mobile and specialized in response to these conditions. Whereas middle palaeolithic sites were mostly at lower elevations, upper palaeolithic sites were both on the lowlands and in the mountains, and the faunal samples tended to be dominated by two species, red deer and steppe horse (*Equus hydruntinus*). Although other species were hunted such as cattle, chamois, fallow deer, ibex, pigs and roe deer, it seemed clear that the human communities increasingly specialized in hunting red deer and steppe horse. These two species would have migrated into the mountains in the summer months, and then returned to lower elevations on either side of the Apennines for the winter. Moreover, upper palaeolithic sites at or near locations such as gorges well suited for intercept or ambush hunting tend to have lithic assemblages dominated by backed blades and points, whereas other sites have more varied assemblages. It was concluded that upper palaeolithic hunting bands moved between winter lowland and summer upland camps following these animals, using in both areas a series of base camps and hunting sites.

The model has been rightly criticized for over-simplification – the concentration on red deer and steppe horse is obviously high at the kill sites, whereas the subsistence system as a whole was certainly more varied. It is also possible that some parts of the coastal plains created on either side of the peninsula by the drop in sea levels may have been sufficiently productive to have supported semi-sedentary hunting bands throughout the year. However, the distinction drawn in 1981 between middle and upper palaeolithic site distributions still holds good, and it does seem clear that upper palaeolithic subsistence in peninsular Italy, in contrast with earlier patterns of settlement, included the use of the Apennine intermontane basins, presumably in the summer in view of the winter conditions of the glacial climate. The Biferno Valley Survey data conforms with this model, with the majority of the lithic material being found at lower elevations but several locations in the upper valley yielding upper palaeolithic material.

Binford (1978a, 1978b, 1979) has proposed the terms 'logistical mobility' and 'residential mobility' to describe the main kinds of mobility practised by hunter-gatherers today. In the former, consumers remain at a more or less permanent base camp, or use one or two base camps through the seasons, while small groups of producers procure distant resources and bring them back to the consumers. In the latter, small groups of producers and consumers move as a unit throughout the seasonal round. Logistical mobility is normal in areas such as the polar regions, whereas residential mobility is practised by several hunter-gatherer peoples in the tropics. In systems of logistical mobility, most tool production takes place in base camps, or at quarry sites, with most knapping at sites like hunting stands being limited to maintenance and repair.

The system of upper palaeolithic settlement proposed for peninsular Italy conforms to Binford's model of logistical mobility, in the evidence for general-purpose residential sites and specialized kill sites in both the lowlands and the uplands, to take advantage of seasonally changing sets of resources. Further corroboration of this model has been provided by Donahue's analysis of lithic material from one of the Gravettian levels in the Grotta Paglicci (Donahue, 1988). Comparison of the microwear on tools from this level with marks made by the experimental use of modern flint tools on various substances indicated hide working and meat preparation going on in the cave but not antler working or plant processing, pointers towards the use of the site in winter. Given the small size of the occupation area, and the scarcity of the main meat-bearing bones in the faunal assemblage, together with the suitability of the site's location in a gorge on the edge of the Gargano mountain for ambush hunting, Donahue concluded that the Grotta Paglicci was a specialized winter 'hunting stand'. Other sites in the Gargano have been identified by Palma di Cesnola (1984) as specialized lithic workshops. An analysis of the contemporary industries of caves in the Salento peninsula has also indicated that most of them were primarily kill sites (Milliken, 1991).

Whilst the Italian site sample is certainly biased by caves, very few of which were probably major residential sites, it seems increasingly likely that upper palaeolithic hunter-gatherers in peninsular Italy were organized in systems of logistical mobility, using networks of base camps or residential sites at the hub of sets of satellite kill sites and other kinds of special-purpose field camps. No major residential site has been identified near the Gargano kill and quarry sites; one possibility is that they were on the coastal plain now submerged, or on the Tavoliere plain, which is covered by thick deposits of Holocene alluvium. Perhaps the Biferno valley was also visited by upper palaeolithic hunter-gatherers from this Tavoliere system, who came to hunt and forage mostly on the plateau and low hills of the lower valley, though occasionally further inland as well.

POSTSCRIPT

Throughout the Italian peninsula, as elsewhere in the Mediterranean basin, the millennia following the end of glacial conditions were marked by a dramatic diversification in subsistence systems involving a mixture of hunting, fishing and gathering, as communities adapted to the climatic amelioration and accompanying ecological transformations (Barker, 1985; Lewthwaite, 1986). There is increasing evidence from the 7th millennium bc onwards for the exploitation of the resources of the sea, lakes and rivers. The industries made by these people in Italy were at first rather similar to those of the final Epigravettian and are often termed 'epipalaeolithic'; rather than mesolithic, to reflect this continuity. Most of them are dominated by small scrapers and backed blades, but geometric microliths and notched or denticulated tools became increasingly common through time.

Given the considerable evidence for the continued use of Epigravettian artefacts as hunting and fishing equipment for some time after the first appearance of neolithic pottery and agriculture (Barker, 1981, 1985; and see Chapter Six), rather little can be said about mesolithic settlement in the Biferno valley on the basis of our undated surface material. Typical Epigravettian artefacts were found such as very small scrapers, notches, borers, backed blades and bladelets, and the single geometric microlith (Fig. 38: E3) – mostly in the lower valley, and particularly adjacent to streams such as the Sinarca. A major focus of settlement at this time could well have been the Adriatic plain now submerged beyond the present estuary of the Biferno.

CHAPTER 6

THE FIRST AGRICULTURAL
COMMUNITIES

Graeme Barker, with contributions by Gill Clark, Chris Hunt,
Caroline Malone, Tim Reynolds and Derrick Webley

THE BEGINNINGS OF FARMING IN ITALY

Zvelebil and Rowley-Conwy (1984) have proposed a model for the transition to farming in northern Europe that seems increasingly apposite for
the central and western Mediterranean, including Italy (Lewthwaite, 1982,
1986, 1987). The model envisages three stages in the adoption of agriculture
by a mesolithic population: an availability phase, when the foragers are in
contact with farmers, and may obtain the cultigens from time to time
through trade (or by force) but make little use of them; a substitution phase,
when the foragers make increasing use of animal and/or plant husbandry
at the expense of their traditional way of life; and a consolidation phase,
when husbandry becomes the predominant mode of subsistence.

Apulia, the southeastern part of the Italian peninsula, is climatically very
similar to Greece, and it is from this region that there is the first evidence
for the establishment of farming communities in the 6th millennium BC,
almost as early as in Greece. Air photography during and after the last war
revealed hundreds of neolithic ditched enclosures on the Tavoliere plain
(Bradford, 1949; Bradford and Williams-Hunt, 1946; Brown, 1991). The
largest sites, such as Passo di Corvo, are several hundred metres in
diameter, with a series of ditches enclosing scores of small circular features
interpreted as 'hut compounds'. Excavations have shown that most of these
were indeed probably the enclosure ditches of small circular huts, though
rectangular houses have also been found at some sites (Cassano and
Manfredini, 1983; Tiné, 1983, 1987). These communities cultivated a
mixture of cereals and legumes, with emmer wheat (*Triticum dicoccum*) and
barley the major crops, and also kept cattle, pigs, sheep and goats (the
latter two in particular). The sites are generally adjacent to areas of *crosta*, a
calcium carbonate crust below the surface which results in lighter soils and
better drainage than on the surrounding alluvium (Jarman and Webley,
1975). The Tavoliere farmers used pottery storage vessels decorated with

incised and impressed designs, part of the family of neolithic 'Impressed Wares' that is generally the first major pottery type throughout the central and western Mediterranean (Barker, 1985).

It is normally assumed that farming was introduced to the Tavoliere from Greece, though whether by information and goods exchange between the indigenous populations or by immigration of farmers from one region to the other is a matter of considerable dispute. Given the time lag between the beginnings of farming here and to the north, there would seem to have been an 'availability phase' between c. 5500 and 4500 bc when there must have been contacts between the Tavoliere farmers and adjacent bands of foragers, but when the new way of subsistence had little or no impact on the old (Lewthwaite, 1987). Farming then began north of the Tavioliere in Molise (as the excavations described later in this chapter show), Abruzzo and Marche (Grifoni Cremonesi, 1992) in the second half of the 5th millennium bc, a process traditionally interpreted in terms of a population migration from the Tavoliere though equally likely to have been a process of local adoption of farming by indigenous foragers within the 'substitution phase' of the Zvelebil and Rowley-Conwy model. Certainly the system of farming changed as farming spread north, for the preference for wheat over barley on the Tavoliere was reversed (Skeates, 1991): although barley is less tolerant of wet soils than wheat, it can tolerate a wider range of soils, and certainly early farming in central Italy was practised on a wider range of soils than on the Tavoliere (Barker, 1981). The chronological break between the first farming in Apulia and further north therefore probably reflects in part the re-adaptation of the Tavoliere crop complex to one better suited to the different ecological conditions further north.

NEOLITHIC SETTLEMENT TRENDS IN THE BIFERNO VALLEY

Thin parallel-sided blades have often been regarded as the typical flint artefacts of neolithic settlements in central Italy. In fact, these artefacts are not dominant on neolithic settlements until the 4th millennium bc, the 'consolidation' phase of agriculture. They are also associated then with fine pressure-flaked arrowheads, presumed to be hunting equipment, though they may well have been as important for prestige as for practical use. The flint assemblages of sites belonging to the preceding phases of neolithic settlement reflect the inter-mixing of subsistence systems discussed in the previous section, as farming was incorporated into, and gradually replaced, the existing pattern of hunting, fishing and gathering. In the case of the Copper Age of peninsular Italy, the best-known flint artefacts are those found in burials, such as superb pressure-flaked projectile points and arrowheads, together with very long fine blades, all generally made of imported high-quality flint. However, the settlements of the period also have lithic assemblages rather similar to those of the Late Neolithic. Bronze age lithic industries also included pressure-flaked arrowheads, at least in the earlier centuries of the 2nd millennium bc, but certainly by the later centuries they tended to be dominated by unworked flakes as domestic technology turned increasingly to bronze, a general trend for the peninsula confirmed by our excavations of bronze age settlements.

Figure 39 shows the large number of findspots at which unpatinated lithic material was found that is likely to date to the Holocene generally, most of it to the Neolithic. For the reasons outlined above, it is impossible to divide this material unequivocally into mesolithic, neolithic, copper age and bronze age groups. However, the paucity of typical mesolithic artefacts such as backed bladelets, small round scrapers and geometric microliths, and the fact that the little material we found was always near the coast, tends to support the hypothesis that little use was made of the valley by foraging groups in the early Holocene, with most settlement restricted to the Adriatic littoral. Similarly, the frequency with which bronze age pottery was found with undifferentiated flakes also suggests that most bronze age material has been identified satisfactorily. Thus, although some of the sites in Figure 39 could date from the earlier or later phases of Holocene flint use in the valley, the likelihood is that most of them date primarily to the 5th, 4th and perhaps 3rd millennia bc, and as such are a fair indication of the nature of settlement during the 'substitution' and 'consolidation' phases of the agricultural economy.

In Figure 39 the lithic collections have been classified into two groups. The larger group ('probably neolithic') consists of sites where most pieces are plain and retouched flakes similar to those of the assemblage found at the principal excavated site with early neolithic pottery, Monte Maulo (B198), which is dated by radiocarbon to the second half of the 5th millennium bc (Fig. 49). The second group (identified securely as 'neolithic') consists of sites with parallel-sided blades typical of the later neolithic phases of settlement; where these have arrowheads, these are also identified (Fig. 40). For the same reason, the sites with neolithic pottery have also been divided where possible into two major chronological groups, an earlier neolithic group with Impressed Ware pottery and a later neolithic group with the various fine wares of the middle and late neolithic typologies (the stylistic divisions of which are discussed later). Two sites have pottery spanning the entire period, A268 and C186.

Fig. 39. Neolithic settlement in the Biferno valley according to the archaeological survey, with the principal sites mentioned in the text identified.

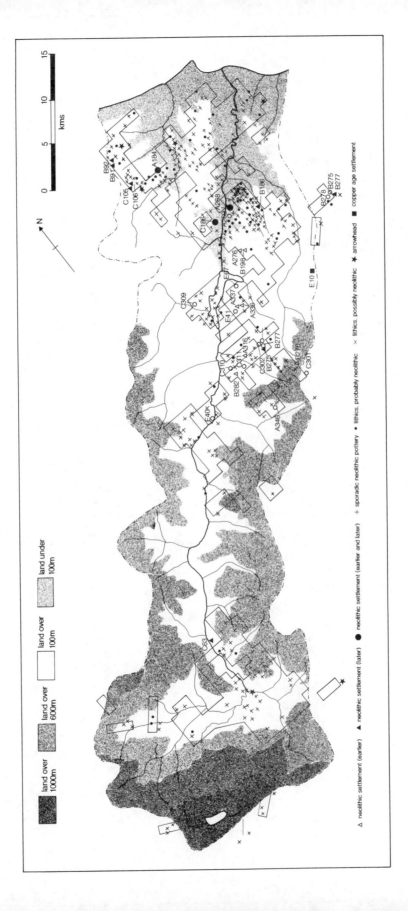

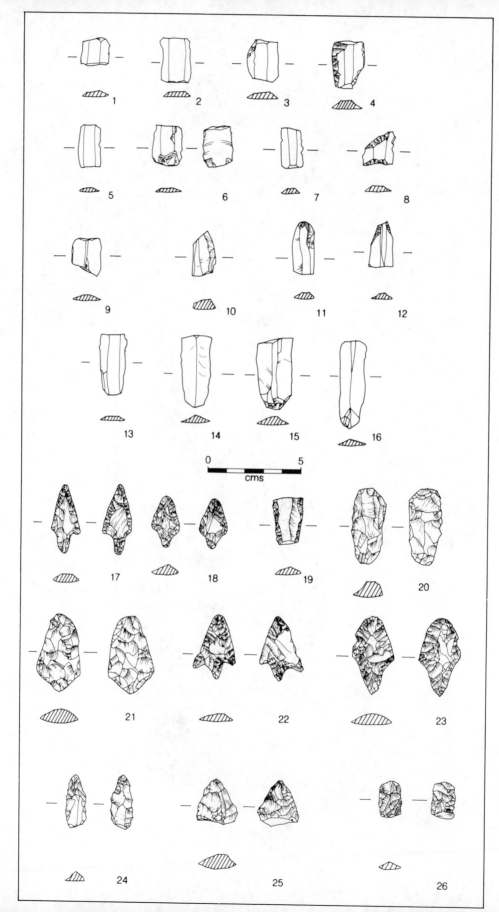

0 ____ 5
cms

Excavations were carried out at four sites with neolithic pottery on the surface; all proved to have been settlements. All of these sites also had numerous lithic artefacts on the surface. Our assumption is, therefore, that the other sites with neolithic pottery associated with numbers of lithic artefacts are also settlements (Fig. 39). Most of the findspots with lithic material of possible or probable neolithic date without pottery consist of very small collections, and seem unlikely to be settlement residues. The adjacency to each other of many of these in many localities suggests that they are the residues of activities creating 'off-site' patterns of spreads of debris such as hunting, gathering and animal herding.

Eight settlements were found with pottery belonging to the earlier phase of neolithic settlement, four in the lower and four in the middle valley. They are located at altitudes varying from 75 to 375 metres above sea level and in a range of topographical situations. Thus one of the settlements in the lower valley (A268) was positioned on the dissected plateau below Larino, at the end of a promontory overlooking the river (Fig. 43), whereas the other three were all on hilltop locations, though their height above the river varies between less than 100 and almost 300 metres (A276, B198, C186). In the middle valley the four settlements are all on spurs some 200 to 250 metres above the river, halfway between the valley floor and the watershed ridge. The findspots with lithic material loosely ascribed to the period of earlier neolithic settlement cluster around these sites in the lower and middle valley. Although no sites with earlier neolithic pottery were located in the upper valley, lithic material possibly of this date was found widely distributed along the margins of the Biferno alluvium and on the spurs overlooking the Boiano basin, between 500 and 700 metres above sea level.

By contrast, most of the settlement sites with later neolithic pottery are in the lower valley, and the two sites elsewhere do not seem to have been normal domestic sites. Of the four main settlements in the lower valley, two are on the dissected plateau below Larino (A268, B186), one is on an isolated hill by the river (C186) and one is on the Biferno/Sinarca watershed ridge (A184). The only site found in the middle valley with (possibly) later neolithic pottery was a quarrying and knapping site, where good-quality chert (some of it palaeolithic in origin) was collected and re-worked (B275). The remaining site with later neolithic pottery and lithic material was a small rock shelter in the upper valley at Ponte Regio (C63), which our excavations indicated can best be interpreted as a seasonal

Fig. 40. Neolithic blades and arrowheads from the Biferno valley. [D47 (1), A130 (2, 6), C121 (3), D87 (4), C106 (5), A124 (7), A268 (8), D46 (9), B216 (10), D97 (11), C224 (12), C63 (13, 14, 15, 16), C102 (17), C111 (18, 19), G4 (20), C121 (21), C186 (22, 23), B230 (24), B210 (25), A249 (26)]

camp, probably for herding animals (Barker, 1974; Fig. 44). The findspots of lithic material assigned to this period also concentrate almost exclusively in the lower valley. Apart from findspots in the vicinity of the quarrying area in the middle valley, the localities with later neolithic blades are almost invariably near the river, and the same is true of the upper valley and Boiano basin.

The survey data therefore indicate considerably more variability in the nature of earlier neolithic settlement compared with later neolithic settlement. The main earlier neolithic settlements were situated in both the lower and middle valley, in a number of topographical situations, and off-site activities ranged throughout the valley. The main later neolithic settlements were in the lower valley, in more restricted topographical situations, and off-site activities in the middle and upper valleys were generally near the river.

SETTLEMENT STRUCTURE

Our principal information on the nature of the earlier neolithic settlements was obtained from our excavations on Monte Maulo (B198), a prominent hill overlooking the lower Biferno valley. Neolithic pottery and stone implements were found by a survey team in the ploughsoil of the summit slope, with a principal concentration of large sherds with fresh breaks in an area some 5 metres in diameter. Removal of the ploughsoil revealed an arc-shaped neolithic occupation deposit, which proved on excavation to cover an irregular depression formed of three pits (Figs. 41, 42). The archaeological deposit overlying these pits was some 10–15 centimetres thick, and extended eastwards beyond them half a metre or so in places – presumably this was part of a larger occupation deposit destroyed by recent deep ploughing. The principal deposit in the depression was the same as that overlying it – the mixture of dark soil rich in charcoal and other organic matter, stones, potsherds, and other archaeological residues. Particle-size analysis indicated that for the most part the sediments in the pits were sandy silts much as the modern ploughsoil.

In places there was clear evidence that the edges of the pits had been formed by hacking or quarrying into the bedrock. Elsewhere, however, the dark occupation soil was interleaved at the edges of the pits with mixed yellow and brown clays devoid of finds, deposits that had either slumped naturally or been trampled into the depression from the surrounding surface. There were also two slabs of a sterile green clay laid down during the filling of the depression with the archaeological deposit, presumably created in situ in waterlogged conditions.

Fig. 41. Excavation at the neolithic settlement of Monte Maulo (B198). (Photograph: Graeme Barker)

Four radiocarbon determinations were obtained from the excavation. One date of 5930 ± 100 bp (3980 bc) was calculated by the Harwell laboratory (HAR-2710) from charcoal collected by water flotation from the main occupation deposit, and three dates were obtained from animal bone submitted to the Oxford laboratory (Gowlett *et al.*, 1987). OxA-652 (6280 ± 70 bp – 4330 bc) and OxA-653 (6210 ± 70 bp – 4260 bc) are from two adjacent cattle bones (a scapula and humerus respectively) taken from a cluster of animal bones in one of the pits, and OxA-651 (6540 ± 80 bp – 4590 bc) dates another cattle bone (a radius) from another. These determinations suggest an occupation in the second half of the 5th millennium bc (uncalibrated), or *c.* 5300–4800 BC (calibrated). Their range also provides further evidence for the length of use of the pit complex. The ceramic repertoire from the site is entirely consistent with these dates.

Pit complexes like that of Monte Maulo are the commonest and best-known structures found at earlier neolithic settlement sites in the Italian peninsula. They are normally shallow, with an irregular oval, circular, or figure-of-eight plan, with no apparent structural elements. For many decades they have been interpreted as 'hut pits' (*fondi di capanne*), the vestiges of sub-surface pit dwellings, as Peet (1909: 89–90) first argued:

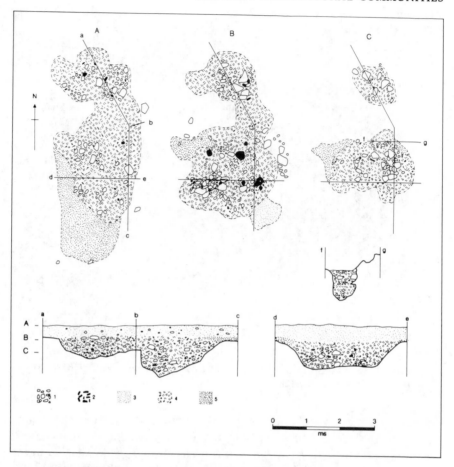

Fig. 42. Plan of the pits at the neolithic settlement of Monte Maulo (B198). 1. cobbles; 2. potsherds; 3. light brown soil, charcoal flecks; 4. dark brown/black soil, charcoal-rich; 5. yellow/green clay

'what is actually found by the excavator is a hole filled with refuse and indistinguishable from the surrounding soil except by the colour of its contents. This simple hole ... formed the foundation, and in part a substitute for the superstructure. This was a hut of wicker- or branch-work, covered with sun-dried clay and perhaps skins. The roof was, at least in some cases, supported by strong vertical poles driven in outside the circumference of the hole or *fondo*. The sockets of such pits are still visible'. On the other hand, large-scale excavations at neolithic settlements in Abruzzo and Apulia have found post-hole settings convincingly interpreted as the remains of substantial above-ground houses (Cassano and Manfredini, 1983; Ducci *et al.*, 1983; Tozzi, 1978), with most of the *fondi di capanne* probably being quarry pits for the clay required for the construction of such houses. However, there are still grounds for supposing that 'hut-pits' were used by some communities, particularly in the transition phase from foraging to farming (Calegari *et al.*, 1986; Tiné, 1983, 1987).

At Monte Maulo, the evidence of the rather complex nature of the pits and of their deposits suggests that the depression we excavated was probably in origin a natural cavity at the junction of the clays and sandstone, but enlarged by deliberate quarrying. There are some indications from the technology of the lithic material that chert was being quarried on site, and this activity may well explain the original purpose of the pits. However that may be, they must have been open to the elements for some time for the wedges of green clay to have formed, and had probably been subject to trampling as well as weathering, but they had also been used – given the evidence of scattered sherds from the same vessels – for quite rapid infilling. Judging from the interleaving of the deposits at the pit edges, there would seem to have been several such episodes before the depression was entirely filled and covered by an occupation surface.

The daub found in the rubbish deposits in the depression included a piece with the impressions of two timbers which must have been some 15 centimetres in diameter, and there were several other pieces with stick impressions of 2 centimetres in diameter and 2–3 centimetres apart, presumably from a structure of vertical posts and horizontally interleaved wattles covered in daub. It is possible that the stone rubble in the depression derives from wall footings. The total amount of daub found in the excavation amounted to about 10 kilograms, whereas Ammerman and Schaffer (1981) have calculated that some 7 tons of clay would have been needed for the walling of a small (5×3 metre) hut of wattle-and-daub construction. Rather than such substantial houses, however, it is perhaps more likely that early neolithic huts were generally more similar to the traditional *pagliara* or *pagliaio* still widely used in the Apennines (Close-Brooks and Gibson, 1966): light huts of branches, reeds, or straw and daub, used variously by farmers, shepherds and charcoal burners for storage or seasonal living accommodation, or as animal shelters (Fig. 60).

The survey recovered very little data on the structure of later neolithic settlements. Trial excavations were conducted at three sites with material predominantly or wholly belonging to the later neolithic periods. At the two major settlements (A268 and C186), it became clear that deep ploughing had more or less entirely destroyed the settlement record, and though daub and other settlement debris were found, no structural evidence remained. At A184, where pottery and other material were found in the ploughsoil of a new vineyard, two test pits between the rows of support posts found a remarkable wealth of cultural debris, again including daub fragments, but the excavations also showed that the vine trenches had gone deep into bedrock, destroying all the archaeology except for a series of parallel segments of the neolithic occupation deposit in between. Animal bone from the excavations at A268 and A184 yielded two radiocarbon dates, of 5840 ± 70 bp or 3890 bc (OXA-655) and 5580 ± 70 bp or 3630 bc (OXA-654) respectively, both consistent with the expected date range suggested by the pottery (Gowlett *et al.*, 1987: 138).

Despite the lack of structural data from these settlements, it does at least seem clear that there was a general trend towards an increase in size between earlier and later neolithic settlements in the valley. Whilst of course we cannot assume a direct relationship between the area covered by surface remains and that of the settlement buried below the ploughsoil – sites like A184 and B198 are clearly only segments of larger sites destroyed by modern ploughing – it is noteworthy that all of the sites with earlier neolithic pottery have surface remains measuring less than 75 metres in diameter (averaging *c.*45 metres), whereas the later neolithic settlement sites are all 100 metres or more in diameter (averaging *c.*120 metres). The distribution of earlier and later neolithic sherds at the major surface sites with both, such as A268 and C186 where the pottery was collected on a 10×10 metre grid, confirms the trend to larger settlement areas in the Later Neolithic. Although the neolithic settlements to the north of Molise are generally bigger, there is the same trend: the earlier neolithic settlements average 4000–8000 square metres, whereas the later neolithic settlements such as Catignano in Abruzzo covered 20,000–30,000 square metres (Pitti and Tozzi, 1976; Tozzi, 1982).

It is also likely that our later neolithic settlements were as substantial in their internal features as Catignano, where excavations revealed the foundations of four houses measuring 13–16×5–8 metres surrounded by pits, some of which were used as grain silos (Costantini and Tozzi, 1983). Geophysical survey at B186 indicated two principal if irregular areas of significantly higher readings, each measuring roughly 10–12×5 metres: whether hut floors or pit clusters, they would seem to indicate settlement structures more substantial than Monte Maulo and more akin to Catignano. Even more persuasive is the evidence of an air photograph taken in 1987 by Derek Riley and Otto Braasch, which shows a promontory cut off by a ditch, with rows of pits suggesting buildings in the enclosed area (Fig. 43). The site is on the immediate edge of the area of surface neolithic pottery recorded as A268, though only sporadic neolithic sherds were found on this promontory during the survey.

In contrast with the extensive open settlements on the lowlands, the Ponte Regio site consisted of a small deposit in the shelter of an overhanging boulder or outcrop of limestone (Fig. 44). The surface area

Fig. 43. The late neolithic promontory settlement at A268, showing the ditch and pit alignments inside. (Aerial photograph: Derick Riley and Otto Braasch, June 1987)

Fig. 44. The shelter at Ponte Regio (C63) in the upper valley, probably used for temporary occupation in the later neolithic period. (Photograph: Graeme Barker)

protected by the outcrop was some 10 metres along the rock face by 3 metres out from the wall. The neolithic occupation deposit was situated in the middle of the sheltered area and consisted of an oval-shaped lens of occupation debris, a dark ash- and charcoal-rich soil, measuring 1.5–2 metres in width and extending 1.5 metres out from the back wall of the shelter (Barker, 1974). The nature of the site and its deposits indicate a temporary shelter of some kind, a satellite camp used by a very few individuals from a permanent settlement elsewhere.

ENVIRONMENT AND SUBSISTENCE

MOLLUSCS (CH)

The species found at Monte Maulo included *Cernella* sp, *Helicella itala*, *Ruminata decollata* and *Helix pomata*. The first three of these species prefer dry, open ground with some rocks or shrubs, whereas *H. pomata* prefers woods, scrub or tall herbage. This species is edible, and another edible species found in the infill was the marine bivalve *Cerastoderma glaucum* – as the crow flies, Monte Maulo is about 20 kilometres from the sea. The land snails recovered from A184 are also suggestive of open ground: in addition to further examples of *Rumina decollata*, *Trichia* aff. *hispida* was identified, a catholic terrestrial species, occurring in most habitats except for the very driest. A268 yielded one specimen of the marine species *Venus striatula*.

CARBONIZED PLANT REMAINS (DW)

Over 2000 litres of soil from the Monte Maulo excavation were processed by froth flotation (Fig. 27), and a sample totalling 146 carbonized seeds was recovered from the resulting residues (Table 4). Half of these were found in the main occupation deposit overlying the depression, in a soil sample less than a quarter of the total processed, but small numbers of seeds were found at most depths and in most parts of the depression. The carbonized plant remains from A268 were recovered from small deposits of undisturbed occupation at the base of the ploughzone, associated with the fragments of animal bone which yielded the late neolithic radiocarbon date.

Little weight can be placed on the numbers and percentages of identified seeds given the very small size of these samples. However, it seems clear that the material is the result of an agricultural system using a variety of cereals and legumes. Furthermore, it is likely that barley and emmer wheat dominated the husbandry regime as well as the plant residues discarded at both sites. These two cereals are invariably the commonest at comparable

Table 4 Carbonized plant remains recovered from neolithic sites in the Biferno valley: B198 (Monte Maulo, earlier neolithic) and A268 (later neolithic)

		B198	A268
CEREALS			
Avena sativa	Common oat	3	–
Hordeum vulgare	Barley	38	24
Panicum miliaceum	Millet	1	–
Triticum aestivum	Bread wheat	1	–
Triticum dicoccum	Emmer wheat	78	40
LEGUMES			
Lens esculenta	Lentil	9	–
Pisum arvense	Pea	5	2
Vicia faba	Horse bean	2	–
OTHERS			
Antica dioca	Nettle	2	1
Galium aparine	Cleaver	6	32
Stellarium media	Chickweed	2	–
Total		146	99

neolithic sites in the Italian peninsula, both as carbonized remains and as seed impressions in daub (Castelletti, 1974–5; Evett and Renfrew, 1971; Malone and Stoddart, 1992), though seeds and other fragments of einkorn (*Triticum monococcum*) were also abundant at Catignano (Costantini and Tozzi, 1983). As noted earlier, the dominance of barley over wheat at early neolithic sites in Abruzzo and Marche, a reversal of these crops' roles on the Tavoliere, could reflect an adaptation from the light *crosta* soils of the Tavoliere to the wider range of soils cultivated to the north. The dominance of barley over wheat at Monte Maulo fits into this trend, and may help to explain the time lag between farming here and further south.

In addition to the carbonized plant remains from these two sites, flotation of samples from the hearth in the Ponte Regio shelter recovered fragments of charcoal (mainly oak) as well as carbonized seeds of blackberry (*Rubus fructicosus*).

ANIMAL BONES (GB, GC)

Small samples of faunal material were recovered from the excavations of the neolithic sites at B198, A268, A184, and C63 (II: Chapter Seven).

Animal bone was poorly preserved in the Monte Maulo deposit, for the most part being very badly crushed in amongst the rubble. None of the bone was burnt. Only 3 species are certainly represented – cattle, pigs, and sheep/goats, although a crushed pelvis may belong to red deer rather than cattle. (Sheep and goat are treated here as 1 species, because most pieces of bone in this kind of badly fragmented material cannot be identified reliably as belonging to either sheep or goat.) The only weathered bone was noted in the surface occupation deposit, so it seems that the bones in the depression had been dumped there relatively quickly after the butchery of the animals, rather than being secondary refuse exposed earlier to weathering, trampling, and the like. Most of the bones were in two clusters, one in the northern pit and the other at a comparable depth in the southern pit, with the pelvis lying between the two. A minimum number of only 1 individual per species is represented – in the case of pig, a female (on the evidence of a canine tooth).

The material from A268 was better preserved, so that almost two-thirds could be identified to the level of bone and over half to the level of species. Cattle and sheep/goats are the principal species represented, with a range of anatomical elements, together with two fragments of pig. Sheep were definitely present according to Boessneck's (1969) morphological criteria on the evidence of a scapula, but there was no positive evidence for goats. The minimum number of individuals represented by this material is 2 sheep/goats, 1 cattle and 1 pig. The faunal sample from A184 is very similar: cattle, pigs, and sheep/goats are all represented, with a minimum of one animal per species. The material from both sites included burnt bones. The neolithic hearth at C63 yielded a minimum number of 2 sheep/goats, 2 pigs, 1 cow, 1 red deer and 1 roe deer. Most parts of the skeleton are present in the faunal samples from the lowland sites, suggesting that the animals kept by the neolithic communities were butchered and consumed, and their remains discarded, at their settlements. The range of skeletal parts of sheep/goats at C63 also indicates that animals were butchered and consumed on site, whereas cattle and pigs are represented only by head and lower-limb bones, possibly suggesting that the main part of the carcass was consumed elsewhere.

The age at which animals were killed in antiquity ought to reflect the husbandry goals of their keepers. It is commonly assumed that prehistoric farmers would have killed stock at a relatively early age if meat production was a priority (surplus males in particular could be killed without damaging the breeding stock), whereas it would have been important to raise more animals to maturity if their secondary products (traction and dairy products in the case of cattle, wool and dairy products in the case of sheep, and the manure from both) were a priority (Payne, 1972b, 1973). Whilst the mortality data from the Biferno neolithic sites are very few (II: Chapter Seven), there is at least a consistent impression from most sites that cattle and sheep were killed as young adults, or as older animals, but not immature (though the C63 sample includes sheep of all three age groups). Pigs do not provide useful secondary products apart from manure, so it is efficient to kill them as soon as they have reached a reasonable body weight. They also breed prolifically, so a herd can withstand systematic culling of most young stock. Modern pigs can be brought to a satisfactory killing weight within a few months, but in primitive husbandry systems fattening took rather longer, and animals up to two years old are common in many faunal samples from prehistoric Europe. The Biferno material is typical: most of the samples include both one- and two-year old animals.

As in the case of the botanical residues, the faunal material from the Biferno valley neolithic settlements is very limited, but does at least share a number of similarities with the contemporary faunal record of neolithic sites in adjacent regions of the peninsula (Wilkens, 1987). In general cattle, sheep/goats and pigs are the dominant species at early neolithic sites, though their frequencies varied considerably, primarily in response to differing environments; most stock were kept for their meat. However, numbers of sheep and goats decreased through time on the lowlands, from an average of 60 per cent on early neolithic sites to 30 per cent on late neolithic sites, and cattle frequencies generally doubled over the same period from 20 per cent to 40 per cent. Inland, several late neolithic sites have high frequencies of sheep and goats. These changes probably reflect the development of increasing specialization in husbandry systems as well as an adaptation (inland) to an increasingly open landscape. Mortality data are not abundant, but there does seem to have been a general trend towards killing older cattle and sheep/goats, suggesting the increasing importance of secondary products such as milk and wool during the course of the 3rd millennium bc, an hypothesis supported by the appearance of spindle whorls and strainer sherds (the latter presumed to be associated with cheese-making) at late neolithic settlements. The mortality data from the Biferno valley sites are not sufficient to show this trend, though interestingly the finds included a strainer sherd from A184 (Fig. 47: 21) and a spindle whorl from A268.

DISCUSSION

Systematic farming seems to have begun in the Biferno valley in the late 5th millennium bc, the botanical and faunal evidence from Monte Maulo indicating an integrated system of crop and animal husbandry. There is little evidence for wild foods, though it must be acknowledged that carbonized plant remains are almost invariably biased towards cereals because processing these, unlike most wild plants, frequently involved the use of parching or roasting. It is impossible to calculate the respective importance of plant and animal foods at the site, though plant foods – and in particular cereals and pulses – are generally assumed to have dominated the diets of most early neolithic farming communities on the Mediterranean lowlands. Halstead (1981, 1987), for example, suggests that in the predominantly forested landscape at this time, it would have been impracticable to maintain large herds of domestic animals as well as uneconomic if, as seems to have been the case, meat was the primary product for which they were kept. In fact, domestic animals may have been valued as much for social as for economic reasons by these societies: a number of apparently ritual deposits of animal bones has now been recognized in central Italian caves, and feasting deposits in others, suggesting that an important function of domestic stock was as wealth on the hoof for sacrifice or exchange (Skeates, 1991; Whitehouse, 1992).

Crop cultivation probably consisted of small-scale horticulture – the working with hoes, mattocks and digging sticks of small plots near the residential sites. The plots may have been fertilized by human manure and household rubbish, and grazing animals on the fields would also have helped maintain their fertility. The pulses grown by neolithic farmers would also have fed nitrogen back into the soil, suggesting that some of the major principles of soil management were understood at this very early date.

The variability in the locations of the early neolithic settlement sites in the valley could imply variability in subsistence practices of the kind predicted for the 'substitution' phase of early farming, but without faunal and botanical data from most of these sites it is impossible to test this hypothesis. What is clear is that later neolithic settlements were in more restricted locations: particle size analysis indicated that all the major lowland sites were on almost identical sandy silts, excellent arable soils in terms of fertility and drainage. The subsistence data are few, but conform with the picture emerging from elsewhere in central Italy of the development of more substantial agricultural settlements on the lowlands in the 'consolidation' phase of farming. It seems likely that the animal husbandry of the lowland Biferno settlements concentrated on sheep and goat herding, and that the shepherds from these sites made use of seasonal herding camps up valley of the kind we found at Ponte Regio. The absence of carbonized cereals but presence of carbonized blackberry seeds and of oak charcoal there is also interesting: one activity requiring the collection of firewood at a pastoral camp would have been the boiling of milk for the production of cheese like the sheep's milk *pecorino* of the modern Italian shepherd (Barker and Grant, 1991).

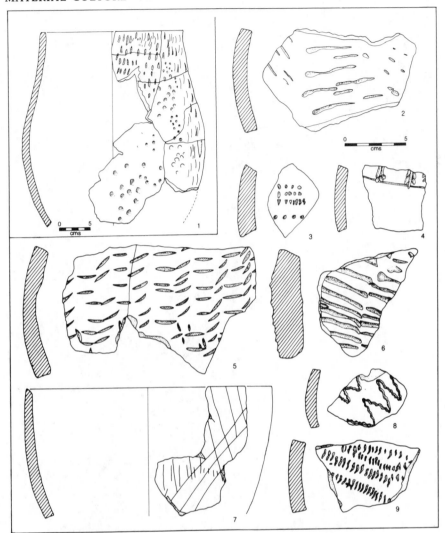

Fig. 45. Earlier neolithic pottery (coarse ware) from Monte Maulo (B198).

MATERIAL CULTURE

POTTERY (GB, CM)

Some 1500 neolithic sherds were recovered from the Monte Maulo excavation, weighing in total almost 70 kilograms, a classic sample of the impressed/incised wares and red-painted *figulina* characterizing the first (and contemporary) phase of pottery use in Abruzzo and Marche (Grifoni

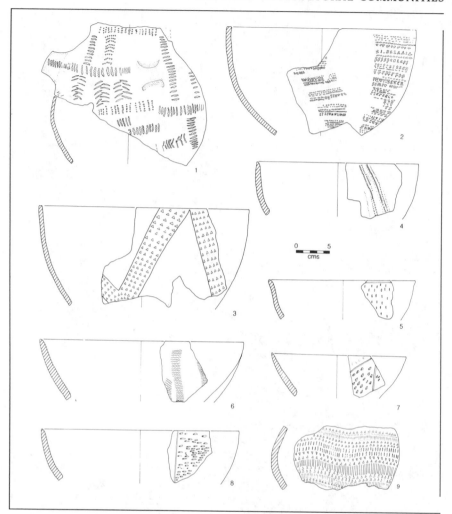

Fig. 46. Earlier neolithic pottery (finer wares) from Monte Maulo (B198). (Above and facing page)

Cremonesi, 1992; Figs. 45, 46). The pottery in fact divides into three principal fabrics, the first two making up the impressed/incised ware. The coarsest ware is poorly fired to a red or brown, has roughly smoothed surfaces, large grit inclusions, and is often 1–2 centimetres thick. The other common ware is finer, of a hard sandy fabric with very small grit inclusions, is lightly burnished, well fired to a pale brown, grey or orange, and is usually less than 5–6 millimetres thick. Sherds of this finer ware were twice as common as sherds of the coarse ware. The *figulina* sample consisted of a handful of sherds, some of them with traces of red paint including one with a pivoting flame design.

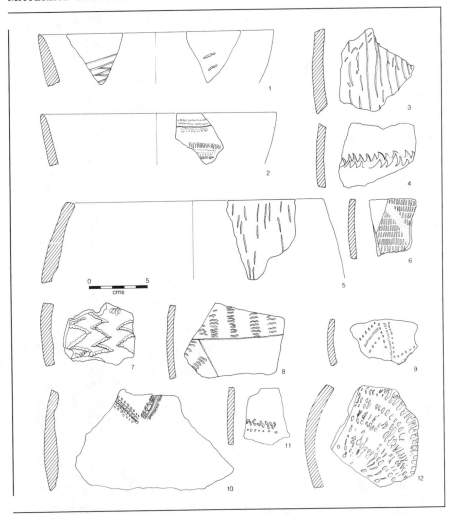

Most of the coarse ware sherds were from large baggy vessels 30–40 centimetres in height, some of which were bottle- or flask-shaped with narrow necks relative to the body (Fig. 45). Bases were rounded or gently flattened. A variety of rounded open bowls was also manufactured, ranging in size from 10 to 30 centimetres at the rim. Handles were small and rounded, fixed either horizontally or vertically to the main body of the vessel. The finer wares (Fig. 46) were normally fashioned into bowls, varying in their rim diameter from 10 to 40 centimetres, with an average diameter of 25 centimetres. The preferred form was rounded with steep sides and a flat base, but more open shapes were also manufactured,

Table 5 Monte Maulo: motifs used on Impressed Ware: (above) detailed occurrences, and (below) major groupings and frequencies

decoration	coarse ware number of sherds	fine ware number of sherds
fingernail, linear	9	1
fingernail, random	40	60
fingernail, zoned	2	–
pinching, random	11	13
shell, linear	4	42
shell, random	90	192
shell, zigzag	9	12
shell, zoned	13	27
stab-and-drag, linear	2	33
stab-and-drag, random	30	51
stab-and-drag, zigzag	1	1
stab-and-drag, zoned	6	8
stick/bone impressions, linear	6	35
stick/bone impressions, random	109	117
stick/bone impressions, zigzag	13	12
stick/bone impressions, zoned	1	5
other	4	13

	coarse ware		fine ware		total	
	N	%	N	%	N	%
fingernail	51	14.6	61	9.8	112	11.5
pinching	11	3.1	13	2.1	24	2.5
shell	116	33.2	273	43.9	389	40.0
stab-and-drag	39	11.1	93	14.9	132	13.6
stick/bone	129	36.9	169	27.2	298	30.7
other	4	1.1	13	2.1	17	1.7

including bowls with straight sides at an acute angle to the rim. Less common shapes were vessels with vertical walls and inturned jars with rounded sides.

About two-thirds of the coarse-ware sherds were decorated, with a repertoire of impressed ware designs typical of those found on the Adriatic side of the Italian peninsula at this time (Cipolloni Sampò, 1992; Gravina, 1987; Grifoni Cremonesi, 1992): finger-pinching to give a coffee-bean effect, fingernail impressions, stick- and bone-impressed and incised patterns, stab-and-drag impressions using a stick or bone, and designs using sea shells, especially the common cockle *Cardium edule* (Figs. 45 and 46; Table 5). A few vessels were decorated with a stick carved into a particular design. Most of the decoration was randomly executed all over the pot. Less commonly, the impressions or incisions were made in rows, or arranged carefully in bands or zones separated by undecorated areas.

Traces of white paste could be seen in some of the impressions, particularly in the finer designs. Approximately half the sherds of the finer fabric were decorated. Many of the techniques were the same as those used on the coarse ware, but zoned and banded decoration was more common, with in some instances carefully arranged geometric patterns of shell incisions, impressed triangles and diamonds, prepared stamps and combs, and lines of shells in rocker patterns.

In its fabrics, shapes and decorative styles, the assemblage has very close similarities with the second or Guadone phase of Impressed-Ware development on the Tavoliere, and there are also similarities with the ensuing La Quercia phase (Tiné, 1983, 1987; Tiné and Bernabo Brea, 1980). The transition between the two phases on the Tavoliere is thought to lie in the middle of the 5th millennium bc. Other comparisons can be drawn with the early Impressed-Ware assemblages of Abruzzo, which are generally dated to the second half of the 5th millennium bc (Ducci et al., 1983). These correlations accord well with the radiocarbon dates from Monte Maulo of c. 4500–4200 bc. A few early neolithic sherds were also recognized at five other sites (A268, A336, A337, B282, C186).

Four sites (A184, A268, A275, E11) produced sherds with the diagnostic fabrics, forms or decoration of the trichrome painted *figulina* styles of Ripoli, Scaloria and Serra d'Alto pottery characteristic of middle neolithic settlement in the mid-4th millennium bc (Cipolloni Sampo, 1992; Grifoni Cremonesi, 1992). The material from Colle del Fico (A184: Fig. 47) demonstrates long continuity of occupation, with material from the earlier Middle Neolithic to the Final Neolithic. One of the earliest diagnostic pieces is a *figulina* rim with a red-painted flame motif much as at Monte Maulo, typical of Catignano (Fig. 47: 1). There was a series of typical middle neolithic rims, including one from a small drinking cup of Ripoli trichrome *figulina*. Typical Serra d'Alto pieces include a rim sherd of a fine, hard *figulina*, highly burnished, and painted with a zig-zag line on the outer rim and filled half-circles on the inner rim (5) and an elaborate handle with a tripartite scrolled upperpart and a 'tongue' over the hole of the handle below, also of a fine, hard *figulina* (6). Middle neolithic *figulina* from A268 had a hard polished surface and included red-painted sherds and rim sherds of typical high-necked flasks, including one with slashed incisions (Fig. 48: 8–10). There was also a grey fabric of *figulina* type. From B275 was a typical Serra d'Alto handle in a fine untempered *figulina*, like the example from A184. The material from E11 included sherds from large simple bowls in a pale *figulina* fabric, with trichrome decoration of dark brown and red paint making semi-geometric curvilinear triangles in a flame pattern.

Late neolithic pottery is well documented at five sites in particular:

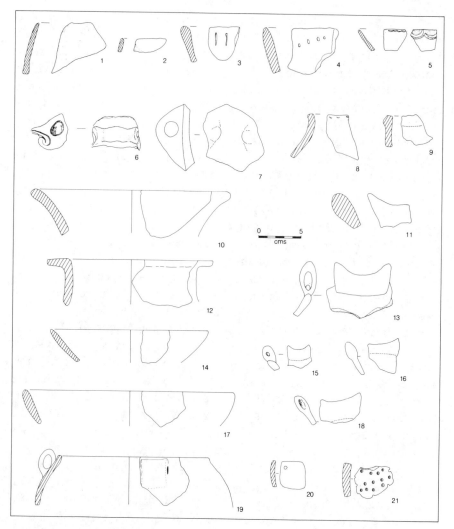

Fig. 47. Middle and late neolithic pottery from Colle del Fico (A184).

A184, A268, B186, B282 and C186. Examples from A184 include 'trumpet' handles typical of the Diana style and red fabric (Fig. 47: 11,13,15,16), and of a highly burnished buff or pink *figulina* fabric (18), together with similar handles made of coarse ware, rims of large open bowls (10) and a strainer sherd (21). From A268 (Fig. 48) there are trumpet handles in the typical Diana red fabric (15,16), *figulina* (17) and a dark micaceous fabric (14), a Diana strap handle (13) and a *figulina* rim decorated with rows of small studs typical of Ripoli (11). B186 produced a collection of sherds of undiagnostic form but of a red burnished fabric likely to be Diana. Most of

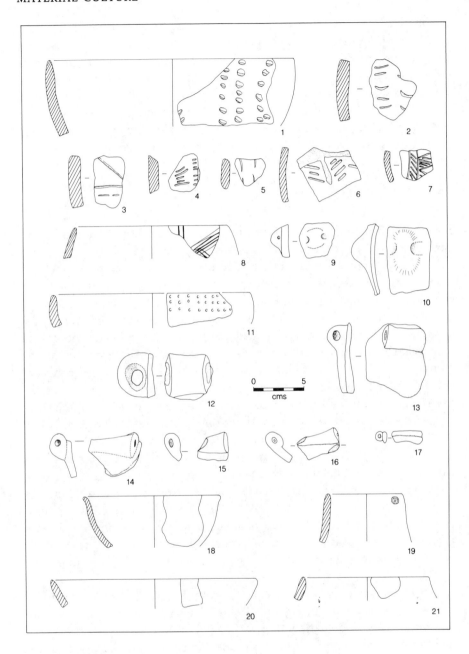

Fig. 48. Middle and late neolithic pottery from site A268.

the material from C186 also consisted of undiagnostic brown-red coarse wares, but loop handles, plain squared-off rims and part of a Diana lug on a carination are all consistent with a late neolithic date. The dark micaceous wares with hard brown-black burnished surfaces at these sites and at the Ponte Regio shelter (C63) are also typical of many copper age assemblages in central Italy, and their association with gritty coarse wares decorated with corrugated rims and impressed cordons, also typical of copper age assemblages, suggests that their occupations probably continued well into the 3rd millennium bc.

THE LITHIC INDUSTRIES (GB, TR)

Some two hundred pieces of chipped stone were found in the Monte Maulo excavation, almost all of a poor-quality local chert, especially of a pale brown colour – only five pieces were of non-local fine flint. The commonest artefacts were crude flakes of the former material, together with blade fragments and cores; only a very few pieces were retouched, as simple denticulated flakes (Fig. 49). All the soil excavated below the ploughsoil was sieved through 1 centimetre and 0.5 centimetre meshes, so it is unlikely that much lithic material was missed during excavation. The complete absence of chipping debris, as well as the low frequency of retouched tools and the very high frequency of cores, suggest that the assemblage is not the typical refuse of a domestic settlement. All the cores and crude flakes are of the pale brown chert, whereas all the tools and retouched pieces are of other kinds of material such as banded grey flint, and brown jasper. A possible interpretation is that the former is debris from quarrying at the site, with material being taken away for secondary working elsewhere, whereas the tools made of exotic cherts and flints were probably brought to the site ready-made. The only other early neolithic sites without admixtures of later neolithic material, A336 and A337, both produced small collections of the same pale brown poor-quality chert (cores and flakes), together with a single flake of a finer grey flint from A337.

The surface collections and excavations of the test pits at A184 produced a small lithic assemblage (Fig. 50). There were some eighty pieces of chert and flint, with a wide variety of raw material being used – grey, black, red and brown cherts, and finer-quality exotic flints, especially honey-coloured or translucent. There were few cores, and numbers of flakes, mostly of the poorer-quality local cherts, but there were also numerous fine blades, mainly unretouched, and mostly made of the finer flint, together with cores and debitage of the same material, showing that both cherts and flints were worked on site. The surface assemblages collected from B186 and C186

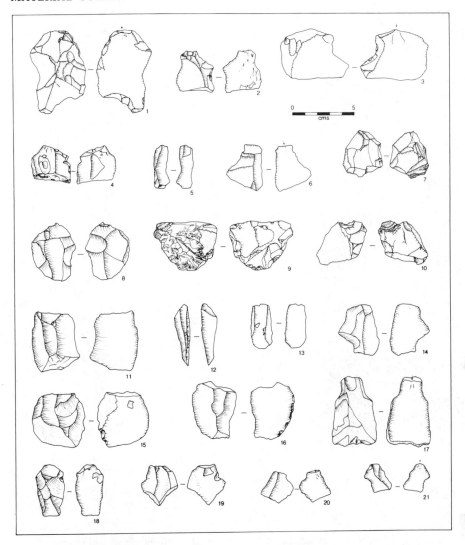

Fig. 49. Chipped stone artefacts from the earlier neolithic settlement of Monte Maulo (B198).

were similar to that of A184 in the range of material and tool types. One of the largest surface collections was made at A268 (Fig. 50), where the pottery indicates occupation throughout the Neolithic: there was a total of 232 pieces, of which 157 were flakes and only 15 were blades or bladelets, with 11 cores (including 2 microflake cores); the very few retouched tools included 4 scrapers and a denticulated flake.

One of the most interesting lithic assemblages is that from the Ponte

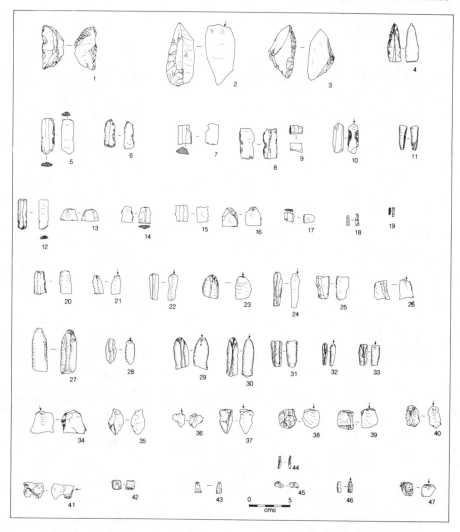

Fig. 50. Chipped stone artefacts from middle/late neolithic settlements in the Biferno valley: flint (1–40) and obsidian (41–7). [Retouched scrapers and points – A268 (1), B186 (2, 3), C64 (4); retouched blades – A184 (5–7), A268 (8–10), C63 (11); plain blades and bladelets – A184 (12–19), A268 (20–3), B186 (24–8), C63 (29–33); flakes – A184 (34–6), A268 (37–9), B186 (40); cores – A184 (41, 42); bladelets – A184 (43, 44), A268 (45); flakes – A184 (46), A268 (47)]

Regio rock shelter (Fig. 50). It was dominated by fine parallel-sided blades and the raw material used was either a milky blue flint or a white chert, both of high quality, but there is no evidence for knapping for making tools (though retouching and repairing took place). The contrast in technology between here and the lowland settlements, with flake-dominated assemblages at A268 and B186, and a mixed flake/blade assemblage at A184, suggests clearly differentiated activities, and the interpretation of the material as the result of a single episode of use is in keeping with the other evidence that the site was a seasonal shelter, perhaps associated with pastoralism.

In addition to the chipped chert and flint assemblages, some of the neolithic sites also produced polished stone artefacts (Fig. 51). Most were found at Monte Maulo (two greenstone polished axes, a variety of cruder implements in a local limestone, three hammerstones and a grindstone), but a fragment of a greenstone axe was also found near the A336 and A337 Impressed-Ware sites (A339), there was a limestone axe at A184, fragments of grindstones were found at A268 and B186, and a fragment of a greenstone axe was found in the upper valley (B26). One other stone artefact was found at C186, a perforated stone 'mace'. All of these artefacts can be matched at contemporary neolithic sites in peninsular Italy.

The primary outcrops of the greenstone used for the finest polished axes found at these sites are all in northern Italy, and a preliminary study of fifty such axes from a selection of sites in the Po valley and down the peninsula demonstrated that size, weight and evidence of wear or damage all decreased with increasing distance from the presumed sources (Evett, 1975). It seems likely that many greenstone axes became non-functional status items once far from the source of the stone – indeed, two of the southern axes studied by Evett had suspension holes drilled in them so that they could be worn as ornaments. Local limestones were therefore used for the heavy groundstone implements needed for normal wood-working and agricultural work. Signs of wear and damage were common on those in Evett's sample. The greenstone axes and axe fragments from the Biferno valley are damaged on the cutting or striking surfaces, but all the limestone tools were either broken or very badly chipped, and were presumably used for heavy work as axes-adzes or mattocks as Evett suggests.

Another commodity that can be probably regarded as a prestige item for neolithic societies in this part of Italy is obsidian. A total of ten pieces was found by the survey, all except one from the middle/late neolithic settlements of the lower valley (Fig. 50): a bladelet core, a bladelet, a larger flake, and a tiny debitage flake from A184, three small flakes and a blade from A268, a blade from C186 and a blade from D85. The obsidian was derived from the island of Lipari off Sicily, some 400 kilometres due south of the Biferno, though studies in Calabria (Ammerman, 1985b) indicate that its exchange was primarily coastal, making its journey to the Biferno valley longer still.

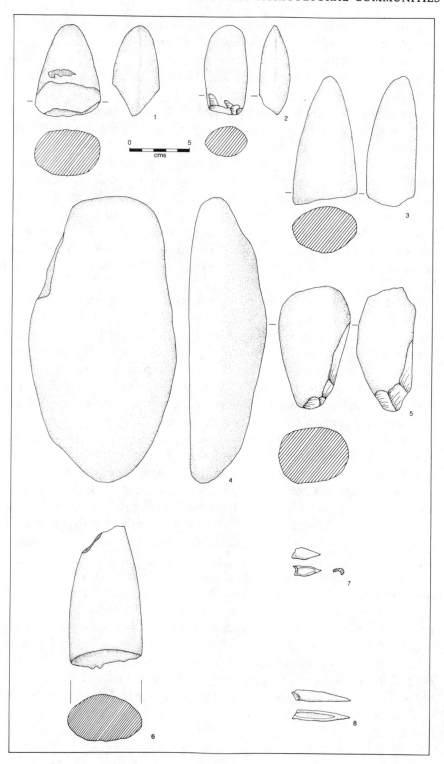

NEOLITHIC SOCIETIES IN THE BIFERNO VALLEY

The earlier neolithic settlements of the Biferno valley, as elsewhere in peninsular Italy, suggest small-scale residential units: farmsteads or homesteads of nuclear or small extended family size. The communities who used them are characterized as having 'a rather undeveloped organization, which did not progress beyond the tribal level of socio-cultural integration and with no signs of even incipient ranking of individuals' (Whitehouse, 1986: 43). Mechanisms are needed for such 'acephalous' societies to maintain themselves and grow, requiring social contacts beyond the immediate kin group (Chapman, 1988). Halstead and Jones (1989) also argue that the vagaries of the Mediterranean environment are such that small-scale neolithic societies could not have existed as self-sufficient units invulnerable to poor harvests and the like, and that 'risk-avoidance' strategies would have been essential – in particular, social mechanisms to promote the exchange of foodstuffs between neighbouring groups in bad years.

Whilst there is no direct evidence for the local exchange of such commodities, which would be very difficult to detect in any case in the archaeological record, it is increasingly clear that during the course of the neolithic period, societies in Italy developed systems of exchange to maintain and promote social cohesion. Malone (1985) argues that there was a three-tier pattern of production and distribution of early and middle neolithic pottery in peninsular Italy: coarse Impressed Ware manufactured and used at the local or domestic level; semi-fine impressed ware used for local exchange between neighbouring groups; and the painted pottery, finely produced in a standardized way as attractive vessels that were also small and lightweight, 'distributed over enormous distances, cutting across local exchange networks . . . an inter-regional commodity of "universal" appeal' (Malone, 1985: 124).

Arguments over the role of Italian neolithic pottery in exchange have been based thus far entirely on stylistic grounds, and it was in this context that a sample of sherds from the main neolithic sites in the Biferno valley was subjected to thin-section analysis (Harvey, 1992). The study found considerable variability in the range and frequencies of inclusions, but almost invariably these could be explained in terms of the local geology. The exceptions were obviously exotic pieces such as the Serra d'Alto rim sherd from A184 (Fig. 47: 5), which contains fine quartz and was fired to a

Fig. 51. Polished stone and bone tools from neolithic sites in the Biferno valley. [Polished axes and adzes – B198 (1–3, 5), A184 (6); grinder – B198 (4); bone points – A184 (7, 8)]

much higher temperature than the other sherds. The most important finding was that, whilst the finest *figulina* and dark burnished fabrics were probably imported, local versions of these fine wares were being produced in the valley as well as the coarser fabrics. Moreover, although coarse wares are usually assumed to have been everyday domestic ware of little status value, the fact that repair holes were present not just in finer wares such as *figulina* (Fig. 47: 20; Fig. 48: 19) but also in coarser wares (for example at Monte Maulo) indicates that the division between domestic and prestige goods was probably not so clear-cut.

The overlapping distribution networks of painted pottery, high-quality flint, greenstone axes and obsidian indicate considerable interaction between neolithic groups throughout the peninsula. The maintenance of these networks probably included activities such as prestige gift-giving between individuals and groups, but the evidence for the deposition of exotic, high-value goods in ritual as well as domestic contexts indicates the importance of symbolic and ritual as well as 'commercial' transactions. A variety of ritual activities has been noted in remote caves in regions such as Apulia and Abruzzo, including elaborate burials, intentional destruction of artefacts, feasting, painting, and even cannibalism (Whitehouse, 1992). Cave sites with underground springs were particularly important as cult sites.

Interpretation is obviously extremely difficult, but it seems likely that neolithic ritual included elaborate initiation rites for particular age and sex groups, as a mechanism for maintaining social boundaries and legitimating traditional authority (Skeates, 1991; Whitehouse, 1990, 1992). The emphasis of earlier neolithic ritual on the promotion of group unity through a concern with 'health, fertility and economic welfare' (Skeates, 1991: 130) makes sense given the nature of the settlement systems and social structures of the 'substitution' phase of farming: there were probably peoples practising different kinds of subsistence in contact with each other, much of this subsistence involved a degree of mobility, and group membership may well have been fluid as well.

During the course of the 4th millennium, as mixed farming became the dominant mode of subsistence in peninsular Italy, settlement units became larger, and there is evidence in both the subsistence data and material culture for increasing specialization in production systems, whether in animal herding or the manufacture of prestige pottery. It is in this context that the emphasis of ritual changed from its concern with the group to a concern with the individual: burials show that a substantial proportion of the exotic goods involved in exchange were now deposited with individuals. In the case of the Biferno valley, it may be significant that human bones were found at the three major later neolithic settlements (A184, A268, C186) but at none of the earlier neolithic settlements. The assumption is that the trends in social and economic intensification apparent in the development of late neolithic societies provided a context which increasingly promoted individuals to higher rank. These people were then able to control aspects of the production, distribution and/or consumption of resources.

SOCIAL ELABORATION IN THE 3RD MILLENNIUM bc

These trends in social change intensified throughout peninsular Italy during the 3rd millennium bc, the Copper Age (Cardarelli, 1992; Guidi, 1992; Pellegrini, 1992). The period is best known for its rich burials: individuals were buried with fine pottery, superb pressure-flaked flint daggers and arrowheads, perforated stone axes and sometimes primitive copper weapons. Most of the metalwork was restricted to within 100 kilometres of the copper ores, such as those of the Colline Metallifere ('Ore Mountains') of Tuscany, a system of local copper exploitation, production and exchange confirmed by trace element analyses (Barker and Slater, 1971). Beyond these zones, high-quality flint provided the equivalent prestige commodity. We must assume that as elsewhere in Europe, the copper age elites of prehistoric Italy were differentiated from the rest of their communities in life by their high-status clothing, ornamentation and weaponry, as they were in death. Certainly the weapons cannot have been of functional importance: the pressure-flaked flint daggers (Fig. 52) are exquisite, but would easily snap in combat, and the alloy composition and structure of the copper daggers make them prone to bend or crumple, but both types of artefact were invariably in pristine condition when they were buried.

The changes in social structure implied by the cemeteries were accompanied by significant changes in settlement patterns: population growth is suggested by a major expansion of sites into previously peripheral zones, a trend accompanied by increasing evidence for deforestation in the pollen diagrams, and the appearance of a few very large sites suggests for the first time the development of settlement hierarchies. The subsistence data indicate the further development of changes in animal husbandry in central Italy, with cattle-keeping increasing in importance on the lowlands and shepherding further inland. In part the trend probably reflects adaptations to ecological change (there is evidence for a more arid climate affecting the central Mediterranean in the 3rd millennium bc), but animals and their products probably also became increasingly important as items of wealth and exchange. Certainly the mortality data of the faunal samples (Wilkens, 1987), and the abundance of

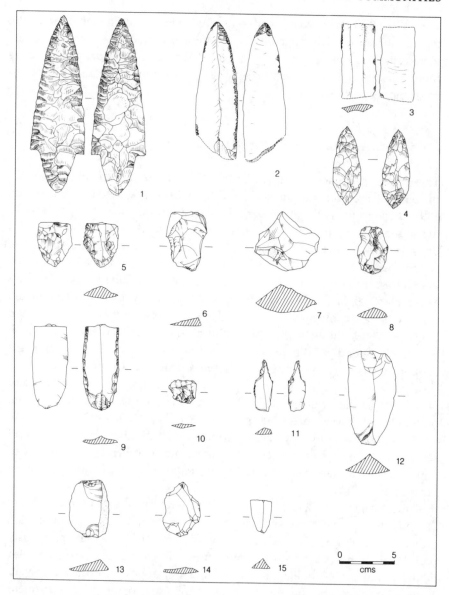

Fig. 52. Chipped stone artefacts of copper age date from the Biferno valley. [Pizzone (1, 2), Campolieto (3), A278 (4), E10 (5–15)]

spindle whorls, demonstrate the increasing importance of animal secondary products for copper age societies.

The principal copper age site known in the Biferno valley was at Masseria Vincelli (E10) near Montorio dei Frentani. According to a local antiquarian, work for a new vineyard in the 1950s destroyed what must have been a very substantial copper age settlement characterized by pits filled with abundant domestic refuse, of which a small sample had been retained. This included grinding-stones, a quantity of lithic material, and almost seven hundred sherds; the fabric of the latter (smoothed but not burnished), the decoration (plain and impressed cordons), and the handles and lug types were typical of the Copper Age. There was also a pressure-flaked dagger of fine translucent honey-coloured flint, together with part of a very long blade of a grey flint, also of a very high quality (Fig. 52), both made from materials exotic to the valley. The faunal sample kept from the site included bones of cattle, pigs and sheep, and red deer antler, and there was also a number of human bones. The indications are that there was a substantial domestic site here, together with burials of high-status individuals.

What was probably another copper age burial was reported by De Blasio (1908) near Saepinum, and the Museo Sannitico in Campobasso has numerous fine pressure-flaked arrowheads collected in the last century and early in this century likely to be from copper age burials, as well as a superb flint dagger from Pizzone (Fig. 52). There seems little doubt that there were people of high status living amongst the Biferno communities by this period, who were buried with the trappings of their authority.

CHAPTER 7

THE SETTLEMENT EXPANSION OF THE 2ND MILLENNIUM bc

Graeme Barker, with contributions by Gill Clark, Chris Hunt, Susan Lukesh and Derrick Webley

INTRODUCTION (GB, SL)

The 'Apennine Bronze Age' of the 2nd millennium bc was first defined by Ugo Rellini in 1931 on the basis of a uform pottery style which he recognized throughout the Italian peninsula: an attractive dark burnished fabric was used to make cups and bowls decorated with carefully incised or excised designs and elaborate handles (Figs. 54 and 55). In 1959 Renato Peroni further classified the pottery into three main typological and chronological groups: 'Apennine', the main phase of decorated pottery and elaborate handles; 'Subapennine', with less decoration and simpler handles; and 'Protovillanovan', a phase with pottery increasingly like that of the Villanovan Iron Age (the phase preceding the Etruscan states in Etruria). Later a 'Protoapennine' stage was also defined, with handles, vessel shapes and decoration intermediate between those of the Copper Age and the developed 'Apennine' style (Cremonesi, 1978). The sequence is conventionally given a precise chronology by Italian prehistorians: Protoapennine (*bronzo antico*) 1800–1400 bc; Apennine (*bronzo medio*) 1400–1300 bc; Subapennine (*bronzo recente*) 1300–1200 bc; and Protovillanovan (*bronzo finale*) 1200–900 bc.

The classification is based on distinctive 'type fossils', but statistical analyses of domestic ceramic assemblages have shown that in fact there is a remarkable degree of underlying similarity (Lukesh, 1975, 1978; Lukesh and Howe, 1978). Given this, it is impossible to assign most of the bronze age sites found by the Biferno Valley Survey to a particular phase or phases. However, analysis of the Biferno valley bronze age pottery by Susan Lukesh indicates the full spectrum of bronze age settlement through the 2nd millennium bc. Some 10,000 sherds from four major assemblages in the valley were studied using the methodology developed for the analysis of the 50,000 sherds from the settlement of Tufariello in Basilicata (Lukesh, 1975): the surface collection from the copper age settlement at Masseria

Vincelli near Montorio dei Frentani (E10); material collected in 1974 by the Superintendency from a cave exposed during road-working operations at Colle Gessari south of Guglionesi in the lower valley (D27); and the assemblages from two sites found and excavated by the survey team, Fonte Maggio in the middle valley (G1) and Masseria Mammarella in the lower valley (A113).

The pottery from these sites divides into fine, medium, and coarse fabrics, but the distinction between the first two is not always clear – both fabrics were well prepared and burnished, and usually dark brown or black in colour depending on firing conditions. The fine ware, 3–6 millimetres in thickness, has fine inclusions and the medium ware is some 7–11 millimetres thick with larger and more varied inclusions. The coarse ware is of a rough and crumbly texture, 12–16 millimetres thick, very variable in colour, and with many large inclusions – the typical domestic ware for cooking and storage at Italian bronze age settlements. A basic set of 18 vessel shapes was found, grouped within five major classes (Fig. 53). The fine and medium wares were used for more or less the full range of shapes, whereas the coarse ware was used predominantly for open storage jars, mostly with straight sides. The Colle Gessari cave contained a burial assemblage, and storage vessels are very rare, with fine cups and bowls predominating. The Fonte Maggio and Masseria Mammarella settlements, on the other hand, have the full range of cups, bowls, and storage vessels, the repertoire being particularly wide at Fonte Maggio.

The typology of Apennine bronze age handles has been studied intensively for indications of chronological and regional variation ever since Trump (1958) pointed out the dominance of horned handles in the northern half of the peninsula and of plainer tab or 'axe' handles in the south. Handles were very rare in the Colle Gessari assemblage, but their frequency at the other sites is shown in Figure 53. Fonte Maggio has the typical range of Apennine forms, whereas the smaller proportion of axe and tongue handles at Masseria Mammarella is a typical feature of Subapennine assemblages.

Storage vessels were mostly undecorated, any decoration being confined to plastic cordons either left plain or decorated with finger-pinching or thumb impressions. Decoration of the finer wares was not abundant at Fonte Maggio, but the classic range of Apennine bronze age decoration is represented (Figs. 54 and 55 and Table 6). Both the frequency of decoration and the range of motifs decreased at Masseria Mammarella, a trend typical of Subapennine assemblages, as are new elements such as bosses (Pannuti, 1969). The burial assemblage at Colle Gessari was almost entirely undecorated. The numerous surface sites elsewhere in the valley which

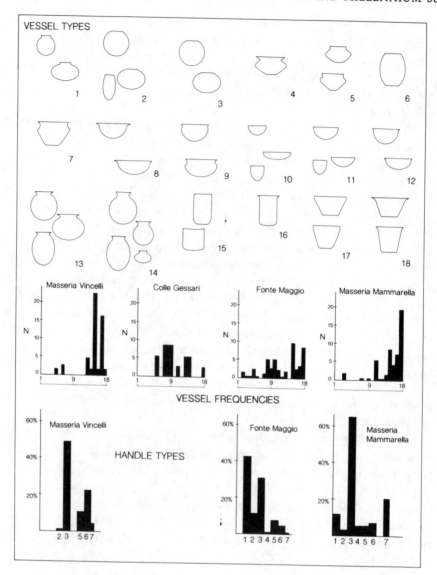

Fig. 53 Pottery development at the major copper and bronze age sites in the Biferno valley: Masseria Vincelli (E10), Colle Gessari (D27), Fonte Maggio (G1) and Masseria Mammarella (A113). Top – the eighteen major vessel types; middle – the frequencies of these eighteen types; bottom – the frequencies of the seven major handle types. (1. axe handle; 2. tongue and loop handle; 3. vertical loop handle; 4. vertical cylinder; 5. ledge handle; 6. horizontal loop handle; 7. horizontal cylinder)

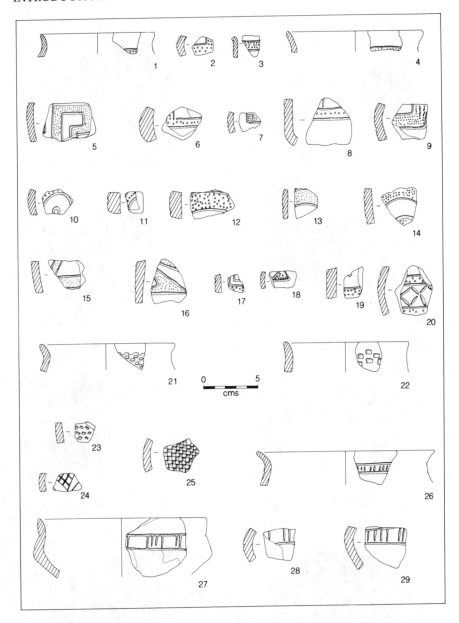

Fig. 54 'Apennine bronze age' decorated pottery from the bronze age settlement of Fonte Maggio (G1).

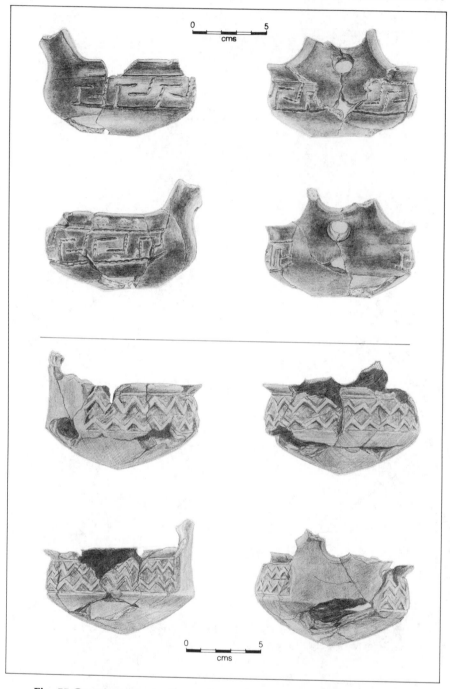

Fig. 55 Complete vessels decorated in the 'Apennine bronze age' style from (above) Fonte Maggio (G1) and (below) Masseria Mammarella (A113).

Table 6 'Apennine' bronze age decoration in the Biferno valley (numbers of sherds)

	G1	A113	A117	B280	B282	C285	D27	E8	E65
punteggio, geometric	26	8						1	
punteggio, curvilinear	9	8	1					2	
incised lines, geometric	27	4		1	2			2	
incised lines, curvilinear	21	1	1		2			1	
excised patterns geometric	24	1					1		4
excised patterns curvilinear	6					1	1		5
chequer pattern	5							1	
laddering	6					1			
impressed triangles	7							1	
nipples, bosses	2								

produced isolated sherds with Apennine bronze age decoration reflect the same range of motifs recorded at the excavated sites (Table 6).

The Colle Gessari burial cave can be assigned quite confidently to the latter part of the *bronzo antico* or earliest *bronzo medio*, in the mid-2nd millennium bc. Fonte Maggio and Masseria Mammarella are typical assemblages, respectively, of the Apennine and Subapennine styles, spanning the latter part of the 2nd millennium and initial centuries of the 1st millennium bc. At the same time, the preponderance of elements such as simple tongue handles at Fonte Maggio suggests an initial phase of occupation within the time range of the Protoapennine tradition. Similar assemblages – primarily Apennine/Subapennine but with recognizable Protoapennine components – were found at B282 and B289 in the middle valley, and a small collection of potsherds from C102 in the same area is probably Protoapennine, post-dating the E10 assemblage but certainly earlier than Fonte Maggio. The majority of bronze age sites found in the survey, however, can only be ascribed very generally to the Apennine/ Subapennine phases of the late 2nd millennium and the beginning of the 1st millennium bc.

SETTLEMENT TRENDS

Bronze age assemblages were identified by the survey at c. 40 localities in the valley, and there were sporadic finds of bronze age pottery at another 15 locations (Fig. 56). Sporadic 'findspots' were defined as finds of single sherds or groups of less than 5 sherds, either found in isolation or identified in site assemblages of later periods (particularly iron age and Samnite). Discrete 'sites' have 20 or more sherds, and the 'possible sites' in Figure 56 have 5–20 sherds. Characteristic incised sherds of the Apennine and Subapennine styles were present at 13 of the main localities and at one of the 15 sporadic findspots. All the other localities consisted of plain sherds that from their fabric and surface appearance can be identified as most likely to belong to this period of settlement by comparison with the major ceramic assemblages.

Most bronze age material was found in the middle valley: 31 sites and 8 findspots. In the lower valley we recorded 10 sites and 7 findspots. The uppermost site with definite Apennine bronze age pottery was at Matrice (A165/E65) 800 metres above sea level, from a pit found underneath the Samnite/Roman villa excavated by John Lloyd after the survey (see Chapters Nine and Ten). The densities of finds in the middle valley may in part reflect the more efficient system of field-walking employed in the last season of fieldwork. However, there may be another factor for the numbers of sites here: some of the 23 sites recorded in the middle valley could well belong to the first half of the 1st millennium bc rather than to the second half of the 2nd millennium bc, a reflection of the isolation of this part of the valley during the Iron Age when the lower valley came into trading contact with Magna Graecia (the Greek colonies of southern Italy and their Hellenized neighbours) and when the styles of fine pottery there – and much else besides – changed dramatically as a result (Chapter Eight).

No pottery definitely decorated with Apennine bronze age motifs was recognized in the upper valley, but it is difficult to separate absence of evidence from evidence of absence. As discussed in Chapter Three, the process of land abandonment in the upper valley made field-walking here more difficult than in the rest of the valley. The discovery of the pit at Matrice deeply buried below the modern ground surface and of bronze age occupation material under 2.5 metres of colluvium at Fonte Maggio (see next section) provides a further cautionary note. However, several sites with definite iron age material were located by field-walking in the upper valley, including one at some 1400 metres above sea level on the Matese

Fig. 56 Bronze age settlement in the Biferno valley according to the archaeological survey, with the principal sites mentioned in the text identified.

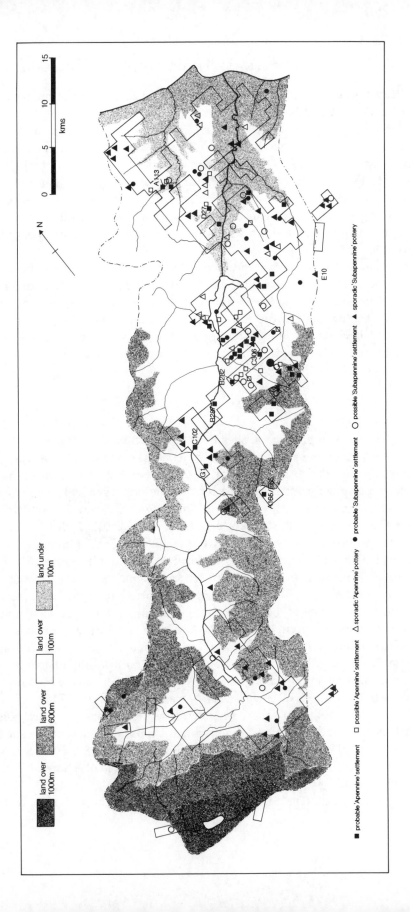

land over
1000m

land over
600m

land over
100m

land under
100m

N

0   5   10   15
kms

■ probable 'Apennine' settlement □ possible 'Apennine' settlement △ sporadic 'Apennine' pottery ○ possible 'Subapennine' settlement ● probable 'Subapennine' settlement ▲ sporadic 'Subapennine' pottery

A113

D27

E10

C306

B282

B267

C102

G1

A166/ E66

plateau, and are of similar surface characteristics to bronze age surface sites further down the valley.

Although (as discussed in Chapter Six) it is difficult to separate many pressure-flaked flint arrowheads into definitely bronze age and definitely pre-bronze age forms, the distribution of late forms extends throughout the catchment. Whilst there may be an element of doubt that some of these arrowheads were simply hunting equipment, the occurrence of bronze age lithic material in the mountains, where no neolithic material was found, surely indicates a significant expansion in the utilization of the uplands.

Taking all these factors into consideration, it seems reasonable to conclude from the survey evidence that the principal zone of permanent settlement embraced the lower and middle valley during the course of the 2nd millennium bc, but did not extend – at least on any scale – into the upper valley at this time. During this period, however, hunting and pastoral activities now extended to the highest elevations.

SETTLEMENT STRUCTURE

Large numbers of bronze age sites have been identified in peninsular Italy, and excavations have been conducted at many of them, but with a few notable exceptions (e.g. Holloway, 1975; Östenberg, 1967), these have yielded remarkably little evidence for the internal organization of bronze age settlements and for the degree of similarity or difference in settlement forms before the closing stages of the period (Guidi, 1992; Pellegrini, 1992).

The first bronze age settlement we investigated, Fonte Maggio (G1), is situated at c.450 metres above sea level in the middle valley (Barker, 1976a). When found in 1974 it consisted of a semicircular zone of surface pottery measuring c.50×30 metres (Fig. 57), but cleaning the bank section on the northern side of the track revealed stratified bronze age sherds, and a trench excavated north of the bank revealed a small pit with bronze age material cut into the clay subsoil, overlaid by some 2.5 metres of colluvium. The area of the settlement must have extended north of the main zone of surface material indicated in Figure 57, perhaps over an area almost as large again. A series of small trenches was excavated in 1974, 1975 and 1976, totalling about 30 square metres. These excavations produced some 6000 sherds, and it is salutary to reflect that similar densities for the site as a whole would result in a total assemblage of some 180,000 sherds, in contrast with the 200 sherds forming the total surface collection when the site was found.

The excavations (Fig. 58) found three pits cut into the subsoil in trench

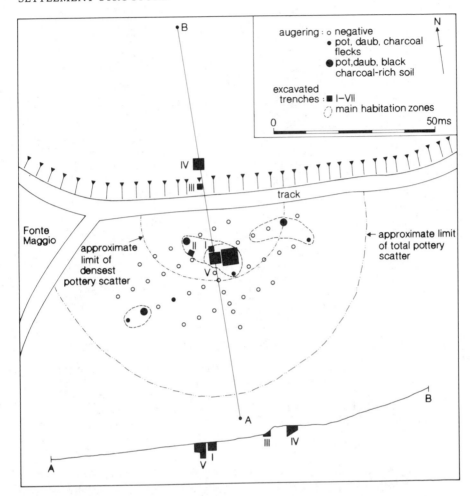

Fig. 57 Plan of (with, below, section across) the bronze age settlement of
Fonte Maggio (G1) showing the surface distribution of finds, the
augering evidence for the principal habitation zones, and the location of
the excavated trenches.

V. The two on the western edge of the trench proved to be Roman in date,
perhaps for olive trees, but the pit in the southeastern corner is a bronze
age feature. Some 70 centimetres deep from the top of the subsoil, it was
semicircular in shape with a near vertical northern edge but otherwise
sloping walls. No postpipe or stone setting was detected, but a concentration of stones in the northern half was probably the packing against a
vertical post. Between 1 and 2 metres beyond the pit was a dense scatter of
limestone cobbles and smaller stones extending into trench VII. The
densities of pottery and bone in each of the metre squares in trench VII
show a very close correlation between the two and, more generally, with

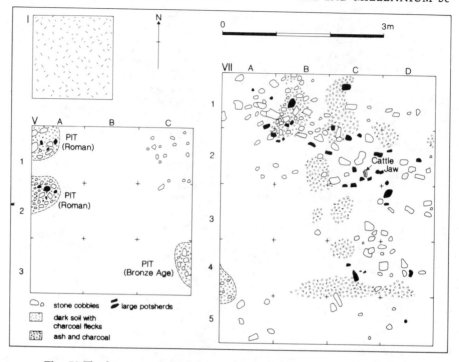

Fig. 58 The bronze age settlement of Fonte Maggio (G1) – plan of the main habitation features: the pit between trenches V and VII probably supported the main timber of a simple conical hut of the kind illustrated in Figure 60, with the midden deposits across the northeast part of Trench VII lying beyond the perimeter of the dwelling.

the stone scatter (Fig. 59). The finds in trench V were not collected according to individual metre squares, but greater densities were observed in the northeastern part of the trench. Patches of ash and charcoal, presumably fire sweepings from a hearth elsewhere, were found in and around this midden zone but not near the pit, as were specimens of burnt bone, the latter having a particular concentration in square C4. Weathered and trampled bone was found almost exclusively in square D3.

It seems likely that the central pit supported the main timber of a simple conical hut. Fragments of daub have the impressions of reeds and light withies, and the rubble could be evidence for stone footings. The evidence suggests we have the residues of a structure not dissimilar to the traditional *pagliara* or *pagliaio* huts in the valley today (Fig. 60). A rather similar hut outside Rome used by transhumant shepherds was planned some years ago (Close-Brooks and Gibson, 1966): measuring 5 metres in diameter and 5.25 metres in height, it had walls of straw and reed leaves between two faces of vertical reeds, a thatch roof, and bunk accommodation for six

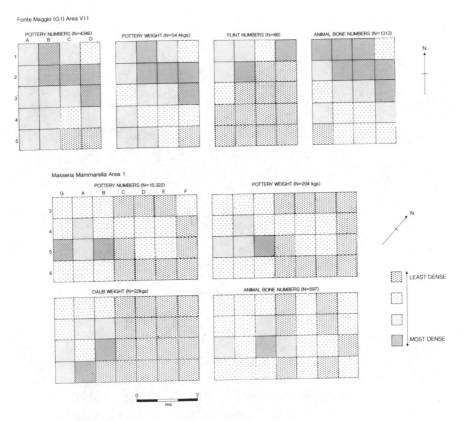

Fig. 59 Finds densities and distributions at the bronze age settlements of Fonte Maggio (G1) and Masseria Mammarella (A113).

shepherds. The huts at Fonte Maggio would have been heavier and more substantial if they had wattle and daub walls. Whether or not the midden deposit in trench VII defines the area immediately outside a hut, the distribution of stone tools and debitage on either side may indicate working areas.

Augering in 1976 suggested that, whilst the excavation undoubtedly investigated the densest area of occupation debris, the settlement probably consisted of four or five discrete zones of such occupation debris (Fig. 57). Assuming that these represent individual structures, mostly for habitation but others for working and storage, and allowing for more in the (now destroyed) northern segment of the site, it seems likely that the Fonte Maggio settlement was the base for between three and five family groups, if the structures were occupied at the same time – perhaps between fifteen and thirty-five people? Four radiocarbon dates were obtained from

Fig. 60 A typical thatched hut in the Biferno valley today. (Photograph: Graeme Barker)

charcoal and animal bone which fit well with the predicted age range according to the Apennine and Subapennine pottery, of the later centuries of the 2nd millennium bc (OxA-656: 3260 ± 60 bp, 1310 bc; OxA-657: 3040 ± 60 bp, 1090 bc; OxA-658: 3070 ± 70 bp, 1120 bc; OxA-670: 3050 ± 80 bp, 1100 bc), together with an anomalous date (OxA-671: 1950 ± 160 bp, '0' AD) presumably from intrusive material of Roman age (Gowlett *et al.*, 1987: 138).

The second site investigated (A113) was near the modern farm of Masseria Mammarella on the first terrace above the modern floodplain of the Sinarca stream, some 12 kilometres from the sea. In 1974 over 150 sherds were collected at the site in an area measuring about 75 metres in diameter and another collection was made (*c.* 100 sherds) in the same area in 1975. In 1976 augering traced a dark charcoal-rich deposit below the ploughsoil extending *c.* 60×60 metres, more or less correlating (as at Fonte Maggio) with the principal zone of surface finds, with four distinct but irregular patches of much darker soil mixed with ash and burnt clay within it (Fig. 61).

In trench I, the main excavation, above *c.* 50 centimetres there was considerable evidence for the re-working of the deposits by flooding –

Fig. 61 Plan of the bronze age settlement of Masseria Mammarella (A113), showing the evidence of the augering and geophysical surveys for the principal habitation zones, and (top) the location of the excavated trenches.

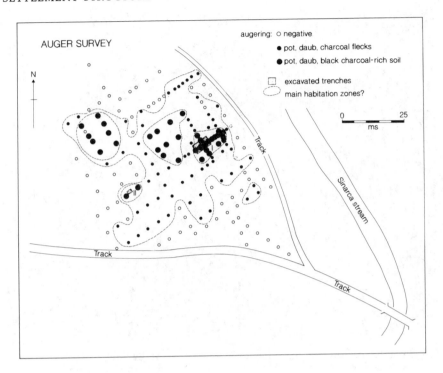

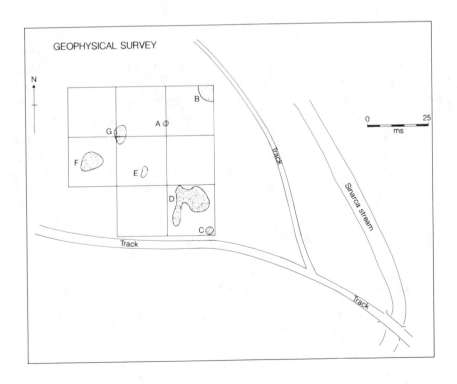

Fig. 62 The bronze age settlement of Masseria Mammarella (A113): the principal hut floor found in the excavation. (Photograph: Graeme Barker)

sherds were often rounded, and there were lenses of gravel and water-rolled pebbles. At 65–70 centimetres' depth, however, there was a circular patch of fired clay *c.* 1.75 metres in diameter, constructed on the undulating surface of the natural subsoil (Figs. 62 and 63). No pits or post-holes were found cut into the clay or into the underlying subsoil, but there were several distinct rounded patches of charcoal which are probably the remains of timbers – two substantial ones in the centre and smaller ones on the margins. Along the southern edge of the clay floor was an area of particularly dark soil containing four pockets of ash. The indications are that the fired clay patch is the floor of a circular hut of the kind inferred with less certainty at Fonte Maggio.

In 1977 the site was also investigated by Richard Linington and Franco Brancaleone of the Lerici Foundation, using an absolute proton magnetometer. Eight 20×20 metre squares were surveyed (Fig. 61). Modern iron caused the anomalies at A, B, and C, but those at D-G of about 10 gamma were regarded by Richard Linington as likely to be areas of occupation

Fig. 63 The bronze age settlement of Masseria Mammarella (A113): plan of the hut floor illustrated in Figure 62, showing the location of the associated midden deposits and artefacts.

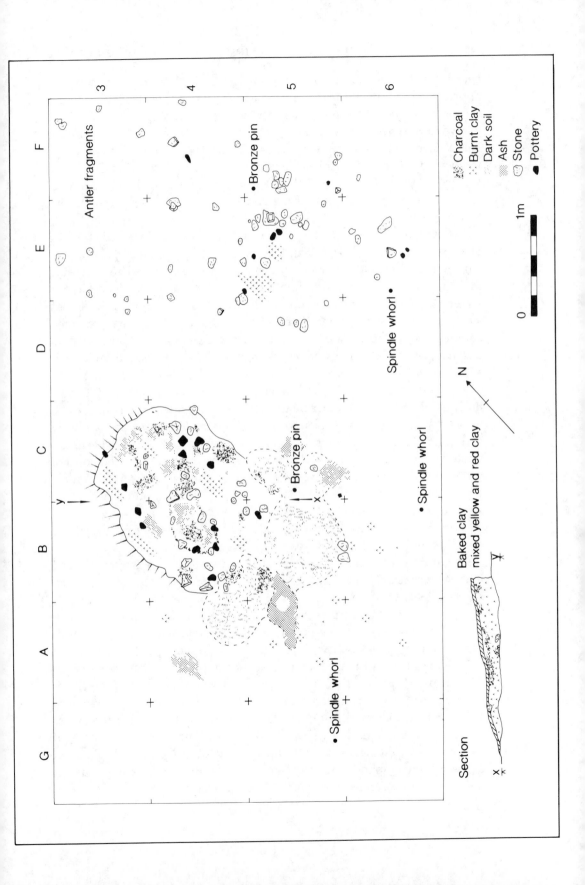

Antler fragments

Bronze pin

Spindle whorl

Bronze pin

Spindle whorl

Spindle whorl

Charcoal
Burnt clay
Dark soil
Ash
Stone
Pottery

0   1m

N

Baked clay
mixed yellow and red clay

Section

X — X
Y — Y

3
4
5
6

G A B C D E F

containing hut floors, hearths, and small pits. D, E, and G all correlate approximately with the patches of charcoal-rich soil located by augering the previous year. Taken together, the augering, geophysical survey and excavation suggest that the settlement consisted of a collection of perhaps half a dozen huts, similar in size to the Fonte Maggio settlement. A single radiocarbon date was obtained, from red deer antler (OxA-672: Gowlett *et al.*, 1987: 139): 2990 ± 80 bp (1040 bc). The pottery is broadly Subapennine, and the C14 date at the end of the 2nd millennium bc is consistent with this.

No obvious entrance to the excavated hut could be discerned, but the black soil and ash pockets along the southern edge of the clay floor (Fig. 63) could indicate either a primary cooking area here immediately outside the entrance, or a primary dump area in the same position for fire sweepings from inside. The fill of the clay floor seen in section also suggests far more wear and tear on the southern side by the presumed entrance. Most of the pottery, daub and fragments of animal bone (and all fragments of burnt bone) were concentrated at the supposed hut entrance and immediately beyond it to the southwest (Figs. 59 and 62). The distributions suggest a regular drop zone for household refuse. At the same time, the distribution of other materials indicates the use of separate zones for craftwork in the space around the hut: there were twice as many flint and chert flakes on the southeastern side of the clay floor as on the southwestern side, large pieces of red deer antler were in a cluster to the north of the floor (one of them yielding the C14 date), three widely spaced spindle whorls formed an arc up the eastern side of the floor, and there was a stone used for burnishing pottery in between. All examples of weathered and trampled bone also occurred to the north-east of the hut floor, perhaps a further indication that this was a working area.

The bronze age surface sites found by the Biferno Valley Survey divided into two principal types. The first category consisted of extremely small collections of surface pottery (usually some ten to thirty sherds) in an area less than 50×50 metres in extent (usually from 10×10 metres to 30×30 metres). In several cases the pottery zone coincided with a zone of much darker soil in comparison with that of the surrounding field. The second category consisted of much larger collections of pottery (commonly one- to two-hundred sherds collected in a single visit, with a combined weight of several kilograms) distributed across a larger area – commonly from 50 to 100 metres in diameter. In general the larger sites also produced a wider range of archaeological material – coarse and fine wares, fragments of animal bone, flint flakes, and fragments of daub, though daub and flint flakes were also found associated with some of the small pottery scatters. The two sites excavated were in the larger category.

BRONZE AGE SUBSISTENCE (GB, GC, DW)

Nearly 600 litres of soil from the trench VII excavation at Fonte Maggio were processed with the froth flotation machine and over 550 carbonized seeds of some 30 species were recovered. A comparable quantity of soil from the Masseria Mammarella excavation was processed in the same way, but there were fewer than 100 carbonized seeds, mostly from immediately above, within, and below the hut floor in trench I – the heavy clay of this site was much more difficult to process efficiently by flotation than the friable loam of Fonte Maggio. However, the range of plants represented at the two sites, over 20 species, is very similar (Table 7). The principal cereals at both sites were emmer wheat and barley, much as they had been at the neolithic settlements in the valley, but new crops included millet, oats, and flax. A range of legumes was cultivated, the horse bean and chick pea being additions to the list recovered from the neolithic excavations. The commonest seeds are wild species, including fruits and nuts (acorn, blackberry, hazelnut, grape), but dominated by plants which today are weeds of cultivated, fallow, and waste land.

Some 3000 fragments of animal bone were recovered from the excavations (II: Chapter 7). At both sites well over 90 per cent of the identifiable fragments were derived from the principal stock – cattle, pigs, and sheep/goats, with game represented only on a small scale (birds, hares, red deer, roe deer). Both sheep and goats are represented according to the half-dozen or so specimens that could be identified using Boessneck's morphological criteria (Boessneck, 1969). According to both the fragment count and the minimum number of individuals (especially if the minor species such as birds, rats, and tortoises and the presumed non-food species cats and dogs are excluded), sheep/goats made up c. 45–50 per cent of the population killed at both sites, pigs c. 20–30 per cent, and cattle c. 15–20 per cent. Whilst extremity bones certainly predominate, all parts of the skeleton of the principal stock are represented, indicating that butchery took place on site. Many of the main meat-bearing bones were smashed into splinters for marrow extraction and further broken up (and often burnt) in cooking.

According to the fusion and tooth eruption/wear data, over half of the sheep/goat population in the two samples died under two years old and most of the rest died in the following two years. The range of deaths suggests a rather generalized system of husbandry, with the flock kept for meat, milk, and wool. Most cattle were probably killed at about three years old, rather later than we would expect in a meat-based system but rather early if they were predominantly older females kept for breeding and milk.

Table 7 Plant remains recovered from the bronze age settlements of Fonte Maggio (G1) and Masseria Mammarella (A113). (Identified by Derrick Webley)

		G1	A113
CEREALS			
Avena sativa	Common oat	2	–
Avena strigosa	Sand oat	4	–
Hordeum vulgare	Barley	30	16
Panicum miliaceum	Millet	1	–
Triticum dicoccum	Emmer wheat	31	50
LEGUMES			
Anthyllis vulneraria	Kidney vetch	–	2
Cicer arietinum	Chick pea	–	1
Pisum arvense	Pea	9	–
Vicia ervilia	Bitter vetch	6	–
Vicia faba	Horse bean	1	1
OTHER CULTIVARS, FRUITS, NUTS			
Corylus avellana	Hazelnut	2	–
Linum usitatissimum	Flax	7	–
Quercus rubor	Oak (acorn)	–	1
Rubus fructicosus	Blackberry	–	1
Vitis sylvestris	Wild vine (grape)	3	1
OTHERS			
Achillea millefolium	Yarrow	–	1
Brassica sp	Brassicas	1	1
Camelina sativa	Gold of pleasure	4	–
Chenopodium album	Fat hen	46	6
Euphorbia helioscopa	Sun spurge	206	–
Geranium dissectum	Cut-leaved cransbill	1	1
Gramineae	Grasses	7	3
Lapsana communis	Nipplewort	1	–
Lychnis sp	Campion	–	1
Lycopsis arvensis	Gipsy wort	–	1
Myosatis sp	Forget-me-not	–	3
Neslia paniculata	Ball mustard	1	–
Onobrychis sativa	Sainfoin	26	–
Picris sp	Hawkweed	–	1
Polygonum aviculare	Knot grass	19	7
Polygonum convolvulus	Black bindweed	82	20
Polygonum persicaria	Red shank	47	–
Prunus institia	Bullace	41	–
Staphylea pionata	Bladderwort	–	2
Trifolium sp	Clovers	1	1

Pigs were killed when they were a year or two old; on the evidence of the canine teeth in the faunal sample, males outnumbered females two to one, as we would expect with an animal kept only for its meat.

The Fonte Maggio settlement was well located for a mixed farming economy. Situated on the spring line at the foot of a limestone outcrop (Fig. 8), the soils immediately downslope are a mixture of light Tertiary sands and *terra rossa*, combining the qualities of both – the fertility of the latter with the suitability of the former for cultivation with hand tools and light ards. The sand oat represented in the botanical sample from the site prefers light soils, as do barley and many of the associated weeds. The limestone outcrop above the site would have provided good grazing, as would the main limestone ridge by the modern village of Petrella. The edible snails identified by Chris Hunt from the Fonte Maggio deposits are mostly species of dry open ground, grassland and light woodland on calcareous soils such as *Helix pomatia* and *Rumina decollata*, and were presumably gathered on these limestone outcrops. On the other hand, the presence of plants such as goosegrass, knot grass, and redshank, all preferring damp heavy soils, indicates gathering activities further afield, perhaps for animal fodder as much as for human needs. Certainly the alluvium of the main valley a kilometre to the west below the site would have provided damp grazing in the summer months and browse for cattle and goats. An indication of the intensity of land use at Fonte Maggio is provided by the very large numbers of nematode cysts found in the flotation residues by Derrick Webley. These are the remains of cereal parasites which build up their numbers when cereals are grown in the same field over many years with little or no rotation or fallow – eventually reaching such densities as to endanger the entire crop.

The location of the Masseria Mammarella settlement on the first terrace of the Sinarca allowed easy access to the range of environments needed for the system of diversified subsistence practised by its inhabitants. The plant remains presumably derive in the main from the lighter drier soils above the site, as do the terrestrial molluscs gathered by the community – again, species of calcareous soils and dry open ground (*Rumina decollata*, *Cernuella virgata*, *Pomatias elegans* and *Chilostoma*) were identified by Chris Hunt. The fine soils of the Sinarca alluvium, traditional grazing and woodland until postwar drainage and cultivation, are immediately below the site, within a few hundred metres, and the stream confluence presumably meant an assured water supply. The similarities between the sites in terms of their plant remains, faunal samples, and locations are striking, with no indication of any significant shift in the agricultural base between the Apennine and Subapennine phases of settlement.

The subsistence systems practised by these bronze age communities are similar in many respects to those documented for this period elsewhere in the peninsula. The botanical remains commonly recovered from bronze age settlements in central Italy include emmer, barley, club wheat, spelt, millet, legumes (bean, vetch, pea), fruits and wild plants much like those of the Biferno valley settlements (Helbaek, 1967; Jarman, 1976). Most communities practised mixed stock keeping, with sheep and goats (especially sheep) the dominant stock (Agostini et al., 1992; Barker, 1976b; Barker and Stallibrass, 1987; Wilkens, 1991, 1992). The dentition and fusion data generally indicate that some sheep died in their first or second years, but that most were older, rather as in the Biferno valley, indicating that meat, milk, and probably now wool were all being produced. In fact, Ryder's (1983) studies of wool from waterlogged sites in the alpine region indicate that the true fleece like that of the modern sheep had been developed by this period, whereas earlier domestic sheep had coarser fleeces that had to be plucked, like those of wild sheep. Cattle husbandry was also mixed: some surplus males were killed quite young for their meat, cows were kept for several years for breeding, and a few cows and bulls lived to a great age, presumably as working animals. As in the case of wool, so too the earliest ploughs in Italy, simple wooden ards, have been found at sites in the Alpine foreland dating to this period (Perini, 1983).

PRODUCTION AND EXCHANGE

For most of the Bronze Age, metal seems to have been in very restricted circulation in the Italian peninsula beyond the Tuscan copper ores (Carancini, 1992). Metal finds are extremely rare at most settlements. Towards the end of the 2nd millennium there was a notable acceleration in the amount of metal in circulation. Metal-working was practised at many domestic sites including those at a distance from the ores, and technical consistency in tin bronze production became the norm. The two principal zones of metal production and use in Italy remained the Po valley and Etruria. The distribution maps suggest that most late bronze age metal was traded from these areas by water, using the Italian coastline and the major rivers (Carancini, 1975; Peroni et al., 1980; V. B. Peroni, 1970, 1979). On the eastern side of the Apennines, most late bronze age metalwork has been found in Marche and northern Abruzzo, and another zone of metal-using was along the Adriatic coast south of the Gargano, but the area in between including Molise has produced virtually nothing. There was a single piece of bronze wire at Fonte Maggio, and two fragments of wire at Masseria Mammarella, one of them perhaps part of a fibula or brooch (Fig. 64).

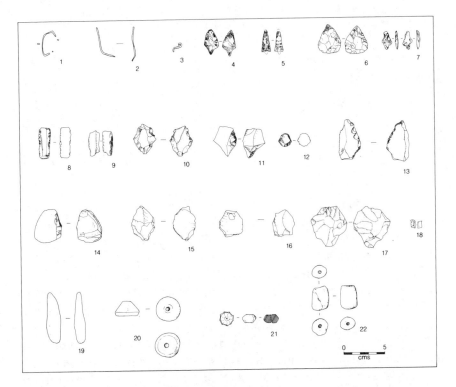

Fig. 64 Metal and stone tools and other artefacts from the bronze age settlements of Fonte Maggio (G1) and Masseria Mammarella (A113). [Bronze wire – G1 (1), A113 (2, 3); flint arrowheads – G1 (4–6), A113 (7); retouched flint blades – G1 (8, 9); retouched flint flakes – G1 (10, 11), A113 (13, 14); flint scraper – A113 (12); flint flakes – A113 (15, 16); flint core – G1 (17); obsidian bladelet – G1 (18); stone ?burnisher – A113 (19); clay spindle whorls – A113 (20); clay beads – A113 (21, 22)]

At both sites, however, a lithic technology continued to be used (Fig. 64). There were about fifty pieces of struck chert at each site, mainly from local river cobbles of brown and grey chert. The majority of pieces consists of either half-worked cores, or primary and secondary flakes struck from them, almost invariably without further edge working, together with small chipping debris. The well-produced blades common at the later neolithic and copper age sites are extremely rare. The few retouched tools are shown in Figure 64 – pressure-flaked arrowheads, simple retouched flakes and blades, denticulated flakes, and occasional scrapers. A single fragment of an obsidian bladelet was also found in the Fonte Maggio excavation, from Lipari like the neolithic obsidian in the valley. Crude flakes and cores were found at most of the surface sites with bronze age pottery recorded by the survey in the valley, and similar assemblages to those of Fonte Maggio and

Table 8 Bronze age fabrics in the Biferno valley and their distribution. (x – present; xx – common; xxx – very common; U – upper valley; M – middle valley; L – lower valley)

	limestone	quartz	siltstone		location
FABRIC GROUP					
A1	xxx	(x)	x	(grey)	U,M,L
A2	xxx	xx	x	(grey)	U,M
B1	xx	x	x	(grey)	M,L
B2	xx	xx	x	(grey)	M
C1	x	xxx	xxx	(orange)	L

Masseria Mammarella were collected at sites such as B282, C102 and C306. Elsewhere in the peninsula, the lithic assemblages of Apennine and Subapennine sites are generally very similar, and microwear analysis of the comparable assemblage from Tufariello indicated an all-purpose toolkit for working bone, wood, and leather (Hartmann, 1975). We can presume that everyday technology for most bronze age communities in the peninsula, and particularly in Molise, was based on the traditional resources of stone, flint, wood, clay, bone, leather, and so on.

A sample of fine, medium, and coarse sherds from about 20 bronze age sites found by the survey was subjected to thin-section analysis, to investigate details of production and of possible areas of manufacture (Nash, 1979). Five fabric groups were recognized (Table 8). The principal inclusions were quartz, limestone, and iron, with siltstones and felspars also being found. All these rock types are local to the valley: limestone, for example, is dominant in the upper valley but occurs as outcrops elsewhere, whereas the quartz and the siltstones are more common in the middle and especially the lower valley. Throughout the valley, the coarse wares tended to contain many inclusions of crushed limestone (Group A1 in Table 8). Amongst the finer wares, however, the analysis indicated four fabric groups with differing quantities of limestone, quartz, and siltstone used as filler. The limestone was predominant in the upper valley (Group A2), orange siltstone and quartz in the lower valley group (C1), and various mixes of quartz, limestone, and grey siltstones were particularly common in the middle valley (Groups B1, B2). The clear implication is that the bronze age pottery of the Biferno valley is likely to be of local manufacture, local not simply to the valley but to particular parts of it, the potters selecting clays and fillers from the vicinity of the settlements.

Yet contrasting with the evidence for local manufacture is the fact that the potters at all these sites took their design motifs from a common repertoire found throughout the peninsula (Cocchi Genick *et al.*, 1992). Apennine and Subapennine pottery decoration has never been subjected to a systematic analysis of regional styles, still less of form and content as a medium of information exchange. At a general level, Trump (1958) pointed out that there were two major geographical groups in terms of handle designs – horned handles were prevalent in the north and axe handles in the south; and that there was a similar geographical distinction in Apennine 'milk-boilers', a funnel type being common in the north and a perforated bowl being preferred in the south. The Biferno valley is at the approximate junction between these two groups, and shares in both with the preference of its inhabitants for 'southern' axe and tongue handles on the one hand and, on the other, the occurrence of strainer sherds of the 'northern' type of milk-boilers at Fonte Maggio and Masseria Mammarella. Susan Lukesh was able to find close parallels for the various design techniques and patterns of the Biferno valley pottery at a series of sites to the north in Marche and Umbria and to the west in Lazio, but the closest parallels were with sites in the immediately adjacent areas to the north in the Abruzzo Apennines and to the west on the other side of the Matese in Campania; far fewer similarities were found to the south in Apulia, few in Calabria, and none in Basilicata.

Mycenaean trading posts and perhaps colonies were established on the southern coasts of the Italian peninsula from the 14th century bc. The Po valley was involved in systematic and regular trade across the alpine passes and was also in trading contact of some kind with Etruria and the Marche by the end of the 2nd millennium; there may have been occasional commercial contact too with Mycenaean Greece. However, there is very little evidence that most communities in central and southern Italy took part in such European or Mediterranean commerce. In Umbria and Tuscany, for example, Stoddart (1987) argues from the distribution of particular types of bronze pins and glass beads that there were systems of regional exchange linking bronze age communities, a single amber bead there being the only clear evidence for contact with a wider world. For the Biferno valley, it is hard to detect even these regional systems of exchange in the 2nd millennium, faced with the evidence of minimal metallurgy, a local lithic industry and local pottery manufacture – the bladelet of Lipari obsidian at Fonte Maggio is the single exotic object.

BRONZE AGE SOCIETIES IN THE BIFERNO VALLEY

The lack of evidence for stratification in Apennine bronze age society has often been remarked upon. The metal daggers of the earlier Bronze Age are assumed to have been status markers like the copper and flint daggers of the 3rd millennium, but there is little other evidence for a permanent elite in Apennine society at this time. There are very few signs of status differentiation amongst the few burials known. Most settlements were simple collections of huts with no evidence for internal differentiation in architecture or material culture that might suggest clear-cut divisions in society. As Ruth Whitehouse (1992) has pointed out, the dominant ritual activities known – food offerings by springs in caves – imply a secretive ritual strikingly different from the conspicuous destruction or discard of material wealth, the elaborate funerary rituals and ceremonial monuments, the complex astronomical rituals and so on found amongst other ranked societies in temperate Europe in the Bronze Age. The indications are of an agricultural society with few social divisions within individual communities or within regional groups. The evidence from the Biferno valley correlates completely with this model: the material culture, the simple habitation structures, the subsistence system, the paucity of metalwork, the minimal level of exchange, the absence of evidence for major social divisions.

Whilst the 'minimal view' of Apennine bronze age society remains apposite for most of the peninsula, two areas were exceptions to the rule, both of which were to impact on life in the Biferno valley in the ensuing Iron Age (Chapter Eight). On the Ionian coast, the instep of the Italian peninsula, a settlement hierarchy developed in the Subapennine phase, and the major settlement, Broglio, sustained specialist craftsmen who produced a wheel-made pottery closely copying an Aegean ware, together with Aegean types of storage jars (Buffa and Peroni, 1982; Peroni, 1984). The agricultural system also included olive and vine cultivation, crops that were critical components of Aegean agriculture at this time (Renfrew, 1972), but probably not part of bronze age subsistence elsewhere in Italy. There is cemetery evidence too for specialized groups of craftsmen and warriors. It is difficult to explain these transformations in technology, agriculture, and social organization except in the context of Mycenaean contact (Bergonzi, 1985).

In south Etruria, there were even more striking changes in settlement towards the end of the 2nd millennium (Galassi, 1986; Peroni and Di Gennaro, 1986). Earlier, the settlement system here had consisted of discontinuous clusters of small sites, which excavations have shown were much like those of the Biferno valley, whose inhabitants practised mixed farming with a strong pastoral component (Maggiani and Pellegrini, 1985; Miari, 1987; Potter, 1976). In the last few centuries of the 2nd millennium the settlement system developed the first indications of hierarchical organization, both within certain settlements and within local settlement clusters, with naturally defended locations increasingly preferred for the main settlements, and the first evidence for defensive walling being found

(Negroni Catacchio, 1981; Negroni Catacchio and Domanico, 1987; Östenberg, 1967). Evidence for intensification in the agricultural system in terms of new crops and increased use of animal secondary products (Barker, 1976a; Jarman, 1976) coincides with other, indirect, evidence for an expansion of arable cultivation (Pacciarelli, 1982). The amount of metal in circulation increased dramatically, and new settlement clusters developed in the vicinity of the metal ores (Giardino, 1984). Competition for mineral resources at this time seems to have been a critical factor in stimulating a process of social transformation that was to culminate a few centuries later in the Etruscan city states.

As observed earlier, the bronze age settlements of the Biferno valley probably divide into hut clusters and single huts. The range of radiocarbon dates at Fonte Maggio could mean that the difference in size is simply a function of the length of occupation, but whilst this may be a factor, it seems extremely unlikely that the single family was the normal living unit – a larger grouping would have been highly desirable for most pre-industrial farmers without recourse to modern labour-saving technology, with cooperation between families essential for the critical tasks of the agricultural year (Fleming, 1985). It is more likely, therefore, that the two sizes of bronze age site found in the survey reflect in greater part a division between the main occupation sites used by groups of families and satellite camps occupied for shorter periods by part of the main community (whether a single family or a particular age or sex group) for specific tasks. Activities necessitating camps away from the main settlement rather than short-distance daily trips could have included hunting, charcoal-burning, and in particular herding.

The process of settlement expansion observed in the Biferno valley during the 2nd millennium bc correlates well with the general settlement trends observed at this time throughout central Italy, of a gradual filling out of the landscape, the permanent occupation of the intermontane basins, and, most noticeably, the first systematic use of the mountains. In central Abruzzo, surface collections of bronze age material have been found at 1500 metres above sea level on the Gran Sasso, the highest mountain of the Apennine range – at such an altitude difficult to interpret as evidence of anything other than a seasonal shepherd camp. In the Cicolano mountains of central Lazio, archaeological survey found pieces of flint likely to be of bronze age date associated with fragments of daub at 1100 metres, perhaps evidence of seasonal camps (Barker and Grant, 1991). Monte Velino, south of the Cicolano, was almost certainly visited by people who occupied a cave in the Val di Varri valley below, for the pottery found in the cave contained inclusions from there (Güller and Segre, 1948). Bronze age material has also been found on the Maiella mountain of Abruzzo at 2000 metres above sea level. The appearance for the first time during the Bronze Age of sites not only on the floors of the Apennine *altopiani*, at altitudes between 1100 and 1500 metres where marginal farming is possible but seasonal pastoralism more realistic, but also above 1500 metres which can only have been occupied in the summer months, surely indicates the development of seasonal exploitation of the Apennines during the 2nd millennium bc, the most likely activity being shepherding. The pollen diagrams available for the Apennines, though still limited, also indicate more open vegetation now in the mountains (Cruise, 1991; Grüger, 1977).

Salvatore Puglisi's 1959 model of large-scale transhumance for the Apennine Bronze Age was undoubtedly exaggerated, and based on unreliable assumptions about the archaeological record: mixed farming was clearly the dominant system of bronze age subsistence. Nevertheless, the evidence accumulated in recent years confirms a core truth of Puglisi's theory, in the growing evidence for the first systematic use of the Apennine pastures during the Bronze Age by what can legitimately be termed a form of short-distance transhumance, albeit on a very limited scale compared with that of historical times (Cocchi Genick, 1991; Maggi and Nisbet, 1991).

The development of more open country on the Apennine plateaux in the later 2nd millennium bc may be a reflection of a climatic trend to aridity (for which there is some evidence in the pollen diagrams and lake levels of central Italy), or of human agency in the form of woodland clearance, or a combination of the two. Either way it seems clear that, as land became available, the agricultural systems of the peninsular Italian Bronze Age were able to expand to exploit it. The use of the high plateaux by shepherds and herders in the later 2nd millennium must have been a factor in the uniformity of the pottery styles of these people down the length of the peninsula. The Apennine mountains were now surely a means of communication and interchange for the communities living on either side rather than a barrier.

Despite the survey evidence for the expansion of settlement throughout the valley during the 2nd millennium bc, the scale of settlement at this time must not be exaggerated. Two lines of evidence indicate that the impact of people on their landscape was still very small. A pollen diagram taken from sediments on the floor of the Adriatic about 30 kilometres from Termoli indicated a predominantly forested landscape on the adjacent mainland in the 2nd millennium, with oak dominating at lower and middle elevations and elm, ash and beech in the mountains (Bottema, 1974). The alluvial sediments in the valley studied by Chris Hunt likewise indicate that later prehistoric farming created only small intermittent clearances in what was still a predominantly closed environment (Chapter Four).

CHAPTER 8

IRON AGE CHIEFDOMS, *c.* 1000–500 bc

Graeme Barker and Marlene Suano, with contributions by Gill Clark,
John Giorgi and Derrick Webley

INTRODUCTION

At the end of the Bronze Age, the Biferno valley was a landscape of hamlets and farms, and as Chapter Seven concluded, there is little evidence for complex stratification in society. A few centuries later, from the end of the Iron Age towards the middle of the 1st millennium BC, the valley emerges into the light of history as the heart of ancient Samnium – the homeland of the Samnites, the renowned opponents of Rome (Salmon, 1967). Although traditionally regarded as a backward and rustic people, archaeology shows that Samnite culture in the later centuries of the 1st millennium BC was far more complex than envisaged even a few years ago, with more or less urban structures developing before Romanization (Chapter Nine). In this chapter we discuss the archaeological evidence for the transformations in settlement and culture between 1000 and 500 BC that projected the village communities of the Bronze Age on the pathway towards urbanization.

These transformations took place alongside two extraordinary cultural changes elsewhere in the peninsula during this period: the development of the Etruscan city states in Etruria, and the establishment of Greek colonies in the south. In Etruria, over the space of a few centuries the hierarchical societies of the Late Bronze Age were replaced by highly stratified societies controlled by regional aristocracies (Spivey and Stoddart, 1990). In southern Etruria in particular there was an elaborate settlement hierarchy of major Etruscan cities, local centres, satellite centres, hamlets, and farms (Barker *et al.*, 1993; Judson and Hemphill, 1981). There were fundamental transformations in the agricultural system and in metal-working, and surplus products from both systems were widely traded outside Italy (Barker, 1988).

From the 9th to the 6th centuries BC the Greeks, like the Phoenicians of the Levant, expanded rapidly across the Mediterranean basin and the Black Sea in search of raw materials and new land for their expanding populations (Boardman, 1980). Greek colonies were established in the Bay of

Naples in the second half of the 8th century BC and in the instep of the peninsula towards the end of the 8th or early in the 7th century BC (Buchner, 1979; De la Genière, 1979; Frederiksen, 1979; Ridgway, 1973). Greek trade with the Italian peninsula in fact preceded the foundation of the colonies and it is commonly assumed that the search for metal ore was the principal stimulus to this contact. Etruria was especially attractive in having both copper and tin deposits in close proximity to one another, and the island of Elba was a rich source of iron ore. Hence the colonies traded directly and also acted in part as 'ports of trade', intermediaries for trade between the Etruscans and the homeland (Ridgway, 1992). By the end of the 8th century Greek and Pithekoussan pottery was being used by the Etruscan elites, Greek artists settled in Etruria, and networks of gift exchange established between Etruscan chieftains were extended to the Greek world (Cristofani, 1975; Torelli, 1971).

This mutually advantageous relationship inevitably deteriorated as Etruscan power expanded southwards during the course of the 7th century, coinciding with a period of territorial expansion by the Greek colonies of the Bay of Naples. In 524 BC an Etruscan invasion force aimed at the destruction of Cumae was instead destroyed, and in 474 BC an Etruscan naval attack was defeated off Cumae (Frederiksen, 1984). The ensuing retreat from Campania marked a watershed in Etruscan history, with the first Etruscan city falling to the expanding power of Rome a century later.

SETTLEMENT TRENDS

In the Biferno valley the survey recorded almost 120 findspots with pottery classified as Iron Age (Fig. 65), an increase of almost 50 per cent over the number of localities with bronze age pottery. As with the latter, the 'probable' sites normally have more than 20 sherds, the 'possible' sites c. 5–20 sherds, and the 'sporadic' findspots have less than 5 sherds. The most common iron age pottery found at these sites is normally termed *impasto* by Italian prehistorians, signifying a coarse handmade ware, though there are in fact two such fabrics. The more common of the two consisted of a thick porous fabric fired to a dark brown or black, normally used for large

Fig. 65 Iron age settlement in the Biferno valley according to the archaeological survey, with the principal sites mentioned in the text identified, together with the cemeteries discovered and excavated by the Archaeological Superintendency. The sites with question marks are Samnite sites post-dating 500 BC with *impasto* pottery that may pre-date 500 BC (see discussion in Chapter Nine).

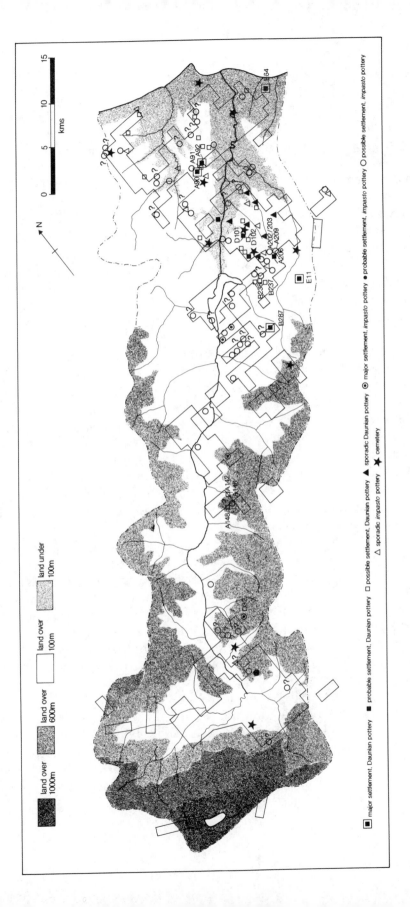

land over 1000m

land over 600m

land over 100m

land under 100m

N

0   5   10   15

kms

A164

A90
A92
A91

D101
D102
D202/203
A208 A209
B238
B237
E11

B287

A148 A142
A146

D92

A?

■ major settlement, Daunian pottery   □ possible settlement, Daunian pottery   ▲ sporadic Daunian pottery   ★ cemetery

■ probable settlement, *impasto* pottery   ⊙ major settlement, *impasto* pottery   △ sporadic *impasto* pottery

● probable settlement, *impasto* pottery   ○ possible settlement, *impasto* pottery

storage vessels and flat cooking plates. The other fabric was of similar colour but harder, thinner, and better fired, and was normally used for small storage vessels and drinking cups. In both fabrics and shapes, these *impasto* wares have their origins in the Bronze Age pottery of the valley.

Associated with *impasto* at many sites are sherds of a fine hard buff fabric, often with traces of dark brown paint. This pottery is very similar to a fabric produced in Apulia termed Daunian ware: the tradition began there in the 9th and 8th centuries with a 'proto-Daunian' geometric style influenced by Geometric and Protocorinthian pottery from mainland Greece, and was followed by Sub-Geometric styles in the 7th and 6th centuries (De Juliis, 1977, 1978). In addition to these definite occurrences of Daunian-type pottery, there are some sites with sherds of the same fabric but without traces of paint which are very likely to derive from the same potting style; probably locally produced, both the painted and unpainted material is referred to as Daunian in this chapter, for the sake of simplicity.

The most immediate characteristic of the distribution of these sites is the bias towards the lower valley – 60 per cent of the total sample: including the cemeteries, there are 58 sites and 12 findspots here, compared with 30 sites and 1 findspot in the middle valley, 12 sites and 1 findspot in the upper valley, and none on the Matese. A few of the sites found by the survey are probably the remains of ploughed-out burials, and are discussed with the major cemetery data later, but the majority of the 56 'definite' and 'probable' sites is probably domestic in character. Certainly all the major assemblages include a range of domestic pottery of both *impasto* fabrics and items such as grindstones and loom weights, suggesting habitation rather than funerary debris.

The most significant feature of the data is the evidence for a far greater degree of settlement hierarchy than in the Bronze Age. Most of the domestic sites consist of spreads of surface debris measuring less than 50×50 metres, but the period was also characterized by massive sites larger than these by a factor of ten. The most important of the latter is the major settlement of Arcora (E64) currently being excavated by the Super-intendency, situated on the edge of the coastal plain near Campomarino. The second is a complex of sites found by the survey at Santa Margherita north of Guglionesi (A90, A91, A92), which probably represents a single major settlement destroyed by quarrying. A third settlement was located near Colle Masilli below Montorio dei Frentani (E11), and a fourth (B287) was just north of Casacalenda a little further inland in the same part of the valley. The fifth iron age settlement was within the later Samnite *oppidum* of Monte Vairano (D32) in the upper valley. A number of other settlement agglomerations is suggested by the occurrence of adjacent small sites: for example, on the ridges below Larino in the lower valley (A202, A203,

A206, A209; B237, B238; D101, D102), on the low-lying terraces of the middle valley (C284, C285), and in a similar location in the upper valley (A142, A146, A148). It seems clear that iron age settlement in the valley was characterized by the emergence of major nucleated sites situated some 10–15 kilometres apart, as well as by a network of smaller sites similar in size to the hamlets and farms of the Bronze Age.

Several of the bronze age sites found by the survey have produced one or two *impasto* sherds of iron age type. However, much more striking is the evidence for continuity between the iron age settlement system and that of the ensuing Samnite period. Most of the 'possible' sites consist of definite Samnite settlements post-dating 500 BC with pottery assemblages which also include a few sherds of iron age *impasto* and Daunian fabrics. As well as the evidence for iron age occupation at Monte Vairano, the clustering of Iron Age settlements around the later urban centres of Fagifulae (near Montagano) and Larinum (modern Larino) is also probably significant. The implication from the survey data is that the Samnite settlement system of farms, villages and local centres described in Chapter Nine had its roots in the settlement hierarchies that developed in the valley during the Iron Age.

SETTLEMENT STRUCTURE

The principal information on iron age settlement structure in the valley has been provided by the excavations at Arcora. The coastal plateau forms a natural peninsula here, the northern flank formed by the plateau edge overlooking the coastal plain and the southern flank formed of the steep bank of a dry valley. Though the area was badly damaged in the last war by the construction of a military airfield and the battle for Termoli, there are some indications of a ditch across the neck of the peninsula, assumed to be contemporary with the iron age settlement it encloses.

Survey by an amateur group in the wake of deep ploughing in the late 1970s mapped some sixty discrete concentrations of archaeological debris (Gravina, 1986; Gravina and Di Giulio, 1982). These concentrations consisted of patches of dark soil mixed with stones (many of them burnt), ash, and artefacts. They were usually sub-rectangular in shape, and measured 6–18 metres on the long axis and 5–9 metres on the short axis. Where these concentrations were cut by a modern road, in the road section could be discerned traces of floor surfaces formed of semi-burnt and trampled clay, post-holes, and pits up to a metre deep filled with dark soil, ash, stones, fragments of wattle and daub, pottery, animal bone and other cultural refuse. A hearth preserved in one of these sections consisted of layers of ash and burnt clay within a setting of pebbles and sand.

Excavations by the Superintendency began in 1982 and have continued to date (Di Niro, 1984, 1991a). Little stratigraphy is preserved below the deep ploughing, but the excavations have confirmed that the stone concentrations are the remains of individual structures. One such structure excavated was roughly rectangular in shape measuring 10×4 metres, with an apsidal end (Fig. 66). The walls of the structure were probably of wattle and daub, on stone footings. For the most part, the floor was constructed of tightly packed river cobbles, but these were substituted around a series of sunken hearths by a surface of semi-fired beaten clay. Given the limited extent of the excavations, and with the results still being assessed, it is impossible to know whether all the structures were residential, or whether some were reserved for storage or labour, and whether residential units were for families or were reserved for particular age and sex groups. However, the evidence clearly suggests a quite substantial community, a nucleated village rather than a hamlet or farmstead.

The surface pottery from the settlement spans a period from the Late Bronze Age to the 5th century BC, with the main occupation thought to divide into two main episodes, the first in the 8th–7th centuries BC and the second in the 6th–5th centuries BC. Charcoal from one of the early structures yielded a radiocarbon date (OxA-609) of 2990 + 80 bp, or 1040 bc (Gowlett et al., 1987: 139). The fine painted Daunian pottery from the village included high-handled cups and vases in the Apennine bronze age tradition. Impasto handmade fabrics of the finer quality were used for a variety of carinated bowls, and large storage buckets were made from coarse impasto. Again, most of the latter are recognisably in the local bronze age tradition. Bronze pieces were very rare at the settlement, consisting mostly of small items of personal ornamentation such as rings, bracelets, and pins. Flint was still used, principally for pressure-flaked flint arrowheads. Some of the most common finds were clay spindle whorls and loom weights (Di Niro, 1991a).

The principal iron age settlement located by the survey was at Santa Margherita north of Guglionesi on the other side of the valley. Several fields here around a large stone quarry produced surface Daunian and impasto pottery (A90, A91, A92), and at the first of them the remnants of two wide, shallow pits like those of the Arcora settlement were found sectioned by the quarry wall. The inhabitants of the locality recalled how large quantities of archaeological materials were found in deposits of dark soil many years ago, and were removed during quarrying operations. It seems highly probable that there was a substantial iron age settlement at Santa Margherita, associated with the cemetery that came to light in 1986 (discussed later in the chapter).

The faces of the two pits were cleaned and cut back (Fig. 67). Separated

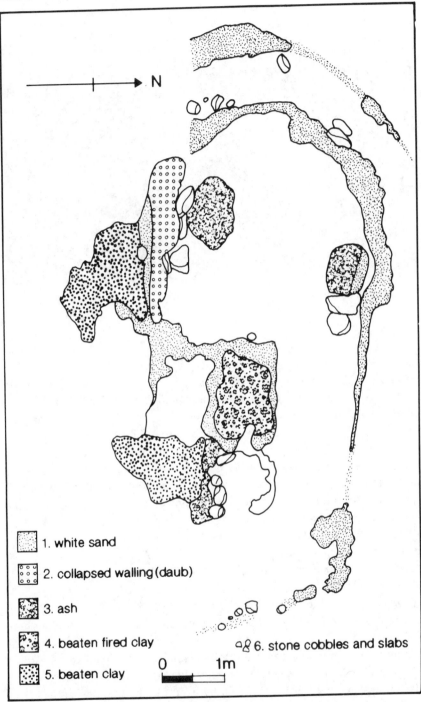

N

1. white sand

2. collapsed walling (daub)

3. ash

4. beaten fired clay

5. beaten clay

6. stone cobbles and slabs

0   1m

Fig. 66 Plan of a house at the iron age settlement of Arcora. (After Di Niro, 1991a: 37)

Fig. 67 Pits exposed in a quarry wall at Santa Margherita, the remnants of an iron age settlement (A90). (Photograph: Graeme Barker)

by only 50 centimetres, they were both about 1 metre deep. Their homogeneous fills consisted of very dark soil, containing a rich assemblage of iron age pottery and other artefacts, fragments of wattle and daub, animal bones, and other organic residues. Daunian sherds from the pits (Fig. 68), of a fine pink or yellow fabric with white and brown painted designs, included pieces which, according to the De Juliis typology, belong to the Geometric Proto-Daunian style of the 8th–6th centuries BC, but the majority of the sherds belongs to the Sub-Geometric Daunian II style of the 6th and 5th centuries BC. A sample of animal bone from the base of one of the pits yielded a radiocarbon date (OxA-674) of 2610 + 80 bp (660 BC), and the basal deposit of the other pit yielded two radiocarbon dates, one from animal bone (OxA-675) of 2480 + 80 bp (530 BC) and the other from charcoal (OxA-673) of 2500 + 80 bp (550 BC) (Gowlett *et al.*, 1987: 139).

The fabric and the workmanship of the Daunian pottery from Santa Margherita, as well as some of the designs (which are unknown elsewhere in Daunia), point to local production – a possible pottery kiln was identified at Arcora. Two particularly handsome pieces of the Late Daunian style at Santa Margherita were handles shaped as ducks' heads. Repair holes on a plain sherd of the same fabric from the site emphasize the status of this pottery. The assemblage also included fine *impasto* sherds from single-handled cups and single- or double-handled cups of the classical

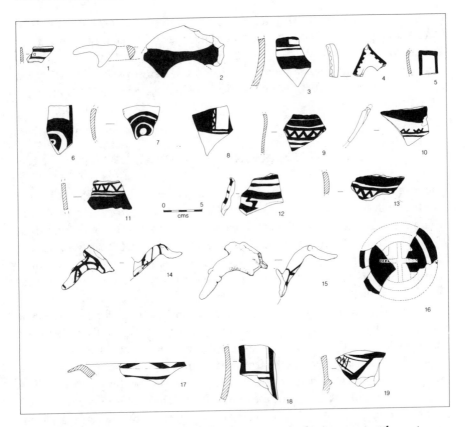

Fig. 68 The development of Daunian pottery at the iron age settlement of Santa Margherita (A90): proto-Daunian (1–5), sub-geometric Daunian I (6, 7), and sub-geometric Daunian II (8–19).

kantharos form, from small *kantharoi* with ribbon handles and miniature cups. Coarser *impasto* was used for large storage jars, buckets, smaller jars, and plates. The latter are presumably domestic items, though storage jars were also used as burial containers in southern Italy at this time, particularly for child burials (De la Genière, 1979). The pits also contained a few struck flint flakes, and there was a single fragment of bronze, probably from a belt buckle.

Little is known of the nature of iron age settlements elsewhere in this part of Italy, but the trends observed in the Biferno valley at this time – the growth of lowland villages, the beginnings of hillfort settlement in the mountains – can be observed elsewhere. In the lowlands of Apulia a settlement hierarchy developed at this time dominated by major regional centres, sometimes defended, though areas without occupation evidence within the enclosed zones suggest that the normal residential populations may not have been very large (Nava, 1982). In the mountainous regions of central and southern Italy isolated hilltops were increasingly selected for settlement, some of which – like Monte Vairano in the Biferno valley – were to develop into substantial *oppida* in the classical period (Anglé *et al.*, 1982; Bonomi Ponzi, 1982; De la Genière, 1979; Gualtieri, 1987; Mattiocco, 1981, 1986).

IRON AGE FARMING (GB, GC, JG, DW)

Evidence for iron age crop farming in the valley is limited to botanical residues collected from the Santa Margherita pits and from Arcora (Table 9). In both cases carbonized vegetal matter was extracted by flotation into a 0.5-millimetre sieve and identified with a binocular microscope with a ×40 magnification. Though the samples are small, they provide significant new information on iron age farming in southern Italy, for which very little reliable data have been available hitherto (De la Genière, 1979).

The whole wheat seeds were almost invariably emmer, *Triticum dicoccum*. A large number of glume bases, spikelet forks and tough rachis nodes and internodes can also be ascribed with some confidence to emmer and are presumably the waste from threshing and cleaning this crop. A few grains of bread wheat were also identified in the two samples. The barley grains and rachis internodes were from two species, six-row hulled barley and naked barley. Single grains of oats were probably weeds within the wheat and barley crops. Peas and beans were common in both samples, and one context from Arcora contained over thirty thousand fragments of the horse bean *Vicia faba*, of a purity indicative of a storage deposit. Several grape pips were found at both sites. It is difficult to distinguish the wild grape (ssp *sylvestris*) from the cultivated grape (ssp *vinifera*), particularly when there are only a few charred seeds present, but the grape specimens from both sites share more morphological similarities with the cultivated than with the wild variety. Other food remains included seeds of fruits and nuts, and the rest of the samples consisted of seeds of plants of arable, fallow and waste land.

The dominance of emmer and barley in the cereal crops from the two sites is just as in the earlier prehistoric systems of crop farming in the valley. The range of legumes, fruits and nuts is also much as before. Rather similar plant remains have also been identified at other iron age sites in southern Italy such as Monte Irsi (Hjelmquist, 1977). However, a significant development in the valley at this time is clearly the evidence for the beginnings of grape cultivation. Taken together with the use of Daunian ware for finely produced and decorated drinking cups, the implication is

Table 9 Plant remains recovered from the iron age settlements of Santa Margherita (A90) and Arcora (E64). Identifications by Derrick Webley (A90) and John Giorgi (E60). Numbers in brackets refer to identifications of fragmentary remains such as internodes and spikelet forks.

| | | Santa Margherita | | Arcora |
		Pit 1	Pit 2	
CEREALS				
Avena sativa	Oat	–	1	2 (1)
Hordeum vulgare	Barley	26	59	14 (1)
Panicum sp	Millet	–	–	2
Triticum dicoccum	Emmer	5	22	9 (143)
Triticum aestivum	Bread wheat	1	1	2
LEGUMES				
Pisum arvense	Pea	–	15	–
Vicia faba	Horse bean	–	3	30,000 +
OTHER CULTIVARS,				
FRUITS, NUTS				
Corylus avellana	Hazelnut	–	–	1
Prunus sp	Plum	–	5	–
Vitis ?vinifera	Vine	–	14	8
OTHERS				
Achillea millefolium	Yarrow	–	1	–
Chenopodium album	Fat hen	11	2	–
Convolvulus arvensis	Bindweed	4	–	–
Euphorbia helioscopa	Sun spurge	3	2	–
Gramineae	Grasses	5	6	–
Lychnis diurna	Red campion	1	–	–
Malva neglecta	Dwarf mallow	1	–	–
Polygonum convolvulus	Black bindweed	4	11	–
Plantago	Plantain	–	–	1
Rumex	Dock	–	–	1
Spergula arvensis	Corn spurrey	–	1	–
Staphylea pionata	Bladdernut	–	11	–

surely that vines were being cultivated especially for the production of wine.

There is widespread archaeological evidence for the practice of viticulture at this time by the Etruscans and by the Greeks of Magna Graecia (Barker, 1988; Frederiksen, 1984). Wine drinking was a critical component of the *symposion*, the banquet that was central to Greek and Etruscan social interactions amongst the nobility. Both societies exported not only wine but also the luxury table services for its preparation and drinking – an Etruscan ship wrecked off the island of Giglio, for example, contained both transport amphoras and table services of *bucchero*, Etruscan fine ware

(Bound, 1985). The material culture of the Biferno valley indicates cultural links with Abruzzo to the north, Apulia to the south, and across the mountains with Campania, and there is no evidence for direct contact with Greeks or Etruscans. However, it does seem likely that the adoption of wine drinking by the emerging elites of the Biferno valley was either directly or indirectly reflecting a mode of behaviour practised by Etruscan and Greek elites. An Etruscan farm excavated recently in the Albegna valley in northern Tuscany had a central room with a hearth, a sunken *dolium* (a large storage vessel) and an associated system of channels for liquids, the whole complex being interpreted as an early wine press (Perkins and Attolini, 1992), and one of the buildings at Arcora had similar facilities (Di Niro, 1984).

There is no direct evidence in the valley at this time for the other major component of polyculture, olive cultivation, which was also practised by the Etruscans and Greeks. However, the pollen core taken off the coast of Termoli contained pollen of olive as well as vine in the part of the diagram thought to be contemporary with iron age occupation in the valley, together with indicators of continued clearance of deciduous forest and the expansion of macchia (Bottema, 1974).

There is little archaeozoological data for animal husbandry in the valley at this time. The animal bones from Arcora have not yet been analysed, but are known to include both wild and domestic animals (Di Niro, 1984). From the Santa Margherita pits, 458 fragments of animal bone were recovered, sheep and goats being most common in terms of identifiable fragments, followed by cattle and pigs. A large proportion of the sample consists of cranial and dental elements, though most parts of the skeleton are represented for the major species by a few fragments. Although the sample is so small, at least it can be said that there is a general resemblance to the larger faunal samples from the bronze age sites in the valley in terms of the species frequencies and range of anatomical elements. One difference is the presence of wild boar in the Santa Margherita material, represented by a single fragment from each pit. Another is the presence of an equid, though whether from a donkey or horse was impossible to tell. The mortality data are limited, but again they fit closely with the mortality data from the bronze age samples.

Faunal evidence for contemporary stock-keeping systems is very limited. The nearest comparisons are with Monte Saraceno, a regional centre in the Gargano peninsula somewhat similar to Arcora in organization and status (Fusco, 1982): sheep and goats dominated this sample and the author concluded that the numbers of adult deaths indicated that secondary products must have been important goals in both sheep/goat and cattle husbandry. The faunal material from Monte Irsi (Barker, 1977) and Gravina

(Watson, 1992) indicates rather similar systems of animal consumption at other iron age centres in southern Italy. In Etruria, the bias towards animal secondary products was even more marked (Barker, 1976b; De Grossi Mazzorin, 1985; Gejvall, 1982; Scali, 1987a, 1987b; Sorrentino, 1981). Artefactual evidence also indicates significant intensification in the use of animal secondary products at this time, particularly the production of wool. Settlement excavations in Etruria and elsewhere invariably produce large numbers of spindle whorls and loom weights, as at Arcora.

Whilst iron age farming in the Biferno valley had a great deal in common with earlier systems of farming, the production of wine and the intensified production of wool marked a radical change in the management of natural resources, as they did elsewhere in the Italian peninsula at this time. In Etruria in particular, the development of the city state system was the critical context for a process of agricultural intensification which served to feed the greatly enlarged rural and urban population, enhance the lifestyles of the elites, and provide critical resources for external trade – wine, oil, and wool (Barker, 1988). The use of donkeys for transport and horses for riding (the latter presumably in the main by the elites) marked a further significant development in iron age stock-keeping in which the valley shared. The changes in farming were certainly at a far smaller scale than in Etruria, like the changes in settlement forms; nevertheless, they still reflect significant developments in social complexity, seen best in the cemetery evidence discussed in the following section.

CEMETERIES AND STRAY FINDS

In the past fifteen years our knowledge of iron age society in the Biferno valley has been transformed by the Superintendency's excavations of four cemeteries, three in the lower valley near the modern settlements of Termoli, Guglionesi, and Larino, and one in the upper valley near Campochiaro (Fig. 65). The first necropolis was situated immediately to the southwest of Termoli at Porticone, overlooking the Sinarca valley. Sixty-nine graves were found, with little patterning in individual orientation, although the cemetery area as a whole consisted of a linear spread of graves restricted to along the plateau edge (Fig. 69). All of the graves consisted of simple trenches, paved with cobbles or beaten clay. The bodies were laid out on their backs with arms and legs fully extended and the gravegoods were placed by their feet. Shallow graves were generally filled with earth and river cobbles to form a low mound, whereas deeper graves were filled with earth and pebbles to the ground surface. Very occasionally, bodies were covered by tiles, either laid horizontally or in the tent-like form of the *a cappucino* style common later in classical times. Most of the gravegoods consisted of pottery, either locally manufactured forms of Daunian ware or coarser *impasto* vessels. Males were buried with their personal weapons, usually a spear and a knife, though one man also carried a sword. Females wore a variety of personal ornaments, the repertoire including iron and bronze fibulae, pendants, rings and bracelets, amber beads, and beads of glass paste (Fig. 69). No child graves are reported. The cemetery was used from the early 6th to the beginning of the 4th centuries BC.

At Santa Margherita, our survey had indicated the likelihood of destroyed iron age graves across the promontory immediately north of the A90 site, and in 1986 intact graves came to light during the construction of new houses (Di Niro, 1986). Nine graves were excavated, 5 dating to the 6th century BC (all adult) and 4 to the 4th century BC (including a juvenile). As at Termoli, the cemetery seems to have consisted of a linear spread of graves of mixed orientations, but in general the graves were richer, containing Daunian vessels of very high quality and some bronze vessels. Female graves also contained pendants of amber and bone, and fibulae of bronze and iron, whilst male graves contained iron knives and arrowheads. One particularly rich individual was buried with vessels of Daunian fine ware, a single vessel of *impasto*, two bronze vessels, a bronze razor, and an iron roasting spit. His personal equipment included a spear, a large knife with a wooden handle and a group of iron nails, perhaps from a shield or coffin. Beyond his head was a collection of charcoal (perhaps the remains of a wooden chest) and a loom weight. Further evidence for the existence of very rich 'warrior graves' here is the sporadic find at the beginning of this century of a bronze helmet and numerous fine bronze bowls that probably derive from this cemetery (Di Niro, 1986: 153).

The Larino cemetery (Di Niro, 1981) was situated at *c.*370 metres above sea level on the southern side of Monte Arcano, a low hill midway down the ridge which extends north from Larino to Monte Maulo, the neolithic settlement discussed in Chapter Six. There were 17 graves, again with no systematic orientation. The trenches were filled with pebbles and stones to form low mounds. Gravegoods were essentially the same as at Termoli: Daunian and *impasto* vessels laid at the feet of the bodies, female personal ornaments including fibulae and pendants, amber beads and glass bead necklaces, and males being equipped with iron spears and knives. The only bronze bowls were also in the male burials.

The Campochiaro cemetery in the upper valley was used from the 6th to the 4th centuries BC (Capini, 1980a). The earlier graves were typical in form to those of the cemeteries in the lower valley, with identical styles of burial. One principal difference can be seen in the gravegoods, however: no

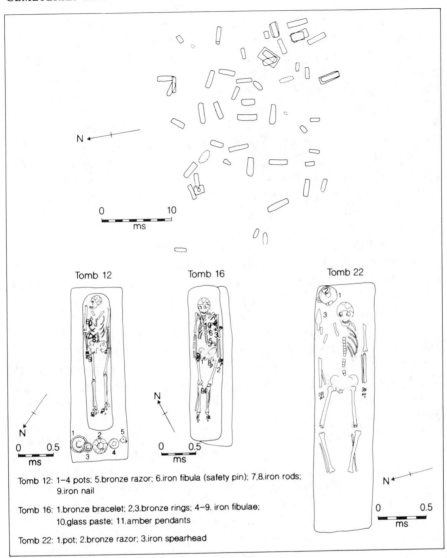

Fig. 69 The Porticone iron age necropolis near Termoli: the general plan of the cemetery and detailed plans of three burials. (Adapted from Di Niro, 1981)

Daunian pottery was used, most of the pottery consisting of locally made *impasto*. Instead of Daunian ware, the fine pottery used was a dark lustrous fabric like Etruscan *bucchero*. Similar fine wares were used in the Pozzilli cemetery near Venafro in the upper Volturno valley (Capini, 1980b), and *bucchero* was the principal fine ware in the contemporary cemeteries of Campania (D'Agostino, 1974, 1977; Frederiksen, 1984).

In addition to the material from the survey and from the recent excavations of settlements and cemeteries, the Superintendency also has a group of stray finds of iron age date from the valley, from collections beginning in the last century. Information on provenance is inevitably very variable, but the majority of these objects almost certainly derives from destroyed graves. The finds are not distributed evenly throughout the valley, reflecting above all processes of urban and agricultural expansion. They concentrate especially around Campobasso, the zone of greatest development during this century, and around the two major settlements of Larino and Termoli in the lower valley. However, they provide further useful insights into the range of material culture of the period and the decorative styles in craftsmanship which linked the valley with other parts of the pensinsula.

About a third of the finds belongs to the earlier part of the Iron Age, down to the 7th century BC. These include two fine cut-and-thrust swords of bronze from the lower valley and a series of bronze spears from the upper valley (Fig. 70). Most of the later iron age material consists of small items of personal ornament typical of the gravegoods from the excavated cemeteries, presumably also deriving from funerary contexts. Such material has been found in both the upper and lower valley. A wealthy hoard of the 6th century was presumably the provenance of some fine metal vessels found near Macchiagódena: an *oinochoe* or jug, a bronze bucket or *situla* with an iron handle, and a bronze *stamnos* (*Sannio*, 1980: 83), thought to have belonged to a Campanian merchant.

The shapes and styles of decoration of most of the small personal ornaments are repeated in the material culture of neighbouring iron age cemeteries, to the north in Abruzzo and west in Campania (D'Agostino, 1980a; Dell' Orto and La Regina, 1978). However, pieces likely to be actual imports from Campania have only been found in the upper valley: the Macchiagódena *oinochoe*, an Etruscan form, was almost certainly manufactured by an Etruscan craftsman in Campania; and the other 'western' pieces, four bronze disc pendants in the Villanovan tradition, were also found in the upper valley, near Sepino (*Sannio*, 1980: 47). Small bronze figurines of Heracles dated to the 6th and 5th centuries BC have been found principally in the upper valley and in the upper Trigno valley. According to the ancient writers, the cult of Heracles was introduced from Campania to the Pentri tribe of the Samnites, whose territory is traditionally located in the upper Trigno and Biferno valleys (Di Niro, 1977). Certainly the cult was important at the sanctuaries in these areas in the Samnite period (Chapter Nine).

The iron age burials of the Biferno valley share a number of similarities with contemporary cemeteries in adjacent regions, though the latter were

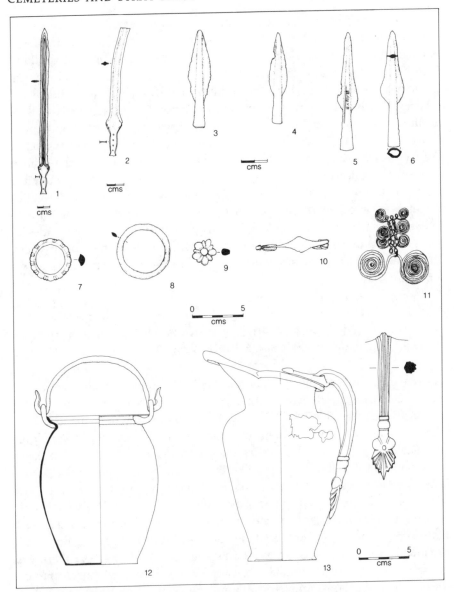

Fig. 70 Stray finds of iron age date from the Biferno valley. [Bronze swords – Larino (1), Montorio dei Frentani (2); bronze spearheads – Guardiaregia (3), Oratino (4), Boiano (5, 6); bronze rings – Torella (7), Montorio dei Frentani (8); bronze bead – Campobasso (9); bronze fibula – Busso (10); bronze pendant – Casalciprano (11); bronze bucket and jug – Macchiagódena (12, 13)]. Main scale refers to 7–13, top right scale to 3–6 (After *Sannio*, 1980)

generally both larger and richer, and there were regional differences in burial customs (Suano, 1991). In both Abruzzo and Apulia, the dominant gravegoods were simple personal ornaments and equipment of the kind found in the Biferno cemeteries: fibulae, razors, knives, and so on. Distinct regional styles have been identified by typological study, the Biferno metalwork sharing in similarities with the adjacent areas both north and south. In terms of pottery, however, whilst the *impasto* funerary vessels in both lower and upper valley cemeteries are typical of the coarse fabrics manufactured at this time throughout the Italian peninsula, the lower valley was on the northern fringe of the production zone of Daunian pottery, whilst the fine wares of the upper-valley cemeteries were like those used to the west. As so often in the valley's history, the lower valley looked primarily to the littoral communities of the Adriatic in its communication networks, whereas the upper valley shared at least as many similarities with the adjacent communities of the Apennines.

IRON AGE SOCIETIES IN THE BIFERNO VALLEY: THE EMERGENCE OF PERMANENT ELITES

As the preceding discussion has described, the Biferno valley witnessed major changes in settlement organization and social complexity in the centuries between 1000 and 500 BC. The survey evidence demonstrates the development of a settlement hierarchy, at the top of which were large nucleated settlements of perhaps two or three dozen houses at least, substantial communities quite unlike the farms and hamlets of the Bronze Age. These villages, clusters of well-built dwellings protected by natural defences and perhaps by enclosure ditches, were probably not only centres of population but also of craft production for commodities such as pottery, metal objects and textiles. Agricultural production now included wine and perhaps olive oil as well as seed crops, and there was probably an increased emphasis on animal secondary products, particularly wool. The large numbers of grindstones and amphoras, as well as the threshing debris, indicate that the villages were centres for the processing and storage of foodstuffs as well as for their consumption. The funerary data demonstrate a parallel elaboration of hierarchy in social organization.

The development of permanent elites is the most striking feature of social change in the Italian Iron Age. The process of stratification was of course most advanced in Etruscan society, but the cemeteries of Abruzzo, Basilicata, Campania, Southern Lazio (Latium) and Apulia have also provided remarkable evidence for the complexity of contemporary societies beyond Etruria (Bietti-Sestieri, 1992; Bottini, 1982, 1986; Cianfarani, 1969; D'Agostino, 1977). In Abruzzo, for example, one male in the Campovalano cemetery was buried with a war cart and equipment for two horses, and a female at Loreto Aprutino wore an iron crown, had at least a dozen bronze fibulae in her hair, elaborate pendants, armbands and a belt of bronze, together with necklaces of amber and glass. An infant at Campovalano was buried with six armbands, an amulet, two iron fibulae each bearing a tiny bronze jug, and an Egyptian scarab. Analyses of the skeletal remains suggest the presence of clearly defined kinship groups, assumed to be patrilocal families, together with an unequal distribution of age and sex classes (Bondioli et al., 1986; Erspamer, 1982; Fornaciari et al., 1984). The populations are dominated by adult males, and this together with the richness of the female graves may be indicative of patrilineal societies in which women were used as vehicles of display for their husbands' wealth (Fig. 71).

Many of the adult male skeletons from the Italian iron age cemeteries have traumatic lesions on the skulls and post-cranial bones, the effects of fighting (Macchiarelli et al., 1981). Furthermore, stone funerary stelae from the major Apulian settlements such as Monte Saraceno frequently show warriors in what seems to be ritualized combat (Nava, 1987). The most extraordinary affirmation of the importance of the warrior in Adriatic society at this time is the remarkable statue of the 'Warrior of Capestrano' found near Capestrano in Abruzzo in 1934 and now in Chieti Museum – a giant figure wearing a tunic and a huge *sombrero*, adorned with arm and neck ornaments and armed with axe, sword, and spear (Fig. 71). The statue is dated to the mid-6th century BC. The evidence seems unequivocal for the emergence of male-dominated elite groups in the Adriatic Iron Age.

The gravegoods of the iron age cemeteries throughout central and southern Italy are the silent witnesses of a quasi-Homeric world of competitive and aggrandizing elites. 'In Homer, we find arms, cauldrons . . . tripods, and iron axes as gifts or exchanges, prizes, payments, or as the *kterea* bestowed on the dead; alongside slaves, women, horses, and rich clothes, these were part of a chieftain's possessions, to be listed with pride, or numbered with exaggeration' (Frederiksen, 1979: 293). Amongst the communities of the Adriatic littoral, this world of ritual combat and aggressive competition for prestige may have extended to piracy at sea: a 6th-century stone stele from a cemetery at Novilara in Marche shows two boats in conflict (Trump, 1965: 163). These craft – long and low, with a crew of perhaps 30 oarsmen and a square sail on a single mast – are seaworthy vessels strongly reminiscent of the world of Odysseus.

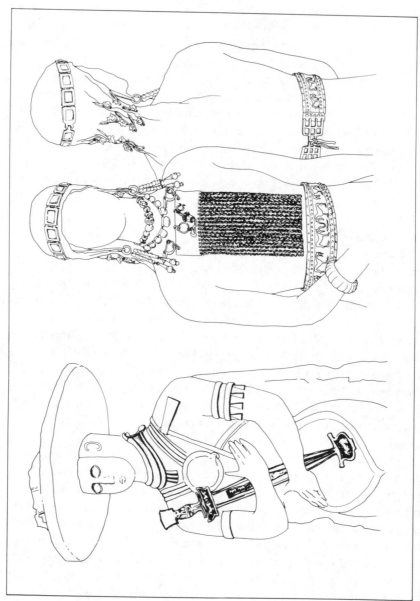

Fig. 71 Male and female status in the Adriatic Iron Age: (left) the costume and weapons of the Warrior of Capestrano and (right) the costume of a woman buried in the Loreto Aprutino cemetery. (Adapted from Cianfarani, 1969: 169 and 186)

The Biferno valley shared in this process of social transformation, but on a much less elaborate scale (Suano, 1991). The richest graves in the Biferno cemeteries are only as rich as those in the middle of the wealth hierarchy of the Abruzzo cemeteries. The absence of child burials, too, compared with the rich infant burials in neighbouring regions, might imply that hereditary power had developed amongst many iron age societies in southern Italy, whereas the emerging elites of the Biferno valley may still have dominated their communities by status achieved in life rather than ascribed by birth. Interesting insights into the lives of these people have been shown by the ongoing analysis of the Guglionesi skeletons and those from Gildone, a contemporary cemetery immediately south of the Biferno valley, indicating much higher mortalities of young males compared with those of the Abruzzo cemeteries – over a third died between twenty and twenty-four (Petrone, 1993). Most of the males had signs of healed traumas and other indications of hard physical labour from a very young age, compared with only a third of the females. The teeth of both sexes, however, were equally in a dreadful condition, again worse than those of contemporary populations in Abruzzo, ascribed to a poor diet very high in carbohydrates.

The process of the emergence of complex societies in peninsular Italy in the Iron Age varied enormously, from the proto-urban and urban communities of the Etruscan city states to the chiefdoms of Apulia, Abruzzo, and Molise. However, every region was characterized by rapid population growth, social hierarchization, and intensification in systems of food production, craft production, exchange and trade. The establishment of the Greek colonies clearly provided an important stimulus to the process of social elaboration, most dramatically in Etruria. Beyond Etruria, distributions of Greek artefacts in cemeteries indicate a primary trading zone stretching some 50–60 kilometres from each colony. The commonest Greek artefacts are pottery associated with wine drinking, together with storage vessels, transport amphoras, small vessels for unguents, and metalwork. The indigenous elites in these areas were probably providing the Greeks with textiles in return for wine, drinking services, and other luxuries, with Greek-style sanctuaries on the edge of the primary trading zones acting as trading emporia (Whitehouse and Wilkins, 1985, 1989).

Systems of gift exchange carried fine table ware and wine in particular beyond the primary trading zone to the elites of outlying regions such as the Biferno valley, as individuals competed for wealth and status (Herring, 1991). Whitehouse and Wilkins conclude that competition for exotic goods provided a critical stimulus to the emergence of local elites in such regions, but that the absence of significant raw materials or opportunities to control critical trade routes prevented the development of the kind of dramatic centralization and nucleation seen in Etruria. The Biferno valley was at the end of this process of change: geographically in terms of exchange links with Greeks and Etruscans; culturally in terms of social elaboration; and chronologically in the tardiness of the process. However, the scale of the transformations in settlement and society in the valley in the first half of the first millennium BC cannot be under-emphasized, particularly in comparison with the preceding millennium. It is tempting to see the emergence of the ethnic groups of the succeeding Samnite period – the Frentani in the lower valley and the Pentri in the upper valley – linked in part at least to the dichotomy in social relations that developed during the Iron Age, with the communities of the lower valley linked in gift exchange networks predominantly with their neighbours along the Adriatic littoral and those in the upper valley sharing more in the Apennine network.

CHAPTER 9
PENTRI, FRENTANI AND THE BEGINNINGS OF URBANIZATION
(c. 500–80 BC)

John Lloyd, with contributions by Graeme Barker, Gill Clark and Derrick Webley

INTRODUCTION

The Biferno valley emerges from the Iron Age as part of ancient Samnium, whose peoples figure prominently in the history of classical Italy. Determined and able warriors, the Samnites led Italian resistance to the expansion of Roman power in a long and bitter series of conflicts from the mid 4th century BC, and were not finally eliminated as a political and military force until the late 80s BC. Thereafter Samnium belonged to Roman Italy until the rise of the Ostrogothic kingdom in the later 5th century AD.

The Romanocentric classical authors portray the Samnites as a hardy, poor and backward mountain people who possessed an archaic political organization and a settlement structure based on the village, supplemented by numerous fortified sites (Brunt, 1971; Salmon, 1967). The terms *urbs* or *polis* were sometimes used of Samnite centres, but none is described as possessing the fine monuments and buildings which to the ancient authors were a defining feature of civilized life. The urbanization of Samnium has therefore usually been regarded as an innovation of the Roman period. Since the 1960s, however, systematic archaeological exploration has accumulated evidence which presents the Samnites in a rather different light – so different, in fact, that the possibility of urban development well in advance of the 1st century BC has begun to be explored (Crawford, 1985: 178; De Benedittis, 1991b: 130; Di Niro, 1991c; La Regina, 1978: 448; Rathbone, 1992, 1993). This chapter examines the extent to which the archaeology of the Biferno valley supports such a reappraisal.

THE HISTORICAL FRAMEWORK

The fragmentary political history of the valley communities in this period relates mostly to the major conflicts in which the Samnites were engaged from the 4th century BC: the three 'Samnite' wars against Rome between 343 and 290 BC; further campaigns against Rome a decade later as allies of Pyrrhus, king of Epirus; the war with Hannibal in the late 3rd century (which split the Samnites); and the war between Rome and the Italian allies – the Social War – of the early 1st century BC (Salmon, 1967).

The upper valley was the heartland of the Pentri, the most resilient of the four tribal Samnite states. There is no doubt that they suffered considerably during the wars of the 4th and 3rd centuries. In the 290s, for example, their capital at Bovianum (modern Boiano) was besieged by Roman troops, who also stormed neighbouring settlements, taking captives and booty, and in the Hannibalic War, when the Pentri, unlike the other Samnites, stood by Rome, the passage of the Carthaginian army through their territory was destructive (Brunt, 1971: 86; Cornell, 1989: 389–91; La Regina, 1989: 428; Salmon, 1967). It is difficult to observe serious long-term effects, however, and they were able to mount formidable armies against Rome in the Social War and again in the late 80s (Brunt, 1971: 443–4).

Rome asserted growing authority over Italy from the 3rd century BC. Although technically independent, the Pentri were obliged, like the other Italians, to sign treaties of alliance with Rome, which compelled them to provide men for the Roman army on demand and probably to pay for their upkeep on campaign (Crawford, 1985: 36; Polybius VI.21.5). Other manifestations of Roman control were the establishment in the 260s BC of a Latin colony at Aesernia (Isernia) and a *praefectura* at Venafrum (Venafro), both within Pentrian territory, and a Latin colony at Beneventum (Benevento) amongst the Samnite Hirpini, about 50 kilometres south of Bovianum. In 180 BC more than forty thousand Ligurians from northern Italy were settled in the Ager Taurasinorum northeast of Beneventum, between the Pentri and the remaining Hirpini (Livy XXXX. 38; Patterson, 1988: 125–7).

The lower valley formed part of the territory of the Frentani, a tribal people not normally considered fully Samnite but closely related by language (Oscan) and probably by ethnic background. A Roman expedition against the Frentani in 320/19 BC is mentioned by Livy (IX. 16.1). In 304 BC they became allies of Rome, with whom they subsequently had friendlier relations than the Pentri. Their leading settlement was Larinum (Larino), which probably acquired a separate political identity (Salmon, 1967: 41; 1982: 21–2). La Regina (1980a: 41) has seen Roman encouragement and the influence of the Latin colony established in 314 BC at Apulian Luceria, about 50 kilometres to the south, in this development. In 217/6 BC Hannibal's troops raided and foraged in Larinum's territory (Polybius III.101), and it was again overrun, by Roman troops, in the Social War (Appian, *Bellum Civile*, 1.52).

The main access to and from the upper valley in this period was probably the Venafrum–Aesernia–Beneventum route through the Apennines, which crossed the head of the valley by Bovianum and Samnite Saepinum, though other routes from Campania crossing the Matese (La Regina, 1984: 208), and from northern Molise, are certain. The valley itself was not an important highway, although the watershed road from Bovianum to Larinum first attested in Roman times was almost certainly the route taken by the Pentrian forces which confronted Hannibal in 217/6 BC (Livy XXII.24.11– 13). Cicero (*pro Cluentio*, 197) hints at regular contacts between Bovianum and Larinum by 66 BC. The main artery of the lower valley was probably the Adriatic highway, which in the Roman period swung inland to Larinum before heading back towards the coast. Other important routes leading to Apulia, mainly via Larinum, can be assumed.

By 80 BC the Samnites had been absorbed within the Roman state. The warfare of the preceding decade (the Social War and Sulla's campaign of terror in 82/1) was probably the most damaging of all the conflicts which touched the region, although Strabo's description (V.4.11) of cities entirely destroyed or reduced to villages is not reliable in all its details (Chapter Ten). The brief but bloody regime of a pro-Sullan faction which came to power at Larinum in the late 80s is described by Cicero in the *pro Cluentio*.

THE ARCHAEOLOGICAL SURVEY: SITE DATING AND DEFINITION

A little south Italian plain and painted fine ware and late 'Daunian' pottery (Chapter Eight) of the 5th/4th centuries BC was found by the survey, but the principal dating evidence for sites of this time period is supplied by Campanian-style black gloss pottery of the later 4th–1st centuries BC. A few sherds of imported Campanian black gloss (Campana A, Campana B and possibly Campana C) were identified amongst the survey finds, but the rest seems to have been made in or near the valley (p. 205). Dating is based mainly on comparisons with the productions of other parts of Italy (Morel, 1981) and will undoubtedly be modified by the building of local sequences, as recent work suggests (De Benedittis, 1990b, with bibliography).

As in other areas of Italy, black gloss wares seem to have circulated until the closing decades of the 1st century BC. The very many surface scatters which produced undiagnostic black gloss sherds could therefore belong in theory to the Samnite or to the early Roman period, or both. However, most of the more closely datable sherds found by the survey seem to belong to the 3rd and 2nd centuries BC (II: Chapter Four). First-century BC

thin-walled wares, which appear in some numbers in a pottery group of
c. 75 BC at Gravina in Apulia (Hayes, forthcoming) are very rare on Biferno
valley sites and none was recognized amongst the survey finds.

Knowledge of the development of Samnite coarse wares is at an early
stage. However, it is likely that *impasto* and 'impastoid' pottery in the iron
age tradition (Chapter Eight) continued to be made into the 4th century
and perhaps beyond (Capini, 1980: 213.9; Di Niro, 1980c: 304.27), with
obvious problems for dating scrappy surface finds. *Impasto*-like sherds
were found at several survey sites with black gloss wares but no clearly
earlier material, and in such cases most probably indicate early Samnite
rather than iron age occupation. Excavated coarse ware groups of the 3rd–
1st centuries BC from the valley are overwhelmingly made up of wheel-
turned wares (which also appear in earlier deposits), and some distinction
between late Samnite and Roman imperial forms can be made on the basis
of finds from the Matrice (A166) excavations (Capini, 1984; De Benedittis,
1988a, 1990b; II: Chapter Four).

The great majority of Samnite and Roman sites appeared as scatters of
pottery and tile, and a number also produced other categories of finds,
including coins, architectural and decorative elements, metal objects,
millstones, loomweights and spindle whorls. In only one case (site D62 in
the upper valley; II: Chapter Three) were standing remains datable to the
Samnite period encountered; *in situ* walls of Roman date were more
frequent but still rare (Chapter Ten). Clearance piles of stone rubble and
tile at the edges of fields and around trees were observed at several
classical sites. Another tell-tale sign was a spread of discoloured (usually
darker) earth within a freshly ploughed field, often closely correlated with
the scatter of archaeological debris. A particularly good example was site
A249 below Larino (Figs. 23 and 89).

Sites have been classified as 'certain', 'probable' and 'possible' according
to the criteria used in Chapter Eight (for the survey methodology see also
Chapter Three). A problem in site definition was posed by multi-period
assemblages, which make up a large percentage of the iron age/Samnite/
Roman sites found by the survey. In such cases the datable 'Samnite' (or
'Roman') material may fall below the notional site threshold, although the
total number of sherds substantially exceeds it. Site A185 is a case in point,
producing three black gloss sherds, six sherds of Roman imperial fine ware
(early to late) and sixty coarse ware fragments, datable only as 'Samnite/
Roman'. Here the view is taken that the black gloss sherds are indicative of
a pre-Imperial phase of settlement. There is support both in the frequency
of such patterning in the survey data as a whole and in the results of
excavation at multi-period sites for this view, as discussed below.
However, an alternative approach, categorizing the black gloss sherds only

as 'sporadic', is clearly possible. Establishing site size for the various phases of a large multi-period scatter is also problematical. Most of the ten or so excavated rural sites in and near the valley seem to have expanded under the early Empire and contracted in the late Roman period, but this was not always the case and no general rule can be inferred.

Where possible, the survey units with Samnite and Roman finds have been divided into four size categories: A (large), with a surface area greater than 7500 square metres; B (medium), 7500-1500 square metres; C (small), less than 1500 square metres; and D, sporadic material or individual finds.

SETTLEMENT TRENDS, *c.*500-350 BC

During the first century and a half of the Samnite period in the valley it is likely that the village-dominated settlement hierarchy established in the late Iron Age persisted without major adjustment. The difficulties of dating in this period are considerable, but about 90 per cent of the 120 or so survey findspots with certain or possible iron age material (Chapter Eight) also produced Campanian-style black gloss wares, suggesting continuity of activity, and a small number of new sites is probable.

Larinum seems to have grown in importance in the 5th and early 4th centuries, as indicated by its wide trading contacts, particularly with Magna Graecia (Di Niro, 1991c; Faustoferri, 1989, 1991). It was perhaps through this centre that the 5th/4th century BC south Italian fine pottery found by the survey at half a dozen or so sites in its vicinity was distributed. Fourth-century and later Gnathia ware, which was made at Taranto and other Apulian centres (Kenrick, 1985: 67-8), also reached the lower valley (Ceglia, 1991; Di Niro, 1991c). Two elaborately decorated loom weights from site A267 below Larinum are probably contemporary (Fig. 78). They have stylistic affinities with material from Apulian Lucera, and like the imported pottery suggest the continuation into the early Hellenistic period of the Daunian exchange networks established in the late Iron Age.

South Italian fine wares seem scarcely to have penetrated the upper valley, with very few finds noted beyond the survey sites A143 (almost certainly the village of Fagifulae) and B65, a little to its north (Fig. 72). The frontier between the Pentri and the Frentani probably fell in this part of the valley (Salmon, 1967: 25).

The upper valley has, nonetheless, produced some remarkable finds suggestive of contacts with the Greek world: at Roccaspromonte, between Oratino and Castropignano (Fig. 72), a near life-size terracotta statue of Athena dating probably to the 5th century BC was dug up in the 18th century, and a Greek marble head, probably of a goddess and dated to the

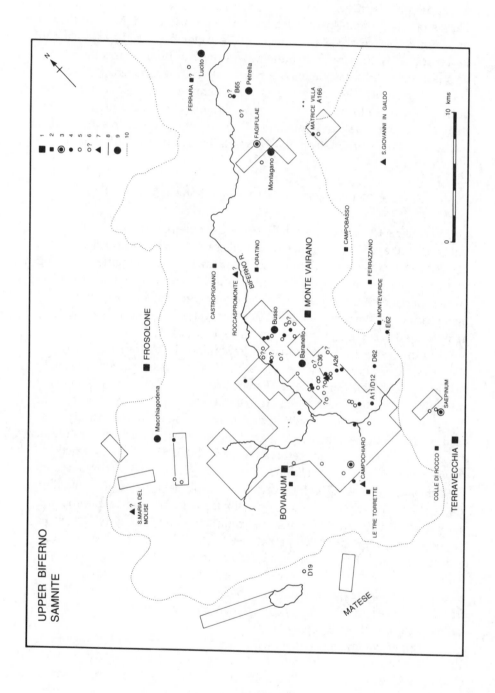

UPPER BIFERNO
SAMNITE

mid 5th century BC, was found built into a nearby church (La Regina, 1978: 305–6; De Benedittis, 1988a: 32; Mirone, 1924; Paribeni, 1984: 105–7). In addition, a stone altar with an Oscan inscription dating probably to the 2nd century BC (Vetter, 1953: 158) was found with the Athena. If the statues were not objects of exchange, plunder or some other kind of movement long after their manufacture, they suggest the early establishment of a rural sanctuary – a kind of site that was to become an important element of the Pentrian landscape, as discussed below – and shed interesting light on the acceptance of Greek gods by the Pentri.

The upper valley seems to have had many fewer sites of this period than the lower valley. The striking difference is perhaps to be explained by a greater preference for nucleated settlement in the uplands, some possibly in defensible positions now overgrown with dense vegetation. The major later hillfort at Monte Vairano has produced sporadic finds of archaic or classical metalwork (De Benedittis, 1980: 324–5), and early activity (preceding their stone fortifications) is also documented at the La Rocca *oppidum* near Oratino (De Benedittis, forthcoming; some *impasto* sherds were found by the survey below it at site D28) and the Civitella sanctuary above Campochiaro (Capini, 1982: 11). It is also noteworthy that late Apennine bronze age pottery has been recovered from the excavated Samnite and Roman rural site at Matrice (A166), although the form of the early settlement is not known and there are too few data to suggest persistence of activity until the period of Samnite occupation, which seems to begin *c*.200 BC (Lloyd, forthcoming). A number of *impasto* or impastoid sherds was found on other dispersed Samnite sites, such as A11/D12; they need not pre-date the 4th/3rd centuries, but it is also possible that they indicate the beginnings of settlement at these sites in the Iron Age – they are the sites marked in Figure 65 by a circle accompanied by a question mark.

SETTLEMENT TRENDS *c*.350–80 BC

Sites producing Campanian-style black gloss pottery are by far the most numerous of any period of comparable length in the valley's pre-modern history. Many of these, including all the major centres, most of the sanctuaries and cemeteries, and several lesser settlements, are known from

Fig. 72 Samnite settlement in the upper Biferno valley (4th–1st centuries BC). 1. major fortified site; 2. minor fortified site; 3. village; 4. sanctuary; 5. farmstead/villa; 6. probable farmstead; 7. cemetery/ tomb; 8. approximate limits of walked areas; 9. modern town/village; 10. valley watershed.

other research. The survey adds just over 100 certain and 80 probable sites, together with 44 possible sites (although the latter can rarely be dated precisely within the Samnite/Roman period). Over 40 sporadic finds of black gloss sherds were also recorded. The abundant data for settlement structures in this period are discussed first for the upper valley and then for the lower valley, with the evidence for economic and social structures then summarized for the valley as a whole.

THE UPPER VALLEY

In the upper valley, this period witnessed a remarkable intensification of Pentrian settlement, which resulted in a highly structured landscape of major and minor hillforts, villages, rural sanctuaries, villas and farmsteads (Fig. 72). The critical period in the formation of this landscape was probably the later 4th and 3rd centuries, with development continuing during the 2nd century BC.

HILLFORTS

Fortified hilltop sites, equated by modern scholars with the *urbes, oppida* and *castella* (and equivalent Greek terms) of the classical writers, are typical of ancient Samnium, with more than 100 examples now identified (Oakley, forthcoming). More than a dozen are known from the upper valley, a density which doubtless reflects the importance of this area as the heartland of the Pentri. They are all located in highly defensible positions on or near the summits of hills and mountains, in some cases more than 1200 metres above sea level. Their fortifications are usually built of rough polygonal masonry and vary enormously in extent and complexity. Most of the larger sites are found on the margins of the Boiano and Sepino plains.

The literary sources leave little doubt that the leading Pentrian settlement was Bovianum (modern Boiano) – already a large and wealthy centre by the late 4th century BC according to Livy (IX. 31.4: *caput . . . Pentrorum Samnitium longe ditissimum atque opulentissimum armis virisque*). Two fortifications are known on the mountain which rises behind Boiano, and traces of what seems to have been a well-organized Samnite settlement are emerging on the lower slopes underneath the present town (De Benedittis, 1977, 1991d). The largest of all the hillforts of the area, however (and the best known archaeologically), was Monte Vairano, 14 kilometres to the north, its *c.* 50 hectares defended by walls stretching for three kilometres, with three main gates and a series of towers, in part probably timber-built

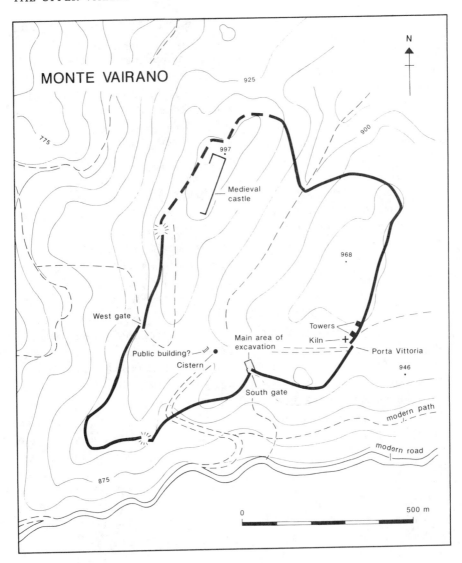

Fig. 73 Monte Vairano: plan of the *oppidum*; house 'LN' and other structures lie in the main excavated area. (After De Benedittis, 1991c: 48 and 50)

(De Benedittis, 1974, 1980, 1988a, 1990a, 1991a, 1991b, 1991c; Fig. 73). The ancient name of the settlement is unknown, but a case has been made for its identification with Aquilonia, near which the elite Samnite 'Linen Legion' was destroyed by the army of Papirius Cursor in a famous engagement described by Livy (X.38–42; La Regina, 1980a: 39–40; 1989: 419–20). The clustering of lesser fortified centres near Monte Vairano is notable.

Pottery, tile and other finds have been discovered at all the major sites and a number of the minor ones (De Benedittis, 1988a; La Regina, 1984; Oakley, forthcoming). The largest centres certainly housed stable communities, at least for some periods of their existence. At Monte Vairano, for example, excavations have brought to light elements of what seems to have been a substantial settlement of the 3rd to early 1st centuries BC. Although only a tiny percentage of the site has yet been investigated, there is evidence for public and private building, artisan and religious activity, and an array of artefacts from many corners of the Mediterranean world. There is no doubt that Bovianum too was permanently occupied, and the same is probably true of Terravecchia, above Saepinum.

Presumably the major hillforts also acted, at times of crisis, as refuges for the surrounding populations. The minor sites were probably temporary refuges in the main, or occupied only seasonally (De Benedittis, 1977; Frederiksen, 1968). Most hillforts controlled access to good upland grazing. Some of the very high small sites dominated routes across the Matese and had a clear military purpose (La Regina, 1984: 208–9).

Networks of hillforts, such as the upper valley group, have been seen as unified defensive systems for territorial control (Conta Haller, 1978; De Benedittis, 1977; Di Niro, 1991f; La Regina, 1975), with the protection of long-distance transhumance routes proposed as an element of this view. A central problem, however, is the dating of their fortifications. Construction technique is not a precise indicator, and so far in the upper valley stratified pottery provides a *terminus post quem* only at Monte Vairano and the minor centre of La Rocca near Oratino, where a date not earlier than the late 4th century is indicated (De Benedittis, 1980: 326ff; De Benedittis, forthcoming), and a *terminus ante quem* at Terravecchia, where a 4th century date for the walls has been suggested (Colonna, 1962). It is very probable that Bovianum had also acquired stone defences by this time, but in our present state of knowledge some of the other fortifications of the area may be later, some conceivably as late as the early 1st century BC (the Social War).

VILLAGES

The ancient authors speak frequently of Samnite villages, and these are usually seen as settlements on open, lower ground, perhaps enclosed by palisades. The village is usually considered to have been the principal form of Samnite permanent settlement and the one best adapted to the limited agricultural opportunities of the uplands and the broken country on the margins (La Regina, 1980a: 37; Patterson, 1988: 115–6; Salmon, 1967: 79–80).

There are three main candidates for villages in the upper valley. San Martino near Campochiaro, 2 kilometres from the sanctuary described below, has surface remains including structures and much pottery of Hellenistic date (Capini, 1982: 10–11; La Regina, 1984: 203). At Saepinum, a town site in the Roman period, abundant traces of a highly developed Samnite settlement of the 2nd and early 1st centuries BC have been found, with several mosaic pavements, part of a house with an *impluvium*, an industrial building interpreted as a *fullonica* (for fulling or washing wool or textiles) and evidence for tile and pottery production (Ambrosetti, 1958; Matteini Chiari, 1982: 19–26). Redeposited material of the 4th century BC has also been recovered. A third village may be indicated by the cluster of sites recorded by the survey near a small rural sanctuary (site C36) on Colle Sparanise (Figs. 24 and 72). The finds included a terracotta architectural revetment and an Oscan tile stamp (II: Chapter Four, F46, 228), which point to a sophisticated building or buildings, possibly of public character. It cannot be ruled out that the pieces belonged originally to the C36 sanctuary, but if so they had been moved several hundred metres by the time of their discovery. The configuration of material around C36 in fact resembles the 10-hectare Samnite settlement discovered near San Vincenzo in the upper Volturno valley, where there is also evidence for a sanctuary and possibly other large-scale buildings (Hodges and Mitchell, 1985: 5–6; Patterson, 1985: 219).

In the middle valley the probable site of the Roman town of Fagifulae (site A143) produced surface finds which date back at least to the 3rd century BC. Its mid-slope position and apparent lack of fortifications suggest another site in the *vicus* category.

SANCTUARIES

The rural sanctuary was also a characteristic element of Samnite settlement. The most elaborate of these was Pietrabbondante in northern Molise, probably the centre of Pentrian cult and an important place of political assembly (La Regina, 1980b; La Regina, 1984: 230–257). The most impressive sanctuary of the upper Biferno valley lay halfway between Bovianum and Saepinum on the lower slopes of the Matese, at Civitella above the modern village of Campochiaro, with splendid views over the Boiano basin (Capini, 1980c, 1982, 1984, 1991). Intensive cult activity seems to have begun here in the second half of the 4th century BC. A stout perimeter wall of neatly fitted polygonal masonry enclosed a roughly triangular *temenos*, measuring some 150×125 metres. The heavily robbed remains of a 2nd century BC prostyle Ionic temple with terracotta architectural decoration and a long stoa-like structure, as yet unexcavated, are the principal known buildings, approached through a handsome gateway. Numerous stamped roof tiles from public workshops suggest a state interest in the sanctuary, while other finds indicate significant wealth and sophistication amongst its clientele. The site has been linked with the *Herculaneum* which Livy mentions as taken by the Roman consul Spurius Carvilius in 293 BC, and the *(fanum) Hercul(is) Rani* of the Peutinger Table (Capini, 1982; La Regina, 1984: 203–8; La Regina, 1989: 422–3).

The Colle Sparanise sanctuary (C36) occupied an equally commanding position on the northern side of the Boiano plain, at a similar altitude (Fig. 7). It was probably visible from Campochiaro. Small-scale excavations undertaken as part of the project in 1975 found part of a building which had a tiled roof, terracotta architectural elements including part of a probable antefix with *potnia theron* scene (comparable with examples from Pietrabbondante), fragments of terracotta statuary, and a bronze club from a Hercules statuette (II: Chapter Three; II: Chapter Four; F25, 41–45). Augering traced a dark charcoal-rich horizon spreading for some 25 metres from the building, and further archaeological deposits over a much larger area. Not enough is known to reconstruct the layout of the site with any confidence, but the minor sanctuary at San Giovanni in Galdo, 18 kilometres to the east, consisted of a rectangular precinct containing a small, almost square shrine and flanking porticoes (Di Niro, 1980b; La Regina, 1984: 295–8; Fig. 74). The finds from C36 are roughly contemporary with those from San Giovanni in Galdo, with the earliest identifiable pottery belonging probably to the 3rd century BC.

A complex sacred landscape can therefore be postulated for the upper valley, with a very few major sanctuaries like Campochiaro situated at nodal points in the communications network, rather more second-order sites like C36 operating mainly at village level and, very possibly, a third and more primitive category of cult site with guardian spirits venerated by local farmers and shepherds (Salmon, 1967: 143–81; cf. Matteini Chiari, 1982: fig.1). We can perhaps glimpse something of this complexity in the widespread distribution of bronze statuettes in Pentrian territory, amongst which Hercules is much the most popular, many from sites with known archaeological remains but many others consisting of isolated finds (Di Niro, 1977).

FARMSTEADS AND VILLAS

Although the literary sources make no mention of isolated farms amongst the Samnites, it is now clear from archaeological discoveries that they were an important element of the settlement pattern (Di Niro, 1991f, 1993; Lloyd,

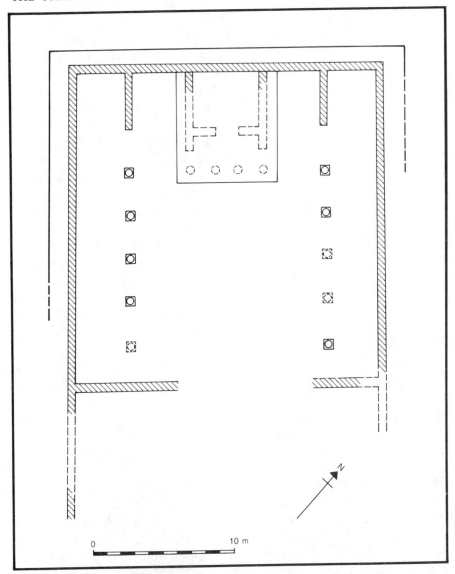

Fig. 74 The Samnite sanctuary at San Giovanni in Galdo, *c.* 100 BC. The reconstructed ground plan of the central shrine or treasury is based on the contemporary small temple at Schiavi d'Abruzzo (La Regina, 1976: 232). (After Di Niro, 1980b: 272 and La Regina, 1984: 297)

1991a; Patterson, 1985, 1987). Given the unfavourable survey conditions of the upper valley (Chapter Three), we should see the 20 certain and 25 probable sites identified, together with 9 possible sites, as the bare minimum of those which once existed in the walked areas. This figure does not include the cluster of scatters close to the C36 sanctuary, which have been interpreted (with C36) as a single nucleated site, as discussed above. It is likely that most parts of the countryside saw some kind of human exploitation, although a concentration in the vicinity of the major centres is clear (Fig. 72). Areas devoid of finds tended to be those where pasture, scrub or forest was at its densest, but even here artefacts were occasionally encountered, as on the *altopiano* of Letino (site D19).

Few sites were discovered on the Boiano and Sepino plains, suggesting that, as today, they were exploited in the main by farmers based in the communities on their edges. Sporadic finds of artefacts, perhaps representing manuring debris, were frequent, however, and together with the site scatters support the geomorphological evidence that post-classical alluviation in the basins has not been extensive (Chapter Four). Away from these 'agro-settlements' isolated farmsteads were fairly common, particularly on the low hills north of the Boiano basin around the modern villages of Baranello and Busso. The distribution of wells and springs here, as well as the light sandy soils well-suited to cereal cultivation, clearly favoured the development of a dispersed settlement system within a few kilometres of Monte Vairano and Bovianum. Around Fagifulae, lower down the valley and in similarly broken topography, the few sites discovered also lay at some distance from the settlement. It is likely that the dispersed farmsteads were occupied on a year-round basis, but some seasonal use cannot be discounted.

Trial excavations were carried out at sites A11/D12, A26 and D62 principally to obtain stratified pottery and faunal and botanical material (II: Chapter Three). Although these were too small-scale to reveal much of the overall plan and organization of the sites, the material culture was strongly suggestive of domestic occupation and agricultural activities dating from the 3rd/2nd centuries BC. The finds included fine and coarse pottery, lamps, storage jars, coins, a loomweight, a millstone fragment, animal bones and carbonized plant remains. An apotropaic phallus carved on the outer wall of D62 finds parallels at several Italian villas (Lugli, 1957: 96). Although plough damage had destroyed most of the archaeology at A11/D12, structural features included stone rubble, traces of beaten earth floors, fragments of daub with wattle impressions and a shallow mortar-lined tank, perhaps a treading-floor or, possibly, an *impluvium*. It seems probable that these sites were farmsteads or *villae rusticae*, not unlike the modest contemporary examples from Etruria, Campania, Apulia and Basilicata (Arthur, 1991a; Carter, 1980; Gadd, 1986; Rossiter, 1978; Volpe, 1990).

Our best evidence for the appearance and organization of a Samnite farmstead comes from recent excavations near Cercemaggiore, 12 kilo-

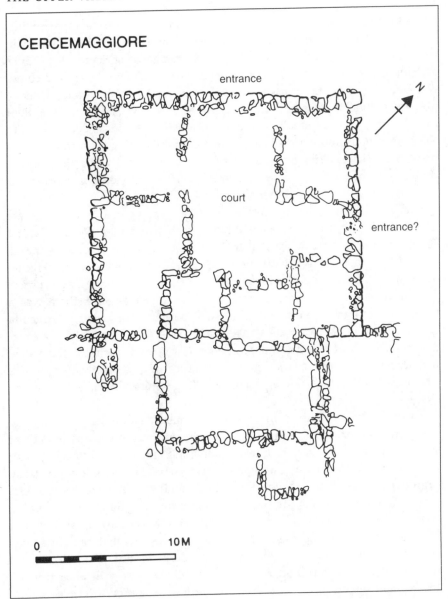

Fig. 75 The Samnite farmstead at Cercemaggiore. (After Di Niro, 1993: 16)

metres southeast of Campobasso (Di Niro, 1991d, 1993). The site dates
from at least the 3rd century BC and was abandoned in the 2nd century BC.
At the end of its life the building consisted of an almost square module
(19×17 metres), adapted at the rear for outbuildings which may have
served as stables (Fig. 75). The main entrance to the farmhouse led to a

central court, around which lay a series of more or less rectangular rooms. Those flanking the entrance contained hearths and were probably the main domestic accommodation. Processing and storage of agricultural produce are indicated by a small mortar-lined basin, several *dolia* and other container vessels. The outer walls at Cercemaggiore were built of heavy polygonal blocks of local limestone, the interior walls (or at least their foundations) were of smaller roughly trimmed limestone blocks, dry-laid. Many iron nails and cramps suggest a plentiful use of timber, and the roof was tiled. The exterior surfaces were of beaten earth, while the internal floors used the natural rock with levelling layers of stone slabs, mortar and tile fragments.

Similar enclosure/terrace walls of rough polygonal masonry were found at the Matrice farm (site A166; Fig. 85) and at D62 (**II**: Chapter Three). Many late Republican villas on the hillsides of northern Campania demonstrate a similar construction method, though with more skilfully dressed and fitted blocks (Arthur, 1991a: 64). Some Samnite *villae rusticae* may have had more elaborate features than Cercemaggiore: there was a limestone column drum at A11/D12 (**II**: Chapter Three), and a terracotta gutter spout, in the form of a male head, was found at Matrice (Lloyd, forthcoming). A domestic building near Capracotta north of the valley had traces of a portico, though the structure may be associated with a sanctuary rather than an agrarian site (La Regina, 1984: 269; Rainini, 1984).

Towards the bottom of the settlement hierarchy in the upper valley were simpler structures, in many cases perhaps no more than cottages or shacks. At Matrice, the rectilinear polygonal masonry farmstead may have been preceded by a small sub-rectangular building of fairly primitive construction (Lloyd 1991a; forthcoming). Archaeology suggests that simple homesteads were probably common throughout Italy (Barker *et al.*, 1986; Perkins and Attolini, 1992). A few sites with pottery but lacking tile might represent the surface traces of thatched buildings similar to the *pagliara* or *pagliaio* of modern Molise (Fig. 60): found normally near the farmhouse but occasionally at some distance from it, the *pagliara* served as a store for straw, fodder or agricultural equipment, but from time to time was used as a temporary home for humans and animals (Sardella and Sardella, 1989). On occasions it could act as a permanent home for the very poor – bringing to mind the destitute market gardener in Apuleius' *Golden Ass* (IX.32) who lived in just such a hut. The small rock shelter frequented in the neolithic period at Ponte Regio (site C63) in the upper valley also produced a few black gloss sherds and is an example of the humblest category of occupation site, perhaps a casual camp for herders (Fig. 44).

THE LOWER VALLEY

The later 4th and 3rd centuries BC seem to mark a watershed in the settlement history of the lower valley, as in the upper valley. Larinum emerged clearly as its leading centre, and the countryside saw much new activity (Fig. 76).

TOWNS AND VILLAGES

Larinum, which controlled the best agricultural land in the lower valley and was the hub of its communications network, began to issue coins in the 3rd century BC and was to acquire municipal status at the very beginning of the Roman period (c. 80 BC, or shortly afterwards). These factors, together with indications that it possessed a well-defined territory by the late 3rd century BC (Livy XXVII. 43.10; Polybius III. 101.3), have long suggested a place of special importance, and its political autonomy in relation to the Frentanian state is likely (above, p. 182).

The archaeology of Larinum strongly supports the idea of an early date for the urban centre. Traces of a carefully laid-out street system of the late 4th or early 3rd century, accompanied by new monumental building techniques using handsome ashlar masonry, have recently come to light, and structures and fittings datable to the 3rd or 2nd century BC include a sacred precinct, an artisan quarter, a large atrium house and mosaic pavements (Di Niro, 1980c, 1991c). The town's coins, together with graffiti on pottery, show the use not only of Oscan but also of Greek and Latin (Cantilena, 1991; Di Niro, 1980c: 286) – a remarkable illustration of cultural penetration.

At about the time that Larinum was emerging as a town, several communities in the middle and lower valley seem to have declined. The late iron age villages just north of Casacalenda (site B287, perhaps the *Kalena* of Polybius III. 101. 3) and at Guglionesi (sites A90, 91, 92) show a relatively slight presence after the 4th century, and much the same picture occurs near Termoli, from a sample of more than 140 tombs (Di Niro, 1991b, 1991c). It is reasonably clear, however, that other villages survived more vigorously, or were founded after the rise of Larinum – as we might expect, given the administrative and organizational needs of a large area with an increasingly dense rural population.

Apart from Kalena, the sites of Gereonium, Buca, Uscosium and perhaps Cliternia emerge from the literary sources as candidates for villages of this period, although very little is known of them (La Regina, 1980a, 1984). The survey offers other possible village sites: in the lower valley, site A198 overlooking the Biferno–Cigno confluence at the edge of the Larino plain,

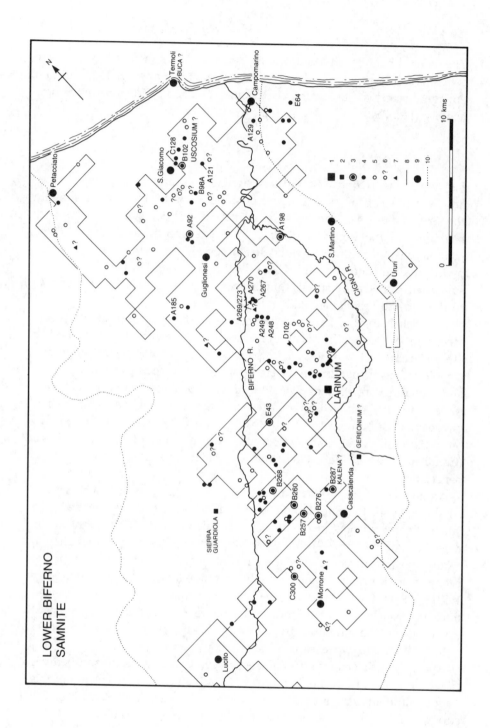

LOWER BIFERNO
SAMNITE

and site B102 on the dissected plateau south of Termoli; and in the middle valley sites B257, B260, B268, B276, C300 and E43 (Fig. 76). Nearly all these sites were inhabited until the late Roman period or beyond, and all were at some point in their existence very large, with surface remains ranging in extent from c.7500 square metres (C300) to a massive 16 hectares (B102). This ranks them in the *vicus*/villa and *vicus* (village) size categories adopted by archaeological surveys elsewhere in southern Italy (Small, 1991: 208). Recent investigations at San Martino (A198), San Giacomo (B102) and Santa Maria Casalpiano (C300) have confirmed the presence of substantial buildings of Samnite and Roman date (Fig. 87), and the latter site has produced several late Republican mosaic pavements similar to those from pre-Roman Saepinum in the upper valley. The sites have been interpreted as villas by their excavators (Ceglia, 1993; De Benedittis *et al.*, 1993: 19), but in the absence of full exploration the possibility that they were villages or hamlets cannot yet perhaps be ruled out – an issue further discussed in Chapter Ten. San Giacomo and B268 probably originated before the 4th century BC, but the other sites seem to begin in the 4th/3rd centuries or later.

In the Frentanian valley there is a dearth of the hilltop fortifications which are so characteristic of Pentrian territory. This may result in part from a comparative lack of exploration – recently, for example, rough polygonal walls have been discovered near Castelmauro and Guardalfiera in the middle valley (De Benedittis *et al.*, 1993: 17), and similar remains are reported from Gerione (possibly Gereonium) between Casacalenda and Larinum (La Regina, 1984: 300). However, no visible traces of wall circuits survive at the other sites discussed above, although some including Larinum itself were situated in elevated, readily defensible positions. They may then have been open settlements; or, more probably, they were enclosed by wooden palisades, in some cases possibly supplemented by earth banks and ditches.

The lower valley also has little to show presently in the way of the rural sanctuaries. Larinum was an important religious centre, but in the countryside evidence is confined at present to a sanctuary of the 3rd/2nd centuries BC near the Roman villa of Arcora (site E64; La Regina, 1984: 307), and to finds of bronze Hercules statuettes (Di Niro, 1977), which are much fewer in number than in the uplands. The distribution of archaic terracotta statuary (Stelluti, 1988: fig. 222; Fig. 77), if these belong to public and not

Fig. 76 Samnite settlement in the lower Biferno valley (4th–1st centuries BC). 1. major centre; 2. minor centre/fortification; 3. *vicus*/villa; 4. farmstead/villa; 5. probable farmstead; 6. possible farmstead; 7. cemetery/tomb; 8. approximate limits of walked areas; 9. modern town/village; 10. valley watershed.

Fig. 77 6th/5th century BC terracotta head from site B198, below Larinum (II: Chapter Four: F40; height 8.5 cms). (Photograph: Graeme Barker)

Fig. 78 Loomweights with head of (?) Athena from site A267, below Larinum (II: Chapter Four: F48–9; scale in cms). (Photograph: Graeme Barker)

private cult, hints at a more dispersed pattern of worship in earlier times, and the centralizing forces associated with the rise of Larinum may have had a religious dimension. Although it is unlikely that the densely populated countryside lacked shrines, they remain for the moment largely invisible.

VILLAS AND FARMSTEADS

The great majority of the 83 certain, 57 probable and 35 possible survey sites of this period appears to have been medium and small scatters, categories B and C. Sites of medium size were much fewer than small sites, although the latter category includes all the examples of 'possible' sites, many of which can only be dated as 'Samnite/Roman'. A high percentage of sites in the certain and probable group also produced iron age and/or Roman finds. There is little doubt that, as in the upper valley, the medium and small range contains a great variety of sites connected with the ancient use of the countryside, and that surface remains may be a very imperfect guide to their character. However, we are probably justified in concluding that most of them represent the remains of villas, farmsteads or buildings related to agricultural or pastoral exploitation.

The development of agrarian economies geared to surplus production may be deduced from the early urbanization of Larinum and from Cicero's *pro Cluentio* of 66 BC, where the wealthy landowning aristocracy of the town is shown possessing large estates by the early 1st century BC (p. 208). As we saw above, some category A sites were probably large villas, and at Santa Maria Casalpiano (C300), part of a wealthy *domus* with at least four mosaic pavements of the late 2nd or 1st century BC may belong to the *pars urbana* of a villa (De Benedittis *et al.*, 1993). However, the clearest archaeological evidence so far for large-scale agricultural production in this period comes from the neighbouring Trigno valley, at Canneto near Terventum (Fig. 88), where excavations have revealed a late Samnite and Roman villa whose installations for wine or oil production rival those of sites like Gragnano in Campania (Di Niro, 1982, 1991g; Rossiter, 1978: 41–3).

Smaller villas, perhaps better characterized as substantial farmsteads, were numerous in the lower valley, especially in the territory of Larinum. They included medium-size sites like A129 and A270, which produced only black gloss finewares and, almost certainly, the early phases of sizeable sites like A248, A249, B98A, E37 and others which survived into the late Roman period. As a general rule, the possible villas of this period tended to be situated at some distance from the large centres, with smaller sites occupying the immediate and middle hinterland, especially around Larinum.

Little can be said about the smaller sites, which rarely produced more than pottery and tile fragments. Most were probably poor peasant farmsteads, similar to those of the upper valley. Some sites were probably tombs, such as D102 (located, significantly, on Colle dell' Uomomorto – 'Dead Man's Hill'), which produced several joining fragments of a south Italian krater. The remains of poor tile graves, often clustered, were found near several villas/farmsteads (A121, A249, A269, A273, C138), but unfortunately they were seldom closely datable within the Samnite/Roman period.

THE AGRICULTURAL ECONOMY (JAL, GB, GC, DW)

The archaeological evidence for Samnite animal husbandry consists primarily of a series of faunal samples, mostly small, which derive from a variety of sites within the settlement hierarchy (II: Chapter Seven). At the invitation of the Superintendency, refuse deposits at the Pietrabbondante sanctuary, between temple A and the theatre-temple complex B, and at the Campochiaro sanctuary, were sampled to provide comparisons with the material from the project excavations at the small rural sanctuary of Colle

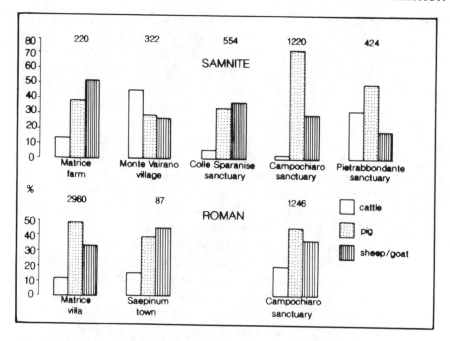

Fig. 79 Stock frequencies at Samnite and Roman sites. The numbers refer to the numbers of identifiable fragments.

Sparanise. Faunal material from domestic contexts consists of samples from occupation deposits by the south gate of Monte Vairano and from the excavations of the Matrice farmstead after the survey (Clark, forthcoming). The total Samnite faunal sample consists of less than three thousand identifiable fragments, but there is a number of repeated associations and contrasts between the different samples that are probably significant (Fig. 79).

All the samples are dominated by the bones of the main domestic species: cattle, pig, and sheep/goat, together with occasional fragments of horse and dog. The best evidence for domestic consumption patterns comes from Matrice, where sheep/goats and pigs were the principal remains (51 per cent and 37 per cent respectively) and cattle very few (12 per cent). The frequencies of these species at Monte Vairano were roughly a third each, but given that the deposits there were not sieved, there is a strong possibility that the smaller species are under-represented, perhaps considerably. Butchery on site is indicated by the presence of head and feet bones of the main food species. The sheep were killed as lambs, shearlings, and as mature animals, the pigs at one or two years old (though sometimes older at Monte Vairano), the few cattle sometimes young but mainly mature. Two cattle phalanges from Monte Vairano had the morphological characteristics of width and foreshortening commonly found in working cattle.

The faunal samples from the sanctuaries show that the animals sent there for slaughter in the cult rites were not a simple cross-section of Samnite domestic stock. At Campochiaro, pigs formed 72 per cent of the sample according to the number of identifiable fragments and 64 per cent according to the minimum number of individuals, with the respective figures for sheep/goats being 28 per cent and 32 per cent. Male pigs were twice as common in the food refuse as female pigs according to the number of canine teeth. The pigs and the sheep were prime animals only a year old, but the few cattle eaten were old animals as on the domestic sites. Colle Sparanise had similar cattle and pigs to Campochiaro, but the sheep and goats were older, suggesting a typical cull from the local subsistence system. Pietrabbondante is unique in the frequency of prime beef cattle. In addition to the main domestic stock, the food refuse at the sanctuaries included birds (mainly domestic fowl) at Pietrabbondante and Colle Sparanise, fish (probably including tunny) at Pietrabbondante and Campochiaro, hare and roe deer at Colle Sparanise, and oysters and other shellfish at Pietrabbondante (II: Chapter Seven). Oysters have also been found at Monte Vairano (De Benedittis, 1988a).

The faunal evidence suggests that Samnite husbandry was little more specialized than that of the Iron Age, with cattle mainly kept as draught animals, sheep for the full range of their products (meat, milk, wool), and pigs for meat. However, it is clear that the domestic system also produced surplus animals for the sanctuaries – ordinary stock going to the local sanctuary, better animals being reserved for a regional sanctuary like Campochiaro, and prime cattle going to the principal Samnite cult site, Pietrabbondante. Keeping beef cattle in most of Italy is an expensive business because of their fodder requirements, and in antiquity the lack of fodder crops meant that feeding a team of plough cattle was a substantial investment – Cato and Columella cautioned the farmer to collect 'whatever leaves are available' to keep them alive between March and September (White, 1970: 282–3). In this light, killing prime cattle as part of temple rituals was almost as conspicuous a form of wealth consumption as the monuments themselves, although perhaps less so in Samnium than in regions of Italy with less grazing. The age of some of the pigs at Monte Vairano compared with those at the sanctuaries also suggests that the better animals produced at the domestic sites were not being consumed on them.

According to the written sources, animal husbandry played a critical role in Samnite agriculture. We hear above all of sheep and cattle, also of pigs and horses (Salmon, 1967: 67–8). The growing urbanization of Italy and the

Mediterranean world in the 3rd and 2nd centuries BC, which was accompanied by military campaigns on a massive scale as Rome's empire expanded, probably led to greater exploitation of Samnium's pastoral resources. The needs of the army alone for textiles and leather must have been very considerable – for example, Livy (XXXXIV.16.4) mentions a contract let at Rome in 169 BC for 6000 togas and 30,000 tunics to be supplied to the legions in Macedonia. Its value has been calculated as nearly one million *denarii* (Badian, 1972: 29). We do not hear of Samnite involvement in such contracts, although the Apulian town of Venusia had supplied togas and tunics in the Second Punic War (Livy XXII.54.2). It has been argued that Samnite hillforts were located to protect transhumance routes (De Benedittis 1991a; Di Niro, 1991f; La Regina, 1975), but it is very difficult to prove that long-distance droveroads crossed the valley much before the 1st century BC (Gabba and Pasquinucci, 1979: 87–91). Direct Pentrian involvement in large-scale transhumance seems unlikely, but smaller local systems, producing animals and animal products for lowland markets, are a different matter.

Intensified production of wool in the lower valley was suggested as a feature of the late Iron Age, and loomweights are common finds from both survey sites and excavated sites of the Samnite period, especially in the lower valley (II: Chapter Four; De Benedittis, 1988a; *Samnium*, 1991; *Sannio*, 1980; Stelluti, 1988). They may indicate no more than household production, but a relative abundance of decoration, graffito initials and longer texts (for example, *Samnium*, 1991: 182) hints at special significance, and an outworking system of textile manufacture like that suggested for Apulia (Brunt, 1971: 370) cannot be ruled out. Particularly noteworthy amongst the survey finds are the loomweights which bear the image of a deity, probably Athena (Fig. 78; for further examples from the Larino area see Stelluti, 1988: fig. 234), or an impressed motif resembling a radiate star – devices which feature prominently in the iconography of the early coinage of Larinum (Cantilena, 1991). Cicero's reference (*pro Cluentio*, 198) to *res pecuariae* suggests that the landed nobility of the town had close interests in stock at the end of the Samnite period, and Larinum's long-standing connections with Apulia, one of the wool trade's more important regions, are worth emphasizing.

The plant remains from Matrice indicate an agricultural regime based on cereal and legume cultivation (Jones and Snowden, forthcoming), bread wheat has also been found at Monte Vairano (De Benedittis, 1988a: 127), and a single carbonized grape pip was found in a small pit with Samnite material excavated at site A26. No plant remains were recovered from the sanctuary excavations despite intensive flotation, apart from one grape pip at Campochiaro, though they all yielded large deposits of wood charcoal, presumably from the fires associated with sacrifice and feasting. Grain was probably the main crop on Samnite farms in the valley, and the territory of Larinum may have been especially productive (Polybius III.101, 107). Cereal, vine and olive pollen are all represented in the contemporary sediments of the pollen core off the coast near Termoli (Bottema, 1974). The upper valley is in the main too high for extensive olive cultivation, but vines can be grown easily. The evidence for possible treading floors on farms here has already been mentioned, but large-scale production of liquids is difficult to document even in the lower valley, and no local amphoras are known. The valley seems therefore not to have been an exporter, though self-sufficiency may have been achieved. Amphoras of the 3rd and 2nd centuries BC from major sites such as Monte Vairano, Campochiaro and Larinum show that whatever was available locally was supplemented by imports, in the main probably for elite consumption.

At Monte Vairano, further artefactual evidence for a system of mixed farming includes iron tools such as a bill-hook, a mattock identical to the one being used in Figure 18, a spade, a large millstone, and a ceramic utensil similar to those used today for boiling sheep's milk for the preparation of *pecorino* and *ricotta* cheese (De Benedittis, 1991c).

MANUFACTURE AND TRADE

Although the surviving written sources give the impression of negligible activity (Brunt, 1971: 357; Salmon, 1967: 65–77), archaeology has provided evidence for a considerable variety and scale of Samnite manufacture in the Biferno valley.

The production of fine and coarse pottery, roofing tiles and terracottas is now abundantly documented. The fullest evidence comes from Monte Vairano, where three kilns are presently known (De Benedittis, 1980, 1988a, 1990b). An evocative recent find has been of a tile with a bilingual stamp – a name (Lukos) in Greek, probably of the artisan, is accompanied by the Oscan initials s k, presumably of the workshop owner (De Benedittis, 1988a: 47–8). Potteries are also known at Bovianum and pre-Roman Saepinum (Matteini Chiari, 1982: 25). It is certain that Larinum had its own workshops from an early date, whose products in the Hellenistic period included painted wares imitating Gnathian vessels and high-quality terracottas (Di Niro, 1980c). Evidence of ceramic production has also been found near Termoli (Di Niro, 1981: 11–13), and a probable kiln spacer (II: Chapter Four; F69) was found at C128, near the major site B102 which was an important centre of pottery and tile manufacture in the late Roman period (Chapter Ten).

The *fullonica* at Saepinum, the artisan quarter at Larinum, the local stone sculpture from various sites (D'Agostino, 1980b), and evidence for iron-working at Larinum (Di Niro, 1991b: 69), Monte Vairano and the Colle Sparanise sanctuary (II: Chapter Five) are further indications of a diverse manufacturing base, and it is surely only a matter of time before direct evidence for the local manufacture of bronze and more precious metalwork – which was a defining feature of Samnite armour and personal ornament – comes to light. The picture is increasingly akin to that of more 'advanced' regions of Italy, although the scale of production is difficult to determine. The most surprising evidence in this respect is a *catillus* of leucitic lava from Monte Vairano, part of a large grain mill of the type familiar from the bakeries of Pompeii and Ostia (De Benedittis, 1991c).

In its trade networks, the valley looked principally to Oscan Italy, Magna Graecia, and, probably indirectly, to the eastern Mediterranean. Regional trade came to be well developed. In the upper valley imported coarse pottery, including *dolia*, points to continuing connections with the volcanic regions of Tyrrhenian Italy, most probably Campania, which much earlier had supplied a little *bucchero* pottery (Capini, 1982: 11; II: Chapter Four), and the nearest possible source for the lava of the Monte Vairano millstone is Roccamonfina in northern Campania, some 60 kilometres across the Apennines as the crow flies. The provenance study of the lava millstones found by the survey throughout the valley suggests southern Italy and Sicily as the sources in this period (II: Chapter Six). The marine foods at the inland sanctuaries could have come from either the Tyrrhenian or the Adriatic coast. The imported fine wares and the stylistic character of the local terracottas of the lower valley attest the continuation of the ancient trade and cultural links with Apulia.

Clear evidence for long-distance networks is provided by amphoras: Monte Vairano, for example, has produced more than one hundred Rhodian amphora handles (De Benedittis, 1980, 1988a, 1991c) and small quantities of Knidian, Black Sea, Punic and south Italian containers have also come to light there and at other sites. Some may have accompanied men of business returning to their homeland from the Mediterranean (Crawford, 1985: 178–9), but the majority is likely to represent commerce. Far-flung connections also appear in finds of 4th/3rd to 1st century coins from the valley and wider Samnium (Cantilena, 1991; Capini, 1984; Catalli, 1980; Crawford, 1985; Mariani, 1901). The mints of Rome, Campania, and, in lesser quantities, Apulia, Lucania, eastern Adriatic cities, Thasos and Balearic Ebusus are represented. The Staii, a leading Pentrian family, are attested in 2nd century BC inscriptions from the trading island of Delos (La Regina, 1989: 335).

Crawford (1985: 178) has suggested that many of the 'foreign' coins in Samnium were brought there by returning soldiers or traders and then lost or discarded as valueless, but the evidence for production and trade described above makes it more likely that they belonged to a complex monetary economy. A small hoard from Larinum of *c.* 100 BC was made up of ten Roman, three Apulian and nine local issues (Di Niro, 1980c: 312ff.), and the mints at Larinum and Aesernia certainly contributed to local exchange. Indeed, it seems likely that minor rural sites in the valley participated in a monetized economy: Republican coins were found in Samnite levels at A11/D12 and A26, some of the nine Republican coins from the extensive excavations at Matrice come from stratified pre-Roman contexts, and sites A198 and A248 each produced a 2nd century BC coin from the surface (II: Chapter Four; Barclay, forthcoming). Presumably these *villae rusticae* and farmsteads looked towards local market centres for manufactured goods – pottery, metalwork, millstones, loomweights – in exchange for their agricultural surplus.

During the Samnite period, therefore, it appears that manufacture and trade grew in sophistication and importance. However, Morel (1991) has argued that even by the 2nd and 1st centuries BC there is little sign that Samnium was an important corridor for east–west trade across the Apennines, and the evidence from the Biferno valley appears to support this view. His proposition that Samnite manufactures were rarely exported also holds good for ceramic products, though not perhaps for leather and textiles. It is clear that something was exchanged in return for the varied imports which reached the valley, and animals, animal products and grain seem the best bet.

SAMNITE SOCIETY: THE BEGINNINGS OF URBANIZATION

The Samnite tribes seem to have conceived their main governmental unit not in terms of the city-state but according to the *touto* (La Regina, 1989: 304ff.; Salmon, 1967: 77–101). Each *touto*, or state, was made up of a number of *pagi*, administrative districts defined territorially. The supreme magistrate of the *touto*, its leader in times of war and probably its chief priest, was the *meddix tuticus*, who was annually elected. Other magistracies and offices, some of which seem to have operated at a local level, are attested. The Pentrian senate was normally based at Bovianum, their capital, but was briefly associated with Aquilonia (perhaps Monte Vairano) in the early 3rd century BC (La Regina, 1989: 305). Otherwise we know nothing of local government. What is clear, however, is that leadership rested in the hands of a small group of aristocratic families.

Literary and epigraphic research reveals the names of the Staii, the Decitii, the Papii, the Pomponii, the Statii and the Egnatii as foremost amongst the records of the Samnites who controlled the major political, military and religious offices, indicating an elite that maintained itself through dynastic succession (La Regina, 1989).

With only a few recent exceptions, ancient and modern assessments have presented the Samnites as a primitive pastoral and agrarian society – *montani atque agrestes* in a phrase of Livy's (IX.13.7), referring to the late 4th century BC. As this chapter has described, however, the archaeology of the Biferno valley reveals a very different picture. The 5th and much of the 4th centuries BC seem to be characterized principally by continuity with the iron age settlement structures described in the previous chapter, but by the later 4th and early 3rd centuries as substantive changes had occurred here as in regions such as Campania (Arthur, 1991a). In the lowlands, the urbanization of Larinum was a crucially important step, implying the development of more elaborate political, social and economic systems: it is tempting to see in the evidence for agricultural settlement (Fig. 76) and production in its environs the emergence of the 'estates, business interests and stock' (*praedia, negotia, res pecuarias*) which Cicero attributes to the leading landowners of the town (*pro Cluentio* 198). In the uplands, the period witnessed the development of the major hillforts and sanctuaries, implying communal organization on a considerable scale. The combined evidence of excavations and survey suggests that the villages, hamlets, local sanctuaries, villas and simpler farmsteads which filled out the landscape of the valley belong in the main to the late 4th, 3rd and 2nd centuries BC.

How urban were the leading centres of the Pentri? Arthur (1991b), drawing on the work of other scholars, has suggested that seven criteria need to be satisfied for a settlement to be defined as a city or town: central place status, the existence of public works, a diversified economy, a significant proportion of non-agricultural adult labour, a social hierarchy, a substantial population and autonomous or semi-autonomous administration. Although our knowledge is still very fragmentary, it seems possible to recognize virtually all of these features in the major upper valley sites. There can be little doubt that Bovianum, Monte Vairano and pre-Roman Saepinum were central places with stable, sizeable populations. Public and private buildings are documented, and an important economic role is certain at Monte Vairano and Saepinum and very probable at Bovianum. A developed social hierarchy can now be hypothesized with some confidence: the presence of elite groups is attested by literature and epigraphy, and archaeologically by imported wines (which seem virtually absent from the countryside), by other relatively exotic objects and by buildings like the house of the Boar Hunt mosaic at Saepinum (Gaggiotti, 1991). Other houses at Saepinum and Monte Vairano suggest less wealthy strata, no doubt including the craftsmen and, perhaps, merchants whose activities are well documented by other evidence. An agrarian peasantry may be assumed. Closely defined hinterlands seem implicit in the local economies linking market centres and farms.

What cannot as yet be demonstrated is developed local government, except perhaps in the case of Bovianum. Local *meddices* are certain, but communities like Monte Vairano and pre-Roman Saepinum are likely to have demanded more complex administration than a single individual – the virtual equivalent of the chief or headman of the Iron Age – could provide. Local offices may well have continued to be monopolized by the traditional aristocracy, but they were probably more diverse than present evidence admits. It may be that the major sites of the upper valley were simply *pagus* centres, but, along with other large Samnite settlements like Alfedena (La Regina, 1984: 260–7; Mariani, 1901, 1902), their resemblance to towns is growing as research proceeds. The occasional use by the classical writers of *urbs* and *polis* to describe Samnite centres seems more understandable in this light. Nonetheless, on present evidence it is easier to compare Larinum with Pompeii, another 'semi-Samnite' town (Rathbone, 1992), than with Monte Vairano. In the uplands, urbanization seems to have been a slower and arguably a more homespun process (cf. La Regina, 1978: 448).

During the 3rd and 2nd centuries the economic life of Samnium developed considerably and the elites clearly prospered. The most striking expression of their resources and sophistication is found in the Hellenizing temples constructed at Pietrabbondante, Campochiaro and several other sanctuaries, whilst at Pietrabbondante the Pentri built a handsome if small stone theatre at least half a century before the first permanent theatre appeared at Rome (La Regina, 1976, 1980b, 1984; Strazzulla, 1973). We know nothing of what was performed on the stage, but, as Rathbone (1992: 18) has suggested, it would be unwise to assume that the Pentri 'could not have appreciated classical Greek drama, or that their own comic theatre was no more than an early version of the Benny Hill show' – a suggestion supported by recent research on the reception of Athenian comedy in southern Italy (Taplin, 1993). The importance of the sanctuaries for social life is also shown by the consumption of high-quality foodstuffs in the rites, probably another means by which the local aristocracies were able to legitimate their authority with the peasantry (Barker, 1989b). They almost certainly had an economic role as well, as focal points for the commerce which attached to festivals. In the lowlands, public works in the nucleated settlements were probably the main channel for wealth display. The remarkable bronze portrait head from San Giovanni Lipioni in the Trigno valley, belonging to a statue probably of the late 3rd or early 2nd century BC, provides a glimpse of the self-image of the local nobility and underlines the means at their disposal (La Regina, 1978: 552–3).

What lay behind the creation of the new prosperity in the valley and its lavish expenditure can only be guessed at. No doubt competition between the Italic elites was as strong, if not stronger, in the Samnite period as it had been in the Iron Age. There may have been pressure to convert personal wealth into public amenities as time progressed, generated by the more complex social stratification which accompanied urbanization. Samnium's relations with Rome were another powerful stimulus: the Roman conquest of the centre-south from the late 4th century removed from the Pentri the possibilities of colonizing or raiding neighbouring territory, traditional Samnite practices, and the eventual imposition of military levies, which probably had to be self-supporting, may have put further strains on the economy. Confined to the mountains, the Pentri may have been forced to diversify. In the lowlands, where more favourable conditions for agriculture existed, the transition to surplus production was almost certainly swifter. Throughout the valley, though, the basis of the economy remained the land and the biggest landholders remained the dynastic aristocracy.

During the last centuries BC profound political and economic change affected most of Italy (Hopkins, 1978). Fuelled by the profits of empire, the city of Rome became a megalopolis, with close to a million inhabitants by the end of the millennium. As the capital of the Mediterranean world, it saw vast and ostentatious expenditure by its competing elites. Smaller towns in Italy also grew in size and sophistication. They drew their wealth largely from the countryside and from trade in its products, for which Rome and its armies and other larger cities at home and abroad provided a ready market. The urban immigrants were in part slaves (two million of whom were imported during the late Republic), but more commonly the dispossessed Italian peasantry. Various factors contributed to the abandonment of their smallholdings, including enforced military service overseas; but possibly the most important was the rise of the large, slave-staffed estate specializing in production for the market place. Recent archaeological research suggests that the great proliferation of the villa system of agriculture in Italy belongs to the 1st century BC (Attolini et al., 1991; Rathbone, 1983: 162), but there is little doubt that it had been established near Rome and on the borders of Samnium during the 3rd and 2nd centuries (Arthur, 1991a; Cornell, 1989: 413–4; Frederiksen, 1984; Toynbee, 1965).

The scanty literary evidence sheds very little light on the extent to which

the Pentri and Frentani were affected by these developments. Salmon
(1967: 305–34) saw the Samnites of the 2nd century as utterly dominated
by Roman exploitation, but this is almost certainly too bleak (Frederiksen,
1968). The expansion of Rome's overseas empire offered opportunities for
the Italians, and service in the legions and participation in trade took them
to many corners of the Mediterranean. Samnites were certainly amongst
them, and some of those who returned had clearly prospered (Crawford,
1985: 178–9; Gabba, 1976: 76). The evidence of archaeology suggests that
Samnite adaptations of the villa and the ranch were features of the
landscape long before the Roman period, and that at least some of the
wealthier landholders turned more actively to the long-distance marketing
of their surplus produce. Although these were probably much smaller in
scale than the estates of the Roman aristocracy, their social and economic
effects may have been similar. The growth of the Matrice, Cercemaggiore
and Santa Maria Casalpiano farmsteads during the period may well have
been at the expense of peasant smallholders, whose emigration from the
countryside would help to explain the swelling of local nucleated settlement. Some may have remained on the land as employees or serfs of the
larger estates. There is scarcely any evidence for slavery in Samnium, but
an underclass may be indicated at least in the early part of the period by
burial evidence: 3 out of the 23 excavated tombs in a cemetery close to the
Cercemaggiore farm have produced no gravegoods and occupy somewhat
marginal positions with regard to the wealthier burials, and there are also a
few tombs without artefacts at Termoli and other cemeteries (Di Niro,
1991d). Analysis of the skeletons from Cercemaggiore (Petrone, 1993)
suggests that rural life was arduous – over a third of the males died
between twenty and twenty-four, and most of the males and many of the
females showed signs of hard physical labour from a very young age. The
teeth of both sexes were in very poor condition, ascribed to a simple diet
very high in carbohydrates.

Trade and cultural patterns suggest that southern Italy was an important
influence in this period, although Roman coinage became prominent
during the 2nd century BC and in the same period Roman political titles –
for example, censor and aedile (in Oscanized form) – were adopted, even if
to describe already existing elements of the Samnite political structure
(Salmon, 1967: 87–91). In the Frentanian valley the use of Latin reached
beyond Larinum, appearing in graffiti on black gloss pottery and a
loomweight from B102 (II: Chapter Four; F230–1, 236) and also, strikingly,
in an inscription – L.Volusius Gallus fecit – on a 2nd/1st century BC mosaic
pavement from Santa Maria Casalpiano (De Benedittis et al., 1993: 40),
although this would be less surprising if the mosaic post-dates the Social
War. The Latin colonies at Luceria, Aesernia and Beneventum are likely to

have had an impact on local developments, although this is difficult to demonstrate in detail.

By 91 BC, therefore, on the eve of the war that was to lead to their incorporation within the Roman state, the settlements of the valley presented a face to the world which had altered radically since the end of the Iron Age. The metamorphosis was remarkable: major centres of population and craft production; imposing sanctuaries deeply influenced by Hellenizing architecture, and a complex ritual landscape beyond them; a hierarchy of rural settlement, including villas; and, linking all these, economic, social and cultural structures reflecting urbanization. The survey has shown that the countryside of the Biferno valley was exploited to a degree unsurpassed in any period before early modern times. The evidence of geomorphology (Chapter Four) likewise suggests that the agriculture of this period created an open environment and erosion rates unparalleled before the modern era.

Clearly the valley communities were affected much more deeply by the processes which transformed Italy and the Mediterranean world in the later 1st millennium BC than the traditional view of Samnite society admits. It is equally clear, however, that with the exception of Larinum and its territory, these processes were relatively modest in their impact. By the early 1st century BC, for example, most towns of Italy could boast more sophisticated and more numerous public and private buildings than have – as yet – come to light in the valley settlements. Nonetheless, we should not underestimate the vigour and enterprise of its peoples, nor how far forms of urbanism had developed before the municipalization which followed the 80s.

CHAPTER 10

ROMAN TOWNS AND TERRITORIES
(*c*. 80 BC – AD 600)

John Lloyd, with contributions by Graeme Barker, Gill Clark and Derrick Webley

INTRODUCTION

As a result of the Social War the Samnite peoples of the Biferno valley acquired Roman citizenship, and in due course a number of their settlements became Roman chartered towns, each administering a closely defined territory. These changes offered a new focus – the Roman city state and empire – for the loyalties and ambitions of the local elites (Patterson, 1987). The towns were to dominate the settlement hierarchy until late antiquity; thereafter, a very different structure emerged, as described in Chapter Eleven.

Samnium has generally been considered a classic backwoods area of the Roman world. Remote, impoverished and thinly populated, its centres were few and unremarkable and it seldom produced individuals of any note. Pastoralism gained ground, and trade and manufacture were scarcely developed (Brunt, 1971: 357–8; Morel, 1991; Salmon, 1967: 387–99). The evidence from the Biferno valley described in this chapter offers support for some aspects of this view; but it also shows a region much more closely in touch with Italy and the Mediterranean world than its historical obscurity and geographical isolation have suggested hitherto.

THE HISTORICAL FRAMEWORK

Strabo, writing in the late 1st century BC, was struck by the deterioration of Samnium following the Sullan devastations: all traces of Samnite culture had disappeared (VI.1.2), several cities had been lost entirely and most of the others, including Bovanium, had been reduced to villages (V.4.11). It has long been known that Strabo exaggerated the decline of settlement, but it has not been doubted that there were considerable demographic and economic difficulties in the post-Sullan period. The late Republic and early Empire brought newcomers to the region – time-expired soldiers granted

plots of land – and some state funds were channelled into urban development, but recovery under the principate is thought to have been modest at
best. The elder Pliny's list of the principal towns in the valley (*Natural
History* III, 103–7, based almost certainly on an Augustan source) identifies
Larinum, Fagifulae and Saepinum as *municipia*, Bovianum as a *colonia*.

Thereafter we have very little literary evidence until the 5th century AD,
when legal texts hint at economic difficulties in Samnium as a whole (De
Benedittis, 1981). Under the Ostrogothic kingdom (AD 493–535) a fair
measure of urban and regional organization was preserved, including
supervision of the transhumance trails which crossed the lower valley
(Wickham, 1983). The Byzantine–Gothic Wars of AD 535–54 and the
Byzantine–Lombard Wars of AD 568–602 almost certainly had damaging
effects, and according to Paul the Deacon (*Historia Langobardorum* V.29),
writing in the late 8th century, many towns and territories in Samnium,
including Bovianum and Saepinum, had been abandoned by the 660s.

A certain amount is known of regional administration. The reorganiz-
ation of Italy under Augustus saw Larinum and its territory assigned to
Regio II (Apulia), the rest of the valley falling within *Regio* IV (Sabina and
Samnium). The lower stretch of the Biferno river was now regarded as the
boundary between the Frentanian and Apulian (Daunian) peoples (Pliny,
Natural History III.103–5; Pomponius Mela, II.65), although Pliny's
description of the Larinates as *cognomine Frentani* indicates a continuing
awareness of their ethnic roots. In the early 4th century Samnium was
joined with Campania for administrative purposes, but by the middle of
that century had become a *provincia* in its own right. Scattered later
references suggest that it remained a recognized unit until at least the mid
6th century. Geographically the region was broadly equivalent to modern
Abruzzo and Molise, thus encompassing Larinum and reaching to the
Adriatic coast (De Benedittis, 1981; Gaggiotti, 1978; Thomsen, 1947).

In the Roman period the principal lines of communication attested in the
Itineraries (Cuntz, 1929; Miller, 1916) passed across rather than along the
valley, continuing the earlier pattern. In the lower valley the coastal
highway swung inland from the Apulian port of Sipontum (modern
Manfredonia) via Teanum Apulum to Larinum, before reaching the coast
again at Histonium (modern Vasto). At the head of the valley the
Aesernia–Beneventum highway, in part a droveroad as we know from the
famous Saepinum inscription (*CIL* IX: 2478), passed through Bovianum and
Saepinum. Droveroads (*calles*) also crossed the lower valley (Cicero, *pro
Cluentio* 161) and probably the middle valley, as in the 16th century
(Chapter Twelve; Fig. 96). A road connecting Larinum with Bovianum
along the eastern valley watershed is first documented by the later Roman
Peutinger Table (Miller, 1916: strecke 63b), but its origins should go back at

least to Samnite times (Chapter Nine). A network of minor roads and tracks also continued in use, as the distribution of lesser settlements attests.

THE ARCHAEOLOGICAL SURVEY: SITE DATING AND DEFINITION

The principal dating evidence for the period c. 80 BC–AD 250 is provided successively by late black gloss pottery, which seems to have been used until the Augustan period, red gloss Italian sigillata (*Conspectus*, 1991), which circulated locally mainly in the 1st and early 2nd centuries AD, and African Red Slip ware (Hayes, 1972, 1980), which took over the fine ware market during the 2nd century AD. As discussed in Chapter Nine, the difficulties of dating scrappy black gloss sherds mean that sites which produced no better dating evidence might be either Samnite or early Roman (late Republican), or both. Assessment of rural settlement in the period from 80 BC to Augustus is therefore problematic.

The most widely useful dating contribution after the fine wares is provided by coarse pottery, which was studied by Paul Roberts using as a control the stratified deposits excavated at Matrice (A166) and San Giacomo (B102) (Roberts, 1988, 1992, 1993). The coarse wares suggest an Imperial phase on several survey sites without contemporary fine wares, and extend the period of occupation indicated by the fine wares at a good many others (II: Chapters One and Four). The findings support recent scepticism about the reliability of *imported* pottery as a guide to the full ancient settlement pattern (Millett, 1991; Patterson, 1987: 137; Wickham 1988, 1989).

Coins and other artefacts are helpful in a few cases, and a clutch of sites displayed building materials and techniques, notably concrete with its various facings, which are very unlikely to have been introduced before the Roman period. *Opus reticulatum*, for example, makes its first closely datable local appearance in the mid-Augustan wall circuit at Saepinum (Fig. 82).

African Red Slip ware was the most popular fine ware in the valley from the 2nd to the early 5th centuries AD. Phocaean Red Slip ware from Asia Minor arrived for a few decades from c. AD 400, and a little Cypriot Red Slip ware reached the lower valley. Only a few imports dating to the later 5th–early 6th centuries AD were found by the survey, and recognizable later forms were wholly absent.

Late Roman red-painted ware, an Italian product which rapidly became popular in much of the centre-south and was to remain so well into the medieval period (Cann and Lloyd, 1984), made its first appearance in the valley a little before AD 400, and there is good reason to believe that most of the survey finds are in fact of local manufacture (Roberts, 1993).

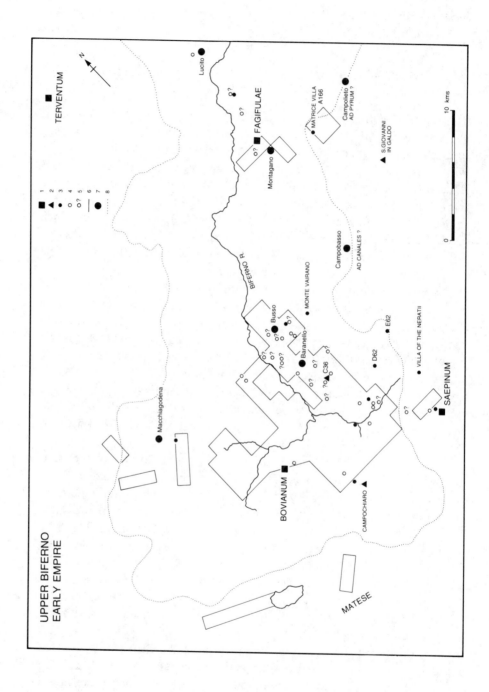

UPPER BIFERNO
EARLY EMPIRE

TERVENTUM

1
2
3
4
5
6
7
8

Lucito

FAGIFULAE

Montagano

MATRICE VILLA
A166

Campolieto
AD PYRUM ?

S.GIOVANNI
IN GALDO

BIFERNO R.

Campobasso

AD CANALES ?

Busso

MONTE VAIRANO

Baranello

C36

D62

E62

VILLA OF THE NERATII

SAEPINUM

Macchiagodena

BOVIANUM

CAMPOCHIARO

MATESE

0   10 kms

Red-painted ware was found on about two dozen sites and may, but does not certainly, indicate later activity than the associated fine wares. The local coarse wares of the later 5th and 6th centuries are not as well known as earlier products. There are therefore significant difficulties in determining the extent of late antique settlement. However, we have a guide to pottery of the 7th century from graves at Saepinum and Vicenne, near Bovianum (De Benedittis, 1988b: 103–8; *Samnium*, 1991: 347–53). These produced debased red-painted ware and crude handmade coarse wares similar in fabric to iron age and early Samnite *impasto* and impastoid vessels. The red-painted ware on late Roman survey sites was generally well preserved and closely akin to 5th-century production in terms of fabric and execution (II: Chapter Four), although some pieces were very worn. Some long-lived classical settlements (for example, the *vicus*/villa sites A198, B102, B260 and B268) produced *impasto* sherds which could conceivably derive from post-Roman vessels, although they are more probably related to the Samnite phase of occupation.

For methods and problems of site definition, the reader is referred to the discussion in Chapters Three, Eight and Nine. The ensuing discussion of settlement trends integrates the survey data with the results of the sample excavations conducted as part of the project at Saepinum, the Campochiaro and Colle Sparanise sanctuaries and a number of minor sites (II: Chapter Three), and with those of the much larger-scale excavations carried out at Larino, Campochiaro, Monte Vairano, San Martino, San Giacomo and Santa Maria Casalpiano by the Molise Superintendency, at Saepinum by Perugia University, and at the Matrice villa (site A166) by Sheffield and Aberdeen Universities (Lloyd 1991a, forthcoming; Lloyd and Rathbone, 1984). The concluding sections of the chapter examine economic and social developments in the valley as a whole during the Roman and post-Roman periods.

SETTLEMENT TRENDS IN THE UPPER VALLEY, c. 80 BC–AD 250

TOWNS

The Romanization of the upper valley began to take effect following Sulla's campaign of 82/81 BC, although its early progress is obscure (Gabba, 1972). However, it is clear that the process of urbanism favoured

Fig. 80 Early Imperial settlement in the upper Biferno valley (1st–3rd centuries AD). 1. town; 2. sanctuary; 3. villa/farmstead; 4. probable farmstead; 5. possible farmstead; 6. approximate limits of walked areas; 7. modern town/village; 8. valley watershed.

the Samnite centres which occupied open, low-lying ground, preferably close to the major routes (Fig. 80). Monte Vairano shows signs of destruction and abandonment in the early 1st century BC (De Benedittis, 1988a, 1991b), and it is probable that other hillforts still in use down to the 80s BC were largely deserted by the Imperial period. At Bovianum which was known to Cicero in 66 BC as an important centre (*pro Cluentio* 197) and where municipal development is attested by the mid 1st century BC (*CIL* IX: 2563, of 48–6 BC), the Roman town grew up on the site of the Samnite settlement close to the Aesernia–Beneventum road. *Municipia* were also established by the Augustan period at Saepinum and Fagifulae (Pliny, *Natural History* III. 107). Bovianum almost certainly received a veteran colony at some time between 48 and 27 BC, probably in the late 40s (Keppie, 1983: 161–3; La Regina, 1980a: 30–1). Saepinum remained a *municipium* throughout the Empire: the Neronian colony attributed by the *Liber Coloniarum* (237, 14–16) is to be rejected (Gaggiotti, 1991; Keppie, 1983:9). However, the centuriation of territory to which the *Liber Coloniarum* refers may survive to the east of the town, where traces of land division have been reported (Gaggiotti, 1982a: 30–1; 1991; see also Chouquer *et al.*, 1987: 147–9).

The well-preserved site of Saepinum offers the fullest insights into the urban centres of the upper valley (Fig. 81). The alignment of the main streets, though not their paving, probably goes back to the Samnite settlement, but the visible remains in the excavated area (about 10 per cent of the whole) are in origin mainly Augustan or slightly later. The city walls (Fig. 82) were completed between 2 BC and AD 4, and virtually the full suite of institutional buildings and amenities appropriate to a fully fledged Roman town was then in place or soon to be acquired – a forum-basilica complex (with temples), theatre, *macellum* (market), baths and other public monuments. Houses, shops and workshops lined the main streets adjacent to the town centre (Fig. 83), and an aqueduct brought water from the hills behind (Gaggiotti, 1991; La Regina, 1984: 209–26; *Saepinum*, 1982). Saepinum, however, was a tiny and rather plain town by comparison with most centres outside the mountains: the fortifications measure less than 1300 metres in length and enclose an area of *c.* 12 hectares, which is small even by Imperial Apennine standards, and the standard building stone was local limestone, with very sparing use of brick and marble.

Public building here was mainly funded by the Imperial government and, as usual, by leading local citizens. A monumental Latin inscription set above the arch of the Bovianum gate (Fig. 82) proclaimed the town walls,

Fig. 81 The Roman *municipium* at Saepinum. (After De Benedittis *et al.*, 1984: end plan)

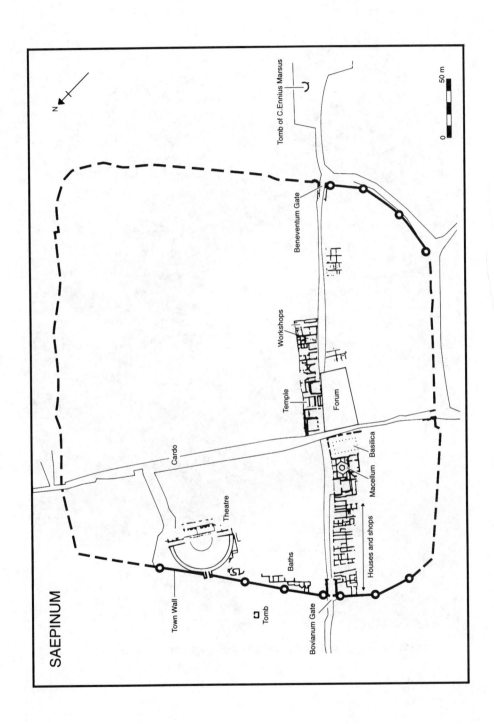

SAEPINUM

N

Tomb of C. Ennius Marsus

Beneventum Gate

Workshops

Temple

Forum

Cardo

Basilica

Macellum

Houses and shops

Theatre

Baths

Town Wall

Tomb

Bovianum Gate

0   50 m

Fig. 82 Saepinum: the Bovianum gate. (Photograph: John Lloyd)

Fig. 83 Saepinum: the main road (*decumanus*) leading to the Bovianum gate. The road was flanked with shops and houses. (Photograph: Graeme Barker)

towers and gates as the gift of two leading members of the Imperial house, Tiberius (later to become Emperor) and his brother Drusus. The flanking sculpture recalled their victories in Germany and Pannonia, and the circuit as a whole was built mainly in *opus reticulatum*, a technique new to the area. This was a potent advertisement of Rome's strength and authority, and the ideology of the Imperial regime was quickly absorbed and promoted by the local elites, amongst whom newcomers to the area – veteran soldiers settled with a grant of land – and their descendants were very prominent. The equestrians C. Ennius Marsus and L. Naevius Pansa are notable examples, and the handsome circular mausoleum of the former stands outside the Beneventum gate (Fig. 84). The C. Papiu[s] who helped pay for the paving of the forum was, however, almost certainly of Samnite descent, suggesting that indigenous families took a share in promoting Romanization.

During the 1st century AD senators with strong local connections are in evidence, including a *patronus* Cn. Pomponius Saturninus (Gaggiotti, 1982d: 513) and members of the *gens* Neratia, who were major local landowners (Gaggiotti, 1982c: 41–9; 1987/8; Torelli, 1982). The Neratii had achieved senatorial rank by the Flavian period and the branch domiciled in Rome was to produce some of the most eminent figures in the Imperial

Fig. 84 Saepinum: the tomb of C. Ennius Marsus. (Photograph: John Lloyd)

government of the later 1st and 2nd centuries AD, including L. Neratius Marcellus, consul in 95 and governor of Britain in 103, and the jurist L. Neratius Priscus whom Trajan considered as his successor (*SHA Hadrian* IV. 9.9). The Neratii and their freedmen were very important contributors to the amenities of Saepinum, and it is likely that the family came to hold an almost baronial grip over the town.

Important monuments were built in the late 1st or early 2nd century AD (Gaggiotti, 1991), but subsequent work – in the excavated area at least – seems to have been concerned mainly with maintenance and refurbishment. Inscriptions of the 3rd century are very few, apart from some dedications to emperors, and fresh building work is scarcely attested until the mid 4th century, when the Neratii re-emerge as patrons.

Little is known of the other towns of the upper valley, but their development seems to have been similar (De Benedittis, 1977, 1991d, 1991f; La Regina, 1984: 193–201, 298–9). Bovianum was probably larger than Saepinum (it may have possessed an amphitheatre), and Fagifulae rather smaller. Precise information on the size of their territories is lacking, but they were perhaps in the order of 500 square kilometres (De Benedittis, 1977), almost certainly a good deal less than the *ager Larinas* in the lower valley. A senatorial connection with Bovianum is possible (Torelli, 1982:

181). Opinion is divided as to whether a second colony was founded there by Vespasian (Keppie, 1984: 97; La Regina, 1984: 197–8), but certainly veteran settlement in Samnium is attested under this emperor and Bovianum may at least have been reinforced. Chouquer *et al.* (1987: 144–7) have claimed two phases of centuriation in its territory on the basis of the IGM maps, but this has not yet been confirmed on the ground.

VILLAGES

Village life shows little sign of vigour, in contrast with the lowlands. The Samnite village below Campochiaro and the possible village near the Colle Sparanise sanctuary (C36) seem to have been virtually deserted under the Empire, although there were a few Roman finds in the latter area, as at the Republican *vicus* of San Vincenzo in the upper Volturno valley (Patterson, 1985). There was some occupation at Monte Vairano, where a little Italian sigillata and two Imperial coins have come to light, as well as a funerary inscription referring to a magistrate of Bovianum (De Benedittis, 1974; 1991c). A Roman-period presence is also attested at the comparable hillforts of Alfedena in northern Samnium and Monte Pallano in Abruzzo (La Regina, 1984: 265, 311; Mariani, 1901: 242–8), and some kind of nucleated settlement probably persisted for a while. If so, these may be examples of the cities reduced to villages about which Strabo was informed (p. 213). The Peutinger Table (Miller, 1916: strecke 63b) lists two road stations, Adeanales (probably Ad [C]anales) and Ad Pyr[um], at 11 and 19 Roman miles respectively from Bovianum along the watershed route to Larinum, but nothing is otherwise known of them.

SANCTUARIES

At sanctuaries throughout Samnium an absence of closely datable finds hints at neglect, possibly even abandonment, in the late Republican period. However, excavation has produced no clear evidence for violent destruction in the 80s BC, and from the Augustan period cult activity comes clearly into view.

At Campochiaro (probably the *(fanum) Hercul(is) Rani* of the Peutinger Table) the *temenos* has produced, amongst other finds, an abundance of Imperial coins, two fragmentary Latin inscriptions and a small marble statue of Hercules. Monumental building or repair is not clearly attested, however (Capini, 1980c, 1982; Cappelletti, 1991). The project excavations at Colle Sparanise (C36) recovered a few coins and lamps of the 1st to 3rd centuries AD, and similar finds have come to light at San Giovanni in Galdo (Di Niro, 1980b) and Vastogirardi in northern Samnium (Morel, 1984).

Campochiaro clearly still attracted some valuable votives, but the simple offerings at the lesser sites suggest a poor clientele – presumably the neighbouring rural population, for whom the sites retained some religious significance. The major focus of elite patronage seems now to have been municipal cult: there is in fact no certainty that the buildings of the rural sanctuaries were in good repair. The great Samnite centre at Pietrabbondante was undoubtedly ruinous, although there is ample evidence for Roman-period activity in the form of makeshift settlement and poor burials within the complex and the remains of a handsome mausoleum belonging to the *gens Socellia* lie not far from the site (La Regina, 1980b; La Regina, 1984: 256–7). All the lesser sanctuaries, with the possible exception of Campochiaro, seem to have been abandoned by the mid 3rd century AD.

VILLAS AND FARMSTEADS

In the upper valley the survey found 11 certain and 15 probable sites of the early to mid Empire, together with 17 possible sites. Only 2 of the certain and probable group seem to have been founded in this period. The 26 sites in this category represent a drop of just over 40 per cent in relation to the Samnite figure (45), virtually identical to the percentage fall found in the lower and middle valley. As noted above, however, it is not inconceivable that some of the smaller Samnite scatters with poorly datable finds are in fact late Republican. If so, they might reflect veteran settlement in the territories of Bovianum and Saepinum (cf. Keppie, 1983: 125–7). The importance of coarse pottery for dating early to mid Imperial activity is well illustrated by the 15 probable sites, of which only three produced contemporary fine wares.

The villa of the Neratii near Saepinum is, not surprisingly, the grandest of all the known upper-valley sites in this category (Gaggiotti, 1984/5). The visible remains (it has not yet been excavated) cover an area *c.* 150×100 metres and include walls of *opus reticulatum* and *opus mixtum*, the latter associated with a facade carrying engaged brick half columns. The villa seems to have developed from a Samnite nucleus, probably in polygonal masonry. A series of honorific inscriptions to the Neratii (*CIL* IX: 2450–3) was set up here by the town of Saepinum in the 2nd and 3rd centuries – an indication of the importance of the Neratii as patrons and perhaps also a hint of changing town–country relationships. There was probably a cemetery at the site, and mausolea and graves are attested at other local villas (sites D62 and E62; De Benedittis, 1977, 1988a).

The fullest picture of villa development, though at a much more modest site, comes from Matrice (A166; Lloyd, 1991a, 1991c, forthcoming; Lloyd and Rathbone 1984; Fig. 85). The Samnite polygonal masonry farmstead was enlarged probably in the 1st century BC and then further extended and partially restructured in the first half of the 1st century AD. Occupation seems to have been more or less continuous up to this point. There are signs of decline from the later 2nd century AD, but active life continued for several centuries beyond. As at the villa of the Neratii, *opus reticulatum* and *opus mixtum* characterize the early Imperial building phase. The villa, though sizeable (c. 2500 square metres in area), was plainly decorated, with only a few fragments of simple frescoes and white mosaic, and some segments (not *in situ*) of brick columns. Flue-tile sherds point to a small bath suite, perhaps similar to the one added to the Posto villa in Campania in the later 1st century AD (Cotton, 1979). A full understanding of the villa's layout was impeded by the modern road which crosses it, and by post-medieval structures within its remains, but it seems to have consisted of three wings grouped round a central yard. In the excavated area the living quarters (at ground floor level) were probably rooms 2–7 in the south wing; one had a concrete floor with a tile hearth. In a corner of the large store-room (1) at the end of this wing stood two substantial container vessels (*dolia*). The east wing was perhaps devoted to storage and stabling. The north wing contained a suite of simple press rooms (10–14) with sunken *dolia*. The firm impression is of a large working farmstead, not unlike the present *masserie* of the valley. It was probably owned by a member of the local aristocracy and run by a tenant or a bailiff. The economic evidence from the site is discussed in later sections.

The smaller sites of the countryside probably represent a range of structures, as in the Samnite period, including peasant farmsteads and outbuildings of the larger estates. Little can be said about their character, except to note that many lacked Imperial fine wares and were identified through coarse pottery. We should be cautious about regarding this as an indication of abject poverty, however, since the non-local sigillata of the early Empire was presumably more costly than the earlier locally made black gloss fine ware. The evidence of both fine ware and coarse ware suggests that two-thirds of all early Imperial rural sites did not survive much into the 3rd century AD, and many seem to have been abandoned a good deal earlier. Survey can offer only a provisional picture of these settlement trends, but the evidence of excavation (admittedly limited) at Monte Vairano and Colle Sparanise supports the view that by c. AD 250 the upper valley landscape was thinly populated by comparison with the early Empire. A very similar picture is found in other parts of upland Samnium and neighbouring regions (Patterson, 1985, 1987). Nucleation of settlement might help to explain the abandonments, but where we can test this hypothesis – at Saepinum and Matrice – the signs are if anything of decline rather than growth.

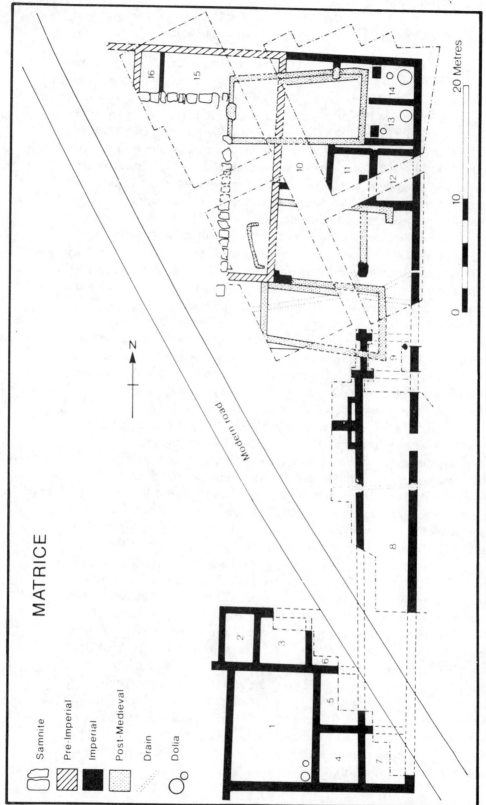

Fig. 85 The Samnite and Roman villa at Matrice (A166).

SETTLEMENT TRENDS IN THE LOWER VALLEY, *c.* 80 BC–AD 250 (Fig. 86)

TOWNS, VILLAGES AND HIGH-RANKING VILLAS

Larinum remained the dominant settlement: its wealth and advanced urbanization allowed the rapid acquisition of municipal status, probably by the late 80s BC (Torelli, 1973). It possessed a medium-sized amphitheatre, the gift of a senator in the late 1st or early 2nd century (De Tata, 1990; Vitiello *et al.*, 1990), and sophisticated early Imperial buildings both in the central public area and in other zones (Di Niro, 1980c, 1991e). Familiarity with concrete construction is evident at the amphitheatre and elsewhere. Marble and bronze statuary, mosaics, and handsome funerary monuments suggest that the prosperity of the urban elites continued into the 3rd century AD (De Caro, 1991b; Morricone Mattini, 1991; Stelluti, 1988).

Many of the local aristocrats who feature in Cicero's *pro Cluentio* were of equestrian rank and thus worth at least 400,000 sesterces, a sum perhaps equivalent to four medium-sized estates (Rathbone, *pers. comm.*). Larinum also produced a number of senators from the Augustan period, who required a fortune of at least 1,000,000 sesterces (Camodeca, 1982; Moreau, 1983: 106–8; Wiseman, 1971: 63 and 274, nos. 488, 491). Around AD 200 the town may have been granted the prestigious title of *colonia* by the emperor Septimius Severus (*RIB* I: 1545; Birley, 1953: 172–4; Taylor, 1960: 321–2), although recent evidence puts this in doubt (De Tata, 1990). The entry for the town in the *Liber Coloniarum* (260) is unreliable.

Larinum's territory probably extended west to the Biferno river, south to the territory of Fagifulae in the upper-middle valley and north to the Adriatic coast, though the *municipium* of Histonium (modern Vasto) owned property east of the river, close to the coast, in the 60s AD (*CIL* IX, 2827; La Regina, 1984: 305–7). To the east the nearest known *municipium* was Teanum Apulum, 27 kilometres away as the crow flies. The land to the west of the river was probably under the overall control of Histonium (lower valley) and Terventum (middle valley). As with the territory of Larinum, these were very large areas, able to support townships and villages and difficult to administer without them. The existence of *pagus* centres in this period is strongly suggested by an inscription from Larinum (*CIL* IX: 726), probably of late Republican date, and an early Antonine inscription found near Guglionesi (*CIL* IX: 2828). The four or five lower-valley communities of this period whose names are preserved probably had this status.

Geron[i]um, presumably the successor of the Gereonium mentioned in the context of the Hannibalic War (Chapter Nine), is located 8 Roman miles

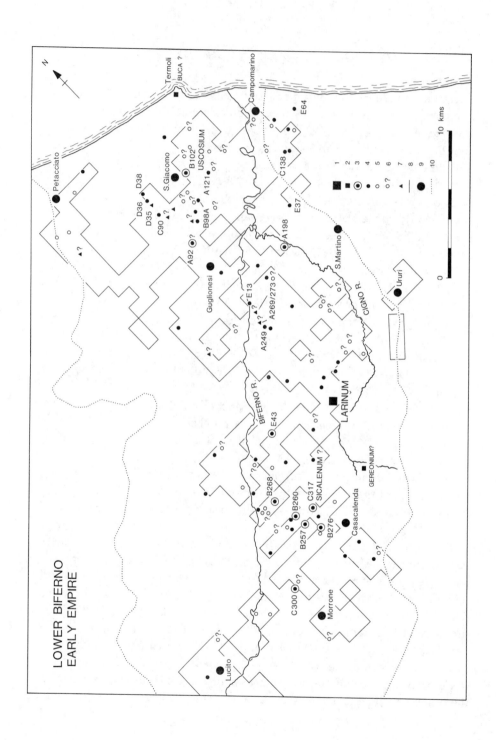

LOWER BIFERNO
EARLY EMPIRE

south of Larinum in the Peutinger Table (Miller, 1916: strecke 63b). Sicalenum, probably the successor of the Kalena mentioned by Polybius (III.101.3), is perhaps to be identified with the category A (*vicus*/villa) site C317, near the church of La Madonna della Difesa just outside Casacalenda. An inscription naming Sicalenum was found here in the late 19th century, and occasional discoveries have included a bronze statuette, decorative stonework, a mosaic and several burials (**II**: Chapter One). Cliternia (Pliny, *Natural History* III. 103; Pomponius Mela II. 65) perhaps lay outside the valley catchment, towards the Fortore river, although the San Martino in Pensilis area has also been suggested as a possible location (La Regina, 1984: 164); a category A site (A198) measuring 7 hectares was found here and subsequent excavations by the Superintendency have revealed part of a substantial settlement (Fig. 87).

West of the Biferno river lay Buca and Uscosium. Buca was known to Strabo (V.4.2; VI.3.11) and later writers (Pliny calls it an *oppidum*), and is perhaps to be linked with the small medieval and modern port of Termoli (La Regina, 1984: 164), though Carroccia (1992) has proposed Campomarino, east of the river. Uscosium appears only in the mid to late Roman Antonine Itinerary, where its location is given as 15 Roman miles from Histonium and 14 Roman miles from Larinum (Cuntz, 1929: section 314). An early proposal (*CIL* IX: 263) for the site was the Monte Antico ridge west of the Slav village of San Giacomo degli Schiavoni. The survey teams located abundant though scattered remains here, including early Imperial tile graves and probable villa/farmstead sites (C90, C90a, D35, D36, D38), and the Superintendency archive records tile graves, Roman Imperial coins and a glass *unguentarium* on the southwest flank of the ridge.

A little to the east of San Giacomo, however, a more likely candidate for Uscosium was located by the survey. The 16-hectare site B102 was by far the largest scatter found during the project, and its surface remains, including standing brick walls, marble veneer, mosaic tesserae, a pottery waster and possible tile graves, suggested a settlement of considerable complexity and some wealth by local standards (Figs. 87, 94). Subsequent excavation has so far brought to light the remains of a major hydraulic complex, focused on a large brick-built cistern datable to the late 1st or 2nd century AD, a group of sunken *dolia*, and evidence for large-scale pottery and tile production in the later Empire (Albarella *et al.*, 1993; Ceglia, 1984, 1985, 1989; Roberts, 1992). The remains bear a close resemblance to the antiquarian description of the

Fig. 86 Early Imperial settlement in the lower Biferno valley (1st–3rd centuries AD). 1. town; 2. village; 3. vicus/villa; 4. villa/farmstead; 5. probable farmstead; 6. possible farmstead; 7. cemetery/tomb; 8. approximate limits of walked areas; 9. modern town/village; 10. valley watershed.

findspot of a marble slab (*CIL* IX: 2828) recording work by *pagani* under Antoninus Pius, which involved the restoration of a *lacus*, a term whose meanings include reservoir or cistern, at a cost of 15,000 sesterces – but the link between the two sites is not certain (II: Chapter One).

In addition to A198, B102 and C317, the survey found several other category A sites which under the Empire are likely to have been either nucleated settlements or large villas (B260, B268, C300, E43, E64 and possibly A92, B257 and B276). Their surface remains generally cover an area no less than the 0.5–1 hectare typical of the valley's deserted medieval villages, whose populations are estimated at about one hundred persons (see Chapter Eleven), and some were considerably larger: at E43, for example, the debris scatter measured *c*. 2 hectares. An interesting comparison is offered by A143 in the upper valley, the probable site of the *municipium* of Fagifulae, where the surface scatter covered only *c*. 1 hectare, less than the villa of the Neratii near Saepinum (*c*. 1.5 hectares).

Nearly all the vicus/villa sites show continuity from the Samnite period (and sometimes earlier) to late antiquity, and seem to have been complex and prosperous: surface finds included fragments of marble veneer, mosaic, painted wall-plaster and terracotta water-pipes. The recent excavation of four mosaics, part of a baths building, and traces of polychrome frescoes at Santa Maria Casalpiano (C300) underlines the impression of wealth (De Benedittis *et al.*, 1993) – though whether the finds belonged to the *pars urbana* of an elegant villa or to the *domus* of a *magister pagi* (village headman) is not perhaps yet wholly certain. An inscription from the site referring to 'the household gods of the cottagers/hut-dwellers' (*lar[ibus] cas[anicis]: CIL* IX: 725) indicates the presence of a community of low economic and social status – the workforce of a large villa or, conceivably, the peasantry of a village.

Cemeteries were commonly associated with category A sites, and their evidence is also somewhat ambiguous with respect to the nature of the settlement. The archaeological remains and most of the funerary inscriptions suggest persons of low rank, including slaves (A198, B102, C300, C317). At A198, however, a young slave, Hymnus, who had died at sixteen before receiving his promised freedom, was mourned in an elaborate metrical inscription set up by his *dominus*, Orestinus (Ceglia, 1984, 1991). At Olivoli (E43) a funerary monument found in 1741 commemorates T. Vibbius Clemens, his wife Babia Prisca, and T. Vibbius Priscus (*CIL* IX: 737). The men are almost certainly connected to the Vibii of Larinum who reached senatorial rank under Augustus (Camodeca, 1982: 145; Torelli, 1973). They had been leading magistrates in a local town – presumably Larinum – and Priscus a patron as well. The monument was erected by municipal decree, bringing to mind the dedications offered by

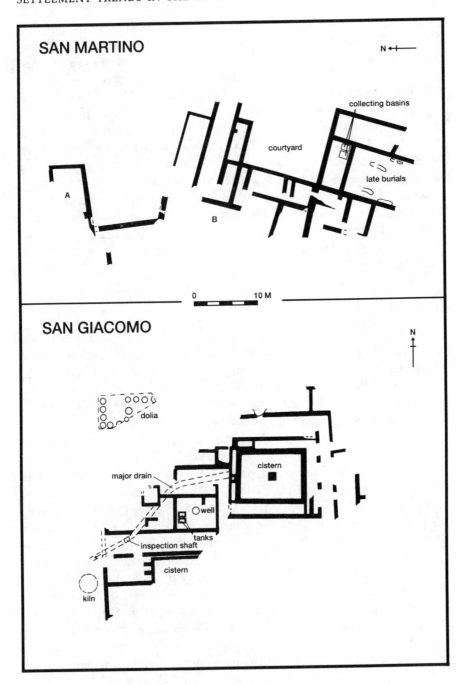

Fig. 87 *Vicus*/villa sites in the lower Biferno valley: San Martino in Pensilis (A198) and San Giacomo degli Schiavoni (B102). (After Di Niro, 1991e: 266 and Albarella *et al.*, 1993: 159)

the *municipes saepinati* at the villa of the Neratii. Olivoli was probably also the site of a wealthy villa. There was another important villa at Arcora, near Campomarino (E64: Fig. 88), belonging to the *fundus Vellanus* owned by the senator Q. Tillius Sassius *c.* AD 60, which had earlier belonged to a Titia Flacilla (*CIL* IX: 2827; La Regina, 1984: 305–7).

There was much new building at these sites in the early Empire, when they probably reached their greatest extent. The evidence includes concrete walls at A198, whose plan (Fig. 87) suggests at least two main phases, brick structures at B102, reticulate and brick (*opus mixtum*) walls at E64 and reticulate at Santa Maria Casalpiano. By the late 2nd or early 3rd century, however, parts of A198 and B102 were no longer being maintained for their original purposes. At A198 a series of poor burials was inserted within earlier buildings, whilst at B102 the vats and drainage channel associated with the cistern were becoming clogged with domestic rubbish (Roberts, 1992: 75).

VILLAS AND FARMSTEADS

In the lower and middle valley the survey found 56 certain and 20 probable early to mid Imperial sites. There are 33 possible sites of this period. Sixteen of the certain and probable group may have been new foundations. As in the upper valley, some scrappy black gloss sites could represent new settlement in the late Republic. The 76 certain and probable sites are about 45 per cent fewer than in the Samnite period (140 sites in this group).

The category B sites of the lower and middle valley seem to have been substantial but fairly plain buildings, with little of the expensive decoration produced by survey sites of comparable size in south Etruria (Potter, 1979: 122–3) or northern Campania (Arthur, 1991a: 109–124). Traces of mosaic and painted wall-plaster were few, and none produced marble. Evidence for building work datable to this period was fairly widespread, however (B98A, C138, D36, E37, E46). Site A249 may have been fairly typical (Fig. 89). Its extent as determined from the surface remains (*c.* 3600 square metres) lies towards the middle of the category B range, and its apparently U-shaped layout finds parallels at sites A121, D36 and C138 and at the excavated villa of Matrice in the upper valley (Fig. 85). Geophysical prospection suggests an earlier phase with a different orientation (II: Chapter Three). Although the site had been deep ploughed just before its discovery (Fig. 23), the only decorative material found was some painted plaster.

Excavation may bring surprises, but we should probably think of these sites as rather like Matrice in their largely utilitarian character and in sharp contrast with western Tyrrhenian villas like San Rocco in Campania, which

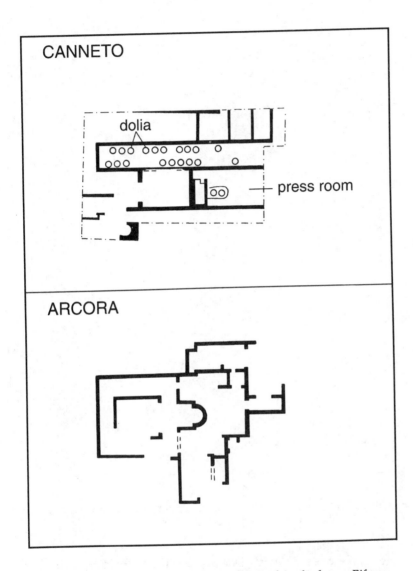

Fig. 88 Roman villas in the Trigno valley and in the lower Biferno valley (not to scale): Canneto in the Trigno valley (after Di Niro, 1982:11) and Arcora (site E64) in the lower Biferno valley (after La Regina, 1984: 305).

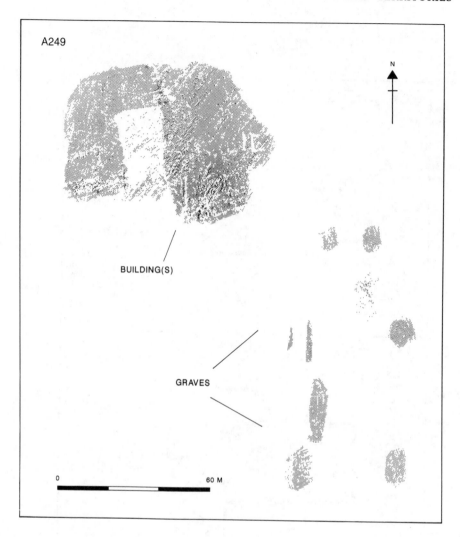

Fig. 89 Site A249, below Larinum: debris scatter from a Samnite and Roman villa, showing main building and associated cemetery.

appears to follow closely Varro's *villa perfecta* in its provision of an elegant and richly appointed *pars urbana* for extended visits by the owner, family and guests (Cotton and Métraux, 1984). The simple decoration (where present) of the Biferno valley sites might suit the status of a bailiff or a moderately well-off tenant or freeholder, but not the rich upper classes of Larinum. Obviously, however, this does not exclude the possibility that many were owned by them.

Simple tile graves were occasionally associated with these sites (A121,

Fig. 90 Part of limestone relief with *bucranion* and garlands from site E13 in the valley floor below Larinum – probably from a funerary monument of the second half of the 1st century BC (**II:** Chapter Four: F27). (Photograph: Graeme Barker)

A249, C138, D35/D36), but only D35, which produced a glass bowl and an Italian sigillata dish, belongs certainly to the early Empire. These burials were probably of the resident labour force, who seem to have been of low rank. The tomb of a villa owner may be represented by the sculpted limestone frieze block (Fig. 90) found in the alluvium of the valley bottom below Larinum (E13). A similar block comes from elsewhere in the *ager Larinas* (Stelluti, 1988: fig. 276). The E13 find, which does not seem to be associated with a category A site, recalls the mausoleum of Didia Decuma at Larinum and other round funerary monuments in the region. It is dated by Amanda Claridge probably to the later 1st century BC (**II:** Chapter Four: 27).

The category C group doubtless includes smaller farmsteads, cottages and agricultural store buildings (**II:** Chapter One: site C90). Their numbers, though considerably fewer than in the black gloss period, nonetheless point to the survival of dispersed smallholdings, and the great majority also produced black gloss pottery. Whether they were independent concerns or leased from larger landholders cannot of course be deduced from the physical remains. Few seem to have survived much into the 2nd and 3rd centuries AD. The pattern of loss from the Samnite period was widespread but especially marked near the major centres, as a comparison between Figures 76 and 86 indicates. It needs to be remembered, however, that the decline of the peasantry may already have been underway before the Social War (Chapter Nine).

SETTLEMENT TRENDS, c. AD 250–600

THE UPPER VALLEY (Fig. 91)

There are a few honorific texts dating to the 3rd century AD at Saepinum, but major new initiatives are not attested there until the middle years of the following century, when several public buildings, including the basilica and the baths of Silvanus, were rebuilt mainly with state-controlled funds (Gaggiotti, 1978, 1982a, 1991). The aim of this programme was almost certainly to restore civic life according to conservative Senatorial ideals (cf. Ward-Perkins, 1984: 27), but it achieved only limited success. The town's theatre was being used as a rubbish dump by the early 5th century, and scattered burials took place there by at latest the 6th or 7th century (Cappelletti, 1982: 160; 1988: 87–9; De Benedittis, 1988b). The forum seems to have undergone a similar evolution (Bergamini, 1986; Matteini Chiari, 1988). The necropolis which developed in the forum (only part of which has survived) perhaps gravitated towards the former basilica, whose 4th century *tribunal*, with later apse, may have been converted into a tiny church (Gaggiotti, 1991). Clearly people were still living at Saepinum c. AD 600, but in physical surroundings much altered since the mid 4th century.

Fourth-century initiatives are also evident at Bovianum (De Benedittis, 1986: 69). We know almost nothing of the town's later history, however, although the survival of traces of the Roman street plan into the modern period, as at Aesernia (modern Isernia), suggests that the town was never completely abandoned. Elsewhere in the upper valley, late 6th or early 7th century tombs have been found at Fagifulae and near Castropignano (De Benedittis, 1988b, 1991f).

In the countryside the survey identified only 7 certain and 2 probable

Fig. 91 Upper Biferno valley: late Roman settlement (c. AD 250–600). 1. town. 2. sanctuary; 3. villa/farmstead site; 4. probable farmstead/ domestic site; 5. possible farmstead/domestic site; 6. possible farmstead/domestic site; 7. approximate limits of walked areas; 8. modern town/village; 9. valley watershed.

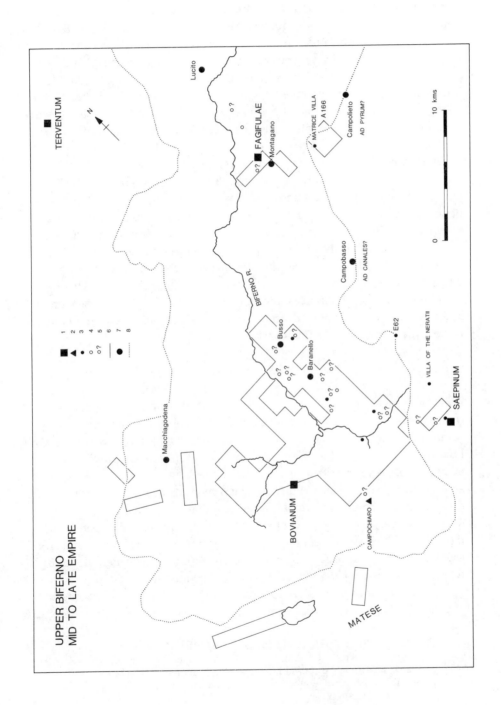

UPPER BIFERNO
MID TO LATE EMPIRE

TERVENTUM

N

FAGIFULAE
Montagano

MATRICE VILLA
A166
Campolieto
AD PYRUM?

BIFERNO R.

Campobasso
AD CANALES?

Busso

Baranello

E62

VILLA OF THE NERATII

SAEPINUM

Macchiagodena

BOVIANUM

CAMPOCHIARO

MATESE

Lucito

1
2
3
4
5
6
7
8

0   10 kms

later Roman sites, compared with 26 certain and probable sites of the early
to mid Empire. Only a handful produced late Roman fine wares and red-
painted ware. There were 16 possible later Roman sites, one fewer than in
the earlier period, but most cannot be dated more closely than 'classical' or
'Roman'. Elsewhere in upland Samnium survey has detected an even
steeper decline in rural settlement by the late Empire (Patterson, 1987: 136).
There is no appreciable trace of village life in this period, and at the
Campochiaro sanctuary some finely decorated glass vessels of the 3rd/4th
centuries seem to be the latest finds (Capini, 1982; Cappelletti, 1991; Lagi,
1991).

At Matrice the villa seems to have declined from the late 2nd and 3rd
centuries, and some of its rooms became dumps for household rubbish. An
indication of harder economic times may be offered by two large pottery
deposits dating to shortly before AD 200 and to shortly before AD 300
respectively. The later group contained 9 vessels of African Red Slip ware
compared with 27 in the earlier group, and a more limited range of coarse
pottery, which was also technically inferior (Roberts, 1988). In the early 5th
century the site may have been abandoned for a while. However,
occupation or re-occupation is attested until c. AD 500, although seemingly
at a low material level and several burials, mostly of infants, were made in
ruinous parts of the villa (Becker, forthcoming).

THE LOWER VALLEY (Fig. 92)

What little we know of Larinum in the later Empire suggests urban
retrenchment. An honorific inscription set up to a 4th century governor of
Samnium, who was also the town's patron, was carved on an early
Imperial statue base (De Caro, 1991b), and subsequent activity in the
excavated areas of the town seems to have been slight (Di Niro, 1991e). The
amphitheatre had lost its original function by c. AD 600 at the latest, when
several inhumation burials took place there (De Tata, 1990). As the tombs
show, however, the town was not deserted in the post-Roman period, and
the only fully excavated grave produced several pieces of bronze and iron
jewellery. None the less, the broad picture is one of substantial decline,
which is matched by the evidence from the countryside.

The survey found 37 certain and 3 probable sites of this period,
compared with 76 certain and probable sites of the early to mid Empire.

Fig. 92 Late Roman settlement in the lower Biferno valley (c. AD
250–600). 1. town; 2. village; 3. *vicus*/villa; 4. villa/farmstead; 5.
probable farmstead; 6. possible farmstead; 7. cemetery/tomb; 8.
approximate limits of walked areas; 9. modern town/village;
10. valley watershed.

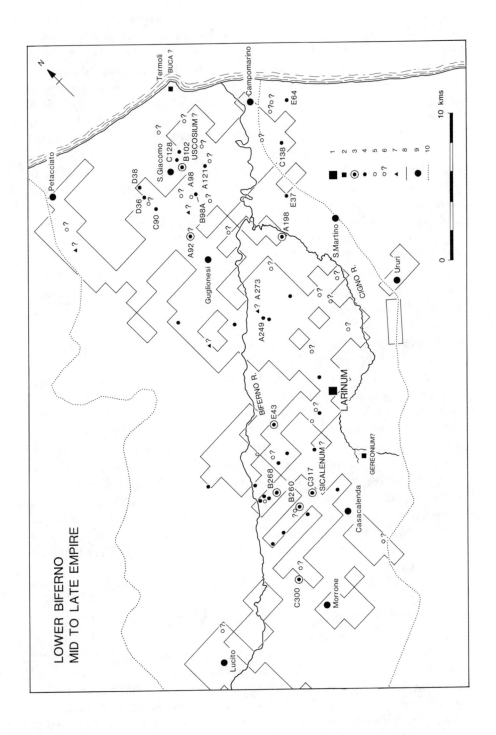

LOWER BIFERNO
MID TO LATE EMPIRE

BUCA ?
Termoli
Petacciato
Campomarino
E64
S.Giacomo o ?
C128
D38
B102
D36
USCOSIUM ?
A98
A121
C90 o ?
B98A
A92
Guglionesi
C138
E37
A198
S.Martino
Ururi
CIGNO R.
A273
A249
BIFERNO R.
E43
LARINUM
B268 o ?
GEREONIUM?
C317
B260
SICALENUM ?
Casacalenda
C300
Morrone
Lucito

1 2 3 4 5 6 7 8 9 10

0   10 kms

There were 29 possible sites (down from 33). The casualties of the c. 50 per cent decline within the certain and probable group seem mostly to have been the smaller sites, following the trend of past centuries. The vicus/villa complexes at A198 and B102 were still vigorous into the early 5th century, with much evidence for long-distance exchange and a possible late mosaic at A198. Subsequently overseas artefacts arrived in very small quantities down to the late 5th or early 6th century, but not beyond. Yet, despite the evidence for a substantial presence well beyond AD 400, the excavated parts of the sites show no sign of restoration after their decline two centuries earlier. The hydraulic installations at B102, for example, saw progressive rubbish-dumping until c. 420–30, when the area seems finally to have closed down (Roberts, 1992, 1993).

A strong late Roman presence is indicated at most of the other category A sites of the lower and middle valley (B260, B268, C300, C317, E43; (?) A92, B257) and at most category B villas. Relatively few sherds of African fine ware of the 3rd and early 4th centuries could be identified, but later African and (from c. AD 400) Phocaean imports were quite plentiful. Closely datable finds of the period beyond c. AD 450 were very few, however.

The scarcity of fine wares, amphoras and other imported pottery after the mid 5th century seems to signal a breakdown in the lower valley's overseas connections. But does it also indicate massive depopulation? Later activity is attested only at a handful of sites: A198, A248, possibly A121, B102, C138 and C181 and now Santa Maria Casalpiano (C300), where recent excavations have brought to light about fifty late antique burials in the ruins of the vicus/villa (De Benedittis, 1991e; De Benedittis et al., 1993). The burials seem to respect a small apsidal building, perhaps a tiny church or chapel. Grave goods are few, but include a gold tremissis of the late 6th century (Justin II, 565–78), some illegible bronze coins and a red-painted ware flagon, probably also of the 6th century. There appears to have been a community of some kind in this fertile and open part of the middle valley close to AD 600, whether descended from the late Roman inhabitants of the area or made up of new settlers.

THE AGRICULTURAL ECONOMY (JL, GB, GC, DW)

The principal faunal sample from the Roman period of settlement is from the Matrice villa – some 3500 fragments of animal bone were recovered from the Roman levels, of which about 3000 were identifiable to species (Clark, forthcoming). Species represented by a few fragments included cat, dog, hare, horse, red and roe deer, but the bulk of the material consisted of the main food species: cattle, pig, and sheep/goat (**II**: Chapter Seven). Little change can be seen in the relative proportions of these species during the several centuries of Roman occupation: the animals most frequently killed were pigs, the bones of which make up between a third and a half of the total sample, followed by sheep/goats (about a third), with cattle bones comprising less than a fifth of the total. The relative proportions of the three species in the later Roman deposits excavated at the Campochiaro sanctuary were very similar to those of Matrice (Fig. 79). In the other two (very small) samples available from the Roman period, from Saepinum (where bones were collected by cutting back domestic deposits near the forum), and from a cistern fill dated to c. AD 430 at the San Giacomo vicus/villa (Albarella, 1993), sheep/goats are slightly more numerous than pigs, with cattle again the least important numerically.

All the samples are poorly preserved, as the numbers of loose teeth (the strongest part of the body) confirm, but the presence of material from all parts of the skeleton indicates *in situ* slaughter at all four sites. The pigs were invariably killed young, at the end of the first or in their second year, as we would expect given their predominant importance for meat. The cattle killed at all four sites were adult animals: whether on the farm, in town or at the sanctuary, it seems that the beef eaten by most people was invariably from breeding cows and bulls and plough animals at the end of their working lives. Sheep, several times more common than goats at Matrice and Campochiaro (on the evidence of the morphological criteria that are used for distinguishing these two species – Boessneck, 1969) at both sites died at a variety of ages as sub-adults and adults, but especially in their second year, and males were noticeably more frequent than females. The likelihood is that most flocks were kept for meat, milk and wool, with sub-adults being killed off for their meat and the older females kept for breeding, milk and wool until their productivity declined.

The bones of all three species have numerous chop marks, especially where the main meat joints had to be separated at the articulations. No chop marks were observed on the few horse and ass bones in the samples, indicating that these animals were not normally eaten, but saw marks show that horse metapodials, red and roe deer antler, and cattle, sheep and goat horns were carefully separated from the rest of the carcass for bone-working. Small cut marks on sheep mandibles and metapodials from Matrice, Saepinum and San Giacomo are evidence of skinning, and similar marks were observed on a cat skeleton from San Giacomo. The most remarkable find from the latter site is the scapula of a camel, the first identification of camel in Roman Italy. Albarella (1993) concludes that it was most probably imported for use as a pack or draught animal. In this respect it is interesting to note that a camel transporting amphoras is depicted on a fragmentary relief, probably of funerary character, from Abruzzo (L'Aquila) and is now in Chieti museum. However, the relief is dated tentatively to the late Republic or early Empire (four centuries or so earlier than the San Giacomo find) and has been explained as symbolizing commerce with the Orient (Romanelli, 1943–5).

Perhaps the most significant feature of the Roman-period faunal samples from the valley, compared with the Samnite samples discussed in the previous chapter, is the broad similarity between the material from domestic and ritual sites (Fig. 79). The shift would appear to reflect the fundamental cultural and economic changes brought to the upper valley by Romanization: the development of a social system in which the city or town was now the dominant focus for the display of power, patronage and wealth, and of an agricultural economy increasingly geared to market production. Whereas pig meat had been reserved especially for local sanctuary feasts in the Samnite period, one feature of Romanization in the towns and villas was the same dietary shift towards pig consumption that we find elsewhere in Roman Italy. Furthermore, the Biferno valley farmers were also exporting pork to market.

Even though pigs are prolific breeders and omnivorous, the fact that they do not provide secondary products like milk or wool (manure being the only product of the live animal) means that they are in some respects a luxury food. The ancient literary sources confirm that pig meat of all kinds was enormously popular with the urban populations of Roman Italy, whether rich or poor (White, 1970), and pigs dominate the faunal samples of towns like Capua, Naples, Pompeii, Ostia and Rome (Barker, 1982; King, 1985). Certainly by the 5th century AD Samnium was an important supplier of pigs to Rome (N. Val. 36.1, in Pharr, 1952), whilst the faunal evidence at Matrice indicates a reversal of the roles of sheep/goats and pigs from as early as the 1st century AD. Like many other villas in Italy in the Imperial period (King, 1985), Matrice was probably engaged in the intensive production of pigs for outside markets, as well as for home consumption. Pork may have been exported on the hoof or as cured pork (laridum): in general curing seems to have been substituted for the driving of herds at a relatively late date (Barnish, 1987: 173), but recent finds from the north Italian Comacchio shipwreck show that jointed pig carcasses were being transported as early as the Augustan period, presumably for sale (Farello, 1991).

Vats, tanks and sunken dolia found at Matrice, San Giacomo and San Martino (Figs. 85 and 87) point towards liquid production, almost certainly wine at Matrice and wine or olive oil in the lower valley. However, only the dolia yard at San Giacomo, as yet unexcavated (Ceglia, 1993), rivals the installations at the Canneto villa (Fig. 88) in the neighbouring Trigno valley, and both seem to have been a good deal smaller than the *cella vinaria* of the well known Pisanella (Boscoreale) villa near Pompeii (Rossiter, 1978: 18–21; White, 1970). It is significant that the small limestone press bed (*ara*) found during the survey near San Giacomo (Fig. 93) is the only example of its kind known from the valley, and the few local amphoras from survey and excavation (Roberts, 1992) do nothing to contradict the impression that olive and vine cultivation in the valley was characterized generally by small-scale production. The products of sites like San Giacomo and Canneto may have travelled regionally, but the contrast between the valley and major wine-producing regions like northern Etruria (Attolini *et al.*, 1991) and Campania (Arthur, 1991a) is very marked.

Agricultural implements from Matrice include a bronze animal bell, an iron pruning-hook and a probable iron scythe, supporting the picture of a mixed economy derived from the faunal and plant remains. A lava grain mill of the smaller Pompeian variety (Moritz, 1958) was also found at Matrice, and fragments of other lava hand mills, all imported, come from thirty or so sites up and down the valley (II: Chapter Six); though some are certainly earlier, many should be of Roman date. None seems to have been as large as the Monte Vairano *catillus* (Chapter Nine) or needs to have had more than a domestic role. However, their frequency is striking by comparison with the finds reported from most other large-scale surveys in Italy, such as those in southern Etruria (Ward-Perkins *et al.*, 1968), northern Campania (Arthur, 1991a) and the Ager Lunensis (Mills, 1986). This might indicate a less sophisticated rural economy, with greater emphasis on self-sufficiency, but could also support the view that cereal production was important, as in the Samnite period. Surplus grain for local centres must be assumed, and at Saepinum a water-driven mill has been identified close to the forum (Matteini Chiari, 1982: 172). We do not hear of exports from Samnium, although Apulia, which included Larinum in the early to mid Empire, was a noted producer of wheat (Brunt, 1971: 369). The combination of cereal cultivation with stock-raising is well-attested in both Roman and medieval Italy (Brunt, 1971: 372–3; Wickham, 1983).

The fullest literary evidence for agriculture in the valley comes in Cicero's *pro Cluentio*, of 66 BC. The orator identifies the *domi nobiles* of Larinum as possessing estates, business interests and stock in the town's territory (*qui in agro Larinati praedia, qui negotia, qui res pecuarias habent: pro Cluentio*, 198), and a further local insight is offered by the account (unchallenged in court) of a violent dispute over grazing rights between the bailiffs (*vilici*) who ran the estate of Cicero's client, Cluentius, and the herdsmen of Ancharius and Pacenus (*pro Cluentio*, 161). Cicero calls this one of the ordinary quarrels which happened between shepherds on the transhumance droveroads (*calles*).

Fig. 93 Press bed (*ara*) for the production of wine or olive oil, found near site C127. (Photograph: Graeme Barker)

Long-distance transhumance between Apulia and Samnium was a factor in the economy throughout the period, as we know from Cicero, Varro (*De Re Rusticae* II.1.16), the famous Saepinum inscription of the later 2nd century AD (*CIL* IX: 2438; Corbier, 1983) and an Ostrogothic text from near Termoli (*CIL* IX: 2826). It flourished under the strong central authority provided by Rome, as it was to again under the control of the Dogana delle Pecore of the post-medieval period (Chapter Twelve). The literary evidence, like the faunal samples, suggests that the major landowners in the valley had interests in stock, but whether they needed to move their animals far, except to more distant markets, is debatable. The local availability of year-round grazing and pannage, already adequate in the Samnite period, should have improved in Roman times with the thinning out of dispersed rural settlement.

Wool production, especially in the lower valley, was suggested as an important feature of the Samnite agricultural economy, and it may also have been significant in Roman times. The valley's close connections with Apulia, renowned for its wool and cloth (Brunt, 1971: 373–4), are again worth remembering. Loomweights were not found in the Roman levels at

Matrice, and were not common on wholly Roman survey sites, but if, as the ancient authors suggest, the warp-weighted loom was being rapidly replaced by other forms of loom in early Imperial Italy (Wild, 1970: 67), this need not be significant.

A Roman-period tannery at Saepinum (De Caro, 1991a: 250–3), like the Samnite *fullonica* there, shows that the town processed animal products at least for local needs. De Caro's discussion of the importance of oak gall in tanning is a reminder that the gathering of woodland products as well as wild plants and fruit, as yet archaeologically invisible, will also have had economic importance (Frayn, 1979: 57–72; Millar, 1981: 73). Hunting, however, does not seem to have contributed much to rural diet. Its products were perhaps mainly consumed in the urban *triclinia* of the wealthy, which may also have been the principal destination of the dormice fattened in the purpose-built jars (*gliraria*) found at San Giacomo and Matrice (Roberts, 1992: 84).

Local farmers seem to have aimed for a diversified base throughout, especially in the more favourable conditons of the lower and middle valley. The geomorphological evidence (Chapter Four) for the early Imperial period suggests an open environment and heavy erosion rates, much as in late Samnite times, whereas from approximately the mid Empire, erosion appears to have slowed considerably, suggesting the contraction of cultivation and the re-establishment of pasture and woodland. There appears to be a close correlation between this development and the substantial drop in the number of dispersed sites after the 2nd/3rd centuries AD.

Whilst it is difficult to isolate the precise cause or causes of the agricultural changes that took place in the valley, it is surely probable that the leading landlords – who included senators – were well aware of economic trends and possibilities elsewhere, especially at Rome. The possibly senatorial villa at Sette Finestre in Etruria seems to have moved into surplus pig-raising c. AD 100, at a time when the capital's grain and wine were being increasingly supplied from overseas (Carandini, 1985b; Purcell, 1988). In the Biferno valley, too, it seems highly likely that the major landowners also responded to changing urban markets, both at Rome itself and elsewhere, expanding the pastoral sector in ways which have left a clear imprint on the geomorphological and archaeological record.

MANUFACTURE AND TRADE

The overwhelming dominance of locally-made pottery and tile in the survey finds is a reminder that the greatest part of the valley's exchange must have been conducted within a small radius. Nevertheless, whilst manufacture and trade were small-scale by comparison with wealthier regions of Italy, the broad picture is one of much busier activity and much closer integration with the Italian and Mediterranean economy than was previously imagined for Roman Samnium (Brunt, 1971: 357; Morel, 1991: 187–203), although Morel's distinction between upland Samnium and the more developed zones on its margins, to which Larinum clearly belonged, is an important one. In the Roman period, as in preceding centuries, the lower and middle valley seems to have looked mainly northwards and southwards for its imports, the upper valley mainly towards Campania.

Larinum is described by Cicero in 66 BC as a market centre (*pro Cluentio* 40) and was clearly the home of a wealthy elite with far-flung social and, possibly, economic connections. Cluentius himself was of equestrian rank (*pro Cluentio* 47), and knights from the central Adriatic coastlands (around Teate, modern Chieti), from Frentanian territory, from Teanum Apulum and Luceria, and from Bovianum and 'the whole of Samnium', came to Rome in his support (*pro Cluentio* 198). Even allowing for some exaggeration on Cicero's part, the network is impressive. It is especially interesting to note Cluentius' ties with the Abruzzo, Apulia and upper Samnium. As Chapters Eight and Nine showed, lower-valley elite connections with Daunia (Apulia) and the Abruzzo are attested as early as the Iron Age, and a link with upland Samnium, though probably a later development, was also long-standing.

There is archaeological evidence for exchange with all these regions, and beyond, in the early Roman period. A northern trade route brought a wide variety of products to Larinum and many rural sites, some of them in the upper valley: middle Adriatic amphoras, millstones from Orvieto, Arretine and north Italian pottery, including Sarius cups, and north Italian lamps (Bailey, forthcoming; *Samnium*, 1991: 237, 275, 287–8, 294; Williams-Thorpe, forthcoming; II: Chapters Four and Six). Contacts with the south ranged from Apulia to Campania (Lamboglia 2, Dressel 1 and Dressel 2–4 amphoras, fine and coarse pottery), and southern Italy and Sicily continued to be the major source for millstones, as in Samnite times (Arthur, forthcoming; Capini, 1982: 67; Soricelli, forthcoming; II: Chapters Four and Six). Campanian goods are found predominantly in the upper valley, with which an institutional trading link existed under the Empire in the form of a periodic market (*nundina*) held at Saepinum. This was part of a circuit linked to several Campanian towns, including Allifae, Telesia and Puteoli (*CIL* IX: 2318).

The eastern Mediterranean links of the later Samnite period were maintained through Rhodian amphoras of the late Republic and early Empire, followed by British Bi, Bii and Biv amphoras in the mid to later

Roman period (II: Chapter Four; Roberts, 1992, 1993). A few eastern sigillata A and B sherds appear amongst the survey finds and at Matrice (Soricelli, forthcoming), and from c. AD 400 Phocaean Red Slip ware arrived in the lower valley, along with Aegean cooking vessels. At San Giacomo eastern pottery accounts for about 20 per cent of an early 5th century deposit containing some 435 vessels (Roberts, 1993). A little Cypriot Red Slip ware also reached the lowlands.

The most successful exporter of pottery to the valley was, however, North Africa. From the 2nd to the 5th centuries AD African fine wares reached every part of the valley, and African amphoras and lamps also arrived (II: Chapter Four; Arthur, forthcoming; Bailey, forthcoming). At San Giacomo, North Africa continued to dominate fine ware and amphora imports in the early 5th century, despite the strong showing of eastern products. Further inland, beyond the middle valley, the penetration of eastern wares was much weaker. A large contemporary deposit at Matrice was well stocked with African fine ware but had scarcely anything from the east (Roberts, 1992), and much the same picture is found at Saepinum (Bergamini, 1986).

The exchange network seems to have been more highly developed under the Roman Empire than it had been earlier. Imports reached every part of the countryside, and coins were found at several rural sites (II: Chapter Four). Ninety coins dating from the 1st to the late 5th centuries AD were found at Matrice: a 4th–early 5th century hoard accounts for one-third of the finds (Barclay, forthcoming). Imperial issues also turn up in plenty at other rural sites in Samnium (La Regina, 1980a; Morel, 1984; Rainini, 1984). There is little doubt that coinage was widely used for exchange purposes, alongside barter and other forms of redistribution, as in most areas of the Roman Empire (Howgego, 1992: 20–2).

Artisans were to be found in all the Roman towns and villages of the valley. The fullest evidence comes from Saepinum: as well as the tannery and water-mill already mentioned, pottery and tile manufacture are documented, and a public slave or freedman, L. Saepinius Abascantus, was responsible for the manufacture of lead water-pipes (Saepinum, 1982: 16, 32, 120). Blacksmithing is also now attested (II: Chapter Five), and the many funerary reliefs from the town suggest local mason-sculptors of reasonable competence. In the case of Larinum, the growing evidence for mosaic and fresco work in the town and its territory suggests that there may have been sufficient work to support local craftsmen with these skills. Given the town's centuries-old association with pottery and terracotta manufacture (Chapter Nine), an intriguing recent find has been the base of an Italian sigillata cup stamped LARI, a mark otherwise unattested (Samnium, 1991: 288). There are many instances of the slave potters in Italian workshops of

Fig. 94 Site B102 (San Giacomo) after deep ploughing for a vineyard.
The surface debris is made up almost entirely of large, fresh tile
fragments. (Photograph: Graeme Barker)

this period taking names from towns – Romanus, Arretinus, Pisanus and
Patavinus are some examples (Oxé and Comfort, 1968). About half of the
survey finds of Italian sigillata cannot readily be attributed to the major
manufacturers, and local production, as at Ordona in Apulia, may be a
possibility (II: Chapter Four).

Local pottery and tile manufacture is best attested, however, at San
Giacomo, where an excavated kiln and many wasters are perhaps just the
tip of a considerable enterprise. Magnetometer survey beyond the area
subsequently excavated encountered major anomalies of the type produced
by kilns or brickwork (II: Chapter Three), and deep ploughing for a
vineyard in 1978 brought to the surface huge quantities of tiles, mostly as
large, freshly broken fragments (Fig. 94). In the late 4th and early 5th
centuries red-painted ware was made at the site, and this accounts for c. 20
per cent of the 435 vessels in the early 5th-century AD deposit mentioned
above (Roberts, 1992, 1993).

Rurally based craft activity may have increased in the late Empire. Apart
from San Giacomo, the Canneto villa near Terventum was also engaged in

pottery manufacture, perhaps from the 3rd century (*Samnium*, 1991: 256), and a late Roman lamp mould is known from Santa Maria Casalpiano (De Benedittis *et al.*, 1993: 67). At Matrice slag and clinker were found only in the late levels, together with a possible anvil, and iron-working waste was found at several vicus/villa and villa sites (II: Chapter Five). The changes may reflect the tendency from the mid-Empire for members of the curial classes, burdened by the expense of holding urban magistracies, to decamp to their rural estates.

Finally, it is appropriate to mention here the *augustales*, special priests of the imperial cult. The institution was confined to rich freedmen, who are generally reckoned to have gained their wealth from commerce and manufacture. *Augustales* are attested epigraphically in all the towns of the valley, including Fagifulae. Some were very well-off indeed, like C. Gabbius Aequalis of Larinum, who received the exceptional honour of admission to the town council and who himself had at least four freedmen (*AE*, 1966: 75). At Saepinum, *augustales* were responsible for a number of building projects and public dedications (Matteini Chiari, 1982: 165).

ROMAN SOCIETY IN THE VALLEY

In Chapter Nine it was argued that although urbanization was a relatively late arrival in the valley, like the social elaboration and long-distance exchange of the Iron Age, there had been considerable movement in this direction from the late 4th/early 3rd centuries BC, especially at Larinum. If this is right, changes in social and settlement structure under Rome may have been more nominal than have been supposed for Samnium as a whole (Gabba, 1972; Patterson, 1987). A very striking feature of classical settlement in the valley is the continuity displayed by its communities and leading farmsteads throughout most of the Samnite and Roman periods. This was more pronounced in the lower valley, certainly, but even in former Pentrian territory much that was done in the Roman period developed from a pre-existing pattern.

There was, nonetheless, much catching-up to do in the way of Roman urban development, and this was probably greater where Sulla had been most damaging and Samnite culture at its strongest. An Augustan impetus was very important in the uplands and may also be considered at Larinum, where Octavian (later Augustus) became patron of the town in the early 30s BC (*AE*, 1966: 73). New settlers of the late Republic and early Empire played a leading role in the growth of the upland towns in the early Principate, although prominent figures of Samnite descent are more numerous than was once thought (Gaggiotti, 1983: 140–2; cf. Salmon, 1967:

397–9). Saepinum illustrates what had been done on the ground by the middle of the 1st century AD. Other forms of Romanization made rapid strides: the cultural transformations included the swift replacement of Oscan by Latin in all public media, the widespread adoption of the Imperial cult, and the emergence of a more complex hierarchical society, headed by senatorial families and supported at its base by slavery. The loyalty of the ruling class to the ideals of the young Imperial regime was widely displayed. A good example comes from Larinum, in the form of a bronze copy of a senatorial decree of AD 19 reasserting earlier bans on public performance in the theatre and amphitheatre by members of the Roman elite (Levick, 1983). Possibly the most important change of all for the local aristocracy, however, was the opportunity which Roman citizenship offered of participating not only in municipal society but also in the political and social life of Rome and in the government of empire (Patterson, 1987).

In the long term, however, the competitive edge introduced by such participation seems to have been disastrous for the majority of the valley's free population. Patterson (1987) has argued that the wealth which funded urban development in early Imperial Samnium came primarily from the growth of landed estates, *latifundia*. Estate-building had almost certainly occurred in the valley before the Social War (Chapter Nine), but land redistribution and veteran settlement subsequently reinforced the peasantry. However, by the 2nd century AD many small dispersed sites had been given up, and abandonments continued into the 3rd century, alongside the last flickerings of activity at the rural shrines. On the other hand, the large vicus/villa and villa sites look at least to have maintained themselves in the early Empire and many, like San Giacomo and Matrice, were enlarged or improved. Although they seem to have faltered in the late 2nd and 3rd centuries, a strong presence continued well beyond. The likely implication is that, as small farmers gave up their isolated homesteads and probably their associated holdings, the more powerful landowners were able to expand their estates – with slaves now an important element of the labour force – to produce the surplus needed to sustain their competitive lifestyles, whether locally or at Rome.

The amenities of the valley towns were improved through elite bene-faction, but absentee senatorial landlords like the Vibii and the Neratii almost certainly took more out of the region than they gave back – a pattern of exploitation that was to become all too familiar in the valley's later history. They may in fact have been at the forefront of latifundist development. This did not necessarily involve the creation of vast unitary estates, as medium-sized holdings were probably the most sensible way of managing the land: inscriptions show that the Neratii owned widely

scattered farms around Saepinum (Gaggiotti, 1982a; *CIL* IX: 2450–3, 2824).
At nearby Ligures Baebiani (where the Neratii also farmed) the well-
known Alimentary Table attests an identical pattern of ownership amongst
larger landowners in the 2nd century AD, with the Emperor an important
landlord as well. At the same time, the accumulation of estates was not
restricted to the wealthy and powerful. When Vespasian settled veterans in
Samnium in the 70s AD some colonists seem to have quickly enlarged their
landholdings (Hyginus 131, 17–20). Whether motivated by the need to
survive, imitation of the powerful (Wallace-Hadrill, 1990) or greed, the
acquisitive peasant is likely also to have been part of the process which led
to an emptier landscape.

The fate of the dispossessed is uncertain (Patterson, 1987, 1991).
Emigration was a well-tried formula in Samnium, whether to nearby towns
and villages or further afield. The city of Rome may have attracted many in
this period. Others may have found employment as labourers or shepherds
on the villa estates, still others may have become brigands. Whatever the
case, the gulf between rich and poor in the valley is likely to have widened,
and the free population almost certainly declined.

It is tempting to interpret what we know of the later history of the valley
towns as in part a reflection of the resulting social and economic
disequilibrium. The principal purpose of Vespasianic colonization in
Samnium was probably revitalization (Keppie, 1984: 106). A generation
later Saepinum, like Ligures Baebiani, was one of the recipients of the
alimentary schemes introduced by the Roman emperors to provide
subsistence for poor children (*CIL* IX: 2472). The motivation for the
schemes has been variously interpreted, most recently as measures to
alleviate rural poverty with military recruitment from the peasantry partly
in mind (Patterson, 1987) and, alternatively, as a form of Imperial largesse
rather than a reaction to economic and demographic crisis (Woolf, 1990).
Whatever the case, there was to be no revival of the smallholder in the
valley, at least in terms of archaeologically-detectable dispersed settlement.
Sometime later, in the 3rd century, we hear of a state-appointed *curator* at
Saepinum and Bovianum (*CIL* X: 4590; *AE* 1975: 349), whose function was
to control their public finances. As with the alimentary schemes, however,
curatores are found widely in Italy during this period, and their
introduction need not signify that local problems were worse than in many
other areas.

The decay of the Italian economy from the late Antonine period
(Carandini, 1989; Frank, 1940: 296–8), and the well-documented 'crisis' of
the 3rd century, which certainly touched Italy (though probably not as
deeply as other parts of the Roman world), will also have been damaging
– above all, perhaps, by reducing the opportunities for external trade. The

middle and lower valley seems to have been able to ride out these difficulties more successfully. Although it shared in the decline of late Roman dispersed settlement which occurred in many other regions of Italy (Arthur, 1991a; Potter, 1987), its better soils and easier access to regional and more distant markets allowed a fairly vigorous response when more settled conditions returned in the 4th century. It is possible that the increased fiscal burden following the lifting of Italy's exemption from the land tax in this period stimulated trade (cf. Hopkins, 1980), and the Adriatic sea-route probably increased in importance following the emperor Constantine's establishment of a 'new Rome' at Constantinople in AD 313. Christian Aquileia was certainly prosperous, and when Ravenna was set up as a western capital in AD 402 further opportunities for exchange were offered, which seem to be reflected in the lower valley by the relatively abundant imports of eastern as well as African pottery and amphoras from around AD 400. In the uplands, there was sizeable investment in Saepinum and Bovianum around the mid 4th century, though this appears to have had little impact on rural settlement. A major earthquake in AD 346, which struck towns in Campania and Samnium, though not certainly the valley (Gaggiotti, 1978, 1991), and another tremor which affected Benevento in AD 375 (Symmachus, *Epistles* 1.3), probably contributed to the weakening of the regional economy.

In AD 413 Honorius granted remission of four-fifths of all taxes for five years, with effect from 411/12, to Samnium, Apulia and several other regions of central-southern Italy (*Cod. Theod.* 11.28.7, in Pharr, 1952). This measure was probably connected with the debilitating effects of the passage of Alaric's Visigoths in AD 410–12 (Christie and Rushworth, 1988: 81). In AD 452 we hear of tax arrears equivalent to 5,400 *solidi* owed by Samnium to the guild of swine-collectors at Rome (*N. Val.* 36.1, in Pharr, 1952). These notices coincide with the archaeological evidence for 5th-century site abandonment or decline in the valley and a huge reduction in imports – matched at Iuvanum in the Abruzzo (Fabbricotti, 1992) and in northern Campania (Arthur, 1991a) – which in combination point strongly to troubled circumstances. Even allowing for the problems of dating in the later 5th and 6th centuries discussed previously, it is difficult not to suppose a much-reduced population both in the countryside and in the towns, whose decaying public monuments were a symbol of more prosperous and settled days.

The loss of evidence for regional and international exchange, though more plausibly explained by political instability in Italy and the Mediterranean and the decline of African production than by a vanishing population (Wickham, 1988: 192–3; 1989), surely also signifies a reduced external market for surpluses. We must assume a local economy gearing more to self-sufficiency, though the Ostrogoths were able to maintain most of the structures developed by Rome, as evidenced by their close monitoring of the transhumance routes of the lower valley. In the 490s two officials of Theoderic's court wished to build a church on an estate near Larinum called Mariana (*PLRE* II: 905). Archaeology too shows that the countryside was not deserted in this period and further amalgamation of rural properties may have taken place, though major estate-centres like San Giovanni in Basilicata (Small, 1986) still await discovery. Beyond the 530s, when Ostrogothic rule collapsed, evidence of any kind, whether textual or archaeological, is very scarce indeed. Nonetheless it is reasonably certain that most town sites saw some form of occupation down to AD 600 and perhaps beyond, and there was some rural continuity, as at Santa Maria Casalpiano. Clearly, too, future investigation may produce the churches, timber buildings and artefacts which have led to a reappraisal of urban vitality at Luni and elsewhere in late antique Italy (Potter, forthcoming; Ward Perkins, 1981; Wickham, 1989).

On present evidence, however, the nature and scale of the transformation of settlement in the 5th and 6th centuries should not be underestimated. The villages and farms which for a thousand years had underpinned a considerable level of civilization seem mostly to have gone, and the towns to have become shadows of their former selves. However it is to be explained, a break with tradition is clearly signalled.

CHAPTER 11

THE EVOLUTION OF HILLTOP VILLAGES
(AD 600–1500)

Richard Hodges and Chris Wickham, with a contribution by Graeme Barker

INTRODUCTION: THE ARCHAEOLOGICAL AND HISTORICAL BACKGROUND

This chapter describes the contribution of the project to the dominant debate amongst Mediterranean archaeologists and historians concerning the post-Roman landscape: the transition from classical antiquity to the Middle Ages characterized above all by the development of nucleated hilltop villages, the process in Italy termed *incastellamento*.

The origins of nucleated villages in Italy will only be fully comprehended once integrated archaeological and historical studies have been executed in all parts of the Italian peninsula. Prior to the Biferno Valley Survey, the main focus of research had been in north-central Italy (Andrews, 1981; Comba and Settia, 1984; Potter, 1979; Toubert, 1973; Ward-Perkins, 1978; Whitehouse, 1970; Wickham, 1978, 1981, 1985). In Molise, post-classical archaeology was almost unknown before the project: research on medieval remains had been limited to the exploration of some possible 'Lombard' tombs at Saepinum, excavations at Boiano and Venafro castles, and the restoration of the well-known Romanesque churches of the region (Trombetta, 1971). Historical documentation implied that the *castelli* or hill villages of Molise were for the most part created in the 10th and 11th centuries, a horizon consistent with the historical process elsewhere in Italy, as well as in much of western and northern Europe (Hodges, 1982b: 131–6), but there was as yet no archaeological evidence to confirm or refute this hypothesis. A major aim of this section of the project was, therefore, to see how much an archaeological approach integrating field survey and excavation could contribute to the debate.

At the end of the Roman period, the Biferno valley, like much of the peninsula, suffered the temporary devastation of several wars, particularly the Gothic Wars of AD 535–54 and the Lombard Wars of AD 568–602. The valley was not a major route, but the Larino-Campobasso ridge was one of the secondary roads across the Apennines and was probably used by the

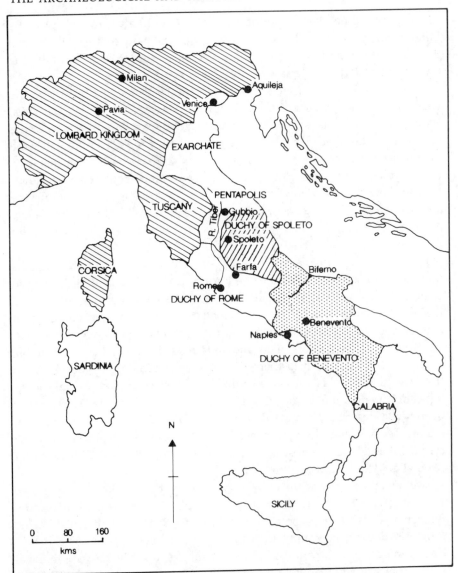

Fig. 95 The Duchy of Benevento in *c.* AD 650 and the political structure of early medieval Italy.

independent Lombard dukes of Benevento of the 570s onwards to extend their rule to the Adriatic (Fig. 95). By the time we have any clear information about the Adriatic coast, in the 7th century, the Duchy of Benevento controlled it from Chieti in southern Abruzzo to the Gargano peninsula in northern Apulia; by AD 700 they had conquered the rest of Apulia as well. The Beneventans (first dukes, then, after the Carolingian conquest of the Lombard kingdom of north-central Italy, princes) ruled the Biferno valley until the Norman conquest of the 11th century. Thereafter the valley was part of the Kingdom of Sicily (or of Naples) until the unification of Italy in the last century.

Within this broad historical framework the local political history of the valley is not easy to characterize. Paul the Deacon, writing in the 790s, claimed that in the 660s the Beneventans handed over the upper part of the valley, including the deserted cities of Bovianum and Saepinum, to the Bulgar duke Alzeco, and that Bulgarian was still spoken there in his own time (Waitz, 1878: 154). Presumably he was right about this last claim, though the total desertion of the cities prior to AD 660 is less likely; but the account tells us nothing else relevant to our study, except that the valley, even though so close to Benevento, was considered extremely peripheral by its dukes.

Its political history thereafter is just of military crossings and divisions into local units. The Arabs used the Larino road in their raiding in the 9th century (Cilento, 1971; Waitz, 1878: 590), and sacked Boiano, Sepino and Larino at various times. The coast road was more often used. German emperors came down it from the north more than once in the 9th–11th centuries, and the coastal plain and hills must have been the vulnerable parts of the valley, both to them and to sporadic raiding by the Arabs in the 11th century. It is, however, unlikely that these events had any long-term detrimental effect on the Biferno communities; the 11th-century documents describe a standard picture of cultivated fields in the coastal region. Termoli was clearly prosperous and expanding already in the 10th century, though its greatest age was perhaps the 12th and 13th centuries (Abulafia, 1976; Petrucci, 1960: 25).

Following a sharp decline of Beneventan power in the 9th century, in the 10th and 11th centuries the valley was split into several, nearly independent, counties, only nominally subject to Benevento: Boiano, Larino (with its dependent county of Campomarino) and Termoli. The better-documented coastal counties were sometimes directly subject to rival states: the Byzantine lands to the south and the Kingdom of Italy/German empire to the north. Termoli in particular was generally dependent on the counts of Chieti, the main political authority on this border of the Kingdom of Italy. The Norman conquest of the late 11th century brought new Norman counties as well. Even after Roger II's re-establishment of centralized political control in the 1140s, the valley was still split (although the local political units got larger): the new county of Molise, centred on Boiano, included the upper basin and middle section of the valley, whereas the county of Loritello controlled the coast.

By 1300 the valley was divided into several small dioceses: Termoli,

Larino, Guardialfiera, Trivento, Boiano, Sepino, parts of Benevento, and – briefly – Limosano; Campobasso, a new city, was not important before the 14th century. By the 13th–14th centuries the county of Molise had crystallized into an administrative unit of the Kingdom of Sicily, extending down as far as Larino. The coastal strip was technically part of Apulia right up to the unification of Italy, and it was only after 1860 that Campobasso was given the whole valley, from Boiano to Termoli, as the core of its province.

THE CHRONOLOGICAL FRAMEWORK

Inevitably, pottery provided the principal means of dating the medieval sites found by the survey and thus the settlement processes they represented, but cannot be used as a straightforward index of past time (Blake, 1980: 3). The production and distribution of distinctive (i.e. datable) ceramics may relate to artificial time-slices rather than ones of historical significance (Hamond, 1978; Plog, 1979). In any ranked society a hierarchy of settlements will exist, and the incidence of particular types of potsherds may do no more than reflect the settlement system: certain types of pottery may occur in some places and not others. In a large and diverse region such as the Biferno valley, we might confidently expect to find – as in previous phases of settlement – several different trading systems in the medieval period and therefore distribution patterns of pottery reflecting these (Arnold, 1985).

Nevertheless, we were constrained to place a great deal of emphasis on the pottery, constructing time sequences or horizons as the best framework for the analysis of the settlement data. Three medieval ceramic horizons were defined, as follows:

Horizon 1: early medieval: 7th–10th centuries
Horizon 2: high medieval: 10th–12th centuries
Horizon 3: late medieval: 13th–15th centuries

The horizons are based largely upon David Whitehouse's pioneering studies of the medieval pottery of southern Italy. He identified the chronological importance of red-painted pottery from central and southern Italy, and developed a typology of it (1966). This included 'Early Christian' red-painted wares of the late Roman period; broad-line painted types belonging to the period c. AD 600–900; and narrow-line painted types dating from the 10th to the 15th centuries. Subsequently, Whitehouse amalgamated the first two types of red-painted wares as broad-line decorated pots (Whitehouse, 1969, 1978). Whitehouse also defined the glazed wares, paying special attention to proto-maiolica in central and southern Italy (1966, 1980, 1986).

The literature on each of these diagnostic wares is now quite considerable (e.g. Buerger, 1979; Dufournier *et al.*, 1986; Johns, 1973; Paroli, 1992; H. Patterson, 1990; Patterson and Whitehouse, 1992). However, in this chapter we shall use the ceramic horizons as we devised them at the end of the project. The detailed bases of Horizons 1 and 2 have already been described by, respectively, Hodges *et al.* (1980) and Hodges and Wickham (1981).

HORIZON 1: THE EARLY MEDIEVAL PERIOD

This archaeological horizon is the most elusive in western Europe. Nevertheless, it was identified in the Biferno valley as a result of the excavations of the settlement of Santa Maria in Civita (site D85) near Guardialfiera in the lower valley (Hodges *et al.*, 1980; Fig. 96). Broad-lined red-painted pottery (and almost no later medieval ware) was a major feature of the ceramic assemblage (Fig. 97), and its dating was tentatively confirmed by a series of radiocarbon dates (II: Chapter One: D85 entry). The radiocarbon dates help to emphasize that there is a chronological basis for the technological distinction between the late Roman red-painted wares defined by Hodges *et al.* (1980) as type Ai and those of *c.* 9th century date defined as type Aii. Aii red-painted wares were almost certainly manufactured with levigated clays and with less investment of labour in their finishing. Only one site of this period was found in the survey, Santa Maria in Civita, though a few sherds that may belong to this horizon occurred at later sites. Several sites of the same antiquity have since been found in the adjacent Volturno valley (Hodges, 1993; Hodges and Mitchell, 1985; Hodges *et al.*, 1984). We assume that site D85 is a model of the earliest medieval hilltop settlements in the Biferno valley.

HORIZON 2: THE HIGH MEDIEVAL PERIOD

This horizon was defined on the basis of pottery from the settlement at Vetrana (site A195) near Guglionesi (Hodges and Wickham, 1981). Three types of pottery were identified, classified as Aii, B and C (Fig. 98). In fact, only three sherds of type Aii broad-lined red-painted wares were found

Fig. 96 Medieval sites in the Biferno valley examined by the survey, and the principal sites discussed in Chapter Eleven. The dashed lines denote the routes of the transhumance droveroads (*tratturi*) in recent centuries.

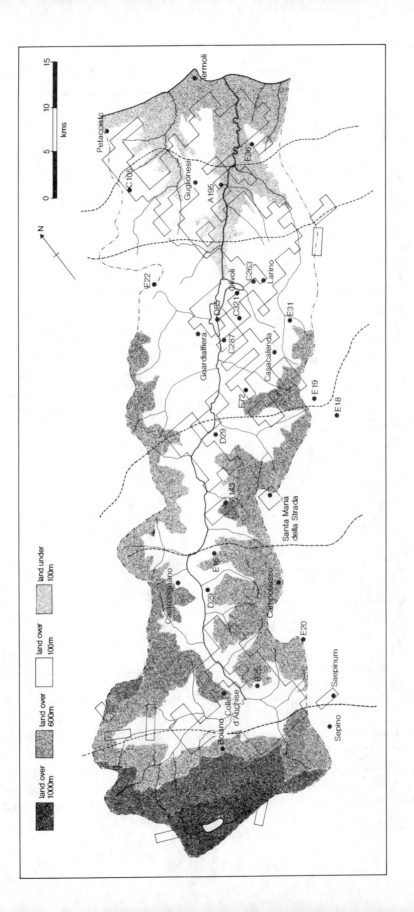

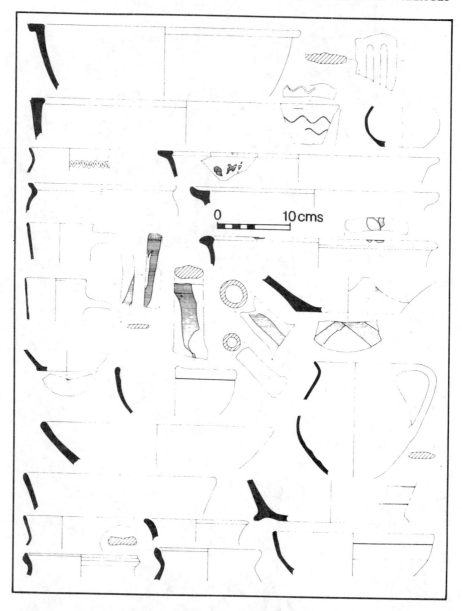

Fig. 97 Horizon 1 pottery from Santa Maria in Civita (D85).

and the remainder of the pottery assemblage consisted of 1396 sherds of type B (59 per cent) and 955 sherds of type C (41 per cent). Type B coarse wares occurred at Santa Maria in Civita in a limited range of forms, while C (a finer undecorated type) is commonly found on later medieval deserted sites in the lower valley. The assemblage appears to fit between that of

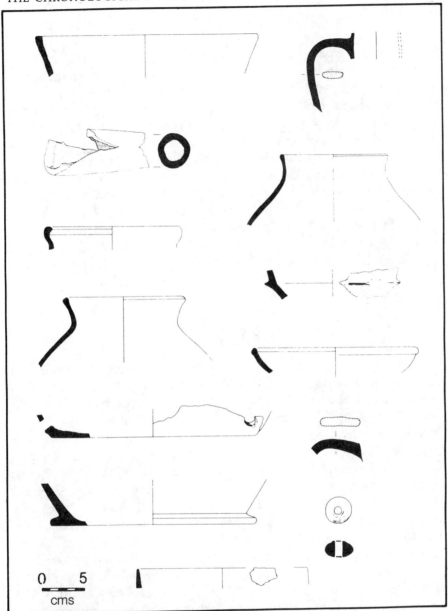

Fig. 98 Horizon 2 pottery and other clay objects from Vetrana (A195).

Santa Maria in Civita and those characteristic of village sites deserted in the 14th and 15th centuries, the site probably being deserted in the 12th century. Vetrana seems to have been a typical small *castello*, a model of nucleated settlements of the age of *incastellamento*, albeit one that was abandoned after only five or six generations.

HORIZON 3: THE LATE MEDIEVAL PERIOD

Two distinctive types of pottery can be attributed to this horizon, besides a number of less common types imported to specific places within the survey zone. Firstly, proto-maiolica glazed types occurred on a number of deserted medieval villages, and were identified as variants of Apulian products discussed by Buerger (1979: 32–3). Secondly, less common narrow-lined red-painted wares were recognized at late medieval sites. The absence of these wares at Vetrana indicates a break between the distribution of broad-line and narrow-line red-painted wares, in contrast with the continuum proposed for Apulia by Whitehouse (1966, 1969). We were able to establish, however, that Horizon 2 ceramics often occurred on Horizon 3 sites.

The chronology and principal characteristics of the main medieval sites studied by the project are summarized in Table 10, and the distribution of the medieval sites and other settlements discussed in this chapter is shown in Figure 96.

EARLY MEDIEVAL SETTLEMENT

The archaeological evidence for the 6th-century Lombard invasions of Samnium is very slight. Rotilli (1986) has published the grave goods associated with rich burials in Benevento, the capital of the duchy created about 571 by Zotto. Excavations at San Vincenzo al Volturno, in northwest Molise, have identified the desertion of a major Roman villa at about this time, and the beginnings of a funerary rite in which the dead were con-spicuously furnished with accoutrements (Hodges, 1993). In the Biferno valley, only the simple graves constructed within the *agora* at Saepinum (Fig. 99) are usually assigned to this period, although a 7th-century cemetery has now been found at Vicenne near Campochiaro (Ceglia, 1988; Fig. 100).

The history of major settlements in the valley at this time is extremely vague. Larinum was still occupied in the 9th century when it was the seat of a bishopric attacked by the Arabs. As noted above, Paul the Deacon, writing in the late 8th century, records the settlement of displaced Bulgars at Bovianum and Saepinum, but the scale of this migration is not known. Only modern excavations of the kind undertaken in northern Italy at Brescia (Brogiolo, 1992), Luni (Ward-Perkins, 1978, 1981) and Verona (Hudson, 1985) will determine how these small classical towns fared in the 6th–10th centuries. There is, however, no particular reason to presume that they remained fully urbanized centres: continuity of occupation may have been restricted to the church and to the use of central zones as homesteads for the

Table 10 Medieval settlements studied in the Biferno valley: chronology and principal characteristics; for their location see Figure 96

Ceramic Horizon	Site Code	Name	Remarks
1	D85	Santa Maria in Civita	Fortified hilltop settlement with two small nuclei of buildings as well as a church (Hodges *et al.*, 1980).
2	A195	Vetrana	Promontory settlement with church overlooking the Biferno (Hodges and Wickham, 1981).
2/3	E36	Portocannone	Promontory settlement, probably moved in the lage 15th century: 2 graveyards and remains of a church at the south end of the spur. Intense occupation over an area about 90×65m. No evidence of a wall around the spur. Lots of Horizon 3 imported pottery.
2/3	E31	Gerione	Walled settlement with remains of a small castle and church. Situated on a spur, covering an area *c.* 150m×75m. A small extra-mural settlement to the south.
2/3	E18	San Pietro	On flat land close to the *tratturo* and overlying a classical settlement. A 13th-century church survives here (Trombetta, 1971: 171) and behind it a grassy mound *c.* 85m×49m.
2/3		Santa Maria della Strada	A promontory settlement *c.* 1 km from the monastery. The remains cover an area *c.* 200×40/25m, with visible buildings including a church and dwellings either side of a road.
2/3	E20	Monteverde	A promontory settlement belonging to Santa Maria di Guglieto with a church and rows of houses either side of a rock-cut street.
3	C105	Serramano	A surface scatter *c.* 50×50m on an exposed hilltop: no visible remains. The site occurs in the *Catalogus Baronum* (Jamison, 1972: 62–3).
3	C321	San Barbato	Promontory scatter relating to a settlement known from the 12th century (Masciotta, 1914: 80) and re-settled with Albanians in the later 15th century (De Gennaro, 1977: 359).
3	E24	Santa Giusta	Small scatter close to an isolated church on a flat hilltop.

Continued overleaf

Table 10 *Continued*

Ceramic Horizon	Site Code	Name	Remarks
3	E26	Covatta	A small scatter on a promontory now largely covered by modern housing.
3	E19	Castello	Small scatter around the base of a prominent castle overlooking a *tratturo*.
1/2/3	B25	Mignaniello	Scatter around the demolished remains of a castle dating from the (?) Norman period: there was also a possible associated hamlet.
3	D29	Torre	Scatter around the base of an isolated tower in the bottom of the Biferno valley: close to a *tratturo*.
3		Casalpino	Scatter around the edge of a small Benedictine monastery.
3	A143	Faifoli	Scatter around the small Benedictine monastery.

Fig. 99 Lombard tombs in the forum at Saepinum. (Photograph: Richard Hodges)

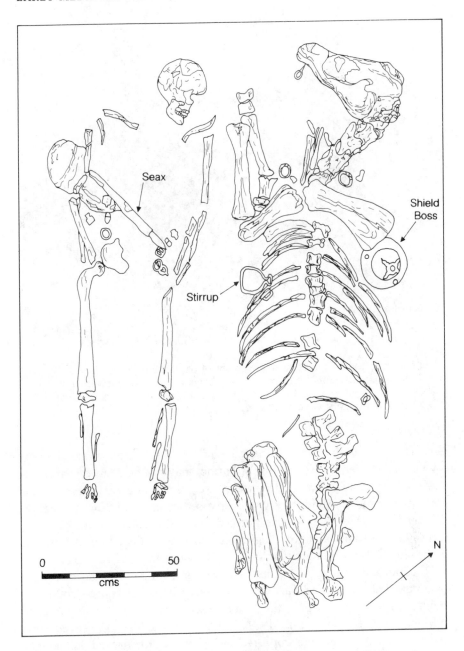

Fig. 100 A Lombard tomb at Vicenne, Campochiaro. (After Ceglia and De Genito, 1991: 337)

Fig. 101 The early medieval settlement of Santa Maria in Civita (D85) (the isolated wooded hill immediately beyond the lake), viewed from the northwest; the church was on the highest point of the hill, to the left. (Photograph: Graeme Barker)

elite. In fact, the absence of early medieval evidence from these classical towns, despite recent excavations at Larino, may not be chance – at most, there was probably small-scale occupation, with minimal provision for craft specialization. Significantly, all three settlements are now on slightly different sites from their Roman antecedents, or have been in the past.

The only substantial archaeological evidence for settlement in this period is the site of Santa Maria in Civita (D85). It was a fortified hilltop site (Fig. 101), commanding one of the major crossings over the Biferno river – it overlooked the bridge of San Antuono before its submergence under the modern lake (Fig. 10). Our small-scale excavations have been reported in full elsewhere (Hodges *et al.*, 1980), but a brief summary is needed here. Before excavation the site appeared as a long saddle-backed hill with a knoll resembling an earthen castle at its eastern end. The hill was gridded with a 10-metre grid, within which the potsherds and tile on the surface were collected. Following this the south-central area of the hill was subjected to a fluxgate gradiometer survey in an attempt to determine the incidence of sub-surface features such as hearths, pits and walls. Finally, a

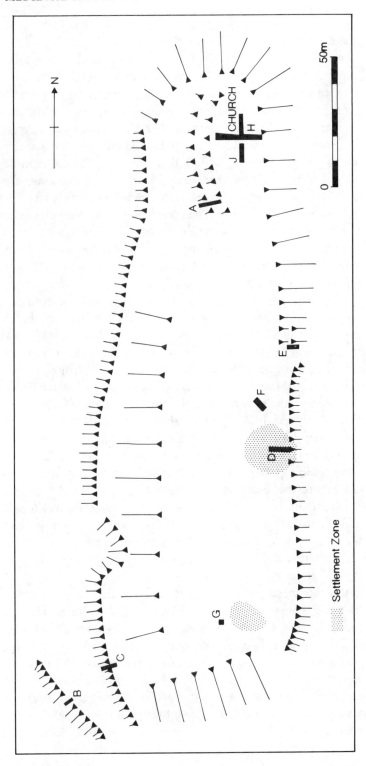

Fig. 102 The early medieval settlement of Santa Maria in Civita (D85): plan of excavations and general features.

selective series of excavations was undertaken to clarify the settlement's history and principal characteristics (Fig. 102).

The radiocarbon dates (II: Chapter One: D85) and the pottery assemblage point to the use of the site from about the end of the 6th century until the 15th century, but the evidence more precisely attests occupation in the late 6th or 7th century and again in the 9th century, the site then being cultivated in the late medieval period. The late Roman phase, represented by a few sherds of broad-line red-painted pottery of type Ai, appears to have been ephemeral: perhaps the hill was a refuge of the kind described by Brown (1978), designed to command the river crossing, though it remains unclear whether such sites were centres of population. By the 9th century, Santa Maria in Civita was certainly a settlement nucleus. The pottery from this phase (Fig. 97) consisted of type Aii broad-line red-painted pottery, which was probably made in Apulia, together with large quantities of a coarser ware (B) which had been made and distributed within the valley since classical times. A small but significant range of glass fragments, mostly pertaining to drinking vessels, was also found.

Traces of a palisade were found on the valley side of the hill, while a thick masonry wall was found on the south side. Our limited excavations showed that in at least two areas wooden structures with clay floors had been constructed up against the masonry wall. Behind these structures, in the centre of the hilltop, were clusters of pits, some of which were clearly used for storage, their contents including large quantities of carbonized grain (Van der Veen, 1985). On the raised knoll at the east end of the hill were the remains of a surprisingly large rectangular church with two aisles, built at this time with newly quarried materials (Fig. 102). A deep pit within the building suggested that a major tomb or reliquary had been removed when the building was demolished. A small cemetery was located around its south and west sides containing 28 skeletons (infants and adolescents as well as adults) buried without gravegoods. Using Narroll's (1962) population constant, it was estimated from the size of the domestic area that the early medieval community consisted of about 50 persons (Hodges et al., 1980: 112).

The large botanical samples recovered from the early medieval settlement included a wide range of cereals and legumes (Table 11). A striking feature of the material found was that it consisted almost entirely of harvested and cleaned crops without threshing debris (Van der Veen, 1985). Some 2700 fragments of animal bone were collected from the excavations, of which just over 1600 were identifiable (Hodges et al., 1980: 97–102). There were complete specimens of cat, dog, donkey and horse, probably from discarded carcasses that were not eaten, and small quantities of bird, fish, red deer and tortoise, but the main species

Table 11 Edible plant remains (seeds and fruits unless otherwise stated) at the early medieval settlement of Santa Maria in Civita. The identifications are of sub-samples taken from the samples collected in the excavations. (After Van der Veen, 1985)

CEREALS

Avena sativa	Common oat	90
Hordeum vulgare	Barley (6-row, hulled)	1193
Hordeum vulgare (rachis internode)	Barley	1
Panicum miliaceum	Millet	337
Triticum aestivum/ Triticum durum	Bread/hard wheat	991
Triticum dicoccum	Emmer wheat	3
Triticum glumebases	Wheat	3
Triticum sp fragments	Wheat	809
Cereal indeterminate fragments		4067

OTHER CROP PLANTS

Coriandrum sativum	Coriander	2
Ficus carica	Fig	307
Lathyrus sativus	Grass pea	37
Linum usitatissimum	Flax, linseed	215
Vicia faba	Horse bean	10
Vitis vinifera	Grape (pips and stalk)	16

COLLECTED FRUITS/NUTS

Quercus sp	Acorn	1
Sambucus edulus	Dwarf elder	5
Sambucus nigra	Elder	3
Fruitstone fragments		5
Nutshell fragments		4
Pulses, fragments		10

represented were sheep/goats (*c.* 57 per cent – mainly sheep according to morphological criteria), pigs (*c.* 28 per cent) and cattle (*c.* 15 per cent). Some lambs were killed after a few months, but most sheep were killed as mature animals, as were the cattle, suggesting the importance of the secondary products of these animals as well as their meat. The pigs were killed between one and two years old. Although the presence of extremity bones of all the main species indicates slaughter on site, the sample was dominated by the main meat-bearing bones.

Structural details revealed by the excavations – repairs to the defensive wall, a dwelling re-floored, fresh pits cut into abandoned ones – point to a short-lived phase of occupation. It ended in a conflagration that burnt the houses and defences and carbonized the grain in the pits. Similar evidence for a massive conflagration at this time has been found in the excavations of the monastery of San Vincenzo al Volturno in upper Molise, a period for which the chroniclers have left a harrowing account of the devastating impact of an Arab attack (Hodges, 1993). We believe that the second, early medieval, phase of occupation at Santa Maria in Civita probably spans the period c. 825–75, ending in the period of Arab raiding.

Although the original excavation report concluded that Santa Maria in Civita was a normal, albeit extremely precocious, early medieval village (Hodges *et al.*, 1980), our increased understanding of rural settlement in this elusive period in the region (Coccia, forthcoming; Hodges *et al.*, 1984) now suggests that this is unlikely. The circuit of defences represents the labour of a large number of people. The prominent position of the church suggests it had a particular, unusual, significance, and the fact that it had a cemetery is also unusual for rural sites of this period (Hodges, 1990). The high proportion (c. 40 per cent) of red-painted pottery made outside the Biferno valley, and the presence of glassware, a prestige commodity at this time, are further indicators of the unusual status of the community. The botanical and faunal remains both suggest that the site was predominantly a centre for the consumption rather than the production of foodstuffs, and it is noteworthy that the hilltop is surrounded by a patchwork of rather poorer soils that those of the comparable territory of Guardialfiera, the nearby 'successful' village on the other side of the valley (Hodges *et al.*, 1980: 103–6).

It is likely that Santa Maria in Civita was an unusually large village for the period, functioning as both a strategic and an economic centre. In AD 801 the Carolingians advanced their southern frontier to the Trigno river, only some 20 kilometres north of the settlement. Given the location of the settlement by a significant river crossing, and the scale of the 9th-century fortifications, the most likely founders of the site are the princes of Benevento, who were more concerned than anyone else with the Carolingian threat. The size of the site, and the location of its church, might well have had a symbolic content, like the far larger San Vincenzo al Volturno monastery, which was a focus for the competing strategies of Carolingians and Beneventans in just this period and which had a similar – indeed, far more impressive – array of prestige material goods (Hodges 1993). Santa Maria in Civita was probably also an estate centre, the focus for the rents (including foodstuffs presumably) and services of dependent tenants, who could, in Italian estates of the period, be scattered over a very wide area (Toubert, 1973; Wickham 1985: 19–23). The site could well have been one of the major collection centres for the Adriatic lands of the Beneventan princes, and possibly the major one for the middle Biferno valley. If so, its stored foods may not have been destined simply to supply a garrison against Carolingian attack, but also, ultimately, the prince's needs in Benevento.

If this is so, however, then Santa Maria in Civita loses any typicality. It was easy enough a site to find – we doubt many others like it remain undiscovered, at least in the middle valley. This is important for the debate about the date of *incastellamento*. Despite several attempts to show that settlement on hills could predate AD 900, often by several centuries, no other clear archaeological example of a fortified settlement founded before 900 has been found on the same scale as Santa Maria in Civita, either in this survey or in those of neighbouring areas such as the Volturno valley. There are some documentary hints that there may have been early concentrated settlements on the Adriatic coast, as we discuss later, but what size or shape they had remain speculative. Whether earlier fortifications in reality underlie still-surviving villages cannot yet be usefully discussed. Nevertheless, the site of Santa Maria in Civita should not be seen simply as an interesting oddity. *Incastellamento* in the 10–12th centuries was not just the creation of new fortified and nucleated villages (and indeed it was this only in some parts of Italy and not others); it was in large part the takeover of formerly public functions by private landowners. If its material form had predecessors and analogues in 9th-century public sites, we should not be surprised. Santa Maria in Civita may, in the end, be a guide not to an ill-documented pre-*incastellamento* but rather to the specific rural forms of local public power in early medieval central-southern Italy, which later fortified villages imitated. It may be a guide to one of the reasons why *castelli* in the centre-south, unlike in most of the rest of Italy (or Europe), were fortified villages at all.

HIGH MEDIEVAL SETTLEMENT: THE DOCUMENTARY EVIDENCE

Nearly all the modern villages of the Biferno valley (Fig. 5) are listed in the *Catalogus Baronum* of AD 1150 (Jamison, 1972), which therefore acts as a reliable *terminus ante quem* for the process of *incastellamento*. Indeed, the earlier we have documents, the earlier we have evidence for *castelli*: the earliest known for the valley is Macchiagódena in AD 1003 (Federici, 1929–33: n.183), and most of the other villages may well go back as early as this (Wickham, 1985: 24–52). However, by far the best historical documentation for the classic *incastellamento* period – in this case, the 11th century – is from the lower valley.

Three features made the lower valley different from the interior in the 8th–12th centuries. The first was the far greater ease of access to it, both by sea and by land (Abulafia, 1976; Bresslau, 1903: nn.465–6482; Federici, 1929–33: n.130; Franchi and Vannucci, 1983; Hoffmann, 1980: 2.6, 31, 52; Petrucci, 1960: I.25, with nn.10,22). Termoli was the most important port between Ancona and Apulia until Mussolini built Pescara, and in the 12th–13th centuries had some political and commercial strength. Even in the

10th–11th centuries it was populous, and men of Termoli are mentioned in a number of monastic texts granting or renting land along the coast or further afield. The narrow river mouths of the Molise coast (the Trigno, Biferno, and even the tiny Tecchio) had their ports in the 11th century – the Tecchio even had tolls that the counts of Chieti thought worth granting a quarter of to the monastery on the Tremiti islands (30 kilometres off the coast of Molise) in AD 1038. Whatever the nature of this trade (in *pietra ollare*, for example? see p. 274), it certainly promoted communications with the interior: there are several references to roads to Termoli in the 11th-century texts for the coastal plain, and these clearly had local importance.

The development of an urban society was the second feature of coastal settlement – there is no sign of it inland until the rise of Campobasso in the late Middle Ages. The third was the fact that as late as AD 800, and in many cases well beyond AD 1000, more or less all the coastline of Molise belonged to the state. Whilst the reasons for this are not well understood, the effect was that state donations of land, for example to churches, tended to be very large and did not get subdivided, so that landholdings in the lower valley remained very large indeed well into the Norman period and beyond.

By the 11th century, with one exception (the 16th-century Slav village of San Giacomo degli Schiavoni), all the major settlements of the lower valley were already present: Petacciato, Montenero, Guglionesi, Termoli, Campomarino, Portocannone (though this village moved to its present position only around AD 1500) and San Martino in Pensilis (Fig. 5). It is possible that several of them predate the classic *incastellamento* period. Guglionesi, for example, first documented as a *castello* in AD 1049 (Petrucci, 1960: n.39), is referred to in the 940s as a *villa* (Hoffmann, 1980: 1.56) with, it seems, already an attached territorial boundary. Similar *villae* (probably open but concentrated centres) are known from Abruzzo predating the fortifications of the *incastellamento* process (Wickham, 1982: 76–8). A striking feature of two other coastal centres when they are first documented, Petacciato in AD 1038 and Campomarino in AD 993, is that they are not called *castra* but *civitates* (Hoffmann, 1980: 2.13; Petrucci, 1960: nn. 2, 22 etc). We cannot imagine that they had bishops (though Campomarino had a count), but they may well have derived their status from a past history – more, anyway, than they would have had if they were only a generation old or less at the time they were first recorded. Of the seven centres listed above, in fact, only Montenero and San Martino were probably new in the 11th century. How early they actually dated from we cannot tell, for none of them has been excavated. Field-walking at the site of old Portocannone (E36), however, found no pottery similar to that at Santa Maria in Civita (below, p. 274), and that site, therefore, probably post-dates AD 900.

There seems to have been a thin but uniform spread of dispersed settlement between the coastal centres, on the evidence of the strikingly high number of rural churches mentioned in the 11th- and 12th-century documents, for example of the Tremiti monastery. Six are recorded for Petacciato, seven for Campomarino, one each for Montenero, Portocannone and Termoli. Rural churches are not universal indicators of settlement, but some of these certainly acted as settlement foci on a small scale, and the numbers of churches involved must be significant.

Petacciato (Fig. 96) is an illuminating example of the phenomenon (Federici, 1929–33: nn.186, 190–1; Petrucci, 1960: nn.10, 22, 105). In 1038 the count of Chieti, the major landowner, gave four pieces of Petacciato's land totalling over 200 hectares to the Tremiti monastery. Each of these pieces had a church on it, two of them on the tops of hills, two of them on the sea coast. A few kilometres south of Petacciato, the area called Serramano (Serramala in the Middle Ages) had two other churches: San Bartolomeo (1010–1318) on the hilltop (Colle Serramano) and San Silvestro (1024–1151) in the Vallone Cupa valley. San Silvestro, a church in 1024, is described as a *casale* (farm) in 1151. San Bartolomeo may have undergone the same development, on the evidence of the survey site C105 found in the same locality – though the richness of the 13th-century pottery assemblage there, including green-glazed wares otherwise absent from the rest of the survey, suggests that it may have been an elite site of some sort, perhaps a hunting lodge. It is more likely that such churches were already settlement foci on a small scale before they developed into *casali*, rather than being isolated religious buildings around which rural settlement was planted *de novo* in the 12th century. On the other side of the valley, too, near Campomarino, the church of Santa Maria *in loco Coronetum* mentioned in 1010 had become the *casale* of Santa Maria *Coroneti* in 1174 (Petrucci, 1960: nn. 2, 106, 119).

Although the documentary record for the central and upper valley is much more fragmentary than for the lower valley, the *Catalogus Baronum* indicates that by the 12th and 13th centuries there was a network of fortified nuclei that determined the political-territorial structure and most of the settlement structure throughout the valley. It was in the hierarchical relationship between these nuclei and their satellite (and universally temporary) minor settlements, that the different zones of the valley differed. In some parts of the upper and middle valley, where the nuclei were fairly small and close together, little other settlement is ever documented at all. In the ample slopes below the large and well-spaced centres of Larino and Casacalenda, on the other hand, many 12th–14th century *casali* are recorded: small centres with a specific history, products of population expansion and the clearance of marginal land, declining as plague and pastoralism made their presence unnecessary and even, perhaps, counterproductive. On the coast, the settlement pattern was more stable, with some dispersal between the major centres in all periods, even if the smaller settlements themselves were not stable. The differences were in degree, not type, but they were real.

HIGH MEDIEVAL SETTLEMENT: THE ARCHAEOLOGICAL EVIDENCE

As in the case of Santa Maria in Civita, the investigations of the settlement of Vetrana (site A195) have been described in detail elsewhere (Hodges and Wickham, 1981), so again only a summary is warranted here. The site lies on a promontory overlooking the Biferno river about 2 kilometres below the village of Guglionesi (Fig. 103). In 1979 the site was ploughed and it was possible as a result to collect all the surface archaeological debris within a 10-metre grid. Subsequent documentary research identified the settlement as the village of Vetrana, which existed from about the 10th to the 12th centuries. The surface scatter suggested that the spur had been occupied by many buildings, but no concentrations of material indicated intra-site structural arrangements. The raised knoll at the north end of the site – the point from which one entered the spur – appears to have been the location of the church, to judge from the incidence of human bone on and around it. No traces of any enclosure wall were discovered, but the deep sides of the spur as well as the outer walls of the dwellings may have provided sufficient defence.

As noted earlier, pottery of two types (B and C) predominated, in a range of forms which extended the variety found at Santa Maria in Civita (Fig. 98). Similar pottery was found at the deserted settlements of Porto-cannone (site E36), Gerione (site E31) and San Pietro a Pianisi (site E18), confirming the existence of these particular villages in the high medieval period (Fig. 96). Most of the pottery used at these sites was of local manufacture and the virtual absence of red-painted pottery at Vetrana indicates that trading links with the production sites in Apulia had been severed. However, evidence for wider trading links included fragments of soapstone (*pietra ollare*) jars at Vetrana and Portocannone which probably derived from alpine factories (Mannoni, 1975), and a 12th-century Byzantine *sgraffito* sherd at Portocannone, probably from Corinth in Greece. The Commercial Revolution, as Lopez (1971) termed it, embraced coastal Molise in the 11th and 12th centuries, even though the hinterland remained more isolated.

Although this period encompasses the Norman occupation, strikingly

Fig. 103 The medieval settlement of Vetrana (A195), viewed from the northwest. (Photograph: Richard Hodges)

little evidence of military strongholds survives in the valley in contrast with, for example, Apulia, Calabria, or northern Sicily. A small keep and its bailey were discovered at Colle d'Anchise in the upper valley, and two possible others were noted at Mignaniello (B25: on the other side of the river in the same part of the valley, below the Colle Sparanise Samnite/Roman sanctuary) and at Gerione (E31) near Casacalenda at the middle/lower valley junction. However, classic mottes such as occur in Apulia (Andrews, 1981: 331) and large isolated castles like those of Sicily (Bresc, 1977) are a feature of the late medieval settlement system of the valley. They were probably associated with the transhumance routes across the valley (Fig. 96), which seem to have regained the importance that they had had in the classical period only after c. 1200 (see below).

The 12th century marked the apogee of ecclesiastical art and architecture in the Biferno valley, material testimony to the wealth of the rich owners of the zone in Norman times. Village churches at Campomarino, Guglionesi and Petrella, as well as the cathedrals at Guardialfiera and Termoli (Trombetta, 1971), reflect the blending of Lombard style with the prevailing European Romanesque tradition (Carbonara, 1979). While these community churches displayed considerable wealth, the monasteries within the valley were of modest scale compared with those of adjacent regions. Santa Maria della Strada, near Matrice, is the best-known community (Jamison, 1938;

Trombetta, 1971: 51–72), but it was a small rural house compared with the magnificent monasteries of Campania such as Casamari, Fossanova and of course Monte Cassino. The other Benedictine house in the valley, at Casalpino near Morrone, was similarly modest in scale. Nevertheless, the ecclesiastical archaeology, like the evidence for exotic trade commodities, provides another useful indicator of the comparative wealth of the Biferno valley in the high medieval period, compared with the 'remote poverty' (Levi, 1947: 12) which developed in the next phase and which has characterized the valley ever since.

LATE MEDIEVAL SETTLEMENT FORMS

Ten deserted medieval villages belonging to this phase were discovered in the survey (Table 10), whilst several castles and church sites, in some cases still partly in use, were also visited. Proto-maiolica sherds and, less commonly, narrow-line red-painted pottery were found on all of these sites. However, the IGM 1:25,000 maps show a great many more abandoned settlements within the survey zone, and post-medieval documentation – usually court-cases relating to disputes over land that had been deserted in late medieval times – makes it clear that comparatively few of these sites were located by the survey. The survey evidence for the late medieval period mapped in Figure 96 can therefore be regarded only as a small sample of the total. Nevertheless, we can at least discern from it the principal characteristics of late medieval settlement forms in the valley.

Portocannone (E36), Gerione (E31), San Pietro a Pianisi (E18), Santa Maria della Strada and Monteverde (E20) were all small villages by the standards of the time. Each measures between half a hectare and a hectare, and would probably have had populations of about a hundred persons. Their morphology was not uniform, however. In the lower valley, for example, Portocannone was situated at 150 metres above sea level on a spur about a kilometre west of the post-15th-century (present) town. Not all of the spur was occupied, and room for expansion still existed at the northern end when the settlement shift took place. By contrast, Gerione was perched high on a limestone hill 600 metres above sea level, nearly an hour's walk from the nearest modern farm and a long walk from the nearest water. Inside its walls are the remains of a small stone-built castle as well as a church and many dwellings; the congestion appears to have been so great that several peasants built homes outside the walls. San Pietro was different again: though quite high (575 metres above sea level), it was sited on a flat plain set back from the south side of the Biferno valley at the north end of a long, low mound (Fig. 104).

Fig. 104 The deserted medieval village of San Pietro (E18) near Santa Elia a Pianisi. (Photograph: Richard Hodges)

In the middle valley, the occupation area of the deserted village of Santa Maria della Strada is similar in size to those of the villages described above; the church and its tiny graveyard lie about two-thirds of the way up to the village (at 800 metres above sea level). The settlement was probably a *casale*, an open settlement dependent on the small monastery of Santa Maria della Strada (Jamison, 1938). In the upper valley, Monteverde above Vinchiaturo was also a *casale*, in this case belonging to the little abbey of Santa Maria di Guglieto, which overlooks the village. The settlement (Fig. 105) was situated on an exposed rocky spur at an altitude of 900 metres. At the end of a road that twisted between the dwellings was a piazza with, to one side, a small church. The dwellings were less packed than at other sites, though several buildings lay outside the defended area.

Many historians have cited the defences common round medieval settlements to explain *incastellamento* in terms of a response to civil insecurity. In the case of the Biferno valley this is not adequate as an explanation – on the evidence of Santa Maria in Civita, fortifications predate the age of *incastellamento* – but it points our attention to the fact that hilltops were readily fortified. At most of the Biferno villages, use was made of natural steep slopes as defences, and also the house-structures themselves. Only Gerione possessed a substantial enclosure wall separated from the dwellings.

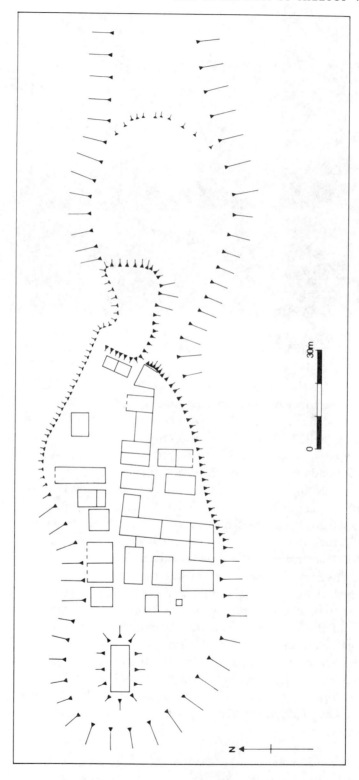

Fig. 105 Sketch plan of the deserted medieval village of Monteverde (E20): the houses were clustered tightly together across the central and eastern part of the promontory on either side of a street that led to the church at the western end.

The layout of roads and piazzas offers clues to village organization. Francovich and Gelichi (1988), for example, have noted the occurrence of regular, perhaps planned, villages in Tuscany from the 12th century, whereas Pesez (1984) has argued that the streets of Brucato in Sicily indicate an irregular, organic, development of the community, and a similar case has been made by Whitehouse (1970) for Satriano in Basilicata. The street bisecting Monteverde was comparable with that serving Satriano: it was designed for animals and people but not wheeled traffic. A single street also bisected the deserted village at Santa Maria della Strada. Two streets, however, almost certainly served Gerione and Portocannone, with small side passages leading off these principal arteries at Gerione. Piazzas do not seem to have been common, although there was a large open space in front of the church at Monteverde and a broad street through the lower half of the village at Santa Maria della Strada. It is difficult without extensive excavations to discern whether the medieval villages of the Biferno valley were planned, but it seems unlikely.

As at Santa Maria in Civita in the 9th century, churches commanded the most prominent positions in the later medieval villages. The church occupied an imposing position at one end of the deserted settlements of Vetrana, Portocannone, Gerione, San Pietro a Pianisi and Monteverde, just like the Romanesque cathedral at the successful village of Guardialfiera opposite Santa Maria in Civita. In some cases there may have been more than one church: this may have been the case at Santa Maria in Civita on the evidence of two graveyards, one associated with the church on the hilltop, the other close to the domestic nucleus. Two graveyards were similarly noted in the field survey at Portocannone. At Santa Maria della Strada, however, the church lay towards the centre of the settlement, perhaps marking the upper extent of the first village, beyond which the later settlement expanded.

The churches in these deserted settlements were relatively modest in size and appearance, but not small. The church at Santa Maria in Civita measured about 12×10 metres, the later church at Gerione about 20×8 metres, and that of San Pietro a Pianisi 11.5×9.8 metres (Trombetta, 1971: 179). The single-celled church at Santa Maria della Strada is 10×8 metres, a little larger in fact than the church of the adjacent abbey (10×5 metres). The church of San Giorgio in the surviving village of Petrella Tifernina in the middle valley indicates just how splendidly decorated these buildings might have been, though admittedly it is twice the size of the churches of the deserted villages (30×16 metres). The surviving churches like those of Petrella, Matrice (Santa Maria della Strada) and Guardialfiera emphasize how small diocesan churches, as well as cathedrals such as those of Larino and Termoli, were decorated in the 12th century. The Biferno valley lay within the orbit of the great church-builders of the Abruzzo on the one hand and those of Apulia on the other (Carbonara, 1979). Churches merited greater investment than any other material structure surviving from the period.

In contrast with the prominence of churches in the region, castles and tower-houses are rare. Great 13th–15th-century fortresses survive at Boiano, Campobasso, Castropignano and Termoli (Trombetta, 1971) and there were similar castles at Casacalenda and Guglionesi, but smaller castles were infrequent. Of the deserted villages investigated by the project, only Gerione contained any form of internal castle – no more than a tower set within a wide ditch at the southern end of the settlement. Why there were so few intra-village fortifications cannot be understood, given the dearth of historical documentation. Certainly the Biferno valley is unlike many other parts of Italy in this aspect of the morphology of its medieval settlements (Andrews, 1981).

Very little is known of ordinary housing. A 14th-century crypt painting at San Pietro a Vincoli, a village 25 kilometres to the north of the Biferno valley, depicts the city of Bethlehem as if it were a Tuscan hilltop settlement such as San Gimignano (Trombetta, 1971: fig. 42). To what extent did the medieval hilltop villages of the valley take this form? Sadly, no village in this region has been thoroughly excavated like Brucato in Sicily (Pesez, 1984) or Rocca San Silvestro in Tuscany (Francovich, 1992). At most deserted sites in the valley, only the general form of the structures sealed beneath rubble and vegetation can be seen: dwellings of either two or three cells, made of rough-hewn rubble lightly mortared together, measuring about 10–14 metres in length and 6–8 metres in width. In size, organization and construction, however, they are broadly similar to late medieval dwellings excavated in other regions of Italy (Beavitt and Christie, 1993; Cabona et al., 1978; Francovich, 1992; Francovich et al., 1980; Pesez, 1984; Whitehouse, 1970). On this basis, we can postulate that the houses of the Biferno valley medieval villages contained two floors, the animals being kept in one ground-floor room, agricultural products and materials in another, and the household occupying the first floor. Our excavations at Santa Maria in Civita suggest that this form of building dates back to the 9th century; it was certainly the predominant type in the earliest *castelli*, and the arrangement has persisted in the valley as elsewhere in the central and southern Apennines (e.g. Barker and Grant, 1991) until modern times.

As described in the previous section, documentary sources of the period such as the *Catalogus Baronum* of AD 1150, papal bulls and tithe lists indicate that, in addition to the main villages, there was also a variety of scattered settlements in the valley such as houses, estate centres and churches, often characterized by brief or discontinuous occupation. In addition to the (?) hunting lodge on Colle Serramano (site C105), other small rural settlements of the period identified by the survey included Casarene (C329), Covatta (E26), Corneto (C263), Canale (C287), and San Barbato (C321). They were all in the middle section of the valley, established in the later 12th or 13th century after the main phase of *incastellamento* as the remaining woodland was colonized. The small size of the pottery scatters (generally measuring under 50×50 metres in extent) indicates very small communities of no more than three or four dwellings. Small *casali* of this kind gradually declined in a combination of economic competition and political pressure from their more powerful neighbours, exacerbated by the Black Death after 1350 (see for one of these, Ururi: Magliano and Magliano, 1895: nn.2–5, 19, 21–6; Masciotta, 1914: iv. 461–76; Tria, 1744: 301–27). All of the late medieval rural settlements located by the survey contracted to single farms in the post-medieval period.

Given the humble nature of the domestic and ecclesiastical archaeology of the valley in this period, it is no surprise that the material culture indicates a very limited level of trade, particularly away from the towns, compared with more prosperous parts of Italy such as Tuscany (Francovich, 1992; Francovich and Hodges, 1989). Portocannone and Colle Serramano were presumably within the market catchments of the Adriatic ports of Termoli and Campomarino, and Apulian proto-maiolica and other decorated table wares constitute up to 8–10 per cent of their assemblages. Rescue excavations in the towns of Larino and Campobasso in the valley and Isernia and Venafro just beyond it have also recovered large quantities of glazed fine wares (De Benedittis, 1983). On the other hand, glazed table wares make up no more than 1–2 per cent of the assemblages collected by the survey from the late medieval rural settlements. The rural population relied on a range of coarse wares from local production centres, like the workshop found recently in Campobasso that probably supplied neighbouring villages such as Monteverde.

LATE MEDIEVAL SETTLEMENT SYSTEMS

By the 13th century the Biferno valley constituted three distinct settlement regions. The coastal hinterland of Termoli and Campomarino formed part of the Adriatic zone, the wealthiest part of the valley, and the most international. The imported pottery at Portocannone and Colle Serramano reflects the impact of this trade at a material level on lower order settlements. Guglionesi possessed 378 hearths (*fuochi*) at this time, indicating a population in excess of two thousand (Masciotta, 1914: 158). Another index of the special nature of this zone is settlement structure, both within the settlements and in the countryside: the new village of Portocannone, for example, had fine walls and a gridded street pattern as if it wished to portray itself as a small town; Ururi, re-founded in the late 15th century, was somewhat similar; and the territories of both settlements were dotted with substantial farms resembling those of the *mezzadria* of northern Italy.

By contrast, the middle valley was hill-country poorly served by markets and, with the exception of the transhumance droveroads, communications. The settlement pattern was if anything denser than on the coast. The IGM maps indicate an average of 4 or 5 *casali* in the territory of every village. The sites we studied varied in size from 2 to 4 dwellings at Santa Giusta (E22) to about 20 at Santa Maria della Strada, suggesting (if we use a household unit of 6 persons) populations in the order of 25–100 people. We know little of village size at this time, though Guardialfiera in the 16th century probably had a population of *c.*600 people (Masciotta, 1914: 158). A reasonable model for the 13th century is that every community in the middle valley comprised a village of about 500 persons and a dispersed population living in three or four hamlets of different sizes containing in total half as many people again – a grand total of about 750 persons. This population is broadly comparable with that estimated for the *castello* of Montarrenti and its territory in an inland zone of central Tuscany (Francovich and Hodges, 1989).

The head of the valley was very densely occupied in late medieval times – the distribution of *casali* around Baranello, for instance, is similar to that around the coastal villages – but the unprepossessing material culture of sites like Monteverde and Sepino clearly resembles the mid-valley pattern. However, communication systems across the Apennines, as so often in the past, offered some advantages to well-placed settlements in this sector: Boiano castle, for example, overlooking the old Roman road from Benevento to Cassino, was abundantly supplied with Apulian narrow-line red-painted ware, proto-maiolica and glazed wares (De Benedittis, 1977, 1986).

Cross-cutting these three zones were the droveroads of the trans-humance shepherds (Fig. 96). As in Roman and post-medieval times, these *tratturi* connected Apulia with Abruzzo (Clementi, 1984). The Normans probably contributed to the revival of long-distance transhumance in the region – certainly they were sufficiently masters of the territory through which the flocks passed to ensure the security of the shepherds. However, it is easy to exaggerate the importance of long-distance transhumance in the medieval period: there was no rationale for producing wool on a large scale before the 12th century, when bulk cargoes could be shipped to the burgeoning cities of northern Italy (Wickham, 1982: 50–8). The survey

found isolated fortifications that are probably related to medieval transhumance, like the many churches, crosses and shrines built beside the *tratturi* in later periods. One example is the hill known as Castello (site E19) near Morrone, which appears to have been artificially flattened and reinforced as if it were once a castle. Another is the single tower near Santa Maria della Strada in the middle valley (site B126), another is the tower on the La Rocca acropolis near Oratino (site D29) in the upper valley, that may be late medieval in date. Each part of the route was monitored and protected and, we may imagine, tolls were charged by the lords of the territories through which the flocks were driven. But the impact of the droveroads on most of the local inhabitants was probably negligible: few of them go near the Biferno village centres at all.

INCASTELLAMENTO, THE EVOLUTION OF HILLTOP VILLAGES, AND THE MAKINGS OF THE 'OTHER ITALY'

With only the evidence of the single – and perhaps atypical – site Santa Maria in Civita, the valley's settlement pattern in the 7th–9th centuries remains a mystery. Given the absence from later deserted medieval villages of material like that found at Santa Maria in Civita, it could in principle be argued that the population was gathered into places where hilltop villages exist today. The hypothesis is difficult to test given the later building on these sites, but it is probably significant that the one such 'successful' site available for study by the survey, the site of the first village of Porto- cannone (E36), had no Horizon 1 ceramics. A reasonable conclusion is that Santa Maria in Civita represents a specific rural form of local power in the 9th century at a time when the rural population was in any case extremely small, rather than the first phase of the process of *incastellamento*.

The major phase of *incastellamento* in the valley, in which the modern landscape of hilltop villages took shape, was in the decades before AD 1000. At this time villages such as old Portocannone, Casacalenda, Guglionesi, Morrone and Petrella were established on or close to the watershed ridge, or on the major spurs running from it, normally spaced a few kilometres apart. In a subsequent phase, satellite settlements – *castelli*, *casali* and monasteries – were founded within the territories of the villages in secondary positions on the middle slopes or even near the valley bottom, probably beyond the bounds of the cultivated ground.

The mapping by Derrick Webley of the 'site catchments' of the medieval settlements, the land within a kilometre's radius thought to be the principal zone of land use for most peasant farming communities (Higgs and Vita- Finzi, 1972), indicated that a hierarchy of agricultural resources can be discerned in the locations of these settlements. The major villages of the lower valley such as Guglionesi and Portocannone tend to be surrounded by good-quality arable soils on elevated but flat situations facilitating easy cultivation particularly of cereals. The villages of the middle and upper valley are frequently on limestone outcrops, with a greater preponderance of steep slopes and a mosaic of soil types around them that are naturally suited to a variety of land use and vegetation forms including cultivation, pasture and forest. The deserted settlements, whether early like Santa Maria in Civita or late like Covatta (E26) and whether situated in the lower (Vetrana, A195), middle (Olivoli, E42) or upper (Monteverde, E20) valley, all tend to be in marginal situations liable to erosion, surrounded by soils most readily used for pasture and forest grazing. As the archaeological record of the medieval period repeatedly shows, these sites were extremely vulnerable in any phase of demographic or economic recession.

The establishment of the extant system of hilltop villages and satellite settlements in the high and late medieval periods coincided with the formation of a series of fluvial sediments (Chapter Four, Table 3). The correlation between the expansion of human settlement and the accumu-lation of river sediments suggests that clearance for agriculture was a significant cause of the latter. The sediments resemble the pre-classical rather than the classical clearance episodes, implying that the scale of cultivation associated with medieval *incastellamento* left substantial parts of the landscape more forested than in the Samnite and Roman phases of settlement, a conclusion supported by the archaeological survey.

But why was the economic promise of the Biferno valley in the early medieval period reversed in the later medieval periods, unlike, for example, in Tuscany? Today, making a comparison between Molise and Tuscany almost appears to be frivolous, yet we need to be reminded that in the 9th century the material culture of the Beneventan principality, at least in its major centres, seems to have far exceeded that of much of Tuscany. In the ensuing centuries, however, in the aftermath of the collapse of the Carolingian empire, Tuscany developed a different social order embodying rights and opportunities for the peasantry that were much more appro-priate to the new states of western and southern Europe (e.g. Wickham, 1993). In striking contrast, the early affluence of Molise and its adjacent regions generated a social order that by AD 1200 was too inflexible and rigid. This feudal regime had outlived its purpose, though as the next chapter describes, it was to keep the southern peasants in its thrall for centuries to come. As we have seen in this chapter, the archaeological evidence from Molise for the wealth and European standing of the Beneventans in the Dark Ages, and for the vitality of *incastellamento* here at the turn of the millennium, stands in stark contrast with Carlo Levi's view of the perennial poverty of peasant life in the Mezzogiorno (Chapter One, p. 16). As far as the Biferno valley is concerned, the Other Italy identified by Levi 'so old that no one knows whence it came, and it may have been here forever' (1947: 13) owes its origins to the aftermath of the Normans, and to the later Middle Ages in particular.

CHAPTER 12

FEUDALISM AND THE 'SOUTHERN QUESTION' (AD 1500 TO THE PRESENT)

Graeme Barker, with a contribution by Peter Taylor

SETTLEMENT TRENDS IN THE VALLEY, 1500–1800

A variety of documentary material on the development of the post–medieval landscape in the Biferno valley was studied by Peter Taylor in the State Archive, the Chamber of Commerce, the Regional Library, and the library of the Superintendency in Campobasso. The material demonstrates that there were two major developments in settlement between the late medieval period and the formal abolition of feudalism in 1806. The first phenomenon was the continuation of the desertion of hill settlements discussed in the last chapter, a process that occurred principally between the 13th and 15th centuries, but which continued with isolated desertions up to the 17th century. The second development consisted of a huge increase in population during the 17th and 18th centuries, when no new hill settlements were founded but when the existing settlements were transformed into 'agrotowns' or 'agrovillages', centres of population for farmers who cultivated their lands around them.

Throughout the period in question, the lower valley was characterized by relatively large but infrequent towns or villages with a lower density of population than the inland part of the valley, where settlements were smaller but far more frequent, and where for several centuries a minority of the population has lived on scattered farms. The settlement desertions of the 13th, 14th and 15th centuries coincided with a sharp decline in population, and they were particularly prolific in the lower valley. As in many other regions of Italy there continued to be a steady decline in population during the 16th and early 17th centuries. The depredations of plague were particularly severe (Lalli, 1978: 116; Table 12), with the lower valley again suffering most – in 1656 the plague killed a quarter of the population of Campobasso, but over half that of Casacalenda, and wiped out that of Covatta (E26) entirely. The lower valley also suffered from attack by the Turks in 1567: ten years later Abbot Serafino Razzi describes the many abandoned burnt houses at Termoli, when much of the population who

Table 12. Population figures (number of 'hearths') for some Biferno valley villages in the years before and after the plague of 1656. (After Lalli, 1978: 116)

	1548	1595	1669
UPPER VALLEY			
Boiano	359	319	214
Campochiaro	–	260	113
Montagano	167	150	119
San Angelo	119	195	87
San Massimo	101	97	94
MIDDLE VALLEY			
Montorio	108	90	81
Morrone	273	225	137
LOWER VALLEY			
Montenero	391	300	204
San Martino	–	215	110
Termoli	239	150	65

had fled to the inland settlements such as Guglionesi (which was prominent in resistance) had still not returned (Carderi, 1970).

The pattern of desertions in the valley was critical in determining the development of hill towns and villages and their territories over the next four centuries. Until 1806 the entire valley was divided into a series of fiefs exploited by predominantly absentee feudatories, either through agents or by selling their feudal privileges for an annual premium (Croce, 1958; Galanti, 1781, 1788). By the 16th century, the fiefs of the Biferno valley fell into two categories: *feudi urbani*, town fiefs which included a hill settlement, and *feudi rurali*, rural fiefs more or less devoid of population, the counterpart of the deserted medieval settlement. Most of the latter were in the lower valley. They were entirely feudal demesne, and although nearby hill settlements were able to establish certain rights of common over them, the feudatory was able to exploit the land without the constraint of an indigenous population. Much of the land was initially reforested. Some fiefs in the lower valley were apparently leased for winter grazing for transhumant flocks.

With the population explosion of the 18th century, the majority of these rural fiefs was again deforested for arable, usually in small plots on short leases to the inhabitants of the nearby hill towns. The data suggest that at least when land was in short supply the *feudi rurali* were more profitable as an investment for the absentee feudatory than the *feudi urbani*. (Although the latter offered opportunities for income, they also entailed civil and criminal jurisdiction over an often hostile population.) The rural fiefs were formally incorporated into the territories of the adjacent hill settlements following the abolition of feudalism in the early 19th century.

Hill settlements were therefore not re-established on these rural fiefs, and the evidence suggests that this is attributable to the policy of the landowners, who despite their legal status preferred to be rentiers rather than feudatories. The distribution of hill settlements in the early 19th century was therefore very much what had been left over after the late medieval desertions. The increases in population of the 17th and 18th centuries were accommodated by an expansion of the established hill settlements (Fig. 106). Similarly, the Slavic immigrants of the 15th and 16th centuries were generally housed in the existing hill towns (albeit in separate quarters), rather than being allowed to found new settlements – some of the deserted settlements and empty fiefs were colonized by Albanian refugees, but most of these foundations were short-lived. The history of the principal exception to this phenomenon, Ururi, demonstrates the difficulties encountered over a period of 150 years by the Slavic refugees who established themselves on this deserted fief, in the face of the opposition of the inhabitants of the nearby town of Larino – who on one occasion drove the inhabitants into the countryside and set fire to the village (Lalli, 1978: 98; Tria, 1744).

In the urban fiefs of this part of the valley, before the land reforms of the early 19th century, the classic division of hilltown territories into radial culture zones corresponded with a division into two property regimes. The inner belt of land (the houses of the hill town and the immediately adjacent gardens and orchards), though often security for loans, was owned outright on an individual basis. The arable and pasture fields in the outer belt were demesne (communal, ecclesiastical, or baronial) and as such subject to a rent in kind and very often *usi civici* (rights of common such as grazing and woodcutting). Something of this radial pattern of land use can be discerned in Petrocelli's drawing of Guardialfiera in 1703 (Fig. 106). Access to the arable and pasture was a matter for negotiation with the town, the church, or the baron. Correspondingly, land sales and mortgages as recorded in the notary books are restricted to the inner belt of land. At the level of the family, the most significant items recorded in dowries and divisions on death are houses, vineyards, and olive groves.

The transition from medieval hill settlement to modern agrotown was complete by the beginning of the 19th century, when the modern system of *comuni* was established and their boundaries laid down (De Sanctis, 1854). The transition was essentially a transformation in scale, both in population and in territory. Population figures – which are available for each hill

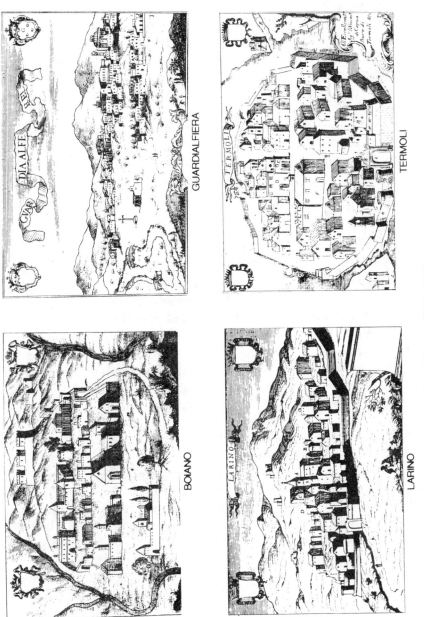

Fig. 106 Some Biferno settlements drawn by E. Petrocelli in 1703.

settlement from the 16th century onwards – suggest that by the end of the
18th century the population of most settlements was at least three times its
level in the 16th century. The expansion in population and territory was
most marked in the lower valley, where the hill towns were able to expand
into, and finally incorporate, the territory of the settlements which had
been abandoned in the late Middle Ages.

The word often used to describe the hill town – the *abitato* – implies
that there was no scattered settlement at all. However, it is clear that in
the upper valley scattered settlement in the post-medieval period has a
history of at least two hundred and fifty years, and it is quite possible that
there was a limited amount of scattered settlement prior to that. In the
18th century the word which is most commonly used to refer to a farm is
massaria or *masseria*. From the contexts in which it is used, it is clear that
the description applies to a peasant farmstead in the upper valley,
whereas in the lower valley it sometimes means a shepherd's temporary
camp, at other times a summer 'farm' used for housing seasonal wage
labour.

By the time the documentary record becomes clear in the early 18th
century, there was considerable scattered settlement in the upper Biferno
valley, though again we must distinguish the urban fiefs from rural fiefs
such as Mignaniello (site B25) or Monteverde (site E20). These, though
cultivated, were almost devoid of permanent housing because of the
policy of the feudatory to let the land on short (six year) leases to peasants
from nearby hill towns. Most of the scattered settlement, therefore, was
within the urban fiefs. It is impossible to treat this scattered settlement
simply as overspill from a crowded hill town. Around an inland village
like Baranello, for example, scattered settlement was prolific in the early
19th century, yet there were some fifty abandoned houses within the
abitato.

Every reference to an inland *masseria* (usually in a deed of sale in a will
or mortgage) refers also to the agricultural land that goes with it – the
garden meadow, *orto prato*, and the arable, *seminatorio* – indicating that the
peasant living in one of these scattered settlements was at least living on a
good part of the land he worked. In some cases it is possible to see the
arrangement more precisely: for example, an extended stem family (a
married couple with two married sons) owning a house in the town and
also two farmsteads, with the old couple in the town house and their
families in the farmsteads. The extent of scattered settlement in the upper
valley around villages such as Baranello, Busso and Colle d'Anchise
indicated by the documentary record was also mirrored in the survey
evidence (Fig. 107).

There would appear to have been two critical factors permitting

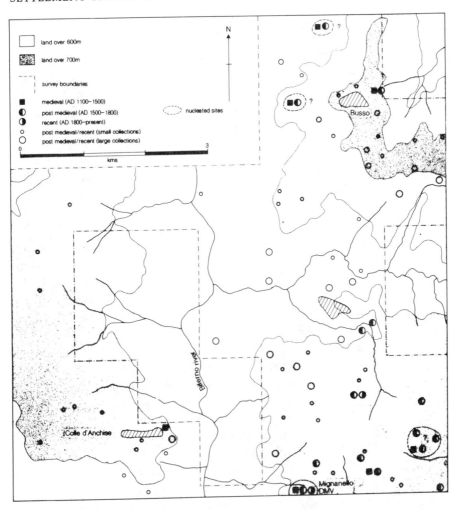

Fig. 107 Distributions of post-medieval and recent pottery found by the survey in part of the upper valley.

scattered settlement in an agricultural context: the ability to assemble in one place a good proportion of the land needed for the agricultural enterprise; and ownership of, or relative security of tenure on, that land. Even before the reforms of the early 19th century, these conditions seem to have applied to a significant minority of the peasantry in the upper valley, whose family economy was of a small-scale subsistence type. In the lower valley, where throughout the past two hundred years most farming has been on a larger scale and more oriented to the market, it was not until the 20th century that those conditions applied to a significant number of the population.

THE FEUDAL LANDSCAPE, 1500–1800

Throughout the valley during this period, both nucleated and scattered settlement avoided the valley bottoms. Roads (basically muletracks) between settlements followed hill crests as far as possible. Cultivation of both cereals and trees was restricted to the higher slopes wherever possible. The lower slopes and valley bottoms were used mainly for pasture. The waters of the Biferno were not used for domestic or agricultural purposes except in the upper valley, where it was possible to channel water from tributaries above the hill settlement or from wells. The exceptions to this rule were water mills, though they were hazardous investments because of their vulnerability to flash floods. The Biferno and its tributaries often marked the boundaries of the fiefs, except in the Boiano basin, where the string of settlements on the northern flank of the Matese needed winter pastures for their animals and their fiefs included both the hill country behind and basin floor in front.

The inland and coastal parts of the valley at this time demonstrated the traditional economic interdependency of the Mediterranean uplands and lowlands but, as before in the valley's history, more commonly with adjacent regions than with each other. There were only two roads in the region, a mountain route from the Abruzzo to Naples (an offshoot meant to connect Naples with Campobasso was stopped when it reached Isernia in 1764) and a coast road, the principal other routes of communication being the transhumant droveroads that crossed the valley linking the Abruzzo and Apulia sheep pastures. As in the recent past (Fig. 16), most of the transhumant sheep which summered on the Matese descended into Apulia, although some were taken to winter grass in the coastal foothills of the valley. The towns of the upper valley provided harvest labour for Apulia, whereas those of the lower valley took in seasonal labour from Abruzzo, with the migrants in each case returning in time for their own harvests, three weeks later in the mountains than on the lowlands. The inland settlements granted special privileges to olive sellers, but the bulk of the trade was either cross-country along the droveroads or with the communities on the other side of the Matese, rather than with the olive-growing regions of the lower valley.

This period was the heyday of the large-scale transhumance between Abruzzo and Apulia that was a critical source of revenue for the State, the vestiges of which in recent centuries are shown in Figure 16. The movement of millions of sheep each year was organized by the Dogana delle Pecore, and a wealth of legislation was promulgated to control the system. Typical was a law of 1549 (when over one million animals were moved) that no flocks from Abruzzo or Molise could begin their journey to

Apulia before September 15th, except in cases of exceptionally bad weather coming early to the mountains, and on no account could they cross the Biferno before October 15th (Di Iorio, 1984: 49). They then had to remain on the pastures around Larino and San Martino in Pensilis until October 31st, during which period the flocks were counted and winter pastures on the Tavoliere assigned. Transgressors of these regulations were liable to ten years' imprisonment. The blatant protectionism of the system by the State caused enormous resentments amongst the peasant population (Di Iorio, 1984).

Braudel (1981: 90) has described the period of European history between 1500 and 1800 as 'a long-lasting biological *ancien regime*', with most rural populations suffering from very high infant mortality, famine, chronic under-nourishment, and formidable epidemics. Of all the depressed areas of southern Europe, none was worse than the Kingdom of Naples, in which the Biferno valley had the misfortune to lie. In 1647 there was widespread rural rebellion against the conditions of grinding poverty. In Molise, the castle of Campobasso was taken and its lord killed, feudatories such as the Duke of Oratino fled, and there was unrest too in the lower valley (Lalli, 1978: 107). Here as elsewhere in the Kingdom the rebellion of Masaniello was savagely suppressed, and the feudal system that caused it was ruthlessly restored (Villari, 1967).

Things were no better in the early 18th century, when Paolo Mattia Doria related how 'the baron has the power to impoverish or ruin his vassal, to imprison him without letting the governor or the village magistrate intervene; having power of life and death, he has anyone he wants murdered and pardons assassins. . . . He abuses his power both against his vassals' property and their honour. . . . To prove a baron guilty of a crime is impossible. . . . The government itself has only indulgence for a powerful baron. . . . These abuses show that some barons are like sovereigns on their own estates' (Villani, 1968: 55). There was a Neapolitan proverb *Chi ha danari compra feudi ed è barone* – 'he who has money buys himself a fief and becomes a baron'. Even in the age of enlightenment, over 50 per cent of the population of the kingdom was subject to feudal justice and the figure was over 80 per cent in certain provinces (Villani, 1968: 97-8). The succinct advice of a Neapolitan economist of the period on how to get results from the peasants was *bastonate, ma bastonate all'uso militare* ('flog them like soldiers') (Braudel, 1982: 264).

We get little sense of what peasant life was like in the valley at this time from the dry notary accounts of mortgages and dowries, though Lalli (1978: 52) described it ironically as a mixture of feudal oppression, starvation, and plague, with earthquakes bringing a little variety from time to time! The grinding poverty of most Italian peasantry has been graphically illustrated by Giorgio Doria's history of Montaldeo, an ordinary community in the northern Apennine foothills for which the documentary record is unusually good (Doria, 1968). Fifty-four families lived here, in wattle and daub cabins. From the production records of the community, Doria estimates that the minimal calorific requirements for a family of four were reached or exceeded by only eight of the fifty-four households, with everybody else living in conditions of chronic malnutrition.

During the course of the 18th century, however, there was a number of examples of some Biferno communities extracting more favourable agreements with their landlords, and by the end of the century leading intellectuals were increasingly inveighing against the feudal system not only in terms of the human degradation it inflicted but also of its gross economic inefficiency (Galanti, 1781; Giampaolo, 1822; Longano, 1788). In his travels round Molise in the late 18th century, Giuseppe Galanti was appalled at the living conditions of the peasants: 'a miserable hovel, roofed with wood or thatch, exposed to the elements. Inside is darkness, smell, filth, misery, and squalor: the bed alongside the pig and the donkey. The better-off have their living space divided off from that of their beasts by a wattle and daub screen. The peasants own nothing and scratch a living, and live a hard life full of troubles that their landlord is ever ready to increase' (Galanti, 1781: 199–206).

Whilst the details of their lives may evade us, the dramatic rise in population of the Biferno valley between the 16th and 18th centuries coincided with the formation of fluvial sediments (Table 3, p. 69), suggesting that, as with *incastellamento* in the medieval period, an extension of the cultivation zone associated with demographic change was the primary factor in producing erosion rates sufficient to be registered in the geomorphological record of the period.

ECONOMIC DEPRESSION AND EMIGRATION, 1800–1914

The 19th century witnessed major changes to the valley's landscape as populations continued to rise, with a shift in the centre of the hill settlements to outside their walls and a steady increase in scattered settlement. The process has continued apace into the 20th century, with the constant expansion of dispersed settlement and the partial desertion of the old centres.

Communications steadily improved during this period with the construction of state highways and the railway, though the Campobasso–Termoli line followed the watershed at a distance from most of the villages, and a projected cross-peninsular rail link between Termoli and Naples that might have transformed the place of the Biferno valley in the wider world was abandoned in favour of one further south, between Foggia and Benevento. However, whilst the formal abolition of feudalism at the beginning of the century offered new hope to the wretched peasants of the South, the following decades in fact brought little but increased misery, the context for mass emigration from the region towards the end of the century.

In the hill settlements, new private housing and public buildings prompted by the administrative reforms of the early 19th century were erected outside the old walls, and the town centres shifted accordingly. Visiting Campobasso (Fig. 108) at this time, the Hon. Keppel Craven described how 'the principal access to it is through a suburb, composed of buildings erected within the last six years on an extensive flat; the level surface of which, as well as the greater regularity of the houses, and their style of architecture, confer upon it a much more attractive character than that retained by the city itself, which is afterwards entered by a gateway, leading into a narrow, dark, and dirty street' (1838: 139–40). Only in a very few *comuni*, such as those on the edge of the Boiano basin, were the new settlements physically separate from the old. The expansion of the hill town beyond its walls continued apace throughout the 19th century.

In the upper valley, the rural population steadily increased during the 19th century (by a third between 1780 and 1842, for example), the increase being especially in the proportion of the population living in scattered farmsteads. After several generations some of the originally isolated farmsteads had become clusters of farmsteads, the inhabitants of which were closely inter-related. In the lower valley, however, the land tax registers of the early 19th century show a total absence of scattered settlement, apart from the *masserie* of the type mentioned above. At Casacalenda, for example, there was no abandoned housing, a relative abundance of land, but no scattered settlement. The absence of scattered settlement is probably closely linked with the cultivation zones and the related system of land tenure described earlier. The first scattered housing in the lower valley developed in the middle of the century, as a greater proportion of land came into peasant ownership following the 19th-century enfranchisement and subsequent land distributions. In parts of the middle valley, however, scattered settlement remained almost entirely absent. According to the 1842 census there were 54,852 people in the upper valley (9,678 of whom were in Campobasso), 29,700 in the middle valley, and 23,967 in the lower valley (with Termoli still a tiny fishing village of just 2,083 inhabitants).

With the abolition of feudal rights and customs in the South, the 'demesne question' – who was to get the common land and the former

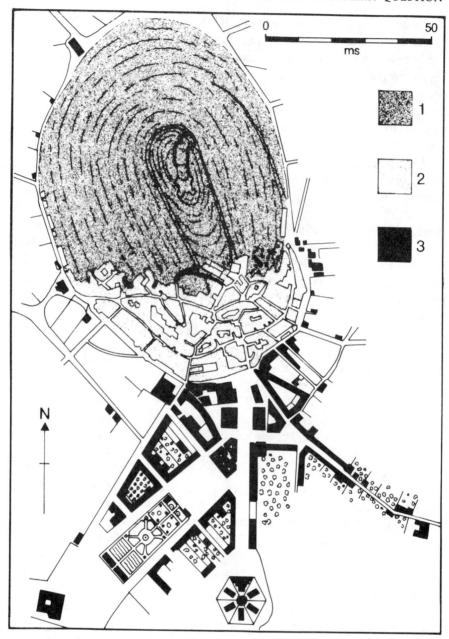

Fig. 108 Plan of Campobasso, adapted from a drawing made by E. Petrocelli in about 1850, showing the three phases of the town's development: 1. the original castle mound; 2. the piecemeal development of medieval settlement on the lower slopes of the hill; 3. the 19th-century planned quarters.

feudal land of each *comune* – was the vital political issue of the period. Local councils managed the sales (which amounted to 265,000 hectares by 1865, and another 50,000 by 1881), but as they were usually dominated by the local major landowners, they tended to protect their own interests and prevent the peasants from buying large amounts of good land, selling it instead to their own relatives. The plots of land allocated to peasants were generally far too small – under 2 hectares – and many of the new landowners, without capital and marketing knowledge, soon lost their land for non-payment of taxes. It was then promptly bought up either by the bourgeoisie or by the aristocrats from whom it had been taken a few years previously. By the middle of the 19th century, most land in the Biferno valley still belonged to absentee landlords. Many peasants scratched a living from tiny plots that were virtually allotments, many did not own or rent any land, and both groups relied on work as day-labourers to survive. Share-cropping was extremely common, with the peasant rarely keeping half the produce.

The effect of the break-up of feudalism was not to lift the peasants out of their poverty trap – indeed, it often made their plight worse – but to create a new rural bourgeoisie. Between 1867 and 1876 another 500,000 hectares were sold off in southern Italy with the expropriation of the ecclesiastical estates, but most of it was bought by these already prosperous landowners, not by peasants. 'A great opportunity for land reform had been lost, and a legacy of bitterness and hatred had been created. . . . The "Southern Question" was not created in these years, but it was made more intractable; so much so that by the 1880s southern Italy was being regularly compared to Ireland' (Clark, 1984: 17). The brigandage of the South that so frightened north Europeans on their Grand Tours (the reason why few ventured further south than Pompeii, and almost never into the interior) had its roots in the rural unrest that was endemic in the region. Many young men from poverty-stricken peasant families headed for the woods rather than the barracks when they received their summons to the five years' compulsory military service. Brigandage was rife throughout Molise, with the Matese being the most notorious for it (Craven, 1838: 136–7).

Food was by far the largest item in the rural dwellers' budget, and observers were constantly surprised at how little, and how badly, the peasants ate – and in winter, when agricultural work was scarce, they ate as little as possible. 'Meat was a rare luxury, eaten only on feast days or family celebrations. Foods which we think of today as typically Italian – tomato puree, for example – were virtually unknown, or far too expensive for most people. Even wine was beyond the means of most peasants, who had to content themselves with *vinello*, mostly water, but passed through the must' (Clark, 1984: 19). Conditions in Molise were amongst the worst anywhere in southern Italy. Many Molise peasants died of hunger in a famine of 1816, in another famine year chestnut flour overtook cereal flour as the staple food, and in the 1830s the staple food for most peasants was a wheat gruel, with bread, pasta, polenta and vegetables reserved for festival days and even most fruit a real luxury (Lalli, 1978: 143, 146). The amount of cereals eaten by Molise peasants according to a census in 1844 was less than anywhere else in Europe, the poverty of the region all the more striking given that most other communities did not have to rely on cereals so heavily.

The North/South economic divide in Italy grew ever stronger through the 19th century, in industry as well as agriculture. The South paid lower taxes than the North, but the income was used to buy demesne and ecclesiastical land, which, as we have seen, had been bought by the elites. The North paid more taxes, but they were used for investment in schools, railways and other major public works: between 1862 and 1897, 267 million lire were spent on land reclamation projects in northern Italy, 188 million lire in the centre, and 3 million in the Mezzogiorno! With a chronic shortage of water, a primitive rural economy, and an elite deriving unearned income in the traditional way from the peasantry, there was little incentive for industrial development in the South (Vitali, 1970).

What little industry existed was small-scale. 'Campobasso is celebrated throughout the kingdom for its manufacture of cutlery. . . . Great was my surprise . . . at finding that the various articles of that nature . . . are all fabricated in small detached workshops, containing little more than a common blacksmith's apparatus. . . . The absence of all mechanical assistance, and the want of efficient instruments and tools to abridge and perfect their labours, renders their final result a matter of surprise and even wonder' (Craven, 1838: 141–2). The unification of Italy in 1871 simply made things worse, as the industrial gap widened. According to the state censuses, 85 per cent of the population of Molise aged over six in 1871 was illiterate compared with 42 per cent in Piedmont in the north, and the gap was still as bad in 1911, when the respective figures were 58 per cent and 11 per cent. Female illiteracy in Molise was the highest in Italy in both periods.

With rising populations steadily making things worse, an increasingly common way in which peasants could escape the miseries of poverty and disease (deaths from cholera, typhoid and malaria in the South were running between 50,000 and 100,000 a year in the 1880s) was to emigrate. Some of this emigration was temporary as men moved to northern Italy or adjacent countries for seasonal work, but most was permanent, increasingly to America (Foerster, 1919). The first recorded emigrants

Fig. 109 Abandoned terraces in the upper Biferno valley. (Photograph: Graeme Barker)

from Molise are in 1866, and between the late 1880s and 1914 tens of thousands of peasants were leaving Molise each year, especially for *La Merica*, so that in the twenty-five to forty-five age group there were less than two men for every three women left. Emigration relieved demographic pressure and thus raised real living standards in the Mezzogiorno, but it made the 'Southern Question' the most acute problem facing the Italian economy by 1914.

Within the Biferno valley, the upper section suffered the most from overpopulation, depressed agriculture, and emigration. The archaeological evidence for the intensity of land use on the better soils consists of the spreads of 19th century pottery found by the survey, for example on the sandy hills around Baranello and Busso (Fig. 107). The silent witnesses of emigration are the huge areas of abandoned terraces along the northern flanks of the Matese (Fig. 109). Throughout the valley, the peasants with the worst land relied on charcoal production to augment their minimal incomes from farming, in turn causing great depredations on forest cover where it was most vulnerable. Other woodland was cut down by peasants desperate for more land, and a great deal of woodland was also cut down for railway sleepers. Deforestation during the first half of the 19th century was so intensive that animal husbandry declined – in 1821 there were 300,000 sheep, 85,000 pigs and 75,000 cattle in Molise, but by 1844 the numbers had fallen to 100,000 sheep, 30,000 pigs and 40,000 cattle. Deforestation also had the effect of dramatically increasing the incidence of malaria – already amongst the worst anywhere in the Mezzogiorno (Pietravalle, 1890) – exacerbated by the digging of drainage ditches along the railway lines. The geomorphological sediments containing 19th-century artefacts, particularly material of the second half of the century (Table 3, p. 69), are surely evidence of the deleterious impact of such activities on the landscape.

FASCISM AND THE CASSA PER IL MEZZOGIORNO

Italy's dramatic industrialization during the First World War worsened the already grave imbalance between North and South in their respective production capacities. In the countryside, although the war forced millions of peasants into the armed forces, leaving the women and the elderly to work the land, the freezing of rents meant that many rural families were able to improve their lot, in some cases entering the money economy for the first time. Government propaganda in the latter part of the war also promised 'land for the peasants' at the end of hostilities. In 1919–20 large amounts of barren or uncultivated land were taken up by ex-soldiers, and many southern *latifundia* disappeared. A million hectares was taken into peasant ownership, doubling the number of peasant landowners compared with the pre-war years, though one effect of these apparently revolutionary agrarian reforms was to reinforce still further the deeply conservative social structure of the Mezzogiorno.

Benito Mussolini became Prime Minister in 1922 and two years later had consolidated his position as the Duce of Italian Fascism, with its slogan 'Everything with the State, Nothing outside the State, Nothing against the State'. Italian Fascism has been described as neither conservative nor revolutionary, just bellicose (Clark, 1984: 261). It was designed to protect the old bureacratic-military ruling class, particularly against the forces of militant industrial and agricultural labour that had been produced by the war and by the political failures and broken promises of its immediate aftermath. When there was no war to fight, the Fascists found surrogates and in 1925, between the Libyan and Ethiopian campaigns, Mussolini proclaimed the 'Battle for Wheat' after a particularly poor harvest necessitated grain imports.

Over the next ten years punitive tariffs were imposed on foreign grain, and Italian farmers were subsidized with seed, fertilizer and machinery to grow grain wherever and however, the harvest going to new (compulsory) marketing agencies. Though total production in Italy went up by a third, yields stayed low by north European standards, and the ecological damage in the Mezzogiorno was enormous (King, 1988). Land well suited for tree crops or pasture was ploughed up, the numbers of cattle and sheep fell by 20 per cent, and olive cultivation was so reduced that for a few years Italy even had to import olive oil. A goat tax was introduced to discourage an animal that the government blamed for erosion, with disastrous effects for impoverished peasants whose goats, living off virtually nothing on waste ground – thorn bushes and sparse grasses – were a critical source of livelihood.

Land reclamation, the other great rural programme that is so often cited as one of Mussolini's most significant achievements (along with making the trains run on time), was largely restricted to the coastal plains of west-central Italy, and fewer than 10,000 peasant families were settled. It was hardly tried in the South. The industrial developments of the Fascist era were also restricted almost entirely to the northern cities. As the North prospered and the South stagnated, the 'Southern Question' became ever more serious after the United States brought in immigration controls in 1921, reducing the number of Italian immigrants from the pre-war 200,000 per year to about 10,000. Emigration continued as the South's safety valve, but especially to Rome and the northern industrial cities. The period 1920–50 was probably the worst in the recent history of the Mezzogiorno economy. In 1945 there were still over two million landless labourers, with an annual income of £35, and the average income of the region in 1950 was about 60 per cent that of 1924.

Quite apart from the grinding poverty of the peasants that so appalled Carlo Levi when he was banished to 'Gagliano' (Aliano), the effects of Fascism on the Mezzogiorno landscape were calamitous in terms of dramatically increased erosion rates. Levi himself said that most of the land under the plough around Gagliano would have been better cultivated for olive and almond trees, or better still, returned to pasture and woodland (Levi, 1947: 183). In the Biferno valley the next set of erosional sediments identified in the geomorphological fieldwork after those of the late 19th century are dated by the artefacts within them to the period 1930–50 (Chapter Four). The change to the river's regime is reflected in a transformation in the topography of the estuary visible on the IGM maps of 1869 and 1957 (Taffetani, 1991: 303). The sediments bear witness to an open landscape eroding on an ever greater scale, a grim reminder of Mussolini's Battle for Wheat and the failure of his much vaunted intention to 'ruralize Italy'. Levi pointed out that the peasants of Aliano were no better off than the landless families of Grassano (another, larger, settlement in Basilicata where he began his banishment), neither group able to make enough to feed themselves and pay their taxes. Peasant landownership in fact declined during the Fascist era.

Life for the peasant population of the Biferno valley during the Second World War was much as in the First – the young men called to arms, the land farmed by the women and the elderly. After the Italian armistice in September 1943 and the Salerno landings, the Allied Forces quickly took control of most of the southern peninsula, arriving in the Biferno valley at the beginning of October (Artese, 1993). The river had been selected as a significant defence line by the retreating German army, linking up with Monte Cassino, and all the bridges were destroyed. Montgomery ordered a joint attack by the Eighth Army at the river estuary, with a commando force landing at Termoli and the main force crossing the river to link up with them. It turned out to be a bloody and near-run thing. The commandos landed successfully at dawn on October 3rd 1943 and established themselves in the port, but it then began to rain heavily, the level of the river rose, and those troops that had crossed the river on a makeshift bridge of boats got completely bogged down. A German panzer group arrived the next day and attacked the two separate groups. There was desperate fighting for the next two days with heavy casualties on both sides before the Allies finally constructed a Bailey bridge heavy enough for tanks to cross the river, and landed more troops by boat at Termoli (Graham and Bidwell, 1986: 112–15).

The inclement weather of this part of Italy clearly came as a nasty surprise to the Allied Forces involved in the Biferno attack. 'How was it possible that twentieth-century Englishmen should have been so ignorant beforehand of the climate of another European country? The only explanation seems to be that peacetime visitors to Italy knew only the big cities and the favoured resorts; that few people penetrated to the eastern side of central and southern Italy; and that Italy was sufficiently near and familiar country for us to have taken it too much for granted in our planning. By now, though, it was obvious that the local inhabitants were used to hard winters. Before the end of October they were wearing fur caps and great black woollen cloaks' (Ray, 1952: 93). A resident of Casacalenda recalled to us his amazement as a boy at seeing Montgomery taking a drink at a water fountain outside the town at this time 'wearing the longest pair of shorts he had ever seen'!

In the immediate post-war years social and economic conditions in the South were extremely depressed. Rural unemployment was between 33 per cent and 50 per cent, a quarter of the adult population was illiterate, the industrial base minimal. The kind of peasant farming photographed by Frank Monaco in the upper Biferno valley in 1953 (Frontispiece, and Figs. 14, 15) could be witnessed around almost every village (King, 1988). Agitation for tackling the 'Southern Question' was as serious in the late 1940s as in the aftermath of the First World War. A series of laws was passed in 1950 establishing new land-reform agencies in the South, with the powers to buy up tracts of uncultivated or badly cultivated estates, improve them, sell them off to peasants at low cost on long mortgages, and provide the peasants with essential services. The land reform broke the power of the big landowners, but in doing so it created a client class entirely dependent on the agencies, which were run by the ruling Christian Democratic party. In fact relatively few peasants actually got land: 700,000 hectares were distributed by the end of 1962, but the 113,000 recipients made up only one per cent of the rural population. Furthermore, as in previous distributions, many holdings were on poor land, and with the efficiency gap widening inexorably in favour of northern farmers, the overall effect was to increase rural poverty in the South and accelerate the flight from the land (King, 1973).

In 1951 the special 'Fund for the South', the Cassa per il Mezzogiorno, was established to invest government funds in the South. It began with development programmes with much of the philosophy (and many of the same officials) as the pre-war Fascist programmes in Libya and Ethiopia, funding roads, houses, and services. In 1957 priorities were switched to industrial development, and tax and credit advantages were offered to investors in designated 'industrial development areas'; there were none in Molise. From the early 1970s, programmes of agricultural modernization and associated public works were increasingly funded through the regional governments, with the Cassa funding a few large industrial projects such as steel plants and oil refineries.

There were a few notable successes, but overall the billions of lire spent by the Cassa in the Mezzogiorno created little permanent employment for the millions of people leaving the land (King and Killingbeck, 1989). Almost two million people emigrated from the South in the 1950s, over two million in the 1960s, and hundreds of thousands more were seasonal migrants to the North. Moreover, many of those who stayed in farming were dependent on state welfare payments, clients of the political party that paid them, as well as the remittances from their relatives abroad: in the late 1950s most emigrants could hope to send back to the family each year twice what they could have earned at home. Average incomes tripled

Table 13. Some recent population statistics for San Polo Matese in the upper Biferno valley (after Spina, 1992: 190–1)

Inhabitants		Recent emigrants	
1861	1112	1962	5
1871	1142	1963	25
1881	1205	1964	18
1901	1042	1965	11
1911	1226	1966	37
1921	709	1967	14
1931	896	1968	142
1951	809	1969	30
1961	619	1970	98
1971	425	1971	–
1981	452	1972	–
1992	502	1973	13
		1974	12
		1975	31

between 1950 and 1975 (though still below the rest of Italy), and education and health improved dramatically: illiteracy was reduced to a few per cent, the amount of meat in the diet doubled, and the average height of eighteen-year old army conscripts from the South increased from 169.50 centimetres in 1947 to 169.60 centimetres in 1969 and 171.48 centimetres in 1975. 'In 1950 the South had been poor and relatively self-sufficient. In 1975 she was better off and utterly dependent. She had gone straight from an agrarian to a post-industrial sociery without the intervening stage of industrialization' (Clark, 1984: 360). It is ironic to note that Antonio Di Pietro, the Milan public prosecutor who has led the corruption investigations that promise finally to destroy the system of political patronage that has bound the Mezzogiorno peasant to poverty, is the son of a peasant family from Montenero in the lower Biferno valley (Clough, 1993).

The post-war history of the Biferno valley has been typical of the 'Southern Question'. Emigration has been such that the population figures for most villages in 1978 (Table 1, p. 27) are much the same as those of 1778, apart from the big villages of the lower valley (which have generally doubled), and the towns: the population of Boiano has more than doubled, that of Termoli has increased eightfold, and Campobasso tenfold. The population statistics of San Polo Matese in the Boiano basin (Table 13) are typical of the trend that left so many Mezzogiorno villages empty shells for much of the year, bustling for a few weeks a year at Christmas and in August when the migrant families returned (King and Killingbeck, 1989).

Fig. 110 The Bifernina road (left), Ponte del Liscione dam (centre distance) and recent alluvial sediments (right). (Photograph: Graeme Barker)

In 1961 there were 131 active farmers at San Polo, but the number had reduced to 96 in 1970 (Spina, 1992). In recent years, however, the increasing demand for meat, cheese, eggs and vegetables by Italian consumers has provided the incentive for a resurgence in the village's farming, with state and EU grants and subsidies helping the *contadini* to invest in modern buildings and equipment. The same funds have aided the development of many small and medium-sized industrial concerns on the floor of the Boiano basin that are providing further incentives for the young to stay in the village. From the late 1970s emigration has been reduced to a trickle, and with the return of several families the village has started to grow again (Spina, 1992: 191).

The combination of the Cassa, regional government and EU funds during the 1970s transformed the Biferno valley most obviously in the construction of the Ponte del Liscione dam and the Bifernina road (Fig. 110). In the 1970s during the survey the lowland villages were commonly restricted to a few hours' piped water a day during the summer, but the dam has ensured a regular water supply not only for these settlements, but also for the new factory complexes around Termoli and the tourist populations on the Adriatic shore in July and August. The road has utterly transformed communications, making the valley an economic and social unit in a way it has never been hitherto, with link roads to the hill villages of the middle valley breaking their traditional isolation from the coast and the interior.

Fig. 111 Typical slope erosion in the Biferno valley in the 1970s.
(Photograph: Graeme Barker)

The massive changes in the 1960s and 1970s to the agricultural landscape
of the valley, particularly the lower valley, were described at the end of
Chapter Two: deep ploughing with caterpillar tractors (Fig. 20), field
enlargement, monoculture, and land drainage. The new technologies, aided
by improved cereal strains and the use of chemical fertilizers, enabled
cereal yields to double here as elsewhere in the South between 1950 and
1970 – but at dreadful costs to the landscape. Whilst land abandonment in
the upper valley has generally had a beneficial effect ecologically, allowing
marginal land to revert to pasture and woodland, erosion rates in the
middle and lower valley since 1960 have been phenomenal (Figs. 111, 112).
Check dams built since 1960 were entirely swamped by sediment from the
slopes above by the late 1970s, and the sediments that have built up behind
the Ponte del Liscione dam since the 1970s are estimated to have already
reduced the size of the water body of the lake by a third. Below the dam
are huge deposits of sediment several metres in thickness deposited in
the past two or three decades (Fig. 110), and satellite photographs show
dark silt-laden waters many kilometres out from the mouth of the Biferno
into the Adriatic every winter. Only now are agriculturalists advising

Fig. 112 Typical storm gullying in the modern arable landscape of the lower Biferno valley. (Photograph: Graeme Barker)

experiments with 'minimal technology' systems of shallow ploughing in these regions, though most farmers are so trapped in high input/high output systems of farming by mortgages and bank loans that they will not be able to change without external intervention.

CHAPTER 13

RETROSPECT: THE EVOLUTION OF A MEDITERRANEAN LANDSCAPE

Graeme Barker

A common criticism of Braudel's history of the Mediterranean has been that, for all the immense value for regional landscape history that his concept of different kinds of historical process working at different timescales offered, he had very little to say about how these processes actually had interacted together. In *Christ Stopped at Eboli*, Carlo Levi wrote that no outsider could ever hope to understand the Italian Mezzogiorno – they just came as enemies and conquerors (1947: 12) – but in the Biferno valley project we hoped that the deliberately inter-disciplinary approach, the size of the research area and the long timescale of the study would provide at least some understanding of the forces that had shaped this particular landscape, rather than just describe them. We hoped to provide some answers to the general question posed by Braudel's study: how had different forces of history – operating variously over millennia, centuries, decades, years and days – shaped life in the valley? Other specific questions included: how had the outside world influenced what had happened? how had the different parts of the valley interacted at different times in the past? what physical impact had the inhabitants of the valley had on their landscape?

The role of the *longue durée* in the history of the valley has obviously been extraordinarily profound. The landscape was not a simple backdrop to the human stage. The topography, climate, resources and natural communications of the different parts of the valley offered different constraints and opportunities for settlement and land use, and the previous chapters have described our findings about the complex ways in which different kinds of societies have reacted to these from early prehistory to the present day. Furthermore, given the long timescale of the study, we have seen how the character of the landscape changed profoundly over its prehistory and history, in response in part to changes in climate and environment, in part to human actions, changes which presented new sets of constraints and opportunities for the inhabitants of the valley. Of course the role of the landscape cannot be reduced to crude environmental determinism, and another thread running through the story has been the role of changing social institutions in shaping the responses to the changing constraints and opportunities of the valley environment.

The exploitation of the Matese is a very good example of this complex interplay between the *longue durée* and settlement forms. The mountain landscape naturally offers extensive woodland and pasture in the summer, but is inhospitable in winter because of the severe weather conditions at this altitude. In fact changing vegetation in response to climatic change meant that in earlier prehistory it was sometimes accessible for grazing animals, but for long periods not, so that for much of the history of human settlement in the valley it was probably only used for occasional hunting and pastoralism. These activities increased in the 2nd millennium BC, and may have been a factor in the opening up of the landscape. The Matese was then used by local communities for pastoralism and woodland exploitation, and for contact with neighbouring communities, but in classical times (perhaps in the Samnite period, certainly after Romanization) its summer pastures were incorporated within long-distance systems of state-organized transhumance, though the local communities continued to make use of the mountain. Between the Roman and modern periods the nature and scale of long-distance pastoralism using the Matese have fluctuated in response to regional and international economic and political structures. The local communities have made constant use of the mountain's resources throughout this time, though in the more recent past the traditional sources of revenue for them expanded from pastoralism and charcoal production to brigandage and, latterly, tourism.

In the main part of the valley, prehistoric farming was at first restricted to the lower valley and only gradually spread to the middle and upper sections. The components of the farming system – cereals, legumes, domestic stock – changed little through this process, though the secondary products of the stock were increasingly important as, alongside the development of more complex social forms, a predominantly subsistence system developed into an economic system producing surplus. The incorporation of viticulture in the lower and middle valley in the Iron Age was also in the context of significant developments in settlement systems and social institutions. Olive cultivation followed in classical times, as well as long-distance transhumance, a period when agricultural products such as cereals, oil and wool were significant sources of wealth for the local aristocracy.

Although this period witnessed the development of arable and pastoral systems that have endured in their essentials to the present day, land use has in fact altered significantly and repeatedly over the past two thousand years in response to changing demographic, social and economic contexts, through Romanization, *incastellamento*, feudalism and Fascism to the EU. The agricultural landscape has changed more profoundly in the past few decades than at any time since Samnite farming, though most of the components of the system are still fundamentally the same. The same is true of cultivation technology, which has probably undergone more profound changes in the past thirty years than the previous two thousand.

If the role of the valley landscape for human settlement has been significant but complex, exactly the same is true of the kind of social, economic and demographic processes which Braudel termed *conjonctures* to differentiate them from the events of traditional political history. He thought of these in terms of a human generation, a quarter of a century or so, but over the long prehistory and history of human settlement in the Biferno valley such trends have been discerned operating at a variety of timescales. The different systems of hunting and gathering adduced for the palaeolithic period lasted many millennia, the transitional phase in which farming supplanted hunting and gathering probably lasted at least a millennium, the social and economic changes of the Late Neolithic can be discerned over a timescale of several centuries, and the same is true of the settlement changes of the Bronze Age. By the Iron Age, the timescale of the changes we can detect has reduced to a few centuries, even one or two, and from the Samnite period onwards the social and economic history of the valley can generally be written in terms of centuries and decades, with the focus sometimes even more telescoped for the recent past.

Ideologies have also profoundly affected life in the valley. We know little of palaeolithic cognitive systems, but if the upper palaeolithic hunters in the valley came from base camps in the Tavoliere as was suggested in Chapter Five, then they certainly had access to (and indeed may have helped make) the kind of cave art that Mithen (1990) argues acted as the critical link between environment and culture at this time. Communal forms of cult involving secrecy, cave sites and water rites characterized the neolithic societies of the region for at least a millennium (Whitehouse, 1992), gradually giving way to the ideologies centred on the individual that endured through later prehistory. Contact with the Greeks introduced the Olympic pantheon to the Samnites, though as the Agnone tablets show, their worship was intermixed with that of a host of local agricultural and natural deities in each *pagus* (Salmon, 1967: 176–7). The role of the Christian church in the life of the valley, whether at the level of local patronage or directly from Rome, needs no emphasis. For Carlo Levi the Church in the Mezzogiorno made up a set of 'paternal, prevailing institutions' which helped bind the peasants to 'this shadowy land, that knows neither sin nor redemption from sin, where evil is not moral but is only the pain residing forever in earthly things' (Levi, 1947: 12).

And what of 'events'? – not the accumulated actions of individuals which have made up the other kinds of settlement histories described above, but the single act of short duration that may have a profound effect on the course of political history. Some we know about historically but cannot detect archaeologically, such as Hannibal's passage through this part of Italy in the late 3rd century BC and the various outsider attacks of the early medieval period. On the other hand, the devastations inflicted on Samnium by Sulla after the Social War of 91–82 BC do seem to be recognizable in the archaeological record in the evidence for a major fall in population at this time, and the fighting associated with Montgomery's crossing of the Biferno in 1943 was also detected by the survey teams in the amount of shrapnel littered across the landscape by the lower river. More significant, obviously, has been the succession of events outside the valley – regionally, nationally, internationally – that has changed the political, social and economic framework in which the valley's inhabitants have operated from the founding of the Greek colonies to the Treaty of Maastricht.

The impact of the outside world has of course been found at every stage in the valley's history, from the arrival of the first scavengers to the agricultural and industrial grants and subsidies from Rome and Brussels today. For most of the valley's history, the immediate contacts have been, in the lower valley, with the Adriatic regions to the north and south, and, in the upper valley, with the western lowlands beyond the Matese. The middle valley has been dissected by the river, the southern side looking as much southwards to Apulia and the northern side northwards to the Trigno as upriver or downriver. The upper palaeolithic hunter-gatherers whose lithic artefacts were found in the middle and lower valley were probably seasonal visitors only, coming from winter camps around the Tavoliere. Agriculture also (and, less likely, agriculturalists) almost certainly came to the valley c. 4500 bc from the same region. The elites that gradually developed amongst these prehistoric societies were involved in exchange systems with equivalent groups in adjacent regions, generally according to the natural communication links described above. Occasional exotic artefacts such as Lipari obsidian reached the neolithic, copper age and bronze age elites, but almost certainly via neighbouring communities, and the same was probably still true of the trade items of the Iron Age, though the impact of Greeks and Etruscans on iron age society in the Biferno seems very clear.

The sphere of interaction expanded dramatically in the Samnite phase of settlement, when archaeology indicates a remarkable level of social and economic complexity bordering on full urbanization before the Roman conquest. The leading Samnite families were actively involved in trade now not only with central and southern Italy but also with the eastern Mediterranean (which some visited), and other Samnites from the valley almost certainly fought in Rome's Mediterranean campaigns. From the 1st century BC the valley was drawn into the 'world system' of the Roman state, and the successive spheres of influence in which the valley was located in medieval times included those of the Lombards, Carolingians, Byzantines, Arabs and Normans. The dominant political unit in post-medieval times has been the Kingdom of Naples, until the development of the modern Italian state in 1871, incorporated within the EU in modern times.

Within the valley, the different components of the landscape have interacted in different ways throughout its history. Palaeolithic, epipalaeo-lithic and neolithic settlement seems to have concentrated in the lower valley, but forays into the interior were probably a feature of upper palaeolithic and neolithic land use. During the course of the 2nd millennium bc the main zone of settlement expanded to include the middle valley, and it was probably at this time that people began to make the first systematic (though no doubt small-scale) use of the Matese mountain for hunting and herding. The establishment of communication systems across the Apennines at this time set the scene for the settlement interactions that were to endure from the Iron Age to the modern period, with the upper valley looking as much across the Matese to Campania as downriver to the lower valley, the lower valley embedded in an Adriatic system, and the communities in between beset by difficult communications across river and with the adjacent parts of the valley.

Of course the uplands and lowlands of the region were not isolated from each other, and from the Bronze Age onwards there are repeated examples of the economic inter-dependence between the two that Braudel identified as a principal theme of Mediterranean history. The transhumant systems documented for the post-medieval period are instructive in this respect, however: some flocks which summered on the Matese were taken directly down river, but most were taken across country to Apulia, and most of the sheep which wintered in the lower valley had likewise been brought across country from the Abruzzo mountains north of the Matese. Only with the construction of the Bifernina road in the 1970s (Fig. 110) have the com-munication difficulties of the middle valley been overcome and the upland, middle, and lowland parts of the valley been brought together within an integrated unit. Having selected the valley for the project in 1974 because it was (a) a coherent settlement unit, and (b) accessible because of its splendid new road, it has been chastening to discover that (b) had largely created (a) more or less as the project began!

The geomorphological sequence of sediments in the valley (Chapter

Table 14 Comparison between the Holocene settlement record and river sediment record (both greatly simplified) in the Biferno valley

SETTLEMENT RECORD	RIVER SEDIMENT RECORD
Mesolithic: lower valley	No evidence
Neolithic: main settlements lower valley, arable-based farming	Phase 1: small-scale clearances
Bronze Age: settlements throughout valley, mixed cereal/stock farming	Phase 1: small-scale clearances
Iron Age: settlements throughout valley, first villages, wine cultivation lower valley?	?Phase 1: small-scale clearances
Samnite: very high rural settlement, polyculture, surplus production, proto-urban economic structure	Phase 2: massive clearance, predominantly open landscape
Roman: declining rural population, estate growth, market economies	Phase 2: continuation of predominantly open landscape
Early medieval: drastically reduced population, small expansion AD 1000–1300, small-scale farming	Phase 3: small-scale clearances as Phase 1
15th, 16th, 17th centuries: second phase of village expansion	Phase 4: increased scale of impact
19th century: dramatic population rise, marginal land cultivated etc.	Phase 5: significantly increased amount of open land and erosion
1920s, 1930s: marginal land taken into cultivation, Mussolini's 'Battle for Wheat' etc.	Phase 6: open landscape, very active erosion
1960s, 1970s: change to mechanization, deep ploughing, construction of dam	Phase 7: dramatically increased erosion rates
1980s, 1990s: expansion of cultivated area, increasing monoculture	Phase 8: massive erosion, dam lake rapidly filling with sediment etc.

Four) is one of the most complex yet identified in the Mediterranean. Whilst tectonics, sea level change and climatic change can all be recognized to have influenced landscape development, especially in the more remote periods of settlement, the repeated correlations between Holocene alluvial sediments and significant episodes of land use suggest that human activities have been the dominant influence over the past five thousand years (Table 14). The impact of prehistoric land use on the landscape seems to have been small but repeated, particularly in the 2nd millennium bc as the settlement zone expanded up the valley (and some activities into the mountains), but the massive aggradations of the Samnite/early Roman period coincide precisely with the archaeological evidence for a dramatic expansion in rural settlement unrivalled until the modern period, and an intensification in land use.

Vita-Finzi (1969) summarized the evidence for climatic change in the Mediterranean region during the 1st millennium AD and concluded that it was the dominant factor in causing the change in river regimes that resulted in the Younger Fill. Although geomorphologists in recent years have increasingly favoured human impact over climate in explaining the various prehistoric, classical, medieval and post-medieval alluvial episodes they have identified (Brückner, 1986; Davidson, 1980; Gilbertson et al., 1983, 1992; Neboit, 1984; Pope and Van Andel, 1984; Van Andel et al., 1985; Wagstaff, 1981), it remains true that the evidence for really large-scale aggradation is invariably classical – though, it has to be said, this evidence is sometimes in the Roman Republican period as in the Biferno valley, sometimes in the phase of Greek colonization earlier, sometimes in the early/middle Roman Empire, and sometimes in late Imperial/early medieval times. Climatic change may well have accelerated erosion rates during the middle centuries of the 1st millennium AD – the documentary sources for the period contain a litany of complaints about more extreme climatic conditions in the Mediterranean (higher rainfall with storm surges and sea flooding in the winter, heat and drought in the summer) that probably reflect a more continental climate (Randsborg, 1991: 24–5). However, the reason that the effects had such a profound impact in terms of erosion remains that, throughout the Mediterranean basin, the classical landscape was predominantly open and cultivated, in a way not repeated until comparatively recent times (Barker and Lloyd, 1991).

In the post-Roman period, the level of correlation between geomorphological change and settlement change in the valley is remarkably good. Parallel with the establishment of the modern system of hilltop villages and their satellite villages from the 10th century onwards is evidence for erosion rather similar in scale to that of the prehistoric period. The sediments of the 17th and 18th centuries coincide with the next major expansion of population and in turn register a greater level of clearance and erosion. The continued expansion of population and scattered settlement in the last century is also mirrored in the geomorphological record. Of the three separate phases of aggradation identified for the 20th century, the inception of the first coincides with Mussolini's Battle for Wheat, when large areas of unsuitable land were ploughed up for cereal cultivation, and the last two, the most dramatic since classical times, with the transformations in farming technology and systems of land use in recent decades (Figs. 111 and 112). In their scale, the modern sediments are rivalled only by those of the classical period, but what is extraordinary is that one is the record of several centuries, the other of scarcely a generation.

Although there has been a great deal of field research on Mediterranean alluviation since Vita-Finzi's pioneering study, understanding its causes has been hampered by the lack of regional studies with integrated sets of data: there have been detailed geomorphological and/or palynological studies where we have little precise information on settlement history, and detailed settlement studies by archaeologists and/or historians without the equivalent data from the region for its ecological history. Studies providing both sets of data have mostly been restricted in their focus to a particular period of the past. One of the most important contributions of the Biferno valley project has been in providing a set of detailed archaeological, historical and geomorphological data for the valley's entire settlement history that is probably unique in the Mediterranean. Of course there are major weaknesses in the data sets, but the repeated correlations between the Holocene geomorphological sequence on the one hand and periods of settlement expansion and/or land use intensification on the other provide powerful evidence for the critical role of Mediterranean farmers in shaping their landscape. In the Biferno valley as throughout the Mediterranean region, their role today, and their responsibility to their successors, have never been more crucial.

BIBLIOGRAPHY

Abulafia, D. (1976) Dalmatian Ragusa and the Norman Kingdom of Sicily. *Slavonic and East European Review* 54: 412–38.

Abulafia, D. (1977) *The Two Italies: Economic Relations Between the Norman Kingdom of Sicily and the Northern Communes*. Cambridge, University Press.

Adams, R. McC. (1974) Anthropological reflections on ancient trade. *Current Anthropology* 15: 239–58.

Adams, R. McC. (1981) *Heartland of Cities: Surveys of Ancient Settlement and Land Use on the Central Floodplain of the Euphrates*. Chicago, University of Chicago Press.

AE *L'Année Epigraphique*.

Agostini, S., De Grossi Mazzorin, J., and D'Ercole, V. (1992) Economia e territorio in Abruzzo durante la media età del Bronzo. *Rassegna di Archeologia* 10: 419–26.

Albarella, U. (1990) La fauna di S. Giacomo degli Schiavoni. *Conoscenze* 6: 115–18.

Albarella, U. (1993) The fauna. pp. 203–21 in U. Albarella, V. Ceglia, and P. Roberts, S. Giacomo degli Schiavoni: a fifth century AD deposit of pottery and fauna. *Papers of the British School at Rome* 61: 157–225.

Albarella, U., Ceglia, V. and Roberts, P. (1993) S. Giacomo degli Schiavoni: a fifth century AD deposit of pottery and fauna. *Papers of the British School at Rome* 61: 157–225.

Alessio, M., Allegri, L., Bella, F., Calderoni, G., Cortesi, C., Dai Pra, G., De Rita, D., Esu, D., Follieri, M., Improta, S., Magri, D., Narcisi, B., Petrone, V. and Sadori, L. (1986) 14C dating, geochemical features, faunistic and pollen analyses of the uppermost 10m core from Valle di Castiglione (Rome, Italy). *Geologica Romana* 25: 287–308.

Ambrosetti, G. (1958) Testimonianze preaugustee da Sepino-Altilia. *Archeologia Classica* 10: 14–20.

Ammerman, A. J. (1985a) Plow-zone experiments in Calabria. *Journal of Field Archaeology* 12: 33–40.

Ammerman, A. J. (1985b) *The Acconia Survey: Neolithic Settlement and the Obsidian Trade*. London, Institute of Archaeology Occasional Publication 10.

Ammerman, A. J. and Shaffer, G. D. (1981) Neolithic settlement patterns in Calabria. *Current Anthropology* 22: 430–40.

Andreolli, B. and Montanari, M. (1983) *L'Azienda Curtense in Italia*. Bologna, CLUEB.

Andrews, D. (1981) The archaeology of the medieval *castrum* in central Italy. In G. Barker and R. Hodges (eds.) *Archaeology and Italian Society*: 313–34. Oxford, British Archaeological Reports, International Series 102.

Anglé, M., Gianni, A., and Guidi, A. (1982) Gli insediamenti montani di sommità nell'Italia centrale: il caso dei monti Lucretili. *Dialoghi di Archeologia* 2: 80–98.

Arnold, D. E. (1985) *Ceramic Theory and Cultural Process*. Cambridge, University Press.

Artese, G. (1993) *La Guerra in Abruzzo e Molise 1943–44*. Lanciano, Casa Editrice Rocca Carabba.

Arthur, P. (1991a) *Romans in Northern Campania*. London, British School at Rome, Archaeological Monographs 1.

Arthur, P. (1991b) Naples: a case of urban survival in the early Middle Ages. *Mélanges de L'Ecole Française de Rome* 103: 759–84.

Arthur, P. (forthcoming) The amphorae. In J. A. Lloyd (ed.) *The Samnite and Roman Villa at Matrice*.

Arthur, P. and Whitehouse, D. (1982) La ceramica dell'Italia meridionale: produzione e mercato tra V e X secolo. *Archeologia Medievale* 9: 39–46.

Ashby, T. (1927) *The Roman Campagna in Classical Times*. London, Bentley.

Attolini, I., Cambi, F., Castagna, M., Celuzza, M., Fentress, E., Perkins, P., and Regoli, E. (1991) Political geography and productive geography between the valleys of the Albegna and the Fiora in northern Etruria. In G. Barker and J. A. Lloyd (eds.) *Roman Landscapes: Archaeological Survey in the Mediterranean Region*: 142–52. London, British School at Rome, Archaeological Monographs 2.

Badian, E. (1972) *Publicans and Sinners*. Oxford, Blackwell.

Bailey, D. (forthcoming) The lamps. In J. A. Lloyd (ed.) *The Samnite and Roman Villa at Matrice*.

Barclay, C. (forthcoming) The coins. In J. A. Lloyd (ed.) *The Samnite and Roman Villa at Matrice*.

Barfield, L. H. (1971) *Northern Italy Before Rome*. London, Thames and Hudson.

Barker, G. (1972) The conditions of cultural and economic growth in the Bronze Age of central Italy. *Proceedings of the Prehistoric Society* 38: 170–208.

Barker, G. (1974) A new neolithic site in Molise, southern Italy. *Origini* 8: 185–200.

Barker, G. (1976a) An Apennine bronze age settlement at Petrella, Molise. *Papers of the British School at Rome* 44: 133–56.

Barker, G. (1976b) Animal husbandry at Narce. In T. W. Potter (ed.) *A Faliscan Town in South Etruria, Excavations at Narce 1966–71*: 295–307. London, British School at Rome.

Barker, G. (1977) Animal husbandry and economic change at Monte Irsi. In A. Small (ed.) *Monte Irsi, Southern Italy*: 265–73. Oxford, British Archaeological Reports, International Series 20.

Barker, G. (1981) *Landscape and Society: Prehistoric Central Italy*. London, Academic Press.

Barker, G. (1982) The animal bones. pp. 81–91 and 96–9 in D. Whitehouse, G. Barker, R. Reece and D. Reece, The Schola Praeconum I: the coins, pottery, lamps and fauna. *Papers of the British School at Rome* 50: 53–101.

Barker, G. (1985) *Prehistoric Farming in Europe*. Cambridge, University Press.

Barker, G. (1988) Archaeology and the Etruscan countryside. *Antiquity* 62 (237): 772–85.

Barker, G. (1989a) The archaeology of the Italian shepherd. *Proceedings of the Cambridge Philological Society* 215: 1–19.

Barker, G. (1989b) Animals, ritual and power in ancient Samnium. In P. Meniel (ed.) *Animal et Pratiques Religieuses: les Manifestations Materielles*: 111–7. Paris, CNRS (*Anthropozoologica*, troisième numéro speciale).

Barker, G. (1991) Approaches to archaeological survey. In G. Barker and J. A. Lloyd (eds.) *Roman Landscapes: Archaeological Survey in the Mediterranean Region*: 1–9. London, British School at Rome, Archaeological Monographs 2.

Barker, G., and Grant, A. (1991) (eds.) Ancient and modern pastoralism in central Italy: an interdisciplinary study in the Cicolano mountains. *Papers of the British School at Rome* 59: 15–88.

Barker, G., and Hodges, R. A. (1981) (eds.) *Archaeology and Italian Society*. Oxford, British Archaeological Reports, International Series 102.

Barker, G., and Lloyd, J. A. (1991) (eds.) *Roman Landscapes: Archaeological Survey in the Mediterranean Region.* London, British School at Rome, Archaeological Monographs 2.

Barker, G., and Slater, E. A. (1971) The development of prehistoric copper and bronze age metallurgy in Italy, in the light of the metal analyses from the Pigorini Museum, Rome. *Bullettino di Palentologia Italiana* 80, n.s.22: 12–44.

Barker, G. and Stallibrass, S. (1987) La fauna. In P. Meloni and D. Whitehouse (eds.) *La Rocca Posteriore sul Monte Ingino di Gubbio (Campagne di Scavo 1975–1977)*: 277–312. Florence, La Nuova Italia.

Barker, G., Grant, A., and Rasmussen, T. (1993) Approaches to the Etruscan landscape: the development of the Tuscania Survey. In P. Bogucki (ed.) *Case Studies in European Prehistory*: 229–57. Florida, CRC Press.

Barker, G., Leggio, T., and Moreland, J. (1988) Insediamento altomedievale ed uso della terra nei dintorni di Farfa: approccio storico-archeologico. *Archeologia Laziale* 9: 424–31.

Barker, G., Lloyd, J. A., and Webley, D.P. (1978) A classical landscape in Molise. *Papers of the British School at Rome* 46: 35–51.

Barker, G., Coccia, S., Jones, D. A., and Sitzia, J. (1986) The Montarrenti survey, 1985: problems of integrating archaeological, environmental and historical data. *Archeologia Medievale* 13: 291–320.

Barnish, S. J. (1987) Pigs, plebeians and potentes: Rome's economic hinterland A.D. c.350–600. *Papers of the British School at Rome* 55: 157–85.

Beavitt, P., and Christie, N. (1993) The Cicolano Mountains project: 1992 interim report. *Archeologia Medievale* 20: 419–51.

Becker, M. (forthcoming) The human skeletal remains. In J. A. Lloyd (ed.) *The Samnite and Roman Villa at Matrice.*

Belasio, M. A. (1975) Studi di geologia e di geografia fisica sul Molise (Matese escluso). *Il Comune Molisano* 5: 37–59.

Belasio, M. A. (1976) Studi di geologia e di geografia fisica sul Matese. *Il Comune Molisano* 6: 5–44.

Bell, M. (1982) The effects of land-use and climate on valley sedimentation. In A. Harding (ed.) *Climatic Change in Later Prehistory*: 127–42. Edinburgh, University Press.

Bergamini, M. (1986) La sigillata africana e orientale di Sepino (scavo 1976). *Annali della Facoltà di Lettere e Filosofia, Perugia: Studi Classici* 23: 89–109.

Bergonzi, G. (1985) Southern Italy and the Aegean during the Late Bronze Age: economic strategies and specialised craft products. In C. Malone and S. Stoddart (eds.) *Papers in Italian Archaeology IV (ii) Patterns in Protohistory*: 355–87. Oxford, British Archaeological Reports, International Series 245.

Berti, F. (1991) *Fortuna Mare: La Nave Romana di Comacchio.* Bologna, Nuova Alfa.

Bertolani Marchetti, D., Accorsi, C.A., Pelosio, G. and Raffi, S. (1979) Palynology and stratigraphy of the Stirone River (northern Italy). *Pollen et Spores* 21: 149–67.

Biddick, K. (1985) Medieval English peasants and market involvement. *Journal of Economic History* 45: 823–31.

Biddittu, I., and Segre, A. G. (1982) Utilizzazione dell'osso nel Paleolitico Inferiore in Italia. In *Il Paleolitico Inferiore in Italia*: 89–105. Florence, Istituto Italiano di Preistoria e Protostoria (Atti della XXIII Riunione Scientifica).

Bietti-Sestieri, A. M. (1992) *The Iron Age Community of Osteria dell'Osa. A Study of Socio-Political Development in Central Tyrrhenian Italy.* Cambridge, University Press.

Binford, L. H. (1978a) *Nunamiut Ethnoarchaeology.* New York, Academic Press.

Binford, L. R. (1978b) Dimensional analysis of behavior and site structure: learning from an Eskimo hunting stand. *American Antiquity* 43: 330–61.

Binford, L. R. (1979) Organization and formation processes: looking at curated technologies. *Journal of Anthropological Research* 35: 255–73.

Binford, L. H. (1986) In pursuit of the future. In D. J. Meltzer, D. D. Fowler, and J. A. Sabloff (eds.) *American Archaeology Past and Future*: 459–79. Washington DC, Smithsonian Institution.

Bintliff, J. (1991) (ed.) *Archaeology and the Annales School*. Leicester, University Press.

Bintliff, J. (1992) Appearance and reality: understanding the buried landscape through new techniques in field survey. In M. Bernardi (ed.) *Archeologia del Paesaggio*: 89–137. Florence, Insegna del Giglio.

Bintliff, J., and Snodgrass, A. M. (1985) The Cambridge/Bradford Boeotian expedition: the first four years. *Journal of Field Archaeology* 12: 123–61.

Bintliff, J., and Snodgrass, A. M. (1988) Off-site pottery distributions: a regional and interregional perspective. *Current Anthropology* 29: 506–13.

Birley, E. (1953) *Roman Britain and the Roman Army*. Kendal, Titus Wilson.

Blake, H. (1980) Ceramica palaeo-italiana. *Faenza* 67: 20–54.

BMC (1923–75) H. Mattingly, R.A.G. Carson and P.V.Hill, *British Museum, Coins of the Roman Empire*. London, British Museum.

Boardman, J. (1980) *The Greeks Overseas: Their Early Colonies and Trade* (3rd edition). London, Thames and Hudson.

Boersma, J., Van Wijngaarden, H., Yntema, D., and Zomer, L. (1990) The Valesio project: 5th interim report. *Babesch* 65: 81–96.

Boessneck, J. (1969) Osteological differences between sheep (*Ovis aries* Linné) and goats (*Capra hircus* Linné). In D. R. Brothwell and E. S. Higgs (eds.) *Science in Archaeology*: 331–58. London, Thames and Hudson.

Bolla, M. (1991) Recipienti in pietra ollare. In D. Caporusso (ed.) *Scavi MM3 3.2 I Reperti*: 11–38. Milan, Edizioni ET.

Bonatti, E. (1961) I sedimenti del Lago di Monterosi. *Experientia* 17 (252): 1–4.

Bonatti, E. (1963) Stratigrafia pollinica dei sedimenti postglaciali di Baccano, lago craterico del Lazio. *Atti della Società Toscana di Scienze Naturali* Ser. A, 70: 40–8.

Bonatti, E. (1966) North Mediterranean climate during the late Würm glaciation. *Nature* 209: 984–5.

Bonatti, E. (1970) Pollen sequence in the lake sediments. In G. E. Hutchinson (ed.) Ianula: an account of the history and development of the Lago di Monterosi, Latium: 26–31. *Transactions of the American Philosophical Society* 60: 5–175.

Bondioli, L., Corrucini, R.S., and Macchiarelli, R. (1986) Familial segregation in the iron age community of Alfedena, Abruzzo, Italy, based on osteodontal trait analysis. *American Journal of Physical Anthropology* 71: 393–400.

Bonomi Ponzi, L. (1982) Alcune considerazioni sulla situazione della dorsale appenninica umbro-marchigiana tra il IX e il V secolo a.C. *Dialoghi di Archeologia* 2: 137–42.

Bottema, S. (1974) Implications of a pollen diagram from the Adriatic sea. *Geologie en Mijnbouw* 53 (6): 401–5.

Bottini, A. (1982) *Principi Guerrieri della Daunia del VII secolo. Le Tombe Principesche di Lavello*. Bari, De Donato.

Bottini, A. (1986) I popoli indigeni fino al VI secolo: Basilicata e Puglia. In *Popoli e Civiltà dell' Italia Antica* 8, 3: 153–351. Rome, Biblioteca di Storia Patria.

Bound, M. (1985) Una nave mercantile di età arcaica all'Isola del Giglio. In *Il Commercio Etrusco Arcaico*: 65–70. Rome, Consiglio Nazionale delle Ricerche (Quaderni del Centro di Studio per l'Archeologia Etrusco-Italica 9).

Bradford, J. S. P. (1949) 'Buried landscapes' in southern Italy. *Antiquity* 23: 58–72.

Bradford, J. S. P. and Williams-Hunt, P. R. (1946) Siticulosa Apulia. *Antiquity* 20: 191–200

Braudel, F. (1949) *La Méditerranée et le Monde Méditerranéen a l'Époque de Philippe II*. Paris, Librairie Armand Colin.

Braudel, F. (1972) *The Mediterranean and the Mediterranean World in the Age of Philip II*. London, Fontana.

Braudel, F. (1981) *Civilization and Capitalism 15th–18th Century 1. The Structures of Everyday Life.* London, Collins.

Braudel, F. (1982) *Civilization and Capitalism 15th–18th Century 2. The Wheels of Commerce.* London, Collins.

Bresc, H. (1977) Contributo ad una etnografia della Sicilia medievale: i marchi del bestiame. *Archeologia Medievale* 4: 331–9.

Bresslau, H. (1903) *Monumenta Germaniae Historica, Diplomata Heinrici II.* Hannover, MGH.

Brogiolo, G. P. (1992) Trasformazione urbanistica nella Brescia longobarda: della capanna regio Longobardi al Barbarossa. In C. Stella and G. Brentegani (eds.) *S. Giulia di Brescia: Archeologia, Arte, Storia di un Monastero Regio dai Longobardi al Barbarossa*: 179–210. Brescia, Comune di Brescia.

Brown F. E. (1980) *Cosa. The Making of a Roman Town.* Ann Arbor, University of Michigan Press.

Brown, K. A. (1991) A passion for excavation. Labour requirements and possible functions for the ditches of the *villaggi trincerati* of the Tavoliere, Apulia. *Accordia Research Papers* 2: 7–30.

Brown, T. S. (1978) Settlement and military policy in Byzantine Italy. In H. McK. Blake, T. W. Potter and D. B. Whitehouse (eds.) *Papers in Italian Archaeology I* : 323–38. Oxford, British Archaeological Reports, International Series 41.

Brückner, H. (1986) Man's impact on the evolution of the physical environment in the Mediterranean region in historical times. *GeoJournal* 13: 7–17.

Brunt, P. A. (1971) *Italian Manpower 225 BC–AD 14.* Oxford, University Press.

Buchner, G. (1979) Early Orientalizing: aspects of the Euboean connection. In D. Ridgway and F. Ridgway (eds.) *Italy Before the Romans*: 129–44. London, Academic Press.

Buerger, J. (1979) The medieval glazed pottery. In J. Buerger, M. R. de Maine, and C. Smith (eds.) *Diocletian's Palace*: 5–126. Split, University of Minnesota.

Buffa, V., and Peroni, R. (1982) Ricognizione di altri siti. In R. Peroni (ed.) *Ricerche sulla Protostoria della Sibaritide*: 147–88. Naples, Institut Français de Naples (Cahiers du Centre Jean Bérard VIII).

Butzer, K.W. (1974) Accelerated soil erosion. In I. Manners and M. W. Mikesell (eds.) *Perspectives on Environment*: 57–78. Washington, Association of American Geographers.

Butzer, K.W. (1982) *Archaeology as Human Ecology.* Cambridge, University Press.

Cabona, I. F., Gardini, A., and Mannoni, T. (1978) Zignano 1: gli insediamenti e il territorio. *Archeologia Medievale* 5: 273–374.

Calegari, G., Simone, L. and Tiné, S. (1986) Ricostruzione sperimentale di una capanna del Neolitico antico. In *Interpretazione Funzionale dei 'Fondi di Capanna' di Età Preistorica*: 9–16. Milan, Istituto Italiano per l'Archeologia Sperimentale, Sovraintendenza Archeologica della Lombardia.

Camodeca, G. (1982) Italia: Regio I, II, III in Epigrafia e Ordine Senatorio II. *Tituli* 5: 101–63.

Cann, S., and Lloyd, J. A. (1984) Late Roman and early medieval pottery from Molise. *Archeologia Medievale* 11: 425–36.

Cantilena, R. (1991) Le emissioni monetali di Larino e dei Frentani. In S. Capini and A. Di Niro (eds.) *Samnium. Archeologia del Molise*: 141–8. Rome, Quasar.

Capini, S. (1978) Campochiaro (CB). *Studi Etruschi* 96: 420–63.

Capini, S. (1980a) La necropoli di Campochiaro. In *Sannio*: 108–12. Rome, De Luca.

Capini, S. (1980b) La necropoli di Pozzilli. In *Sannio*: 112–28. Rome, De Luca.

Capini, S. (1980c) Il santuario di Ercole a Campochiaro. In *Sannio*: 197–229. Rome, De Luca.

Capini, S. (1982) Archeologia. In *Campochiaro: Potenzialità di Intervento sui Beni*

Culturali: 9–80. Campobasso, Soprintendenza Archeologica e per i Beni Ambientali Architettonici Artistici e Storici del Molise.

Capini, S. (1984) La ceramica ellenistica dallo scarico A del santuario di Ercole a Campochiaro. *Conoscenze* 1: 9–57.

Capini, S. (1991) Il santuario di Ercole a Campochiaro. In S. Capini and A. Di Niro (eds.) *Samnium: Archeologia del Molise*: 115–19. Rome, Quasar.

Capini, S., and Di Niro, A. (1991) (eds.) *Samnium: Archeologia del Molise*. Rome, Quasar.

Cappelletti, M. (1982) Il Teatro. La campagna di scavo 1978. In M. Matteini Chiari (ed.) *Saepinum: Museo Documentario dell' Altilia*: 160–2. Campobasso, Soprintendenza Archeologica e per i Beni Ambientali Architettonici Artistici e Storici del Molise/Istituto di Archeologia dell' Università di Perugia.

Cappelletti, M. (1988) Il teatro di Sepino. *Conoscenze* 4: 87–9.

Cappelletti, M. (1991) La fase romana del santuario di Campochiaro. In S. Capini and A. Di Niro (eds.) *Samnium: Archeologia del Molise*: 237–9. Rome, Quasar.

Carancini, G. L. (1975) *Die Nadeln in Italien. Gli Spilloni dell' Italia Continentale*. Munich, Beck (Prähistorische Bronzefunde 13,).

Carancini, G. L. (1992) L'Italia centro-meridionale. *Rassegna di Archeologia* 10: 235–54.

Carandini, A. (1985a) (ed.) *La Romanizzazione dell' Etruria*. Milan, Electa.

Carandini, A. (1985b) (ed.) *Settefinestre. Una Villa Schiavistica nell' Etruria Romana*, 3 vols. Modena, Panini.

Carandini, A. (1989) Italian wine and African oil: commerce in a world empire. In K. Randsborg (ed.) *The Birth Of Europe: Archaeology and Social Development in the First Millennium AD*: 16–31. Rome, L'Erma di Bretschneider.

Carbonara, G. (1979) *Iussu Desiderii. Monte Cassino e l'Architettura Campano-Abruzzese nell' Undicesimo Secolo*. Rome, Università degli Studi.

Cardarelli, A. (1992) Le età dei metalli nell' Italia settentrionale. In A. Guidi and M. Piperno (eds.) *Italia Preistorica*: 366–419. Rome, Laterza.

Carderi, B. (1970) (ed.) *S. Razzi: Viaggi in Abruzzo*. L'Aquila.

Carroccia, M. (1992) Contributo topografico all' identificazione di Buca nel territorio Frentano. *Athenaeum* 80: 199–206.

Carta del Utilizzazione del Suolo d'Italia (1959) Milan, Touring Club Italiano and Consiglio Nazionale delle Ricerche (Centro Studi di Geografia Economica).

Carter, J. (1980) *Excavations in the Territory, Metaponto, 1980*. Austin, University of Texas.

Cassano, M., and Manfredini, A. (1983) *Studi sul Neolitico del Tavoliere della Puglia*. Oxford, British Archaeological Reports, International Series 160.

Castelletti, L. (1974–75) Rapporto preliminare sui resti vegetali macroscopici della serie neolitico-bronzo di Pienza (Siena). *Rivista Archeologica dell' Antica Provincia e Diocesi di Como* 156–7: 243–51.

Catalli, F. (1980) Larino: le monete. Monte Vairano: le monete. In *Sannio: Pentri e Frentani dal VI al I sec. a.C.*: 312–17, 350–7. Rome, De Luca.

Ceglia, V. (1984) S. Giacomo degli Schiavoni. S. Martino in Pensilis. *Conoscenze* 1: 220–4.

Ceglia, V. (1985) S. Giacomo degli Schiavoni: campagna di scavo 1984. *Conoscenze* 2: 135–7.

Ceglia, V. (1986) San Martino in Pensilis (Campobasso). *Studi Etruschi* 52: 451.

Ceglia, V. (1988) Lo scavo della necropoli di Vicenne. *Conoscenze* 4: 31–48.

Ceglia, V. (1989) Le ville rustiche di S. Giacomo degli Schiavoni e S. Martino in Pensilis. V Settimana Beni Culturale *Tutela: Catalogo della Mostra*: 73–82. Campobasso, Soprintendenza Archeologica.

Ceglia, V. (1991) La villa rustica di S. Martino in Pensilis: le anfore del riempimento del pozzo. In S. Capini and A. Di Niro (eds.) *Samnium: Archeologia del Molise*: 273–76. Rome, Quasar.

Ceglia, V. and Di Genito, B. (1991) Le necropoli altomedievale di Vicenne a Campochiaro. In S. Capini and A. Di Niro (eds.) *Samnium: Archeologia del Molise*: 325–8. Rome, Quasar.

Ceglia, V. (1993) The site. pp. 157–62 in U. Alborella, V. Ceglia, and P. Roberts, S. Giacomo degli Schiavoni: a fifth century AD deposit of pottery and fauna. *Papers of the British School at Rome* 61: 157–225.

Chapman, J. C. (1988) Ceramic production and social differentiation: the Dalmatian Neolithic and the western Mediterranean. *Journal of Mediterranean Archaeology* 1/2: 3–25.

Cherry, J. F. (1983) Frogs around the pond: perspectives in current archaeological survey projects. In D. R. Keller and D. W. Rupp (eds.) *Archaeological Survey in the Mediterranean Area*: 375–416. Oxford, British Archaeological Reports, International Series 155.

Cherry, J. F., Davis, J. L., and Mantzourani, E. (1992) *Landscape Archaeology as Long Term History: Northern Kheos in the Cycladic Islands*. Los Angeles, UCLA Institute of Archaeology, Monumenta Archeologica 16.

Chisholm, M. (1968) *Rural Settlement and Land Use*. London, Hutchinson University Library.

Chouquer, G., Clavel-Lévêque, M., Favory, F., and Vallat, J.-P. (1987) *Structures Agraires en Italie Centro-Méridionale: Cadastres et Paysage Ruraux*. Rome, Ecole Française de Rome.

Christie, N. (1991) (ed.) *Three South Etrurian Churches*. London, British School at Rome, Archaeological Monographs 3.

Christie, N. and Rushworth, A. (1988) Urban fortification and defensive strategy in fifth and sixth century Italy: the case of Terracina. *Journal of Roman Archaeology* 1: 73–88.

Cianfarani, V. (1969) (ed.) *Antiche Civiltà d'Abruzzo*. Rome, De Luca.

Cianfarini, V., Dell'Orto, L. F. and La Regina, A. (1978) *Culture Adriatiche Antiche d'Abruzzo e di Molise*. Rome, De Luca.

Ciarlanti, G. V. (1664) *Memorie Storiche del Sannio*. Isernia (reprinted 1823 Campobasso, tipi di Onofrio Nuzzi).

CIL: *Corpus Inscriptionum Latinarum*.

Cilento, N. (1971) *Italia Meridionale Longobarda*. Milan, R. Ricciardi, 2nd edition.

Cipolloni Sampó, M. (1992) Il Neolitico nell' Italia meridionale e in Sicilia. In A. Guidi and M. Piperno (eds.) *Italia Preistorica*: 334–65. Rome, Laterza.

Clark, G. (forthcoming) The animal bones. In J. A. Lloyd (ed.) *The Samnite and Roman Villa at Matrice*.

Clark, M. (1984) *Modern Italy 1871–1982*. London, Longman.

Clementi, A. (1984) La transumanza nell' alto medioevo. *Bullettino della Deputazione Abruzzese di Storia Patria* 74: 31–47.

Close-Brooks, J., and Gibson, S. (1966) A round hut near Rome. *Proceedings of the Prehistoric Society* 32: 349–52.

Clough, P. (1993) Mr Clean and his computer nail the crooks. *The Independent* March 4th: 10.

CNI: *Corpus Nummorum Italicorum*. Rome, 1910–43.

Coarelli, F. and La Regina, A. (1984) *Guide Archeologiche Laterza: Abruzzo Molise*. Rome, Laterza.

Cocchi Genick, D. (1991) La pratica della transumanza dal Neolitico all' età del Bronzo nella Toscana settentrionale: evidenze archeologiche. In R. Maggi, R. Nisbet and G. Barker (eds.) *Archaeologia della Pastorizia nell' Europe Meridionale* I: 241–63. Bordighera, Istituto Internazionale di Studi Liguri.

Cocchi Genick, D., Damiani, I., Macchiarola, I., Peroni, R., Keller, R. P., and Vigliardi, A. (1992) L'Italia centro-meridionale. *Rassegna di Archeologia* 10: 69–103.

Coccia, S. (forthcoming) Excavations at Colle Castellano. In R. Hodges (ed.) *Excavations at San Vincenzo al Volturno* 4. London, British School at Rome, Archaeological Monographs.

Coccia, S. and Mattingly, D. (1992) (eds.) Settlement history, environment and human exploitation of an intermontane basin in the central Apennines: the Rieti survey, 1988–1991, part 1. *Papers of the British School at Rome* 60: 213–90.

Colonna, G. (1962) Saepinum. *Archeologia Classica* 14: 80–107.

Coltorti, M., Cremaschi, M., Delitala, M.C., Esu, D., Fornaseri, M., McPherron, A., Nicoletti, M., van Otterloo, R., Peretto, C., Sala, B., Schmidt, V., and Sevink, J. (1982a) Reversed magnetic polarity at an early lower palaeolithic site in central Italy. *Nature* 300: 173–6.

Coltorti, M., Cremaschi, M., Guerreschi, A., Peretto, C., and Sala, B. (1982b) L'accampamento preistorico di Isernia la Pineta. In *Il Paleolitico Inferiore in Italia*: 577–87. Florence, Istituto Italiano di Preistoria e Protostoria (Atti della XXIII Riunione Scientifica).

Comba, R. and Settia, A. (1984) (eds.) *Castelli: Storia e Archeologia*. Turin, Regione Piemonte, Assessorato alla Cultura.

Conspectus: see Ettlinger (1991)

Conta Haller, G. (1978) *Ricerche su Alcuni Centri Fortificati in Opera Poligonale in Area Campano-Sannitica*. Naples, Accademia di Archeologia, Lettere e Belle Arti di Napoli.

Corbier, M. (1983) Fiscus and patrimonium: the Saepinum inscription and transhumance in the Abruzzi. *Journal of Roman Studies* 73: 126–31.

Cornell, T. J. (1989) The conquest of Italy. In *The Cambridge Ancient History* 7 Part 2: 351–419. Cambridge, University Press.

Costantini, L., and Tozzi, C. (1983) Les plantes cultivées et la conservation des grains pendant le néolithique des Abruzzes (Italie centrale): le témoignage du village de Catignano (Pescara). *Actes du Colloquium de Nice: Longue Durée et Innovation dans le Monde Méditerranéen, Societés Agricoles et Techniques Agraires*: 19A–19H. Nice, CNRS.

Cotton, M.A. (1979) *The Late Republican Villa at Posto, Francolise*. London, British School at Rome.

Cotton, M.A. and Métraux, G. (1984) *The San Rocco Villa at Francolise*. London, British School at Rome.

Craven, K. (1838) *Excursions in the Abruzzi*. London, Bentley.

Crawford, M. H. (1974) *Roman Republican Coinage*. 2 vols. Cambridge, University Press.

Crawford, M. (1985) *Coinage and Money under the Roman Republic*. London, Methuen.

Cremonesi, G. (1978) L'Eneolitico e l'Età del Bronzo in Basilicata. *Atti della XX Riunione Scientifica dell' Istituto Italiano per la Preistoria e Protostoria*: 63–86. Florence, Parenti.

Cristofani, M. (1975) Il 'dono' in Etruria arcaica. *Parola del Passato* 30: 132–52.

Croce, B. (1958) *Storia del Regno di Napoli*. Bari, Laterza.

Cruise, G. M. (1991) Environmental change and human impact in the upper mountain zone of the Ligurian Apennines: the last 5000 years. In R. Maggi, R. Nisbet and G. Barker (eds.) *Archaeologia della Pastorizia nell' Europa Meridionale* II: 169–94. Bordighera, Istituto Internazionale di Studi Liguri.

Cuntz, O. (1929) (ed.) *Itineraria Romana* I. Lipsiae, Teubner.

D'Agostino, B. (1974) *La Civiltà del Ferro nell' Italia Meridionale e nella Sicilia*. Rome, Biblioteca di Storia Patria (Popoli e Civiltà dell'Italia Antica II).

D'Agostino, B. (1977) *Tombe Principesche dell' Orientalizzante Antico da Pontecagnano*. Rome, Monumenti Antichi dei Lincei, Serie Misc. II–1.

D'Agostino, B. (1980a) L'età del ferro e il periodo arcaico. In *Sannio: Pentri e Frentani dal VI al I sec .a.C.*: 15–27. Rome, De Luca.

D'Agostino, B. (1980b) Le sculture italiche. In *Sannio: Pentri e Frentani dal VI al I sec.a.C.*: 230–45. Rome, De Luca.

Davidson, D. A. (1980) Erosion in Greece during the first and second millennia BC. In R. A. Cullingford, D. A. Davidson, and J. Lewin (eds.) *Timescales in Geomorphology*: 143–58. New York, Wiley.

De Benedittis, G. (1974) *Il Centro Sannitico di Monte Vairano*. Campobasso, Soprintendenza Archeologica (Documenti di Antichità Italiche e Romane 5).

De Benedittis, G. (1977) *Bovianum ed il Suo Territorio*. Campobasso, Soprintendenza Archeologica (Documenti di Antichità Italiche e Romane 7).

De Benedittis, G. (1980) L'oppidum di Monte Vairano ovvero Aquilonia. In *Sannio: Pentri e Frentani dal VI al I sec.a.C.*: 321–41. Rome, De Luca.

De Benedittis, G. (1981) Saepinum: città e territorio tra tardo impero e basso medievo. *Archivio Storio per le Province Napoletane* Ser. 3, 20: 7–30.

De Benedittis, G. (1983) (ed.) *Delle Antichità di Larino: l'Anfiteatro*. Campobasso, l'Airone.

De Benedittis, G. (1986) Le schede Chiovitti relative alle iscrizioni romane di Bovianum. *Conoscenza* 3: 67–94.

De Benedittis, G. (1987) Larinum e la 'Daunia settentrionale'. *Athenaeum* 65: 516–21.

De Benedittis, G. (1988a) *Monte Vairano: La Casa di 'LN': Catalogo della Mostra*. Campobasso, Soprintendenza ai B.A.A.A.S. del Molise/I.R.R.S.A.E. del Molise.

De Benedittis, G. (1988b) Di alcuni materiali altomedievale provenienti dal Molise centrale. *Conoscenze* 4: 103–8.

De Benedittis, G. (1990a) Monte Vairano: tratturi, economia e viabilità. *Conoscenze* 6: 13–27.

De Benedittis, G. (1990b) Monte Vairano: la ceramica a vernice nera della fornace di Porta Vittoria. *Conoscenze* 6: 29–70.

De Benedittis, G. (1991a) Note sull' uso del territorio in un' area del Sannio interno nel periodo preromano. In R. Maggi, R. Nisbet and G. Barker (eds.) *Archeologia della Pastorizia nell' Europa Meridionale* I: 179–91. Bordighera, Istituto Internazionale di Studi Liguri.

De Benedittis, G. (1991b) L'abitato di Monte Vairano. In S. Capini and A. Di Niro (eds.) *Samnium. Archeologia del Molise*: 127–30. Rome, Quasar.

De Benedittis, G. (1991c) Monte Vairano. In *La Romanisation du Samnium aux IIe et Ier Siècles av. J.-C.*: 47–55. Naples, Centre Jean Bérard.

De Benedittis, G. (1991d) Bovianum. In S. Capini and A. Di Niro (eds.) *Samnium. Archeologia del Molise*: 233–9. Roma, Quasar.

De Benedittis, G. (1991e) La necropoli di Casalpiano a Morrone del Sannio. In S. Capini and A. Di Niro (eds.) *Samnium. Archeologia del Molise*: 346. Rome, Quasar.

De Benedittis, G. (1991f) Fagifulae. In S. Capini and A. Di Niro (eds.) *Samnium. Archeologia del Molise*: 259–60. Rome, Quasar.

De Benedittis, G. (forthcoming) La Rocca di Oratino. *Conoscenze*.

De Benedittis, G., Gaggiotti, M., and Matteini Chiari, M. (1984) *Saepinum. Sepino*. Campobasso, Edizioni Enne.

De Benedittis, G., Terzani, C., Fracassi, M.C., and Civerra, C. (1993) *S. Maria in Casalpiano*. Pescara, Zemrade Microeditoria.

De Blasio, A. (1908) Capanna-sepolcro dell'epoca neolitica. *Rivista d'Italia*: 160–5.

De Caro, S. (1991a) Una conceria a *Saepinum*. In S. Capini and A. Di Niro (eds.) *Samnium. Archeologia del Molise*: 250–4. Rome, Quasar.

De Caro, S. (1991b) Base di statua con iscrizione opistografa da *Larinum*. In S. Capini and A. Di Niro (eds.) *Samnium. Archeologia del Molise*: 268–70. Rome, Quasar.

De Gennaro, G. O. (1977) L'immigrazione degli Albanesi nel territorio di Larino nel XV secolo. *Almanacco del Molise*: 357–68.

De Giuli, C. and Sala, B. (1988) Vertebrate palaeontology. *Il Quaternario* 1: 63–70.

De Grossi Mazzorin, J. (1985) Reperti faunistici dall'acropoli di Populonia: testimonianze di allevamento e caccia nel III secolo a.C. *Rassegna di Archeologia* 5: 131–71.

De Juliis, E. (1977) *La Ceramica Geometrica della Daunia*. Florence, Sansoni.

De Juliis, E. (1978) Centri di produzione ed aree di diffusione commerciale della ceramica daunia di stile geometrico. *Archivio Storico Pugliese* 31: 3–23.

De Juliis, E. (1984) L'età del ferro. In M. Mazzei (ed.) *La Daunia Antica dalla Preistoria all'Altomedioevo*: 137–84. Milan, Electa.

De La Genière, J. (1979) The Iron Age in southern Italy. In D. Ridgway and F. Ridgway (eds.) *Italy Before the Romans*: 59–93. London, Academic Press.

Delogu, P., Maetzke, G., Tabaczynska, E. and Tabaczynska, S. (1976) *Caputaquis Medievale* 1. Salerno, Laveglia.

Dell'Orto, L.F., and La Regina, A. (1978) *Culture Adriatiche Antiche d'Abruzzo e de Molise*. Rome, De Luca.

Del Re, G. (1836) *Descrizione Topografica Fisica Economica de' Reali Dominj al di Qua del Faro del Regno delle Due Sicilie*. Naples.

Dennis, G. (1848) *Cities and Cemeteries of Etruria*. London, John Murray.

De Sanctis, G. (1854) *Elenco Alfabetico delle Provincie, Distretti Circondarii, Comuni e Villaggi del Regno di Napoli*. Naples.

De Tata, P. (1988) Sepolture altomedievale dall'anfiteatro di Larinum. *Conoscenze* 4: 94–103.

De Tata, P. (1990) L'anfiteatro romano di *Larinum*: le campagne di scavo 1987–8. *Conoscenze* 6: 129–37.

Di Cicio, P. (1966) Il problema della Dogana delle Pecore nella seconda metà del XVIII secolo. *Il Capitanata* 4: 63–72.

Di Iorio, A. (1984) Transumanza e tratturi demaniali. *Molise Economico* 1: 35–89.

Di Nino, A. (1899) Termoli e S. Giacomo degli Schiavoni. *Notizie degli Scavi*: 449–51.

Di Niro, A. (1977) *Il Culto di Ercole tra i Sanniti, Pentri e Frentani*. Campobasso, Soprintendenza Archeologica (Documenti di Antichità Italiche e Romane 9).

Di Niro, A. (1978) San Giovanni in Galdo (CB). *Studi Etruschi* 46: 444–56.

Di Niro, A. (1980a) La necropoli di Termoli; Larino, la necropoli di Monte Arcano; Montorio nei Frentani; Macchiagódena. In *Sannio: Pentri e Frentani dal VI al I sec. a.C.*: 52–84. Rome, De Luca.

Di Niro, A. (1980b) Il santuario di S. Giovanni in Galdo. In *Sannio: Pentri e Frentani dal VI al I sec. a.C.*: 269–81. Rome, De Luca.

Di Niro, A. (1980c) Larino: la città ellenistica e romana. In *Sannio: Pentri e Frentani dal VI al I sec. a.C.*: 286–306. Rome, De Luca.

Di Niro, A. (1981) *Necropoli Arcaiche di Termoli e Larino. Campagne di Scavo 1977–78*. Campobasso, Soprintendenza Archeologica.

Di Niro, A. (1982) *La Villa Romana di S. Fabiano e il Sistema di Produzione Schiavistico*. Campobasso, Soprintendenza Archeologica.

Di Niro, A. (1984) Campomarino, sito preistorico. *Conoscenze* 1: 189–91.

Di Niro, A. (1986) Guglionesi, necropoli arcaica. *Conoscenze* 3: 153–64.

Di Niro, A. (1991a) Il villaggio protostorico di Campomarino. In S. Capini and A. Di Niro (eds.) *Samnium. Archeologia del Molise*: 35–49. Rome, Quasar.

Di Niro, A. (1991b) Le necropoli dell' area interna; le necropoli della zona costiera. In S. Capini and A. Di Niro (eds.) *Samnium. Archeologia del Molise*: 61–71. Rome, Quasar.

Di Niro, A. (1991c) La zona frentana tra IV e I sec. a.C. In S. Capini and A. Di Niro (eds.) *Samnium. Archeologia del Molise*: 131–4. Rome, Quasar.

Di Niro, A. (1991d) Cercemaggiore-Gildone: la casa, le tombe e il sacello. In S.

Capini and A. Di Niro (eds.) *Samnium. Archeologia del Molise*: 121–6. Rome, Quasar.

Di Niro, A. (1991e) *Larinum*. In S. Capini and A. Di Niro (eds.) *Samnium. Archeologia del Molise*: 263–7. Rome, Quasar.

Di Niro, A. (1991f) Introduzione. In S. Capini and A. Di Niro (eds.) *Samnium. Archeologia del Molise*: 101–5. Rome, Quasar.

Di Niro, A. (1991g) *Terventum*. In S. Capini and A. di Niro (eds.) *Samnium. Archeologia del Molise*: 255–7. Rome, Quasar.

Di Niro, A. (1993) Insediamenti di epoca sannitica nel territorio circostante la valle del Torrente Tappino (Campobasso, Molise). *Papers of the British School at Rome* 61: 7–31.

Donahue, R. E. (1988) Microwear analysis and site function of Paglicci Cave level 4a. *World Archaeology* 19: 357–75.

Doria, G. (1968) *Uomini e Terre di un Borgo Collinare*. Milan.

Dramis, F. (1988) Periglacial geomorphology. *Il Quaternario* 1: 45–6.

Drinkwater, J. (1983) *Roman Gaul*. London, Croom Helm.

Drinkwater, J. (1987) Urbanization in Italy and the western empire. In J. Wacher (ed.) *The Roman World* I: 345–79. London, Routledge Kegan Paul.

Ducci, S., Perazzi, P., and Ronchitelli, A. (1983) Gli insediamenti neolitici abruzzesi con ceramica impressa di Tricalle (Ch) e Fontanelle (Pe). *Rassegna di Archeologia* 6: 65–128.

Dufournier, D., Flambard, A.M., and Noyé, G. (1986) A propos de céramique (RMR): problèmes de définition et de classement, problèmes de répartition. In R. Francovich (ed.) *La Ceramica Medievale del Mediterraneo Occidentale*: 251–76. Florence, Insegna del Giglio.

Duncan, G. C. (1958) Sutri (Sutrium). *Papers of the British School at Rome* 26: 63–134.

Empereur, J.-Y. and Picon, M. (1986) A la recherche des fours d'amphores. In J.-Y. Empereur and Y. Garlan (eds.) *Recherches sur les Amphores Grecques*, BCH Suppl. 13: 103–26.

Erspamer, G. (1982) Altri resti scheletrici umani provenienti dalla necropoli di Monte Saraceno (Gargano). *Taras* 2: 35–40.

Esu, D. (1988) Continental malacology. *Il Quaternario* 1: 29–30.

Esu, D. and Girotti, O. (1974) La malacofauna continentale del Plio-Pleistocene continentale dell'Italia centrale. 1. Palaeontologia. *Geologica Romana* 13: 203–94.

Ettlinger, E. (1983) *Novaesium IX: Die Italischer Sigillata von Novaesium*. Berlin, Mann.

Ettlinger, E. (1991) *Conspectus Formarum Terrae Sigillatae Italico Modo Confectae*. Bonn, Habelt.

Evett, D. (1975) A preliminary note on the typology, functional variability and trade of Italian neolithic ground stone axes. *Origini* 9: 35–54.

Evett, D., and Renfrew, J. (1971) D'agricoltura neolitica italiana: una nota sui cereali. *Rivista Scienze Preistoriche* 26: 403–9.

Fabbricotti, E. (1992) Cambiamenti di vita a Iuvanum I. In E. Herring, R. Whitehouse and J. Wilkins (eds.) *Papers of the Fourth Conference of Italian Archaeology* 4, Part 2: 77–82. London, Accordia.

Farello, P. (1991) I reperti faunistici. In F. Berti, *Fortuna Mare: la Nave Romana di Comacchio*: 118–30. Bologna, Nuova Alfa.

Faustoferri, A. (1989) Osservazioni su una tomba Larinate di età classica. *Conoscenze* 5: 7–26.

Faustoferri, A. (1991) I rapporti con l'Apulia: la ceramica di argilla depurata. In S. Capini and A. Di Niro (eds.) *Samnium. Archeologia del Molise*: 72–5. Rome, Quasar.

Federici, V. (1929–33) *Chronicon Vulternense*. Rome, Istituto Storico Italiano, 3 volumes (Fonti per la Storia d'Italia).

Fleming, A. (1985) Land tenure, productivity, and field systems. In G. Barker and C.

S. Gamble (eds.) *Beyond Domestication in Prehistoric Europe: Investigations in Subsistence Archaeology and Social Complexity*: 129–46. London, Academic Press.

Foerster, R. (1919) *The Italian Emigration of our Times*. Cambridge, Mass., Harvard University Press.

Foley, R. (1981a) Off-site archaeology: an alternative approach for the short-sited. In I. Hodder, G. Isaac, and N. Hammond (eds.) *Pattern of the Past: Studies in Honour of David Clarke*: 157–83. Cambridge, University Press.

Foley, R. (1981b) *Off-site Archaeology and Human Adaptations in Eastern Africa*. Oxford, British Archaeological Reports, International Series 97.

Follieri, M. (1958–61) Interpretazione cronologica preliminare della diatomite a Pterocarya di Riano Romano. *Quaternaria* 5: 261–3.

Follieri, M. (1979) Late Pleistocene floristic evaluation near Rome. *Pollen et Spores* 21: 135–48.

Follieri, M. and Castelletti, L. (1988) Palaeobotanical research in Italy. *Il Quaternario* 1: 37–41.

Follieri, M., Magri, M., and Sadori, L. (1988) 250,000–year pollen record from the valle di Castiglione (Roma). *Pollen et Spores* 30 (3–4): 329–56.

Fornaciari, G., Brogi, M.G., and Balducci, E. (1984) Patologia dentaria degli inumati di Pontecagnano (Salerno): VII–IV sec. a.C. *Archivio per l'Antropologia e la Etnologia* 114: 95–120.

Franchi, R., and Vannucci, S. (1983) Rapporto preliminare sulla recinzione medioevale di Termoli: lo scavo archeologico alla torre 'Torniola'. *Archeologia Medievale* 10: 417–37.

Francovich, R. (1985) Un villaggio di minatori e fonditori di metallo nella Toscana del medioevo: S. Silvestro (Campiglia Marittima). *Archeologia Medievale* 12: 313–402.

Francovich, R. (1992) *Rocca San Silvestro*. Rome, Leonardo de Luca.

Francovich, R. and Gelichi, S. (1988) Insediamento sparso e insediamento accentrato medievale nelle ultime ricerche archeologiche in Toscana e Emilia-Romagna: alcune considerazioni. In G. Noyé (ed.) *Structures de l'Habitat et Occupation du Sol dans le Pays Méditerranéens: Les Méthodes et l'Apport de l'Archéologie Extensive*: 467–78. Rome, Ecole Française de Rome.

Francovich, R., and Hodges, R. (1989) Archeologia e storia del villaggio fortificato di Montarrenti (SI): un caso o un modello? *Archeologia Medievale* 16: 15–38.

Francovich, R., Gelichi, S., and Parenti, R. (1980) Aspetti e problemi di forme abitative minore attraverso la documentazione materiale nella Toscana medievale. *Archeologia Medievale* 7: 173–246.

Francovich, R., Hodges, R., Ippolito, L., Mills, C.M., Parenti, R., Roncaglia, A., Rovelli, A., and Ward, R.G. (1985) Il progetto Montarrenti (Siena): relazione preliminare. *Archeologia Medievale* 12: 403–46.

Frank, A. H. E. (1969) Pollen stratigraphy .from the Lake of Vico (central Italy). *Palaeogeography, Palaeoclimatology and Palaeoecology* 6: 67–85.

Frank, T. (1940) *Rome and Italy of the Empire. An Economic Survey of Ancient Rome* 5. Baltimore, Johns Hopkins Press.

Frayn, J. (1979) *Subsistence Farming in Roman Italy*. London, Centaur Press.

Frazzetta, G., and Lanzafame, G. (1977) I dissesti nel medio e basso bacino del F. Biferno (Molise). *Geologica Romana* 16: 87–111.

Frederiksen, M. (1968) Review of E.T. Salmon, *Samnium and the Samnites. Journal of Roman Studies* 58: 224–9.

Frederiksen, M. (1979) The Etruscans in Campania. In D. Ridgway and F. Ridgway (eds.) *Italy Before the Romans*: 277–311. London, Academic Press.

Frederiksen, M. (1984) *Campania*. London, British School at Rome.

Freed, J. (1982) *Late Roman Pottery from San Giovanni di Ruoti and its Implications*. University of Alberta, unpublished PhD dissertation.

Fusco, V. (1982) Ricerche faunistiche a Monte Saraceno (Gargano). *Taras* 2: 7–33.

Gabba, E. (1972) Urbanizzazione e rinnovamenti urbanistici nell'Italia centro-meridionale del I A.C. *Studi Classici e Orientali* 21: 73–112.

Gabba, E. (1976) *Republican Rome, the Army and the Allies*. Oxford, Blackwell.

Gabba, E. (1985) La transumanza nell'Italia romana. Evidenze e problemi. Qualche prospettiva per l'età altomedievale. *XXXI Settimana di Studio sull'Alto Medioevo, Spoleto 1985*: 373–400. Spoleto, Centro Italiano di Studi sull'Alto Medioevo.

Gabba, E. (1988) La pastorizia nell'età tardo-imperiale in Italia. In C. R. Whitaker (ed.) *Pastoral Economies in Classical Antiquity*: 196–209. Cambridge, Cambridge Philological Society, Supplementary Volume 14.

Gabba, E. and Pasquinucci, M. (1979) *Strutture Agrarie e Allevamento Transumante nell' Italia Romana*. Pisa, Giardini.

Gadd, D. (1986) The Roman farmstead at site 9. pp. 109–118 in C. Delano-Smith, D. Gadd, N. Mills and B. Ward-Perkins: Luni and the *Ager Lunensis*. *Papers of the British School at Rome* 54: 81–146.

Gaggiotti, M. (1978) Le iscrizioni della basilica di Saepinum e i rectores della provincia del Samnium. *Athenaeum* 16: 143–69.

Gaggiotti, M. (1982a) Il periodo romano. In M. Matteini Chiari (ed.) *Saepinum: Museo Documentario dell' Altilia*: 27–35. Campobasso, Soprintendenza Archeologica e per i Beni Ambientali Architettonici Artistici e Storici del Molise/Istituto di Archeologia dell' Università di Perugia.

Gaggiotti, M. (1982b) La stratificazioni sociale. In M. Matteini Chiari (ed.) *Saepinum: Museo Documentario dell' Altilia*: 36–40. Campobasso, Soprintendenza Archeologica e per i Beni Ambientali Architettonici Artistici e Storici del Molise/Istituto di Archeologia dell' Università di Perugia.

Gaggiotti, M. (1982c) La *gens Neratia*. In M. Matteini Chiari (ed.) *Saepinum: Museo Documentario dell' Altilia*: 41–9. Campobasso, Soprintendenza Archeologica e per i Beni Ambientali Architettonici Artistici e Storici del Molise/Istituto di Archeologia dell' Università di Perugia.

Gaggiotti, M. (1982d) Nuovo testo da Saepinum. Epigrafia e Ordine Senatorio. *Tituli* 4: 513.

Gaggiotti, M. (1983) Tre casi regionali Italici: il Sannio Pentri. In *Les 'Bourgeoisies' Municipales Italiennes au IIe et Ier Siècles av. J.-C.* Naples, Centre Jean Bérard.

Gaggiotti, M. (1984/5) La villa dei *Neratii* nel territorio di Saepinum. *Annali della Facoltà di Lettere e Filosofia, Perugia. Studi Classici* 22: 115–24.

Gaggiotti, M. (1987/8) Frammenti epigrafici inediti da Saepinum pertinenti alla Gens Neratia. *Annali della Facoltà di Lettere e Filosofia, Perugia. Studi Classici* 25: 129–40.

Gaggiotti, M. (1991) Saepinum. In S. Capini and A. Di Niro (eds.) *Samnium. Archeologia del Molise*: 243–6. Rome, Quasar.

Galanti, G. M. (1781) *Descrizione dello Stato Antico ed Attuale del Contado di Molise*. Naples, Società Letteraria e Tipografica, 2 vols.

Galanti, G. M. (1788) *Nuova Descrizione Storica e Geografica delle Sicilie*. Naples, Società Letteraria e Tipografica, 4 vols.

Galassi, R. (1986) Problemi di tipologia degli insediamenti dell' età del bronzo nell' Etruria meridionale. In G. L. Carancini (ed.) *Gli Insediamenti Perilacustri dell' Età del Bronzo e della prima Età del Ferro: il Caso dell'Antico Lacus Velinus*: 151–92. Perugia, Istituto di Archeologia dell' Università di Perugia.

Gamble, C. S. (1986) *The Palaeolithic Settlement of Europe*. Cambridge, University Press.

Gejvall, N.-G. (1982) Animal remains from Zone A in Acquarossa. In M.-B. Lundgren and L. Wendt, *Acquarossa III: Zone A*: 68–70. Stockholm, Skrifter Utgivna av Svenska Institutet i Rom 4, 38 (3).

Giampaolo, P. N. (1822) *Dei Disordini Fisici ed Economici che Han Luogo nel Sistema Agrario nel Regno di Napoli*. Naples.

Giardino, C. (1984) Insediamenti e sfruttamento minerario del territorio durante la media e tarda età del bronzo nel Lazio: ipotesi e considerazioni. *Nuova Bullettino Archeologico Sardo* 1: 123–41.

Gilbertson, D. D., Holyoak, D. H., Hunt, C. O., and Paget, F. N. (1983) Palaeoecology of Late Quaternary floodplain deposits in Tuscany: the Feccia valley at Frosini. *Archeologia Medievale* 10: 340–50.

Gilbertson, D. D., Hunt, C. O., Donahue, R. E., Harkness, D. D., and Mills, C. M. (1992) Towards a palaeoecology of the medieval and post-medieval landscape of Tuscany. In M. Bernardi (ed.) *Archeologia del Paesaggio*: 205–48. Florence, Insegna del Giglio.

Gowlett, J. A. J., Hedges, R. E. M., Law, I. A., and Perry, C. (1987) Radiocarbon dates from the Oxford AMS system: archaeometry datelist 5. *Archaeometry* 29, 1: 125–55.

Graham, D., and Bidwell, S. (1986) *Tug of War: the Battle for Italy 1943–45*. London, Hodder and Stoughton.

Grant, A. (1982) The use of tooth wear as a guide to the age of domestic ungulates. In B. Wilson, C. Grigson, and S. Payne (eds.) *Ageing and Sexing Animal Bones from Archaeological Sites*: 91–108. Oxford, British Archaeological Reports, British Series 109.

Gravina, A. (1986) Annotazioni sul popolamento Daunio nel territorio a nord e a nord-ovest di Foggia. *Profili della Daunia Antica*: 283–96. Bari.

Gravina, A. (1987) Alcuni aspetti del Neolitico medio-finale nella Daunia centro-settentrionale. Elementi di topografia. In *Il Neolitico d'Italia: Atti della XXVI Riunione Scientifica del'Istituto Italiano di Preistoria e Protostoria*: 733–41. Florence, Istituto Italiano per la Preistoria e Protostoria.

Gravina, A., and Di Giulio, P. (1982) *Abitato Protostorico presso Campomarino in Localita Difensola: Nota Preliminare*. Campomarino, Archeoclub.

Grifoni Cremonesi, R. (1992) Il Neolitico nell' Italia centrale e in Sardegna. In A. Guidi and M. Piperno (eds.) *Italia Preistorica*: 306–33. Rome, Laterza.

Grüger, E. (1977) Pollenanalytische Untersuchung zur würmzeitlichen Vegetationgeschichte von Kalabrien (Suditalien). *Flora* 166: 475–89.

Gualtieri, M. (1987) Fortifications and settlement organisation: an example from pre-Roman Italy. *World Archaeology* 19: 30–46.

Guerreschi, A. (1992) La fine del Pleistocene e gli inizi dell' Olocene. In A. Guidi and M. Piperno (eds.) *Italia Preistorica*: 198–237. Rome, Laterza.

Guidi, A. (1992) Le età dei metalli nell' Italia centrale e in Sardegna. In A. Guidi and M. Piperno (eds.) *Italia Preistorica*: 420–70. Rome, Laterza.

Güller, A., and Segre, A.G. (1948) La stazione enea del grottone di Val di Varri nell' Appennino abruzzese. *Rivista di Antropologia* 36: 269–81.

Halstead, P. (1981) Counting sheep in neolithic and bronze age Greece. In I. Hodder, G. Isaac and N. Hammond (eds.) *Pattern of the Past: Studies in Memory of David Clarke*: 307–39. Cambridge, University Press.

Halstead, P. (1987) Man and other animals in later Greek prehistory. *Annual of the British School of Archaeology at Athens* 82: 71–83.

Halstead, P. (1989) The economy has a normal surplus: economic stability and social change among early farming communities of Thessaly, Greece. In P. Halstead and J. O'Shea (eds.) *Bad Year Economics: Cultural Responses to Risk and Uncertainty*: 68–80. Cambridge, University Press.

Halstead, P., and Jones, G. (1989) Agrarian ecology in the Greek islands: time stress, scale and risk. *Journal of Hellenic Studies* 109: 41–55.

Hamond, F. W. (1978) The contribution of simulation to the study of archaeological processes. In I. Hodder (ed.) *Simulation Studies in Archaeology*: 1–9. Cambridge, University Press.

Harding, J. L. (1992) *Holocene Environmental Change through Natural Processes and*

Human Influence in Salento, Southeast Italy: an Integrated Geomorphological and Palynological Investigation. Sheffield University, unpublished PhD thesis.

Hartmann, N.B. (1975) Stone and bone objects. pp. 72–5 in R. Ross Holloway (ed.) Buccino: the early bronze age village of Tufariello. *Journal of Field Archaeology* 2: 11–81.

Harvey, D. (1992) *Neolithic Pottery from the Biferno Valley, Italy. Results of a Thin Section Study.* Leicester University, unpublished MA thesis.

Hayes, J. (1972) *Late Roman Pottery.* London, British School at Rome.

Hayes, J. (1980) *Supplement to Late Roman Pottery.* London, British School at Rome.

Hayes, J. (forthcoming) The pottery. In A. Small, A pit group of c.75 BC from Gravina. *Papers of the British School at Rome* 63.

Helbaek, H. (1967) Agricoltura preistorica a Luni sul Mignone in Etruria. Appendice II. pp. 277–9 in C. E. Östenberg (ed.) Luni sul Mignone e problemi della preistoria d'Italia. *Acta Istituti Romani Regni Sueciae* 4, 25: 1–306.

Herring, E. (1991) Power relations in iron age southeast Italy. In E. Herring, R. Whitehouse and J. Wilkins (eds.) *Papers of the Fourth Conference of Italian Archaeology 2: the Archaeology of Power Part 2:* 117–33. London, Accordia Research Centre.

Higgs, E. S. and Vita-Finzi, C. (1972) Prehistoric economies: a territorial approach. In E. S. Higgs (ed.) *Papers in Economic Prehistory:* 27–36. Cambridge, University Press.

Hill, P.V., Kent, J.P.C., and Carson, R.A.G. (1960) *Late Roman Bronze Coinage, A.D.: 324–498.* London, British Museum.

Hjelmquist, H. (1977) Economic plants of the Italian Iron Age from Monte Irsi. In A. Small, *Monte Irsi, Southern Italy:* 274–81. Oxford, British Archaeological Reports, International Series 20.

Hodder, I., and Malone, C. (1984) Intensive survey of prehistoric sites in the Stilo region, Calabria. *Proceedings of the Prehistoric Society* 50: 121–50.

Hodges, R. (1981) Excavations and survey at San Vincenzo al Volturno, Molise, 1980. *Archeologia Medievale* 8: 483–502.

Hodges, R. (1982a) Excavations and survey at San Vincenzo al Volturno, Molise. *Archeologia Medievale* 9: 299–310.

Hodges, R. (1982b) *Dark Age Economics.* London, Duckworth.

Hodges, R. (1986) Rewriting history: archaeology and the Annales paradigm. In *Alltag und Fortschritt im Mittelalter:* 137–49. Österreichischen Akademie der Wissenschaften, Philosopisch-historische Klasse Sitzungberichte 470. Vienna, Verlag der Österreichischen Akademie der Wissenschaften.

Hodges, R. (1988a) *Primitive and Peasant Markets.* Oxford, Blackwell.

Hodges, R. (1988b) Charlemagne's elephant and the beginning of commoditisation in Europe. *Acta Archeologica* 59: 15–168.

Hodges, R. (1990) Rewriting the rural history of early medieval Italy: twenty-five years of medieval archaeology reviewed. *Rural History* 1.1: 17–36.

Hodges, R. (1991) A fetishism for commodities: ninth century glass making at San Vincenzo al Volturno. In M. Mendera (ed.) *Archeologia e Storia della Produzione del Vetro Preindustriale:* 67–90. Florence, Insegna del Giglio.

Hodges, R. (1993) (ed.) *San Vincenzo al Volturno I: The 1980–86 Excavations, Part I.* London, British School at Rome, Archaeological Monographs 7.

Hodges, R. and Mitchell, J. (1985) (eds.) *San Vincenzo al Volturno: the Archaeology, Art and Territory of an Early Medieval Monastery.* Oxford, British Archaeological Reports, International Series 252.

Hodges, R. and Wickham, C. (1981) *Vetrana:* un villaggio abbandonato altomedievale presso Guglionesi nella valle del Biferno (Molise). *Archeologia Medievale* 8: 492–502.

Hodges, R., Barker, G. and Wade K. (1980) Excavations at D85 (Santa Maria in

Civita): an early medieval hilltop settlement in Molise. *Papers of the British School at Rome* 48: 70–124.

Hodges, R., Heming, P., Higgins, V., Grierson, P., Nowakowski, J.A., Patterson, H., and Wickham, C. (1984) Excavations at Vacchereccia (Rocchetta Nuova): a later Roman and early medieval settlement in the Volturno valley, Molise. *Papers of the British School at Rome* 52: 148–93.

Hoffmann, H. (1980) (ed.) *Die Chronik von Montecassino*. Hannover, Hann (Monumenta Germaniae Historica, Scriptores 34).

Holloway, R. R. (1975) (ed.) Buccino: the early bronze age of Tufariello. *Journal of Field Archaeology* 2: 11–81.

Hopkins, K. (1978) *Conquerors and Slaves*. Cambridge, University Press.

Hopkins, K. (1980) Taxes and trade in the Roman empire (200 BC–AD 400). *Journal of Roman Studies* 70: 101–25.

Howgego, C. J. (1992) The supply and use of money in the Roman world 200 B.C.–A.D. 300. *Journal of Roman Studies* 82: 1–31.

Hudson, P. (1985) La dinamica della insediamento urbano nell' area del cortile del Tribunale di Verona. L'età medievale. *Archeologia Medievale* 12: 281–302.

Hunt, C.O. and Eisner, W.R. (1991) Palynology of the Mezzaluna core. In A. Voorrips, S. H. Loving, and H. Kamermans (eds.) *The Agro Pontino Survey Project*: 49–59. Amsterdam, Studies in Prae- en Protohistorie 6.

Hunt, C.O., Gilbertson, D.D. and Donohue, R. (1992) Palaeoenvironmental evidence for agricultural soil erosion from late Holocene deposits in the Montagnola Senese, Italy. In M. Bell and J. Boardman (eds.) *Soil Erosion, Ancient and Modern*: 163–74. Oxford, Oxbow.

Hunt, C., Malone, C., Sevink, J. and Stoddart, S. (1990) Environment, soils and early agriculture in Apennine central Italy. *World Archaeology* 22, 1: 33–44.

Ietto, A. (1971) Assetto strutturale e ricostruzione paleogeografica del Matese occidentale (Appennino meridionale). *Memorie Società Naturalisti in Napoli* 80: 441–72.

Iker, R. (1971) La Tombe LX. In J. Mertens (ed.) *Ortona* III: 39–82. Wetteren, Imprimerie Universa.

Ippolito, F. (1970) Nuovi aspetti della geologia applicata in relazione alle recenti concezioni sulla geologia dell'Appennino centro-meridionale. *Bollettino della Società Geologica Italiana* 89: 435–46.

Isings, C. (1957) *Roman Glass from Dated Finds*. Groningen, J. B. Wolters (Archaeologica Traectina 2).

Jamison, E. (1938) Notes on S. Maria della Strada at Matrice. *Papers of the British School at Rome* 14: 32–97.

Jamison, E. (1972) (ed.) *Catalogus Baronum*. Rome, Istituto Storico Italiano (Fonti per la Storia d'Italia 101).

Jarman, H.N. (1976) The plant remains. In T. W. Potter (ed.) *A Faliscan Town in South Etruria – Excavations at Narce 1966–71*: 308–10. London, British School at Rome.

Jarman, H. N., Legge, A. J., and Charles, J. A. (1972) Retrieval of plant remains from archaeological sites by froth flotation. In E. S. Higgs (ed.) *Papers in Economic Prehistory*: 39–48. Cambridge, University Press.

Jarman, M. R., and Webley, D. (1975) Settlement and land use in Capitanata, Italy. In E. S. Higgs (ed.) *Palaeoeconomy*: 177–221. Cambridge, University Press.

Johns, J. (1973) The medieval and renaissance pottery. pp. 49–111 in J. B. Ward-Perkins (ed.) Excavation and survey at Tuscania, 1972: a preliminary report. *Papers of the British School at Rome* 41: 45–154.

Jones, G. D. B. (1962) Capena and the Ager Capenas, Part I. *Papers of the British School at Rome* 30: 116–207.

Jones, G. D. B. (1963) Capena and the Ager Capenas, Part II. *Papers of the British School at Rome* 31: 100–58.

Jones, G., and Snowdon, K. (forthcoming) The plant remains. In J. A. Lloyd (ed.) *The Samnite and Roman Villa at Matrice.*

Judson, S. (1963) Erosion and deposition of Italian stream valleys during historic time. *Science* 140 (3569): 898–9.

Judson, S., and Hemphill, P. (1981) Sizes of settlements in southern Etruria, 6th–5th centuries BC. *Studi Etruschi* 49: 193–202.

Keeley, L.H. (1980) *Experimental Determination of Stone Tool Uses: a Microwear Analysis.* Chicago, University Press.

Keller, D. R., and Rupp, D. W. (1983) (eds.) *Archaeological Survey in the Mediterranean Area.* Oxford, British Archaeological Reports, International Series 155.

Kelly, M. G. and Huntley, B. (1991) An 11000–year record of vegetation and environment from Lago di Martignano, Latium, Italy. *Journal of Quaternary Science* 6 (3): 209–24.

Kenrick, P. (1985) *Excavations at Sidi Khrebish, Benghazi (Berenice) Vol III Part I: Fine Pottery.* Tripoli, Department of Antiquities and London, Society for Libyan Studies.

Keppie, L. (1983) *Colonisation and Veteran Settlement in Italy 47–14 B.C.* London, British School at Rome.

Keppie, L. (1984) Colonisation and veteran settlement in Italy in the first century A.D. *Papers of the British School at Rome* 52: 77–114.

King, A. (1985) I resti animali. In A. Ricci (ed.) *Settefinestre. Una Villa Schiavistica nell' Etruria Romana 2: La Villa e Suoi Reperti*: 278–99. Modena, Panini.

King, R. (1973) *Land Reform: the Italian Experience.* London, Butterworth.

King, R. (1988) Carlo Levi, Aliano and the rural Mezzogiorno in the 1930s: an interpretative essay. *Journal of Rural Studies* 4 (4): 307–21.

King, R. (1990) Carlo Levi, artist and geographer. *Geographical Magazine* April 1990: 41–5.

King, R., and Killinbeck, J. (1989) Carlo Levi, the Mezzogiorno and emigration: fifty years of demographic change at Aliano. *Geography* 14 (2): 128–43.

Knapp, A. B. (1992) (ed.) *Archaeology, Annales, and Ethnohistory.* Cambridge, University Press.

Lagi, A. (1991) Vetri incisi dal santuario di Campochiaro. In S. Capini and A. Di Niro (eds.) *Samnium. Archeologia del Molise*: 240–2. Rome, Quasar.

Lalli, R. (1978) *Conoscere il Molise.* Campobasso, Edizioni Enne.

Lanzafame, G. and Tortorici, L. (1976) Osservazioni geologiche sul medio e basso bacino del F. Biferno (Molise, Italia centro-meridionale). *Geologica Romana* 15: 199–222.

La Regina, A. (1975) Centri fortificati preromani nei territori sabellici dell'Italia centrale adriatica. *Posebna Izdanja* 24: 271–82.

La Regina, A. (1976) Il Sannio. In P. Zanker (ed.) *Hellenismus in Mittelitalien* 1: 219–48. Göttingen, Vandenhoek and Rupprecht.

La Regina, A. (1978) *Culture Adriatiche Antiche d'Abruzzo e di Molise.* Rome, De Luca.

La Regina, A. (1980a) Introduzione: (b) Dalle guerre sannitiche alla romanizzazione. In *Sannio: Pentri e Frentani dal VI al I sec.a.C*: 29–42. Rome, De Luca.

La Regina, A. (1980b) Pietrabbondante. In *Sannio: Pentri e Frentani dal VI al I sec.a.C.*: 129–96. Rome, De Luca.

La Regina, A. (1984) Molise. In F. Coarelli and A. La Regina, *Guide Archeologiche Laterza: Abruzzo e Molise.* Rome, Laterza.

La Regina, A. (1989) Samnium. In *Italia Omnium Terrarum Parens*: 301–94. Milan, Garzati.

Leggio, T. (1991) Medieval and post-medieval settlement: documentary sources. pp. 37–41 in G. Barker and A. Grant (eds.) Ancient and modern pastoralism in central Italy: an interdisciplinary study in the Cicolano mountains. *Papers of the British School at Rome* 59: 15–88.

Levi, C. (1947) *Christ Stopped at Eboli.* New York, Farrar Strauss and Co.

Levick, B. (1983) The *Senatus Consultum* from Larinum. *Journal of Roman Studies* 73: 97–115.

Lewthwaite, J. (1982) Ambiguous first impressions: a survey of recent work on the Early Neolithic of the West Mediterranean. *Journal of Mediterranean Anthropology and Archaeology* 1(2): 297–307.

Lewthwaite, J. (1985) From precocity to involution: the Neolithic of Corsica in its West Mediterranean and French contexts. *Oxford Journal of Archaeology* 4, 1: 47–68.

Lewthwaite, J. (1986) The transition to food production: a Mediterranean perspective. In M. Zvelebil (ed.) *Hunters in Transition: Mesolithic Societies of Temperate Eurasia and their Transition to Farming*: 53–66. Cambridge, University Press.

Lewthwaite, J. (1987) Three steps to leaven: applicazione del modello di disponibilità al neolitico italiano. In *Il Neolitico d'Italia: Atti della XXVI Riunione Scientifica dell' Istituto Italiano di Preistoria e Protostoria*: 89–102. Florence, Istituto Italiano per la Preistoria e Protostoria.

LIMC II (1984) *Lexicon Iconographicum Mythologiae Classicae.* Munich, Artemis.

Lloyd, J. A. (1991a) Farming the Highlands: Samnium and Arcadia in the Hellenistic and early Roman imperial periods. In G. Barker and J.A. Lloyd (eds.) *Roman Landscapes. Archaeological Survey in the Mediterranean Region*: 180–93. London, British School at Rome, Archaeological Monographs 2.

Lloyd, J. A. (1991b) Forms of rural settlement in the early Roman empire. In G. Barker and J.A. Lloyd (eds.), *Roman Landscapes: Archaeological Survey in the Mediterranean Region*: 233–40. London, British School at Rome, Archaeological Monographs 2.

Lloyd, J. A. (1991c) The Roman villa at Santa Maria della Strada, Matrice. In S. Capini and A. Di Niro (eds.) *Samnium. Archeologia del Molise*: 261–2. Rome, Quasar.

Lloyd, J. A. (forthcoming) *The Samnite and Roman Villa at Matrice.*

Lloyd, J. A., and Barker, G. (1981) Rural settlement in Roman Molise: problems of archaeological survey. In G. Barker and R. Hodges (eds.) *Archaeology and Italian Society*: 289–304. Oxford, British Archaeological Reports, International Series 102.

Lloyd, J. A., and Rathbone D. W. (1984) La villa romana a Matrice. *Conoscenze* 1: 215–19.

Lona, F., and Bertoldi, R. (1972) La storia della Plio-Pleistocene italiano in alcune sequenze vegetazionali lacustri e marine. *Atti della Accademia Nazionale dei Lincei Memorie* 11 (3): 1–45.

Longano, F. (1788) *Viaggi per lo Contado del Molise.* Naples, Tipografia Domenico Sangiacomo.

Lopez, R. (1971) *The Commercial Revolution of the Middle Ages.* New Jersey, Englewood Cliffs.

LRBC: see Hill *et al.*, 1960.

Lugli, G. (1957) *La Tecnica Edilizia Romana I.* Rome, Bardi.

Lukesh, S. S. (1975) The pottery. pp. 36–59 in R. Ross Holloway (ed.) *Buccino: the early bronze age village of Tufariello. Journal of Field Archaeology* 2: 11–81.

Lukesh, S.S. (1978) Tufariello (Buccino): preliminary reconsiderations of bronze age sequences in the south Italian context. *Rivista di Scienze Preistoriche* 33: 331–57.

Lukesh, S.S. and Howe, S. (1978) Protopennine vs. Subapennine: mathematical distinction between two ceramic phases. *Journal of Field Archaeology* 5: 339–47.

Macchiarelli, R., Salvadei, L., and Dazzi, M. (1981) Paleotraumatologia cranio-cerebrale nella communità protostorica di Alfedena (VI–V sec.a.C., area medio-adriatica). *Antropologia Contemporanea* 4: 239–43.

Maggi, R. and Nisbet, R. (1991) Prehistoric pastoralism in Liguria. In R. Maggi, R. Nisbet and G. Barker (eds.) *Archeologia della Pastorizia nell' Europa Meridionale* I: 265–96. Bordighera, Istituto Internazionale di Studi Liguri.

Maggiani, A., and Pellegrini, E. (1985) *La Media Valle del Fiora dalla Preistoria alla Romanizzazione*. Pitigliano, Comunità Montana Zona 'S' Colline del Fiora.

Magliano, G., and Magliano, A. (1895) *Considerazioni Storiche sulla Città di Larino*. Campobasso, Stab. tip. Ditta Giovanni e Nicola Colitti.

Malatesta. A. (1985) *Geologia e Paleobiologia dell' Era Glaciale*. Rome, Nuova Italia Scientifica.

Malone, C. (1985) Pots, prestige and ritual in neolithic southern Italy. In C. Malone and S. Stoddart (eds.) *Papers in Italian Archaeology IV (i): Prehistory*: 118–51. Oxford, British Archaeological Reports, International Series 244.

Malone, C., and Stoddart, S. (1992) (eds.) The neolithic site of San Marco, Gubbio (Perugia), Umbria: survey and excavation 1985–7. *Papers of the British School at Rome* 60: 1–69.

Manfredini, M. (1964) *Utilizzazione Irrigua del Fiume Biferno: Diga di Ponte Liscione: Carta e Sezioni Geologiche*. Campobasso, Cassa per il Mezzogiorno.

Mannoni, T. (1975) *La Ceramica Medievale a Genova e nella Liguria*. Bordighera and Genova, Istituto Internazionale di Studi Liguri.

Mariani, L. (1901) Aufidena. *Monumenti Antichi* 10: 225–638.

Mariani, L. (1902) Alfedena. *Notizie degli Scavi*: 517–25.

Martin, J. M. and Noyé, G. (1991) *La Capitanata nella Storia del Mezzogiorno Medievale*. Bari, Editrice Tipografia.

Martindale, J. R. (1980) *The Prosopography of the Later Roman Empire*, volume 2. Cambridge, Universtity Press.

Masciotta, G. B. (1914) *Il Molise dalle Origini ai Nostri Giorni*. Naples, Di Mauro.

Matteini Chiari, M. (1982) (ed.) *Saepinum; Museo Documentario dell' Altilia*. Campobasso, Soprintendenza Archeologica e per i Beni Ambientali Architettonici Artistici e Storici del Molise/Istituto di Archeologia dell' Università di Perugia.

Matteini Chiari, M. (1988) Sepolcreto altomedievale dell'area forense di Sepino. *Conoscenze* 4: 89–94.

Mattingly, H. and Sydenham, E. A. (1923–) *Roman Imperial Coinage*. London.

Mattingly, H., Carson, R.A.G., and Hill, P.V. (1923–75) *British Museum, Coins of the Roman Empire*. London, British Museum.

Mattiocco, E. (1981) *Centri Fortificati Preromani nel Territorio dei Peligni*. Sulmona, Museo Civico.

Mattiocco, E. (1986) *Centri Fortificati Vestini*. Sulmona, Soprintendenza Archeologica dell'Abruzzo and Museo Civico.

Mertens, J. (1981) *Alba Fucens*. Brussels, Centre Belge de Recherches Archéologiques en Italie Centrale et Meridionale.

Mezzena, F. and Palma di Cesnola, A. (1972) Scoperta di una sepoltura gravettiana nella Grotta Paglicci (Rignano Garganico). *Rivista di Scienze Preistoriche* 27: 27–50.

Miall, A. D. (1977) A review of the braided-river depositional environment. *Earth Science Review* 13: 1–62.

Miari, M. (1987) La documentazione dei siti archeologici dei bacini del Fiora e dell' Albegna: criteri di classificazione e analisi dei modelli di insediamento dell' età del bronzo. *Padusa* 23: 113–45.

Millar, F.G.B. (1981) The world of the *Golden Ass. Journal of Roman Studies* 71: 63–75.

Miller, K. (1916) *Itineraria Romana*. Stuttgart, Strecker.

Millett, M. (1991) Pottery: population or supply patterns? The *Ager Tarraconensis* approach. In G. Barker and J. A. Lloyd (eds.) *Roman Landscapes: Archaeological Survey in the Mediterranean Region*: 18–26. London, British School at Rome, Archaeological Monographs 2.

Milliken, S. (1991) *Aspects of Lithic Assemblage Variability in the Late Palaeolithic of Southeast Italy*. University of Oxford, unpublished D.Phil. thesis.

Mills, N. (1986) The *Ager Lunensis* archaeological survey. pp. 83–109 in C. Delano Smith, D. Gadd, N. Mills and B. Ward-Perkins, Luni and the *Ager Lunensis*. Papers of the British School at Rome 54: 81–146.

Miozza, P. (1964) *Breve Storia del Santuario della Madonna della Difesa*. Larino, Nicola Marrone.

Mirone, S. (1924) La statue d'Athéna en terre cuite de Rocca d'Aspromonte. *Arethuse* 1: 141–50.

Mithen, S. (1990) *Thoughtful Foragers. A Study in Prehistoric Decision-Making*. Cambridge, University Press.

Moreau, P. (1983) Structures de parenté e d'alliance à Larinum d'aprés le *pro Cluentio*. In *Les Bourgeoisies Municipales Italiennes au IIe et Ier Siècles av. J.-C.* Naples, Centre Jean Bérard.

Morel, J.-P. (1981) *Céramique Campanienne: les Formes*. Rome, Ecole Française de Rome.

Morel, J.-P. (1984) Gli scavi del santuario di Vastogirardi. In *Sannio: Pentri e Frentani dal VI al I sec.a.C: Atti del Convegno 10–11 Novembre 1980*: 35–41. Campobasso, Enne.

Morel, J.-P. (1991) Samnium. In *La Romanisation du Samnium aux IIe et Ier siècles av. J.-C.* Naples, Centre Jean Bérard.

Moreland, J. (1986) Ricognizione intorno Farfa, 1985: resoconto preliminare. *Archeologia Medievale* 13: 333–43.

Moreland, J. (1987) The Farfa survey: second preliminary report. *Archeologia Medievale* 14: 409–18.

Moreland, J. F. (1992) Restoring the dialectic: settlement patterns and documents in medieval central Italy. In A. B. Knapp (ed.) *Archaeology, Annales, and Ethnohistory*: 112–29. Cambridge, University Press.

Moritz, L. A. (1958) *Grain Mills and Flour in Classical Antiquity*. Oxford, Clarendon Press.

Morricone Matini, M. (1991) Pavimenti musivi a *Larinum*. In S. Capini and A. Di Niro (eds.) *Samnium. Archeologia del Molise*: 271–2. Rome, Quasar.

Mueller, J. W. (1975) *Sampling in Archaeology*. Arizona, University Press.

Napoleone, I. and Follieri, M. (1967) Pollen analysis of a diatomite near Mazzano (Rome). *Review of Palaeobotany and Palynology* 4: 143–8.

Narroll, R. (1962) Floor area and settlement pattern. *American Antiquity* 27: 187–9.

Nash, S. (1979) *Thin Section Analysis of Bronze Age Pottery in Molise, Central Italy*. Sheffield University (Department of Archaeology and Prehistory), unpublished BA thesis.

Nava, M.L. (1982) Aspetti e problemi dell'età del bronzo e del ferro nel Gargano. In *La Ricerca Archeologica nel Territorio Garganico*: 141–70. (Atti del Convegno di Studi, Vieste 1982).

Nava, M.L. (1987) *Pietre del Gargano: Scultura Protostorica della Puglia Settentrionale*. Turin, il Quadrante.

Neboit, R. (1984) Erosion des sols et colonisation grecque en Sicile et en Grand Grèce. *Bulletin, Association des Géographes Français* 499: 5–13.

Negroni Catacchio, N. (1981) (ed.) *Sorgenti della Nova. Una Comunità Protostorica ed il Suo Territorio nell' Etruria Meridionale*. Rome, Consiglio Nazionale delle Ricerche.

Negroni Catacchio, N., and Domanico, L. (1987) I modelli abitativi dell' Etruria protostorica. *Annali Benacensi. XI Convegno Archeologico Benacense Simposio Internazionale 1986*: 515–85.

Oakley, S. (forthcoming) *The Hill-Forts of the Samnites*. London, British School at Rome, Archaeological Monographs.

Orombelli, G. (1988) Glacial geology. *Il Quaternario* 1: 25–7.

Östenberg, C.E.(1967) Luni sul Mignone e problemi della preistoria d'Italia. *Acta Istituti Romani Regni Sueciae* 4, 25: 1–306.

Oxé, A. and Comfort, H. (1968) *Corpus Vasorum Arretinorum: a Catalogue of the Signatures, Shapes and Chronology of Italian Sigillata*. Bonn, Habelt.

Pacciarelli, M. (1982) Economia e organizzazione del territorio in Etruria Meridionale nell' età del Bronzo media e recente. *Dialoghi di Archeologia* 2: 69–79.

Pacicchelli, E. (1703) *Il Regno di Napoli*. Naples.

Paganelli, A. and Bartolani Marchetti, D. (1988) Research in palynology in Italy. *Il Quaternario* 1: 55–61.

Palma di Cesnola, A. (1975) Il Gravettiano della Grotta Paglicci nel Gargano. *Rivista di Scienze Preistoriche* 30: 3–177.

Palma di Cesnola, A. (1982) Il Paleolitico Inferiore in Puglia. In *Il Paleolitico Inferiore in Italia*: 225–48. Florence, Istituto Italiano di Preistoria e Protostoria (Atti della XXIII Riunione Scientifica).

Palma di Cesnola, A. (1984) Il Paleolitico. In *La Daunia Antica, dalla Preistoria all' Altomedioevo*: 9–54. Milan, Electa.

Pannuti, S. (1969) Gli scavi di Grotta a Male presso L'Aquila. *Bullettino di Paletnologia Italiana* 78, n.s. 20: 147–67.

Paribeni, E. (1984) Una testa femminile da Casalciprano. In *Sannio: Pentri e Frentani dal VI al I sec.a.C: Atti del Convegno 10–11 Novembre 1980*: 105–7. Campobasso, Enne.

Paroli, L. (1992) *La Ceramica Invetriata Tardoantica e Altomedievale in Italia*. Florence, Insegna del Giglio.

Pasquinucci, M. (1979) La transumanza nell'Italia romana. In E. Gabba and M. Pasquinucci, *Strutture Agrarie e Allevamento Transumante nell'Italia Romana*: 79–182. Pisa, Giardini.

Patterson, H. (1985) The late Roman and early medieval pottery from Molise. In R. Hodges and J. Mitchell (eds.) *San Vincenzo al Volturno*: 83–111. Oxford, British Archaeological Reports, International Series 252.

Patterson, H. (1990) *The Later Roman and Early Medieval to Medieval Pottery from San Vincenzo al Volturno, Molise: Production and Distribution in Central and Southern Italy, AD 400–1100*. University of Sheffield, unpublished PhD thesis.

Patterson, H. and Whitehouse, D. B. (1992) Medieval domestic pottery. In F. d'Andria and D. W. Whitehouse (eds.) *Excavations at Otranto, Vol. II: The Finds*: 87–196. Lecce, Dipartimento dell' Antichità, Università degli Studi di Lecce.

Patterson, J. (1985) The upper Volturno valley in Roman times. In R. Hodges and J. Mitchell (eds.) *San Vincenzo al Volturno*: 213–26. Oxford, British Archaeological Reports, International Series 252.

Patterson, J. (1987) Crisis, what crisis? Rural change and urban development in imperial Apennine Italy. *Papers of the British School at Rome* 55: 115–46.

Patterson, J. (1988) *Sanniti, Liguri e Romani/Samnites, Ligurians and Romans*. Benevento, Auxiliatrix (bilingual publication).

Patterson, J. (1991) Settlement, city and elite in Samnium and Lycia. In J. Rich and A. Wallace-Hadrill (eds.) *City and Country in the Ancient World*: 147–68. London, Routledge.

Payne, S. (1972a) Partial recovery and sample bias: the results of some sieving experiments. In E. S. Higgs (ed.) *Papers in Economic Prehistory*: 49–64. Cambridge, University Press.

Payne, S. (1972b) On the interpretation of bone samples from archaeological sites. In E. S. Higgs (ed.) *Papers in Economic Prehistory*: 65–91. Cambridge, University Press.

Payne, S. (1973) Kill-off patterns in sheep and goats: the mandibles from Asvan Kale. *Journal of Anatolian Studies* 23: 281–303.

Peacock, D. P. S. (1977) Roman amphorae: typology, fabric and origins. In *Méthodes*

Classiques et Méthodes Formelles dans l' Etude des Amphores: 261–278. Rome, Ecole Française de Rome.

Peet, T. E. (1909) *The Stone and Bronze Ages in Italy.* London, Oxford University Press.

Pellegrini, E. (1992) L'età dei metalli nell' Italia meridionale e in Sicilia. In A. Guidi and M. Piperno (eds.) *Italia Preistorica*: 471–516. Rome, Laterza.

Peretto, C., Terzani, C., and Cremaschi, M. (1983) (eds.) *Isernia La Pineta: un Accampamento Più Antico di 700.000 Anni.* Bologna, Calderini.

Perini, R. (1983) Der frühbronzezeitliche Pflug von Lavagnone. *Archaologisches Korrespondenzblatt* 13 (2): 187–95.

Perkins, P., and Attolini, I. (1992) An Etruscan farm at Podere Tartuchino. *Papers of the British School at Rome* 60: 71–134.

Peroni, R. (1959) Per una definizione dell' aspetto culturale 'subappenninico' come fase cronologica à se stante. *Atti Accademia Nazionale Lincei* Ser.8, 9: 3–253.

Peroni, R. (1984) (ed.) *Nuove Ricerche sulla Protostoria della Sibaritide.* Rome, Paleani.

Peroni, R., and Di Gennaro, F. (1986) Aspetti regionali dello sviluppo dell' insediamento protostorico nell' Italia centro-meridionale alla luce dei dati archeologici e ambientali. *Dialoghi di Archeologia* 4 (2): 193–200.

Peroni, R., Carancini, G.L., Bergonzi, G., Lo Schiavo, F., and von Eles, P. (1980) Per una definizione critica di facies locali: nuovi strumenti metodologici. In R. Peroni (ed.) *Il Bronzo Finale in Italia*: 9–87. Bari, De Donato.

Peroni, V.B. (1970) *Die Schwerter in Italien.* Munich, Beck.

Peroni, V.B. (1979) *I Rasoi nell' Italia Continentale.* Munich, Beck.

Perrazzelli, N. (1976) (ed.) *Viaggio nel Molise.* (Edited volume of Francesco Jovine's 1941 letters to *Giornale d'Italia.*) Isernia, Libreria Editrice Marinelli.

Pesez, J. (1984) Brucato. *Histoire et Archéologie d'un Habitat Médiéval en Sicilie.* Rome, Ecole Française.

Peterson, G. M., Webb, T., Kutzbach, J. E., Van der Hammen, T., Wijmstra, T. A., and Street, F. A. (1979) The continental record of environmental conditions at 18,000 bp: an initial evaluation. *Quaternary Research* 12: 47–82.

Petrone, P. P (1993) Gildone: mortalità, stress nutrizionali e da attività lavorativa in un campione di Sanniti del V-IV sec. a.C. *Papers of the British School at Rome* 61: 33–49.

Petrucci, A. (1960) (ed.) *Codice Diplomatico del Monastero Benedittino di S. Maria di Tremiti.* Rome, Istituto Storico Italiano per il Medioevo.

Pharr, C. (1952) *The Theodosian Code. A Translation with Commentary, Glossary and Bibliography.* Princeton, University Press.

Pietravalle, M. (1890) *La Malaria della Provincia di Molise: Note d'Igiene Pubblica.* Campobasso, Jannicelli.

Pigorini, E. (1992) Le età dei metalli nell' Italia meridionale e in Sicilia. In A. Guidi and M. Piperno (eds.) *Italia Preistorica*: 471–516. Rome, Laterza.

Piperno, M. (1992) Il Paleolitico inferiore. In A. Guidi and M. Piperno (eds.) *Italia Preistorica*: 139–69. Rome, Laterza.

Piperno, M., and Segre, A.G. (1982) Pleistocene e Paleolitico Inferiore di Venosa: nuove ricerche. In *Il Paleolitico Inferiore in Italia*: 589–96. Florence, Istituto Italiano di Preistoria e Protostoria (Atti della XXIII Riunione Scientifica).

Pitti, C., and Tozzi, C. (1976) Gli scavi nel villaggio neolitico di Catignano (Pescara). *Rivista Scienze Preistoriche* 31: 87–107.

PLRE II – Martindale, J. R. (1980) *The Prosopography of the Later Roman Empire,* volume 2. Cambridge, University Press.

Plog, F. (1979) Alternative models of prehistoric change. In C. Renfrew and K. L. Cooke (eds.) *Transformations. Mathematical Approaches to Culture Change* : 221–36. New York, Academic Press.

Poccetti, P. (1979) *Nuovi Documenti Italici a Complemento del Manuale di E. Vetter.* Pisa.

Pope, K. O., and Van Andel, Tj. H. (1984) Late Quaternary alluviation and soil formation in the southern Argolid: its history, causes and archaeological implications. *Journal of Archaeological Science* 11: 281–306.

Potter, T. W. (1972) Excavations in the medieval centre of Mazzano Romano. *Papers of the British School at Rome* 40: 135–45.

Potter, T. W. (1976) *A Faliscan Town in South Etruria. Excavations at Narce 1966–71.* London, British School at Rome.

Potter, T. W. (1979) *The Changing Landscape of South Etruria.* London, British School at Rome.

Potter, T. W. (1987) *Roman Italy.* London, British Museum Publications.

Potter, T. W. (forthcoming) *Towns in Late Antiquity. Iol Caesarea and its Context.* Sheffield University, Fourth Ian Sanders Memorial Lecture in Classical Archaeology.

Potter, T. W. and Whitehouse, D. B. (1984) Il castello di ponte Nepesino e il confine settentrionale del ducato di Roma. *Archeologia Medievale* 11: 63–147.

Prag, A. J. N. W. (1992) Black Glaze ware. In A. Small (ed.) *Gravina: An Iron Age and Republican Settlement in Apulia. Volume II: the Artifacts*: 66–131. London, British School at Rome, Archaeological Monographs 5.

Puglisi, S. (1959) *La Civiltà Appenninica. Origine delle Communità Pastorali in Italia.* Florence, Sansoni.

Purcell, N. (1988) Review of A. Carandini (ed.) *Settefinestre. Una Villa Schiavistica nell' Etruria Romana*, 3 vols. *Journal of Roman Studies* 78: 195–98.

Radmilli, A. M. (1962) *La Piccola Guida della Preistoria Italiana.* Florence, Sansoni.

Radmilli, A. M. (1964) *Abruzzo Preistorico. Il Paleolitico Inferiore-Medio Abruzzese.* Florence, Sansoni.

Radmilli, A. M. (1982) Il Paleolitico Inferiore in Abruzzo. In *Il Paleolitico Inferiore in Italia*: 165–75. Florence, Istituto Italiano di Preistoria e Protostoria (Atti della XXIII Riunione Scientifica).

Rainini, I. (1984) Capracotta. *Conoscenze* 1: 201–7.

Randsborg, K. (1991) *The First Millennium A.D. in Europe and the Mediterranean: An Archaeological Essay.* Cambridge, University Press.

Ranieri, L. (1956) *La Media ed Alta Valle del Biferno. Studio Antropogeografico.* Rome, Consiglio Nazionale di Ricerche, Memorie di Geografia Antropica 12,1.

Rathbone, D.W. (1981) The development of agriculture in the 'Ager Cosanus' during the Roman Republic: problems of evidence and interpretation. *Journal of Roman Studies* 71: 10–23.

Rathbone, D.W. (1983) The slave mode of production in Italy. *Journal of Roman Studies* 73: 160–8.

Rathbone, D. W. (1992) Salvaging the Samnites. *JACT Review* 2nd series 10: 15–18.

Rathbone, D. W. (1993) Review of *La Romanisation du Samnium aux IIe et Ier Siècles av. J.-C.* (Naples, Centre Jean Bérard). *Journal of Roman Studies* 83: 193–4.

Ray, C. (1952) *Algiers to Austria: a History of 78 Division in the Second World War.* London, Eyre and Spottiswoode.

Rellini, U. (1931) Le stazioni enee delle Marche di fase seriore e la civiltà italiana. *Monumenti Antichi* 34: 129–280.

Renfrew, C. (1972) *The Emergence of Civilisation.* London, Methuen.

Renfrew, C., and Wagstaff, M. (1982) (eds.) *An Island Polity: the Archaeology of Exploitation in Melos.* Cambridge, University Press.

RIB: *Roman Inscriptions of Britain.*

RIC: see Mattingly and Sydenham (1923–)

Riccardi, M. (1976) (ed.) *Collana di Bibliografie Geografiche delle Regioni Italiane VIII.*

Abruzzo e Molise. Rome, Consiglio Nazionale delle Ricerche, Comitato per le Scienze Storiche, Filologiche e Filosofiche.

Ridgway, D. (1973) The first western Greeks: Campanian coasts and southern Etruria. In C. F. C. Hawkes and S. Hawkes (eds.) *Greeks, Celts, and Romans*: 5–36. London, Dent.

Ridgway, D. (1992) *The First Western Greeks*. Cambridge, University Press.

Roberts, P. C. (1988) *Pottery and Settlement in the Province of Molise during the Roman Imperial Period*. University of Sheffield, unpublished MPhil thesis.

Roberts, P. C. (1992) *The Late Roman Pottery of Adriatic Italy*. University of Sheffield, unpublished PhD thesis.

Roberts, P. (1993) The pottery from the cistern. pp. 163–203 in U. Albarella, V. Ceglia, and P. Roberts, S. Giacomo degli Schiavoni: a fifth century AD deposit of pottery and fauna. *Papers of the British School at Rome* 61: 157–225.

Roberts, P. C. (forthcoming) The pottery. In J. A. Lloyd (ed.) *The Samnite and Roman Villa at Matrice*.

Romanelli, P. (1943–5) Un rilievo inedito di L'Aquila. *Bullettino della Commissione Archeologica Communale di Roma* 71 (appendice): 3–8.

Rossiter, J. J. (1978) *Roman Farm Buildings in Italy*. Oxford, British Archaeological Reports, International Series 52.

Rotilli, M. (1986) *Benevento Romana e Longobarda: l'Immagine Urbana*. Benevento, Banco Sannitica.

Roy, J., Lloyd, J.A., and Owens, E.J. (1992) Two sites in the Megalopolis basin. In J. M. Sanders (ed.) *PHILAKON: Lakonian Studies in Honour of Hector Catling*: 185–92. London, British School at Athens.

Rust, B. R. and Koster, E. H. (1984) Coarse alluvial deposits. In R. G. Walker (ed.) *Facies Models*: 53–69. Toronto, Geoscience Canada Reprint Series 1.

Ryder, M. L. (1983) *Sheep and Man*. London, Duckworth.

Saepinum: see Matteini Chiari (1982).

Sala, M., Rubio, J.L., and Garcia-Ruiz, J. M. (1991) (eds.) *Soil Erosion Studies in Spain*. Zaragoza, Geoforma Edicionez.

Salmon, E. T. (1967) *Samnium and the Samnites*. Cambridge, University Press.

Salmon, E. T. (1982) *The Making of Roman Italy*. London, Thames and Hudson.

Samnium (1991) S. Capini and A. Di Niro (eds.) *Samnium. Archeologia del Molise*. Rome, Quasar.

Sannio: Pentri e Frentani dal VI al I sec.a.C. (1980). Rome, De Luca.

Sannio: Pentri e Frentani dal VI al I sec.a.C: Atti del Convegno 10–11 Novembre 1980 (1984). Campobasso, Enne.

Saracino, L. M. (1985) Terra Sigillata nord-italica. In *Enciclopedia dell'Arte Antica Classica e Orientali. Atlante delle Forme Ceramiche* 2: 175–230.

Sardella, A. and Sardella, P. (1989) La pagliara: esempio di architettura rurale in estinzione. *Conoscenze* 5: 91–104.

Scali, S. (1987a) Bolsena – Gran Carro: i resti faunistici. In *L'Alimentazione del Mondo Antico: Gli Etruschi*: 67–70. Rome, Istituto Poligrafico e Zecca dello Stato.

Scali, S. (1987b) Blera: i resti animali. In *L'Alimentazione del Mondo Antico: Gli Etruschi*: 86. Rome, Istituto Poligrafico e Zecca dello Stato.

Schiffer, M. B., Sullivan, A. P., and Klinger, T. C. (1978) The design of archaeological surveys. *World Archaeology* 10: 1–28.

Segre, A. G., Biddittu, I., and Piperno, M. (1982) Il Paleolitico Inferiore nel Lazio, nella Basilicata e in Sicilia. In *Il Paleolitico Inferiore in Italia*: 177–206. Florence, Istituto Italiano di Preistoria e Protostoria (Atti della XXIII Riunione Scientifica).

Sella, P. (1936) (ed.) *Aprutium-Molisium. La Decime dei Secoli*. Rome, Città del Vaticano.

Shackleton, J.C., Van Andel, T. T., and Runnels, C. N. (1984) Coastal palaeogeography of the central and western Mediterranean during the last 125,000 years and its archaeological implications. *Journal of Field Archaeology* 11: 307–14.

Silver, I. (1969) The ageing of domestic animals. In D. R. Brothwell and E. S. Higgs (eds.) *Science in Archaeology*: 283–302. London, Thames and Hudson.

Simoncelli, R. (1972) *Il Molise. Le Condizioni Geografiche di una Economia Regionale*. Rome, Kappa.

Skeates, R. (1991) Caves, cult and children in neolithic Abruzzo, central Italy. In P. Garwood, D. Jennings, R. Skeates, and J. Toms (eds.) *Sacred and Profane*: 50–64. Oxford, Oxford University Committee for Archaeology, Monograph No.32.

Small, A. (1986) S. Giovanni di Ruoti (Basilicata). Il contesto della villa tardo-romana. I. La villa e la sua storia. In A. Giardina (ed.) *Società Romana e Impero Tardoantico III: le Merci, gli Insediamenti III*: 97–113. Rome, Laterza.

Small, A. (1991) Late Roman rural settlement in Basilicata and western Apulia. In G. Barker and J. A. Lloyd (eds.) *Roman Landscapes: Archaeological Survey in the Mediterranean Region*: 204–22. London, British School at Rome, Archaeological Monographs 2.

Small, A. (1992) (ed.) *Gravina. An Iron Age and Late Republican Settlement in Apulia*. 2 vols. London, British School at Rome, Archaeological Monographs 5.

Soricelli, G. (forthcoming) The Italian sigillata. In J. A. Lloyd (ed.) *The Samnite and Roman Villa at Matrice*.

Sorrentino, C. (1981) The fauna. In E. Berggren and K. Berggren, *San Giovenale II.2: Excavations in Area B. 1957–1960*: 58–64. Lund, Skrifter Utgivna av Svenska Institutet i Rom 4, 36 (II.4).

Sparkes, B. and Tallcott, L. (1970) *The Athenian Agora Vol. 12. Black and Plain Pottery of the 6th, 5th and 4th centuries B.C.* Princeton, University Press.

Spina, A. (1992) *San Polo Matese. Un Paese Molisano*. San Polo Matese, privately printed.

Spitzer, D. C. (1942) Roman relief bowls from Corinth. *Hesperia* 11: 162–92.

Spivey, N., and Stoddart, S. (1990) *Etruscan Italy: an Archaeological History*. London, Batsford.

Sprengel, U. (1975) La pastorizia transumante nell' Italia centro-meridionale. *Annali del Mezzogiorno* 15: 271–327.

Starkel, L. (1991) Fluvial environments as a source of information on climatic changes and human impact in Europe. In B. Frenzel (ed.) *Evaluation of Climate Proxy Data in Relation to the European Holocene*: 241–54. Strasbourg, European Science Foundation.

Stelluti, N. (1988) *Mosaici di Larino*. Pescara, Tipolitografia G. Fabiani.

Stelluti, N. (1992) Samnium frentano. *Il Ponte* 5, 19: 11–15.

Stevenson, R.B.K. (1947) The neolithic cultures of south-east Italy. *Proceedings of the Prehistoric Society* 13: 85–100.

Stoddart, S. (1987) *Complex Polity Formation in Central Italy in the First Millennium BC*. Cambridge University, unpublished PhD thesis.

Strazzulla, M.J. (1973) *Il Santuario Sannitico di Pietrabbondante*. Campobasso, Soprintendenza ai Monumenti alle Antichità e alle Belle Arti del Molise (Documenti I).

Suano, M. (1986) *Sabellian-Samnite Bronze Belts in the British Museum*. London, British Museum Occasional Papers 57.

Suano, M. (1991) A princeless society in a princely neighbourhood. In E. Herring, R. Whitehouse and J. Wilkins (eds.) *Papers of the Fourth Conference of Italian Archaeology 2: the Archaeology of Power Part 2*: 65–72. London, Accordia Research Centre.

Taffetani, F. (1991) Il litorale nord dell' antica 'Capitanata' della storia di un patrimonio naturale dissipato alla tutela delle ultime preziose testimonianze. *Almanacco del Molise* 1: 293–351.

Taplin, O. (1993) *Comic Angels*. Oxford, Clarendon Press.

Tatton-Brown, V. (1992) Loomweights, bobbins and spindle whorls. In A. Small (ed.) *Gravina. An Iron Age and Late Republican Settlement in Apulia. Vol. II: Artifacts*: 218–26. London, British School at Rome Archaeological Monographs 5.

Taylor, L. R. (1960) *The Voting Districts of the Roman Republic*. Rome, American Academy.

Thomsen, R. (1947) *The Italic Regions from Augustus to the Lombard Invasions*. Copenhagen, Gyldendal.

Tiné, S. (1983) *Passo di Corvo e la Civiltà Neolitica del Tavoliere*. Genoa, Sagep Edetrice.

Tiné, S. (1987) Considerazioni sul Neolitico della Puglia. In *Il Neolitico d'Italia: Atti della XXVI Riunione Scientifica del'Istituto Italiano di Preistoria e Protostoria*: 321–7. Florence, Istituto Italiano per la Preistoria e Protostoria.

Tiné, S., and Bernabo Brea, M. (1980) Il villaggio neolitico del Guadone di S. Severo (Foggia). *Rivista Scienze Preistoriche* 35, 1–2: 45–74.

Tite, M. S., and Linington, R. E. (1986) The magnetic susceptibility of soils from central and southern Italy. *Prospezioni Archeologiche* 10: 25–36.

Torelli, L. (1882) *Carta della Malaria d'Italia*. Florence, Pellas.

Torelli, M. R. (1971) Gravisca (Tarquinia) – scavi nella città etrusca e Romana. Campagne 1969 e 1970. *Notizie degli Scavi*: 195–299.

Torelli, M. R. (1973) Una nuova iscrizione di Silla da Larino. *Athenaeum* n.s. 51: 336–54.

Torelli, M. R. (1982) Italia: Regio IV. In Epigrafia e Ordine Senatorio II. *Tituli* 5: 165–99.

Toubert, P. (1973) *Les Structures du Latium Médiévale*. Rome, Ecole Française de Rome.

Toynbee, A. J. (1965) *Hannibal's Legacy*. London, Oxford University Press.

Tozzi, C. (1978) Un aspetto della corrente culturale della ceramica dipinta in Abruzzo: il villaggio di Catignano (Pescara). *Quaderni de la Ricerca Scientifica* 100: 95–111. Rome, CNR.

Tozzi, C. (1982) La transition du Néolithique ancien au Néolithique moyen dans la côte adriatique (Abruzzo-Marche). In *Le Néolithique Ancien Méditerranéen*: 319–25. Montpellier.

Tria, G. A. (1744) *Memorie Storiche Civile ed Ecclesiastiche della Città e Diocesi di Larino*. Rome, G. Zempel.

Trombetta, A. (1971) *Arte Medievale nel Molise*. Campobasso, Nocera.

Trump, D.H. (1958) The Apennine culture of Italy. *Proceedings of the Prehistoric Society* 30: 165–200.

Trump, D. H. (1965) *Central and Southern Italy Before Rome*. London, Thames and Hudson.

Turq, A. (1978) Note preliminaire sur l'outillage en quartzite entre Dordogne et Lot. *Bulletin de la Société Préhistorique Française* 75: 136–9.

Van Andel, Tj. H., Runnels, C. N., and Pope, K. O. (1985) Five thousand years of land use and abuse in the southern Argolid, Greece. *Hesperia* 55: 103–28.

Van der Veen, M. (1985) An early medieval hilltop settlement in Molise: the plant remains from D85. *Papers of the British School at Rome* 53: 211–24.

Vetter, E. (1953) *Handbuch der italischen Dialekte*. Heidelberg, Carl Winter.

Villani, P. (1968) *Feudalità, Riforme, Capitalismo Agrario*. Bari, Laterza.

Villari, R. (1967) *La Rivolta Antispagnola a Napoli*. Bari, Laterza.

Vita-Finzi, C. (1969) *The Mediterranean Valleys. Geological Changes in Historical Times*. Cambridge, University Press.

Vitali, O. (1970) *Aspetti dello Sviluppo Economico Italiano*. Rome.

Vitiello, A., Schizzi, A., Antonicelli, M., and Wrzy, D. (1990) L'anfiteatro di Larino. Studio architettonico. *Conoscenze* 6: 73–114.

Volpe, G. (1990) *La Daunia nell' Età della Romanizzazione. Paesaggio Agrario, Produzione, Scambi.* Bari, Edipuglia.

Wagstaff, J. M. (1981) Buried assumptions: some problems in the interpretation of the 'Younger Fill' raised by recent data from Greece. *Journal of Archaeological Science* 8: 247–64.

Waitz, G. (1878) (ed.) *Monumenta Germaniae Historica: Scriptores Rerum Longobardicarum et Italicarum.* Hannover, MGH.

Wallace-Hadrill, A. (1990) The social spread of Roman luxury: sampling Pompeii and Herculaneum. *Papers of the British School at Rome* 58: 145–92.

Ward-Perkins, B. (1978) Luni: the decline and abandonment of a Roman town. In H. Blake, T.W. Potter and D.W. Whitehouse (eds.) *Papers in Italian Archaeology* 1: 313–21. Oxford, British Archaeological Reports, International Series 55.

Ward-Perkins, B. (1981) Two Byzantine houses at Luni. *Papers of the British School at Rome* 49: 91–8.

Ward-Perkins, B. (1984) *From Classical Antiquity to the Middle Ages. Urban Public Building in Northern and Central Italy, AD 300–850.* Oxford, Clarendon Press.

Ward-Perkins, J.B. (1962) Etruscan towns, Roman roads and medieval villages: the historical geography of southern Etruria. *Geographical Journal* 128: 389–405.

Ward-Perkins, J. B. (1964) *Landscape and History in Central Italy.* Oxford, Second J. L. Myres Memorial Lecture.

Ward-Perkins, J. B., and Claridge, A. J. (1976) *Pompeii AD 79.* Bristol, Imperial Tobacco Limited.

Ward-Perkins, J. B., Kahane, A., and Murray-Threipland, L. (1968) The Ager Veientanus north and east of Veii. *Papers of the British School at Rome* 36: 1–218.

Watson, J. (1992) The mammals. In A. Small (ed.) *Gravina: an Iron Age and Republican Settlement in Apulia*: 93–120. London, British School at Rome, Archaeological Monographs 5.

Watts, W.A. (1985) A long pollen record from Laghi di Monticchio, southern Italy. *Journal of the Geological Society* 142: 491–9.

White, K. D. (1970) *Roman Farming.* London, Thames and Hudson.

Whitehouse, D. B. (1966) Medieval painted pottery in south and central Italy. *Medieval Archaeology* 10: 30–44.

Whitehouse, D. B. (1969) Red-painted and glazed pottery in western Europe from the eighth to the twelfth century. *Medieval Archaeology* 13: 137–41.

Whitehouse, D. B. (1970) Excavations at Satriano: a deserted medieval settlement in Basilicata. *Papers of the British School at Rome* 38: 188–219.

Whitehouse, D. B. (1978) The medieval pottery of Rome. In H. McK. Blake, T. W. Potter and D. B. Whitehouse (eds.) *Papers in Italian Archaeology* 1: 475–505. Oxford, British Archaeological Reports, International Series 55.

Whitehouse, D. B. (1980) The medieval pottery from Santa Cornelia. *Papers of the British School at Rome* 48: 125–56.

Whitehouse, D. B. (1986) Apulia. In *La Ceramica Medievale nel Mediterraneo Occidentale*: 573–86. Florence, Insegna del Giglio

Whitehouse, R. (1968a) Settlement and economy in southern Italy in the neothermal period. *Proceedings of the Prehistoric Period* 34: 332–67.

Whitehouse, R. (1968b) The early Neolithic of southern Italy. *Antiquity* 42: 188–93.

Whitehouse, R. (1969) The neolithic pottery sequence in southern Italy. *Proceedings of the Prehistoric Period* 35: 267–310.

Whitehouse, R. (1971) The last hunter-gatherers in southern Italy. *World Archaeology* 2: 239–54.

Whitehouse, R. (1986) Siticulosa Apulia revisited. *Antiquity* 60: 36–44.

Whitehouse, R. (1990) Caves and cult in neolithic southern Italy. *Accordia Research Papers* 1: 19–37.

Whitehouse, R. (1992) *Underground Religion: Cult and Culture in Prehistoric Italy.* London, University of London, Accordia Research Centre.

Whitehouse, R. D. and Wilkins, J. B. (1985) Magna Graecia before the Greeks: towards a reconciliation of the evidence. In C. Malone and S. Stoddart (eds.) *Papers in Italian Archaeology IV. Part iii. Patterns in Protohistory*: 89–109. Oxford, British Archaeological Reports, International Series 245.

Whitehouse, R.D. and Wilkins, J.B. (1989) Greeks and natives in southeast Italy: approaches to the archaeological evidence. In T. C. Champion (ed.) *Centre and Periphery; Comparative Studies in Archaeology*: 102–27. London, Unwin Hyman.

Wickham, C. (1978) Historical and topographical notes on early medieval South Etruria. *Papers of the British School at Rome* 47: 132–79.

Wickham, C. (1981) *Early Medieval Italy: Central Power and Local Society 400–1000.* London, Macmillan.

Wickham, C. (1982) *Studi sulla Società degli Appennini nell'Alto Medioevo: Contadini, Signori e Insediamento nel Territorio di Valva (Sulmona).* Bologna, CLUEB.

Wickham, C. (1983) Pastoralism and underdevelopment in the early Middle Ages. *Settimane di Studio (Spoleto)* 31: 401–55.

Wickham, C. (1985) *Il Problema dell' Incastellamento nell'Italia Centrale: l'Esempio di San Vincenzo al Volturno.* Florence, Insegna del Giglio.

Wickham, C. J. (1988) Marx, Sherlock Holmes, and late Roman commerce. *Journal of Roman Studies* 78: 183–93.

Wickham, C. J. (1989) Italy and the early Middle Ages. In K. Randsborg (ed.) *The Birth of Europe. Archaeology and Social Development in the First Millennium AD*: 140–51. Rome, L'Erma di Bretschneider.

Wickham, C. (1993) *Comunità e Clientele nella Toscana del XII Secolo.* Florence, Olschki.

Wild, J. P. (1970) *Textile Manufacture in the Northern Roman Provinces.* Cambridge, University Press.

Wilkens, B. (1987) *Il Passaggio dal Mesolitico al Neolitico attraverso lo Studio delle Faune di Alcuni Siti dell' Italia Centro-Meridionale.* Pisa University, unpublished PhD thesis.

Wilkens, B. (1991) Il ruolo della pastorizia nelle economie preistoriche dell' Italia centro-meridionale. In R. Maggi, R. Nisbet and G. Barker (eds.) *Archeologia della Pastorizia nell' Europa Meridionale* II: 81–94. Bordighera, Istituto Internazionale di Studi Liguri.

Wilkens, B. (1992) I resti faunistici di alcuni insediamenti dell' età del Bronzo nell' Italia centro-meridionale. *Rassegna di Archeologia* 10: 463–9.

Williams-Thorpe (forthcoming) The millstones. In J. A. Lloyd (ed.) *The Samnite and Roman Villa at Matrice.*

Wiseman, T. P. (1971) *New Men in the Roman Senate 139 BC–AD 14.* Oxford, Clarendon Press.

Woolf, G. (1990) Food, poverty and patronage: the significance of the epigraphy of the Roman alimentary schemes in early imperial Italy. *Papers of the British School at Rome* 58: 197–228.

Zvelebil, M. and Rowley-Conwy, P. (1984) The transition to farming in northern Europe: a hunter-gatherer perspective. *Norwegian Archaeological Review* 17, 2: 104–28.

INDEX

Note: Page numbers in **bold** type refer to **figures** Page numbers in *italic* type refer to *tables*